WAR With the Remnant

THE HIDDEN NARRATIVE OF TERRORISM AND THE CHURCH OF JESUS CHRIST OF LATTER-DAY SAINTS

MATTHEW A. HUGHES

CFI
AN IMPRINT OF CEDAR FORT, INC.
SPRINGVILLE, UTAH

ISBN 13: 978-1-4621-3711-4

Published by CFI, an imprint of Cedar Fort, Inc.
2373 W. 700 S., Springville, UT 84663
Distributed by Cedar Fort, Inc., www.cedarfort.com

LIBRARY OF CONGRESS CONTROL NUMBER: 2020945613

Cover design by Wes Wheeler
Cover design © 2020 Cedar Fort, Inc.
Edited and typeset by Valene Wood

Printed in the United States of America

10 9 8 7 6 5 4 3 2 1

Printed on acid-free paper

I dedicate this work to the Saints directly affected by terrorism, especially the people of Chile. Also, to the fearless Saints who preach the gospel and remain true to the faith, as well as those who apply their expertise in protecting the Church from those with malicious intent.

CONTENTS

TABLES

FIGURES

ACKNOWLEDGMENTS

I am grateful God guided me to research this topic and prepared me to see His hand in the affairs of the Saints and His Church. His direction in my professional studies and military assignments led me to develop analytical skills and prepared me through experience to discern trends and study the adversary's tactics, conveying analysis in ways by which others may benefit. Service as a full-time missionary in Chile blessed me with the language skills necessary to obtain additional facts and personal accounts of attacks in South America through interviews in the native tongue.

My wife, Laura, played an instrumental role as I completed this project through her constant encouragement and mentorship as a gifted writer. I am grateful to several friends and acquaintances for their contributions of time in reading early drafts and providing feedback. Finally, special thanks to the team at Cedar Fort, especially Heather Holm and Valene Wood for their attention to detail while editing and Wes Wheeler for excellent cover design.

AUTHOR'S NOTE

In July 2017, I began sifting through terrorist attack incident summaries while researching terrorism trends in Chile as part of a personal project. Unexpectedly, I encountered a block of incidents targeting The Church of Jesus Christ of Latter-day Saints. Despite having served as a full-time missionary in the Chile Santiago West Mission between 2007 and 2009, I had never heard of any terrorism targeting Latter-day Saint chapels or members there. Intrigued, I began to search for other terrorist attacks targeting the Church in recent decades. I eventually compiled the comprehensive list of attacks contained in Appendix A. I decided to write a book on the topic, as I realized during my search that no such book or database existed. Rather, disparate data in government records, church files, a handful of journal articles, and other open sources held information on attacks against the Church, but this was mainly raw, unanalyzed data.

In this book, I attempt to provide the reader with a breadth and depth of understanding of the relationship between contemporary terrorism and The Church of Jesus Christ of Latter-day Saints. I introduce this analysis by investigating the spiritual and temporal roots of the conflict, focusing on man's thoughts and emotions. This is the core of terrorism, a method employed to influence people to act in desired ways through the application of violence to provoke fear. I provide historical context and incorporate government sources and media reports to explain why various perpetrator groups attacked the Church. Analyzing statistics and perpetrator attack trends exposes Satan's role and tactics in this conflict. Testimonies of miracles and tragedies of Church members involved in attacks against the Church or other targets manifest the hand of a loving and patient God in the face of such heinous acts. Studying scripture and modern counsel through an analytical lens focused on terrorism reveals important aspects of doctrine, including warnings and counsel. Finally, I frame assessments of future terrorism involving the Church in terms of theories proposed by subject matter experts and prophecies in scripture and latter-day revelation.

Ultimately, I hope to allay fears propagated through terrorism and violence by demonstrating through analysis that God is aware of the unique challenges of our day and that there is meaning in these trials. In the face of such threats that seem to fill headlines more frequently as we enter the future, hope can seem forlorn; nevertheless, the restored gospel of Jesus Christ will continue to penetrate every continent and touch the hearts of men. As prophecies foretell, the last days hold more challenges for Latter-day Saints, but gaining a better knowledge of past trials and anticipated threats through study offers greater peace and strengthened resolve.

Matthew A. Hughes

INTRODUCTION

Opposition is a fundamental principle of nature. The enduring conflict between good and evil forces described in scripture continues today. Men and women have gained spiritual enlightenment by studying the many forms and effects of this enduring conflict, such as war. Terrorism is another form of opposition in this world. In the moral ambiguity plaguing society today, where practices once considered wicked are now condoned and applauded, terrorism is one evil still recognized and labeled by most as evil. Many books define, investigate, and analyze contemporary terrorism from a secular perspective, but few people have studied terrorism through the lens of the gospel of Jesus Christ, seeking meaning and spiritual lessons.

This book explores the spiritual applications of terrorism studies through the lens of restored doctrines and teachings, focusing on terrorism targeting The Church of Jesus Christ of Latter-day Saints. This investigation begins with analysis regarding the role and significance of terrorism in the last days with special emphasis on prophecies and historical vernacular from the restored Church of Jesus Christ. Examining the battleground of hearts and minds helps to understand Satan's objectives through the application and timing of violence. A thorough analysis of the diverse ideologies and motives, tactics, and organizations of terrorists helps to explain why and how people attacked Church buildings and members in recent decades. Accounts of miracles and tragedies involving terrorism reveal a loving Father's merciful hand at work in behalf of His Saints in extremely personal ways. Shrouded among the evil machinations of men lies evidence of Satan's strategies; he leverages all weapons in his arsenal, including terrorism, to counter the spread of the gospel and other vital missions of the restored Church of Jesus Christ. Finally, formulating predictive analysis regarding future terrorist threats the Church may encounter explores what may lie ahead as Satan continues to rage against the Lord's Church on the earth.

Granted, the terrorist attacks targeting the Church within the past few decades hardly rival the opposition faced by Church members at other times. Latter-day Saints suffered many trials at the hands of wicked mobs and under unjust political leaders shortly after the Restoration and formal establishment of the Church of Jesus Christ of Latter-day Saints in 1830. Persecution in the United States drove these early members westward, leading thousands of pioneers to abandon their homes and head to the Rocky Mountains. Members from Europe, many of whom faced persecution or other tribulations, also joined these Saints traveling westward. Mobs razed communities and murdered members, political figures issued decrees targeting Saints, and other forms of intimidation and persecution ensued. Elder Jeffrey R. Holland described this era of the early church, stating, "at its worst, this was the most difficult and dangerous time—may I say 'terror-filled'—that the Church had ever known."[1] These early Saints maintained hope throughout this difficult period and even endured other challenges during the trek westward, until they eventually settled new communities in the western United States.

Although recent terrorist attacks against the Church generally involved fewer casualties and inflicted less damage than attacks in earlier periods of Church history, analyzing these recent attacks and exploring personal accounts offers powerful spiritual lessons. We refer to those who crossed the plains in the westward trek as pioneers, yet many of those affected by recent terror attacks are also pioneers in a sense, as they were spiritual trailblazers in areas where the Church was young and budding. In Church meetings, members often share experiences of early pioneers to show how divine intervention saved them from death or misfortune at the hands of mobs, but few share, or know of, more recent experiences involving terrorism. Studying these experiences and investigating the nature of these attacks offers rich spiritual insights and growth.

Literature Review

There is little academic material or research on spiritual lessons of terrorism, attacks against Latter-day Saint targets, or publicly available predictive analysis or speculation regarding what the future may hold concerning terrorism affecting the Church. Articles and books are replete with valuable insights on the war chapters of the Book of

Mormon and applications for physical and spiritual warfare in the last days, yet there is an extremely limited amount of literature addressing terrorism, through either a secular or spiritual lens.

The only texts or media addressing terrorism's spiritual lessons, through the perspective of a Latter-day Saint, are a handful of works written by Latter-day Saint authors sharing personal experiences or encounters involving terrorism (not necessarily attacking Latter-day Saint targets) or a few Latter-day Saint movie directors portraying individual instances of terrorism involving members of the Church. While these biographical works do not follow the outline or methodology typical of a case study, they are the closest forms of text resembling an investigation of individual events. Mason Wells describes his experiences in three separate terrorist attacks in his coauthored work, *Left Standing: The Miraculous Story of How Mason Wells's Faith Survived the Boston, Paris, and Brussels Terror Attacks.* Wells shares commentary on the spiritual impacts of these attacks on his life and how he grew as a result of these experiences. Alissa Parker also shares personal experiences about an act of terror in her book *An Unseen Angel: A Mother's Story of Healing and Hope After Sandy Hook.* She explains the comfort and understanding she gained through spiritual experiences following the Sandy Hook school shooting, where her young daughter, Emilie, was tragically killed. These works, written by Latter-day Saint authors, provide personal insights on a handful of terrorist attacks and offer unique perspectives regarding God's response in the wake of such incidents. The attacks did not directly target members of the Latter-day Saint faith; rather, the attackers indiscriminately targeted people of all ages, religions, and other characteristics. A secondary source demonstrating the miraculous experiences of Church members is T. C. Christensen's *The Cokeville Miracle.* This movie reflects the amazing experiences and circumstances concerning an attack in 1986 in Cokeville, Wyoming affecting a predominantly Latter-day Saint community. The perpetrator, while possibly motivated by disdain for members of the community or personal vendettas, demanded a ransom, congruent with crimes, as opposed to carrying out an act to incite fear, more representative of terrorism. These works provide unique insights on the nature of violence through a spiritual lens. Lessons shared by the authors or contributors are lessons conveyed to them through the Holy Ghost, as opposed to secular theories or analysis devoid of spiritual matters often found in other texts discussing terrorism.

North and South American television news, radio broadcasts, and newspaper articles from the late 1980s and 1990s reported on anti-Latter-day Saint terrorism in South America. Several devoted airtime or article space to certain events, such as the murder of missionary companionships on two occasions. Others cited experts or commentators providing basic analysis on attack frequency and trends during periods of heightened attacks against the Church. Usually, when individual attacks occurred, local South American newspapers and radio stations would at least provide information about the alleged perpetrators and attack timing, location, and weapons. Attack descriptions sometimes included in-depth background on perpetrator groups and reports of how government entities sought to identify attackers and hold these individuals accountable. Many of these foreign language materials were inaccessible to researchers and analysts in the United States in the 1980s and 1990s, when terrorism targeting the Latter-day Saint Church peaked, which might help to explain the lack of publicly available analysis.

Government documents are a rich source of raw data, or information that has not undergone processing or analysis, and simple objective analysis regarding terrorism impacting the Church. The Foreign Broadcast Information Service (FBIS), a government entity translating foreign radio broadcasts into English for analysis, produced hundreds of translations in the late 1980s and early 1990s covering attacks against Latter-day Saint targets. These translations corroborate reporting elsewhere and sometimes include additional details about attacks, including addresses of attack sites, names of perpetrators or victims, and estimated damage costs. Such work enables English-speaking analysts without knowledge of a foreign language to bypass obstacles associated with foreign language materials. FBIS summaries and reports offer a large swath of data for analysis, information which may reside in now-inaccessible South American newspapers. While these translations provide verbatim translations of broadcasts, the reports constitute raw data, lacking any analyst comments or notes regarding the information within translations. The Global Terrorism Database

(GTD) is another valuable source of relevant raw data. This open source database was developed and made available to the public by the National Consortium for the Study of Terrorism and Responses to Terrorism (START), a Department of Homeland Security Center of Excellence led by the University of Maryland. The GTD is a tertiary source which includes filterable attack details. This source is an excellent fount of quantitative data and facilitates analysis of perpetrator groups, casualty counts, attack locations, and other attack characteristics. Again, however, this source lacks analyst comments or lengthy descriptions of attacks. Additional government materials relevant to this research include some country studies and intelligence agency reports, now available to the public after declassification. These reports mention attacks targeting Latter-day Saint meetinghouses and members or provide analysis on attack tactics and perpetrator ideologies, often elaborating on evidence linking groups to attacks and providing analysis about the likelihood of future attacks. These materials provide unique and generally reliable information useful in corroborating attack descriptions recorded in other sources.

Although rare, some journal articles include analysis on terrorist attacks targeting the Church. These materials provide a unique blend of objective data and subjective analysis and opinions. David Knowlton, professor of anthropology at Utah Valley University, authored a series of articles and spoke at some lectures in the 1990s, focusing on such attacks against the Church in South America. His analysis constitutes some of the only publicly available information about populations' social and cultural dynamics, as he asserts some of these factors largely influenced attack trends.

The Church also possesses records within the scope of this study, but many of these files are closed to the public. The Church History Library has written volumes, photos, and oral histories referencing terrorism that are closed to research. Examples of such closed files include communications the Church received from terrorist groups, which would likely aid in determining or substantiating assertions about motives among groups targeting members and meetinghouses. The Church Security Office also conducts analysis and maintains files closed to public access. These records would help to complete and render a more comprehensive list of terror attacks targeting the

Church, contained in Appendix A. Such information would fill gaps and include hoaxes, threats, and attacks not included in media reports or other open sources. Due to the lack of public accessibility to these files, Appendix A and analysis on attack trends relies on attacks reported in media, government reports, and other open sources.

Generally, the subject of terrorist attacks targeting the Church is a mostly uncharted field of research. As mentioned, many authors have explored parallels between war and the spiritual battle between good and evil by studying ancient warfare described in the war chapters of the Book of Mormon or other scriptures and extracting spiritual truths about integrity, daily conduct, and decision-making. Few authors, however, have investigated such spiritual principles as they apply to modern-day terrorism. The limited amount of material exploring acts of terrorism through a spiritual lens involves biographical accounts, wherein the authors share personal insights, rather than analysis on multiple attacks to extract trends and application of gospel principles to develop spiritual insights. Few people have studied terrorist attacks against the Church to identify attack trends or explore reasons behind attacks. Those who have shared their studies, although they contain detailed observations and sound conclusions, presented opinions on a narrow scope of attacks rather than a large sampling pool of attacks. There is an information gap, at least in open source materials, regarding a comprehensive analysis of terrorism affecting The Church of Jesus Christ of Latter-day Saints. No open source materials examine large numbers of attacks, taking into account the various ideologies fueling more recent attacks and threats. These attacks have not been studied under the application of analysis tools or methods, normally applied by experts to identify patterns and identify characteristics of terrorism targeting specific populations.

Defining Contemporary Terrorism and the Scope of Study

The definitions of terrorism and descriptions of what constitutes terrorism vary among sources and experts. What everyday people perceive as terrorism also varies, depending on era, culture, and perspective.

While there is no single, universally accepted definition for terrorism, the following definition developed and used by the National Consortium for the Study of Terrorism and Responses to Terrorism concisely describes the principle objectives and characteristics of terrorism:

> "The threatened or actual use of illegal force and violence by a non-state actor to attain a political, economic, religious, or social goal through fear, coercion, or intimidation."[2]

This definition includes hoaxes within the purview of terrorism and acknowledges the varying motives and ideologies behind attacks. This description also distinguishes acts of terrorism from other crimes, as there must be some objective to incite fear and influence others in some way. Hostage taking, for instance, can be a terrorist act if satisfying certain criteria, but if failing to do so, this would constitute crime, likely focused on monetary objectives through ransoms. While this definition is succinct and logical, the definition does not define the intended target, either as non-combatants or some other noun denoting a group of non-belligerents.

Another commonly referenced definition is that drafted by the US Department of State, which describes terrorism as, "premeditated, politically motivated violence perpetrated against non-combatant targets by subnational groups or clandestine agents."[3] This definition includes an explanation of the perpetrator and target, as well as the characteristics of violence and motive qualifying an event as an act of terror. However, the definition may be too narrow to account for terrorism conducted by lone wolves or jihadists with religious motives, which became increasingly more frequent in recent decades. The definitions of terrorism will likely continue to adapt as motives, targets, and other factors change. To elaborate on the evolving sense of a definition and put the term in proper context, Table 1.1 lists terms and concepts most frequently included within definitions of terrorism found in academic literature. Most of these terms involve desired effects on the hearts and minds of the target audience. Satan portrays terrorism as a viable and effective method to achieve desired changes in society not attained through non-violent or otherwise peaceful means.

Table 0.1: Frequency of Terms in Definitions of Terrorism

Term/Concept	Frequency (Percentage) of Term Appearing in Definition
Violence, force	83.5
Political	65
Fear, terror emphasized	51
Threat	47
(Psych.) effects and (anticipated) reactions	41.5
Victim-target differentiation	37.5
Purposive, planned, systematic, organized action	32
Method of combat, strategy, tactic	30.5
Extranormality, in breach of accepted rules, without humanitarian constraints	30
Coercion, extortion, induction of compliance	28
Publicity aspect	21.5
Arbitrariness; impersonal, random character; indiscrimination	21
Civilians, noncombatants, neutrals, outsiders as victims	17.5
Intimidation	17
Innocence of victims emphasized	15.5
Group, movement, organization as perpetrator	14
Symbolic aspect, demonstration to others	13.5
Incalculability, unpredictability, unexpectedness of occurrence of violence	9
Clandestine, covert nature	9
Repetitiveness; serial or campaign character of violence	7
Criminal	6
Demands made on third parties	4

Source: Alex P. Schmid, Albert J. Jongman, et al. Political Terrorism: A New Guide to Actors, Authors, Concepts, Data Bases, Theories, and Literature (Amsterdam: North Holland, Transaction Books, 1988), p. 5–6.

The START and US Department of State definitions and these associated terms provide a litmus for distinguishing acts of terrorism from crime, not analyzed in this work. Crime may involve violent acts of revenge targeting a particular member of the Church, kidnapping missionaries for ransom money, or other actions reflecting distinct motives not associated with terrorism. Terrorists, however, seek to usurp power, control others, and motivate supporters through violence. These tactics and terms, such as fear, coercion, and intimidation, rely on influencing hearts and minds of a target audience, and they are stark contrasts to faith, agency, and peace. They are antonyms of Paul's list of the fruits of the Spirit in Galatians 5, as such terms are fruits of contention and Satanic alternatives to peaceful conflict resolution.

This study focuses on attacks targeting The Church of Jesus Christ of Latter-day Saints between 1979 and 2018. While *modern terrorism*, as described by experts like David Rapoport, dates back to anarchist groups targeting heads of state in the late 1800s, this study concentrates on *contemporary terrorism*, a term herein used to describe any terrorism occurring after 1979. While the term appears infrequently in literature, the post-1979 period aligns with Rapoport's latest wave of modern terrorism, known as the "religious wave" for the defining characteristic of religious ideologies driving attacks.[4] This demarcation also suits the time frames associated with databases logging terrorist events. The Global Terrorism Database, an open source database containing information on terrorist attacks throughout the world since 1970, is a vital tertiary source in the identification and analysis of attacks targeting the Church. Given the time frame of events included in this source, identifying attacks before 1970 presents challenges. The RAND Database of Worldwide Terrorism Incidents (RDWTI), another reliable tertiary source, compiles attacks using similar criteria between 1968 and 2009. There is a lack of registered attacks against the Church within the first decade of these databases, corroborated by a lack of accounts in open source media and other government sources, but attacks registered in these databases corroborate other open source reporting of a terrorism targeting the Church in 1983 and thereafter.

The general objectives and methods of terrorism are consistent throughout recent decades, but ideologies and motives fueling terrorism varied. Motive is a fundamental factor in assessing whether or not an event meets criteria for inclusion in this study. Appendix

A, the raw data behind much of the terrorism analysis in this work, contains summaries of terrorist attacks against Latter-day Saint targets after 1979 that meet criteria to categorize those events as acts of terrorism. The qualifying characteristics are a blend of criteria applied by START and the RAND Corporation in categorizing events as terrorism. In assessing which acts of violence they should include in the Global Terrorism Database, START applies the following criteria:

> *Criterion I:* The act must be aimed at attaining a political, economic, religious, or social goal.
>
> *Criterion II:* There must be evidence of an intention to coerce, intimidate, or convey some other message to a larger audience (or audiences) than the immediate victims.
>
> *Criterion III:* The action must be outside the context of legitimate warfare activities.[5]

The GTD includes incidents that meet at least two of the three listed criteria. The RAND (Research and Development) Corporation uses a broader set of parameters for inclusion in their RAND Database of Worldwide Terrorism Incidents (RDWTI), which includes incidents between 1968 and 2009. According to the RAND Corporation, key factors of terrorism include:

- violence or the threat of violence
- calculations to create fear and alarm
- intentions to coerce certain actions
- motives that include a political objective
- generally civilian targets
- actions by a group or an individual[6]

This study investigates events that qualify as terrorism by these standards. Discrepancies may exist, as some attacks in Appendix A cite North or South American newspapers or other secondary sources, rather than a tertiary source (GTD or RDWTI), as database staff members acknowledge that information contained in their databases may be incomplete and is continually undergoing revisions or updates, as needed. Raw data in Appendix A feeds quantitative analysis for charts and graphs depicting trends relating to terrorism targeting the Church. Appendix A strictly contains those acts of terrorism targeting the members and buildings of the Church; however, the rest of this work also contains acts of terrorism wherein members were victims or otherwise affected, but not necessarily targeted because of their membership in the Church. Exploring such events reveals the hand of God and grants spiritual insights regarding God's awareness of the Saints.

Assumptions

There are various assumptions influencing this investigation, all of which are necessary to proceed in the absence of some facts. One significant assumption regarding this research is that Appendix A, containing a chronological list of 315 terrorist attacks targeting The Church of Jesus Christ of Latter-day Saints, is incomplete. This list contains a large enough pool of events to analyze and identify general trends and important details about attacks, and with a strong degree of reliability in most circumstances, but the list fails to include every terrorist attack targeting the Church between January 1, 1979 and December 31, 2018. In fact, this book includes information about threats, plots, or attacks that meet criteria to be considered terrorism, but they are not included in Appendix A due to very limited information (e.g., a bomb threat against an meetinghouse in a town without a specific date or even a precise year). Although comprehensive, gathered from primary, secondary, and tertiary sources from multiple languages and types of media, this list comprises only information contained in open sources or details gathered from databases or personal interviews. Commentary in some academic works alludes to attacks in general terms, listing bomb threats against chapels in a particular city, for instance, without providing specifics as to date or perpetrator. Such information provides some context and background about tactics but lacks the definitive information for inclusion in Appendix A and analysis.

The list of attacks in Appendix A does not include attacks not reported by the Church, either, which occasionally occurred in Central and South America. For instance, after members of the Zarate Willka Armed Forces of Liberation bombed a Latter-day Saint meetinghouse in the Villa Victoria sector of La Paz, Bolivia in the late 1980s, the Church repaired the damages without reporting the incident.[7] Other times, there is not definitive or precise information regarding dates or locations, due to single-source reporting or other factors influencing reliability. At some point in the late 1990s, for example, terrorists threw a bomb at a chapel in Colombia and it landed inside the outdoor handcart members had made for the anniversary of pioneers arriving in Salt Lake City, whereupon it exploded, preventing destruction to the chapel or harm to anyone nearby.[8] Appendix A does not contain a variety of such instances without precise dates, locations, or descriptions. Similarly, this list does not contain information found in portions of the Church History Library closed to research, nor does the list include data from the Church Security Department. Such details may contain personally identifiable information, the release of which would violate privacy rights or eliminate the anonymity currently in place for victims or other persons involved in events. Such data, especially recent reports and analysis, might pose a threat to the Church or members if released to the public, revealing security vulnerabilities or other concerning information. Similarly, classified reports and documents of the US Government or other foreign governments likely contain additional insights and analysis which would contribute to better understanding threats. Access to these reports or materials concerning additional attacks, hoaxes, and threats would strengthen the reliability of analysis, producing a larger and more complete sampling pool of attacks, but this potential gain in reliability and completeness would come at a cost of compromised security and privacy.

Another assumption addresses the reliability and accuracy of government records. Personal accounts of victims contradict event summaries in some government sources, raising discrepancies in reporting. These short or incomplete summaries often provide a lead for spiritual accounts, when, for instance, a summary explains there were zero injuries or all hostages were released in incidents perpetrated by armed assailants with seemingly no reservations for harming those involved. Such discrepancies, however, pose concerns for the accuracy of some data, but the assumption is that such discrepancies are seldom;

no discrepancies are so significant as to alter the reliability or accuracy of identified trends, overall conclusions, or predictive analysis.

Significance of Analysis

The study of terrorism, much like that of peace, war, charity, theft, or other manifestations of good or evil, holds lessons about Jesus Christ and His gospel. After all, the Lord explained to Adam:

> "And behold, all things have their likeness, and all things are created and made to bear record of me, both things which are temporal, and things which are spiritual; things which are in the heavens above, and things which are on the earth, and things which are in the earth, and things which are under the earth, both above and beneath: all things bear record of me."[9]

The study of all things, even terrorism, holds valuable lessons about gospel principles. Terrorism is one field offering new insights, as few have investigated its spiritual lessons.

This work aims to investigate this unexplored field. By following the charge to "seek learning even by study and also by faith," truths manifest themselves and reaffirm the veracity of various gospel principles.[10] This study includes the following specific objectives:

- Consider terrorism in general, in the context of Latter-day Saint doctrine and teachings.
- Identify, investigate, and analyze terrorist attacks targeting the Church.
- Explore spiritual lessons and applications of terrorism.
- Strengthen testimonies of readers through accounts and analysis.

This study contains analysis and commentary based on quantitative and qualitative research. This work contains personal accounts and testimonies of victims, objective scrutiny of trends, case studies, exploration of the motives behind terrorism, and conjecture about future events. Some important benefits of studying and analyzing terrorism's effects on the Church and members include the following:

- Reveals the hand of God through miracles and divine intervention.
- Demonstrates God's awareness of the Saints and their trials, as many accounts describe how Saints found solace and understanding in the wake of tragedy.
- Enlightens those seeking to answer the important question of the soul, "Why does God allow evil and suffering to occur?"[11]
- Experiences reflect truths about important Gospel principles (e.g., physical protections available through the garment, prayer, healing, angels, prophecy, comforting power of the Holy Ghost, and the Holy Ghost guiding Saints to safety).

Trends and case studies, especially when analyzed through a spiritual lens, expose some of Satan's strategies and tactics in the last days. Comparisons to ancient practices of Gadianton Robbers and other secret combinations uncover recurring ideologies and motives fomenting violence. Personal accounts and lessons garnered through study restore hope in a time plagued with evil and iniquity.

The approach taken in this study draws from the framework of mission analysis and analytical tools and methods used by the US Army and intelligence agencies, which help to identify and explore trends and facets of terrorism. Investigating the role of terrorism in the last days, along with perpetrators' tactics and ideologies, yield insights about why groups and individuals have targeted the Church. Studying trends exposes aspects of Satan's strategy in combating the Church and curbing missionary work and other aspects of the gospel of Jesus Christ. Predictive analysis based on secular and spiritual takeaways identifies forthcoming threats and considers how to best prepare for them. Such analysis produces more objective and sound conclusions than what mere opinion might yield.

CHAPTER 1

TERRORISM IN THE LAST DAYS

"Everything in the arsenal of the adversary will eventually be used."

—Elder Neal A. Maxwell, "All Hell is Moved," Devotional given at Brigham Young University, November 8, 1977

Relevance of Contemporary Terrorism

Nephi and other prophets foresaw the challenges of these last days, among which is the bloodshed associated with terrorism. They recorded their visions and revelations in the compilation of scripture penned by prophets known as the Book of Mormon. David Brent Marsh of the Priesthood and Family Department for the Church explained that the Book of Mormon was preserved and brought forth in our day to help Saints with the challenges of this dispensation, stating that, "of the 239 chapters in the Book of Mormon, 174 (73 percent) deal with war, terrorism, murder, political conspiracies, secret combinations, threats, family collusions, and other hostilities."[12] The last days are rife with violence. People all over the world witnessed terrorism increase in frequency and impact in recent decades, influencing many facets of life, from security procedures at airports to apprehensions about sending our children to school.

Latter-day Saints do not readily come to mind as a unit of people directly affected by contemporary terrorism, yet many have been deliberately targeted in attacks or have become the victims of indiscriminate targeting in broader terrorism campaigns. In fact, at one time in recent history, the Church was the most frequently targeted organization in anti-US attacks in Latin America.[13] While attacks waxed in the late 1980s and early 1990s and waned in the following years, the Church remains a target. Saints have been victims of attacks not specifically targeting the Church, as well, with Saints perishing or suffering injuries in the Oklahoma City Bombing, the 9/11 attacks, and other events.

Terrorism has been the subject of scriptural prophecy, as well as counsel and warnings of modern-day prophets. While armed conflict still produces more fatalities than do acts of terrorism, the frequency of terrorist attacks in the world and perpetrators' indiscriminate nature of targeting makes this a chief factor of concern among people, especially members of younger generations bombarded by terrorism in the media for most of their lives. Future generations will undoubtedly continue to confront the perpetual and ever-evolving threat of terrorism.

Brigham Young's Prophecy on the Power of Satan in the Last Days

Satan's power and influence in the world are often difficult to quantify, given gradual shifts in public policy on issues of morality, changing perceptions of polemic issues across generations, and evil practices adopted and accepted as norms as society grows more distant from God. Terrorism, however, differs from many of the shifting societal norms, as terrorism remains one aspect of opposition in the world most people still recognize as evil. Aspects of terrorism are quantifiable, revealing trends over time.

By nature, terrorism incites fear that can counteract the faith and hope of the gospel of Jesus Christ. Commenting on the opposition countering the spread of the Church, Elder Neal A. Maxwell, a member of the Quorum of the Seventy at the time, stated the following:

> "President Brigham Young observed that it would be at the very time when the Church was reaching out to all the nations of the world, when it was prospering and growing, that there would be in proportion to the spread of the gospel a rise in the power of Satan."[14]

In other words, assigning variables to certain phrases in this prophecy, with an increase in missionary work and Church membership, there will be a proportional increase in evil. In the context of terrorism, one manifestation of Satan's power in the world, comparing key indicators of the variables listed in Brigham Young's prophecy reveals a proportional correlation. The graph depicted in Figure 1.1 compares changes in Church membership (primary vertical axis) and the number of full-time missionaries (secondary vertical axis) to key indicators of terrorism (also secondary vertical axis) over time.

Generally, key variables representing the occurrence and impacts of terrorism changed *in proportion to* the number of full-time missionaries over the depicted 47-year time frame. Key indicators of terrorism closely followed changes in the number of full-time missionaries throughout the depicted time period, with marked similarities in slope. The rise in terrorism after 1979 marks a changing tide in predominant ideologies fueling terrorism, shifting from violence perpetrated by leftist groups to religious terrorism conducted by extremist factions. Despite a lull in attacks from 1998 to 2005, casualty counts remained relatively high, especially on September 11, 2001. Global Church membership consistently increased at a relatively constant rate, but the number of full-time missionaries varied in recent decades. President Thomas S. Monson's announcement in the October 2012 General Conference, lowering the minimum age of male missionaries from 19 to 18 and of women missionaries from 21 to 19 contributed to the subsequent momentary spike in the number of full-time missionaries. Interestingly, a proportional increase in the number of terrorism-inflicted casualties accompanied this dramatic increase in the preaching of the gospel, partially due to the resurgence of the Islamic State in 2011 during the Syrian civil war. Similarly,

Figure 1.1: Key Indicators for Church Growth and Global Terrorism

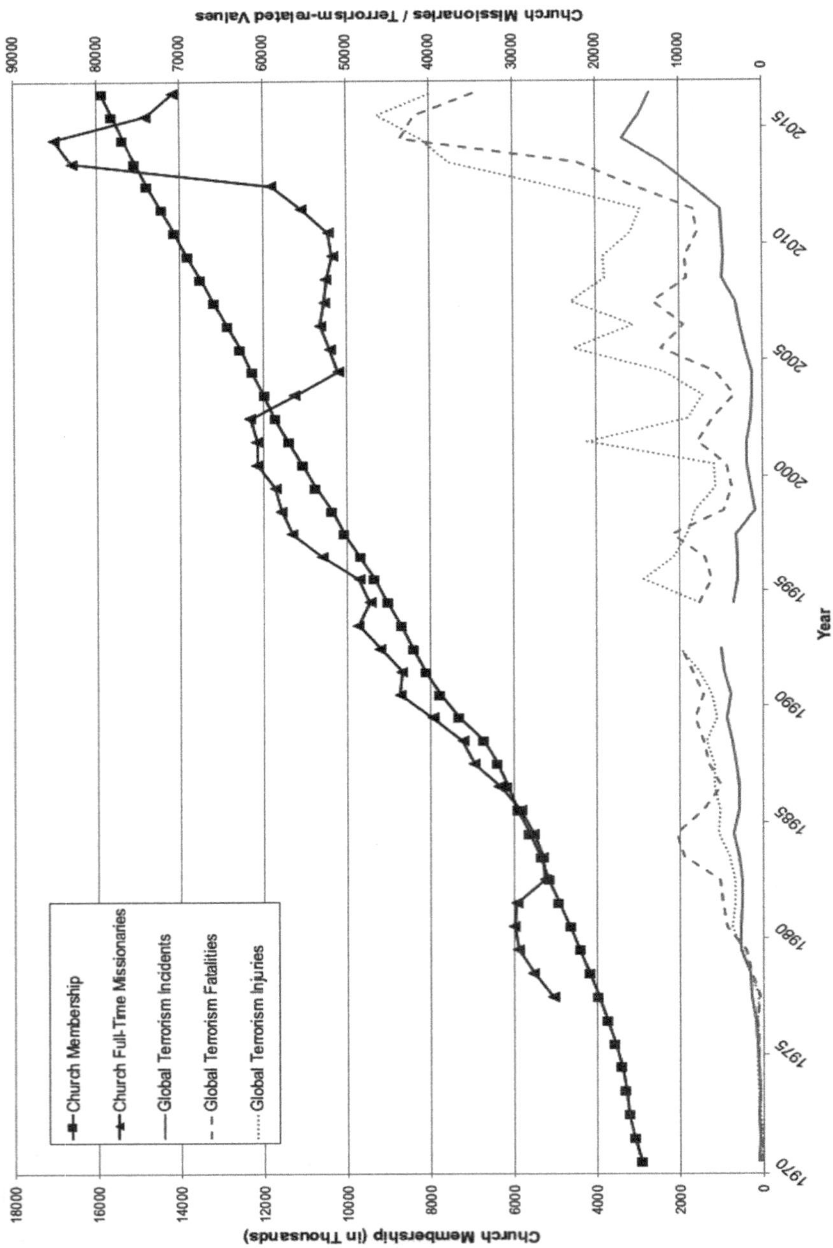

Source: Values for Church membership and full-time missionaries compiled from statistics presented in each General Conference. Terrorism figures compiled from the National Consortium for the Study of Terrorism and Responses to Terrorism Global Terrorism Database. Terrorism statistics for 1993 are not included in the GTD.

casualty numbers decreased between 2015 and 2017, accompanying a decline in the number of full-time missionaries.

Missionary work represents one of the most formidable tools combating Satan's focus on the spiritual and eternal state of man, so correlations between degrees of evil and terrorism and missionary work seem practical. Missionaries are the front line of the Lord's work, so as their ranks increase in size and spread to new countries, a logical reaction from Satan would be to increase his efforts to spread chaos and sow seeds of strife. In addition to Brigham Young's prophecy concerning evil, supported by terrorism trends compared to Church statistics, many other General Authorities have spoken on the topic of terrorism and violent opposition.

Rebuke, Chastisement, and Other Associations

Terrorism plays a significant role in warnings and prophecies associated with the last days. Due to the relative newness of the term *terrorism*, that role may not be as readily apparent as other foretold events and aspects of the last days that prophets overtly describe in scripture in translated terms still used today, such as wars and rumors of wars. Analyzing the context of terror in scriptures especially relevant to the latter days, such as the Book of Mormon and General Conference addresses, helps to fill this gap of knowledge and understanding and exposes terrorism as another topic included among revelations.

Since the Restoration, many General Authorities mentioned *terror* in their general conference addresses. The word cloud depicted in Figure 1.2 reflects words occurring most frequently in close proximity to the term *terror* and related terms in General Conference addresses. In the word cloud, the size of the word reflects the word frequency—the larger the word, the greater the frequency of that word.

The word cloud reveals three of the most common words associated with *terror* in General Conference addresses are *death*, *war*, and *famine*, reminiscent of the Four Horsemen of the Apocalypse. Descriptions vary among scholars, but the *New Testament Institute Student Manual* asserts the following possible interpretations regarding symbolism in Revelation 6: white horse, victory; red horse, bloodshed;

Figure 1.2: 100 Most Common Words Associated with Terror in General Conference Addresses (1851–2017)

Source: Word cloud generated using site http://www.wordclouds.com. Utilizing the Latter-day Saint General Conference Corpus, a collection of text containing historical General Conferences (1851-2017) addresses accessible at https://www.lds-general-conference.org, this word cloud displays the 100 most frequent words/terms correlated with *terror**** (within a four-word span to the left and to the right of the search term).

black horse, famine; and pale horse, death.[15] Other scriptural accounts and prophetic statements describing how God chastises man and punishes the wicked mention variations of four elements, listing death, war (bloodshed, the sword, or strife), famine (hunger or drought), and pestilence (plague, disease, or sickness).

Helaman 12:3 mentions the four elements in this model of rebuke and chastisement with one particular variation. The verse reads as follows (italics added):

> "And thus we see that except the Lord doth chasten his people with many afflictions, yea, except he doth visit them with death and with *terror*, and with famine and with all manner of pestilence, they will not remember him."

This echoes the description of afflictions plaguing man in other accounts, with the important distinction of the word *terror* taking the place normally occupied by *war* or a reference to war. While the meaning of the term *terror* varies throughout each book of scripture, prophets emphasize the Book of Mormon was written for our time and holds special significance for the latter days. The verse does not reference a specific group of people or time period, as opposed to the preceding verses in Helaman 12:1–2 describing the Lord's dealings with the Nephites. Hence, *terror* is likely one form of chastisement tailored to this phase of the last days. Regarding this likening of scripture to present day conditions, Elder Dallin H. Oaks once stated (italics added):

> "The idea that scripture reading can lead to inspiration and revelation opens the door to the truth that *a scripture is not limited to what it meant when it was written but may also include what that scripture means to a reader today.* Even more, scripture reading may also lead to current revelation on whatever else the Lord wishes to communicate to the reader at that time. We do not overstate the point when we say that the scriptures can be a Urim and Thummim to assist each of us to receive personal revelation."[16]

The rarity of the term *terror* in scripture, especially in this context, further bolsters the possibility that the verse relates to these latter days and holds a unique meaning for readers today that differs from the meaning understood in the times of the Nephites. President Boyd K. Packer, in his 2004 General Conference address "Do Not Fear," also mentioned Helaman 12:3 in discussing events leading up to the Lord's return, and posed the question, "Have you noticed that word terror in that prophetic Book of Mormon warning?"[17] Book of Mormon prophets foresaw these last days; their writings hold special meaning in our modern interpretations.

The substitution in Helaman 12:3 of *terror* for the more commonly used *war* or *sword* holds more significance when investigating the literal replacement of war with terror by casualty count. While the number of casualties inflicted by terrorism remains lower than that resulting from armed conflict, the rate of deaths and injuries caused by acts of terrorism has risen dramatically in recent decades. One study by Duncan Green, a strategic adviser for the poverty-focused non-governmental organization Oxfam Great Britain, revealed terrorism caused 13,186 deaths in 2010, compared to 63,910 caused by armed conflict (war) around the same time.[18] Despite this difference in casualty counts, terrorism is often more prevalent in people's minds, given media coverage and domestic threats. Younger generations worry more about school shootings and lone wolf gunmen than nuclear nightmares of past generations. As such, the Lord may leverage the term *terror* in scripture for the intended effect of calling the wicked to repentance and in chastening His people, given the more palpable fear and connection than with other terms. Along this vein of insight, Elder Bruce C. Hafen of the Quorum of the Seventy Presidency shared the following shortly after the 9/11 attacks:

> "So now the question for all of us is the one Elder Henry B. Eyring asked at October Conference about all the people who've started praying since the terrorist attack. 'I hope the change lasts,' said Elder Eyring. His concern, and mine, is that, as Mormon wrote, 'Except the Lord doth chasten his people with many afflictions [and] visit them with . . . terror . . . they will not remember him."[19]

Elder Hafen's interpretation of Helaman 12:3 takes a modern approach to the word *terror* with a direct reference to the 9/11 attacks. While terrorism will not necessarily supplant the sword in an era characterized by wars and rumors of wars, acts of terror will serve as one method to chasten the wicked and call people to repentance.

American Religiosity in the Wake of 9/11

For weeks following the 9/11 attacks, church attendance reached record highs as religiosity returned to America. Many wondered whether the attacks altered the spiritual state of Americans for the foreseeable future, as evidenced by this religious fervor and increased church attendance. Over the course of the following months, however, church attendance began to decrease and then returned to percentages near those prior to 9/11. Studies reflect this shift, as a September 21–22, 2001 Gallup poll showed 47 percent of Americans said "they had attended church or synagogue in the past seven days," but by November, subsequent polls showed "church attendance had dropped back to 42 percent," levels consistent with those of previous years.[20] The spiritual rejuvenation experienced after similar attacks is regrettably fleeting. Such events awaken people to the fragility of life, but ultimately fail to produce an enduring change of behavior, the same type of change associated with repentance.

Evolution of *Terror* and Associated Terms in Latter-day Saint Vernacular

The frequency and meanings of the term *terror* within the Church changed over time, generally reflecting changes in term meaning among the greater public as media and political conditions prompted the term to evolve. Textual analysis reveals three distinct periods in which General Authorities used the term more prevalently. These periods also reflect different meanings for the term and associated words, based on context in General Conference addresses.

Early Church Growth, Tyranny, and Death (1850s–1890s)

Shortly after the Restoration, General Authority use of the word *terror* predominantly followed one of three themes: the unstoppable spread of the Gospel, tyranny and compulsion, or physical death. The leading theme associated with terror held a positive connotation involving the spread of the Church. In 1856, for instance, President Brigham Young said the following:

> "The very report of the Church and kingdom of God on earth is a *terror* to all nations, wheresoever the sound thereof goeth. The sound of 'Mormonism' is a *terror* to towns, counties, states, the pretended republican governments, and to all the world. Why? Because, as the Lord Almighty lives and the Prophets have ever written the truth, this work is destined to revolutionize the world and bring all under subjection to the law of God, who is our lawgiver."[21]

Figure 1.3: Prevalence of Terror and Associated Terms in General Conference Addresses by Decade

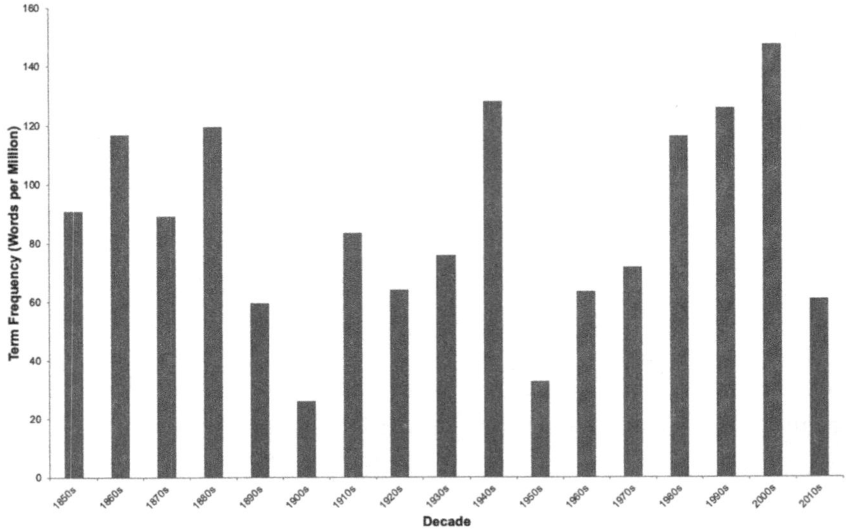

Source: Generated using the General Conference Corpus with the search term terror*** and the frequency by decade for this term. This search yielded 268 occurrences of 12 related terms (e.g., terror, terrorism, terrorist, terrorists) in the corpus. The General Conference Corpus, a text analysis tool developed by BYU Linguistics Professor Mark Davies, is accessible at http://www.lds-general-conference.org.

The term, thus, referred to emotions associated with uprooting secular institutions. The principle of revolution remains associated with modern uses of these terms, as political change is the common objective of modern terrorism. President John Taylor's words two years later echo similar positive sentiments of terror after the Restoration when he said, "Zion will become a terror to all nations," referring to the growth of the Church as an unstoppable force.[22] Similar phrases exist among the addresses of other early Church leaders, reflecting a connotation to the Church that faded over time as interpretations of terror with negative connotations replaced former meanings.

A second common theme associated with terror reflected the secular use of the term, referring to tyranny and political oppression after the model of France. The term *terrorism* originated from the 1793–4 *régime de la terreur* in France as political leaders used fear and intimidation tactics to maintain order during a phase of anarchy, but quickly became an expression describing "the abuse of office and power" during

Robespierre's reign.[23] Some church leaders used the term with this connotation to tyranny commonly used in Europe. This meaning is evident in the words of Charles W. Penrose, spoken in 1883:

> "Some people say they can not understand how it is that these Latter-day Saints are so united, unless they are held together by some secret bond or some kind of tyranny. They can not understand how it is that when the leaders of the people speak, the people are willing to move in a body, with scarcely a dissenting voice, unless it is that they are terrorized or coerced by some power that is not known on the outside. Now, all the bondage and terrorism that exist in this church is the terrorism and bondage—if such a thing can be—of conscience."[24]

This definition and usage reflects compulsion and overriding agency through threats and inspiring fear in a group of people. This characteristic of the term gained momentum and it remains a fundamental characteristic in the word's meaning today.

Death, and the fear associated with departing the mortal frame, became a third predominant theme linked to *terror* in the early Church. In this sense, the term held a negative connotation and reflected uncertainty and fear related to the unknown hereafter. In 1860, John Taylor used the term as follows:

> "He [God] has planted within us, through the principles of eternal truth, the germs of everlasting life; so that Death, which has been a terror to all nations for generations past, which has caused men to quail, and through which the Jews all their life long were subject to bondage, has lost its terrors on the minds of men who live their religion, who walk according to the laws of the holy Priesthood, and cultivate the Spirit of God."[25]

This meaning faded over the subsequent decades, or at least the term's association to death or fear appeared less frequently. The term *terror* and associated terms became less prevalent around the turn of the century, regaining use as the world erupted in armed conflict.

The Desolation of War (1910s–1940s)

A resurgence in the usage of the word *terror* and associated terms took place between the 1910s and 1940s, aligned to two world wars and reflecting the horror and devastation of armed conflict. During these times, General Authorities used the term *terror* to describe the sweeping destruction of military forces and the fears felt by civilians. In the 1918 General Conference, Joseph B. Murdock used the term *terror* as he contrasted Christ's temperament and charity to Kaiser Wilhelm II, the German Kaiser and King of Prussia during World War I:

> "He [Christ] said 'Suffer the little children to come unto me, for of such is the kingdom of heaven.' That was the testimony of the Savior, in whose footsteps we are striving to follow. What a vast difference between that and the statement of the monster to his armies, to the effect: 'Leave your mark when you go through the great cities, that you may strike terror to the inhabitants of the world, even to the extent of killing, crucifying women and children, soldiers, prisoners or any one, that terror may come into the hearts of the people! That the fear of the sword and of the aim of the Kaiser, (who falsely represents that he is a representative of the Almighty) might strike terror to the hearts of the people."[26]

Other church leaders used the term *terror* to describe the effects of war and militarism, alluding to physical devastation and emotional damage inflicted through fear. Many conveyed the futile application of despotic rule over a people and advocated for liberty and tenets of democracy.

Terrorism as a Political Tool to Engender Change and Incite Fear (1960s–Present)

After another lull in the use of *terror* and related terms, these terms reemerged in the 1960s. The gradual increase from the 1960s into the 1980s emphasized fear, anarchy, and war. In the late 1970s, *terror* and associated terms took on the distinct meaning of violence conducted by individuals and networks pursuing political change. In the October 1979 General Conference, Barbara B. Smith, General President of the Relief Society, discussed the harrowing times and vulnerability of Saints throughout the world in the midst of new threats, commenting:

> "My heart was deeply touched by the obedience of sisters I recently met in a country at war. I heard the branch Relief Society president commend them for their commitment to the work of the Lord and to each other during the perilous times they faced each day. She said, 'You never know when you step outside your door whether you will be attacked by terrorists, yet you do your visiting teaching and attend all of your church meetings. You are courageous women who do a mighty work quietly in such a time as this."[27]

In the execution of their religious duties, Saints began to face threats of physical violence. That danger continued into the next decade, as the likelihood of violence also increased in areas where North American missionaries and Latter-day Saint chapels constituted vulnerable and symbolic entities associated with the United States, at least in the eyes of many anti-US terrorist groups.

This steady increase in the frequency of the terms *terror* and *terrorism* in General Conference addresses took place during a time when persecutions targeting chapels and missionaries increased, mainly in South America. In the wake of the assassinations of Latter-day Saint missionaries Todd Ray Wilson and Jeffrey Brent Ball in Bolivia on May 24, 1989, Elder M. Russell Ballard stated the following in the October 1989 General Conference:

> "Our missionaries have not participated in this great work without serious challenges, tribulations, and difficulties. Parents of missionaries have always known the risk of losing a loved one serving in the mission field due to accident or illness. Now, we must add to the risk of missionary service the possibility of acts of terrorism. Terrorism is centuries old but perhaps has never before been so open and blatant nor had such extensive news coverage. Terrorism has many victims. They include the innocent and law-abiding people residing in

> a troubled region who are striving to provide for their families and to do what is right. Missionaries live among the peoples of the world; and even with the protection of the members, they also can become innocent victims of acts of violence."[28]

Terrorism took on a new and more personal meaning, as threats of violence seemed to pervade previously safe communities in Western countries. Communist extremist groups and others emerged in the Western Hemisphere, determined to attack US facilities and citizens abroad as political statements, such as to protest US military actions in the Middle East.

This ever-present danger and possibility of violence with political objectives increased in frequency into the new millennium. In his dedicatory prayer of the Conference Center, the new site of all General Conferences in Salt Lake City, Utah, President Gordon B. Hinckley incorporated protection from such threats among the invoked blessings upon the edifice. He said, "Protect it from [. . .] the desecrating hand of the vandal and destroyer. Preserve it from conflict and acts of terrorism."[29] General Conference addresses reflected this evolving and pervasive threat as General Authorities counseled Saints on how to supplant fear with faith. Many likened the scriptures unto our day, including President Boyd K. Packer when he spoke on terrorism and stated, "We are not blind to the conditions in the world," and then continued, "Isaiah promised, 'In righteousness shalt thou be established: thou shalt be far from oppression; for thou shalt not fear: and from terror; for it shall not come near thee (Isaiah 54:14).'"[30] The most prevalent period of General Conference references to terrorism occurred in the five years following the 9/11 attacks, but General Authorities continue to provide guidance on how to endure such evils.

President Gordon B. Hinckley's General Conference Address Following the 9/11 Attacks

Within one month of the 9/11 attacks, President Hinckley spoke on peril and threats associated with terrorism, describing the plan involving hijackings and subsequent attacks as, "cruel and cunning, an act of consummate evil." He discussed fundamentals of the gospel of Jesus Christ, including the importance of prayer, emphasizing that strict observance to commandments would provide protection and peace. Discussing the uncertain economic future in the United States and elsewhere, he provided counsel on tithing and personal finance. He also discussed the Constitution as a model for other nations to follow, emphasizing safeguards for freedom and liberty included therein. President Hinckley described Satan's role in the world's history of violence, remarking, "Treachery and terrorism began with him. And they will continue until the Son of God returns to rule and reign with peace and righteousness among the sons and daughters of God."[31]

CHAPTER 2

BATTLEGROUND OF HEARTS AND MINDS

"Therefore he had accomplished his design, for he had hardened [their] hearts [. . .] and blinded their minds, and stirred them up to anger, insomuch that he had gathered together a numerous host to go to battle . . . "

—Alma 48:3

The Center of Gravity

War, ancient and modern, teaches a perpetual truth: the hearts and minds of men play a central role in every conflict. Failed generals ignored this concept, while their most adept counterparts leveraged men through influence, appealing to men's emotions and thoughts to accomplish their purposes. In his work *On War*, Prussian military theorist Carl Von Clausewitz introduced the concept of the center of gravity, defined in modern military regulations as, "the source of power that provides moral or physical strength, freedom of action, or will to act."[32] The center of gravity in conflict often involves civilians and how belligerents gain or lose their collective support.

Some leaders attempt to exert control over or eliminate civilians from the equation through genocide. Many instill fear in the populace through brutality. Others assimilate defeated peoples, integrating the conquered forces or people among their ranks to curb revolts. In recent conflicts, especially insurgencies in the Middle East and Asia, leaders focused on providing security to locals and establishing legitimacy in efforts to gain lasting support and inspire change. Generals and statesmen must acknowledge the crucial role of hearts and minds in conflict and address them through action. Evidence of attempts to do so are plentiful, most apparent in budget allocations on non-lethal targeting to influence people or in political speeches and military strategies replete with the phrase *hearts and minds*.

This collective will sustains a force in a war of attrition and emboldens people in the face of a powerful enemy. Regarding the American Revolution, a classic example of a struggle for freedom and delivery from oppression against a formidable foe, John Adams penned:

> "The Revolution was in the minds and hearts of the people; a change in their religious sentiments of their duties and obligations [. . .] This radical change in the principles, opinions, sentiments, and affections of the people, was the real American Revolution."[33]

The outward physical rebellion of the Colonies and resulting series of battles against British forces constitutes the conflict known as the American Revolution, but, as Adams reflects, the true revolution began and took place within the minds and hearts of Americans. The most important battles occurred on an invisible battleground among thoughts and emotions.

Further illustrating the perpetual importance of this theme in warfare, American politicians and generals often referred to hearts and minds during recent conflicts. In 1965, US President Lyndon Baines Johnson declared, "We must be ready to fight in Vietnam, but the ultimate victory will depend upon the hearts and the minds of the people who actually live out there."[34] Fate revealed the pivotal role of resolve on the home front, as well, as American hearts and minds critical of the war effort altered the course of that war. Decades later, General David Petraeus and other strategic leaders employed the phrase in Iraq. In 2003, posters throughout military facilities in Iraq read, "What have you done to win Iraqi hearts and minds today?"[35] This concept played a central role in information operations and strategies during counter-insurgency campaigns in Iraq and Afghanistan. This battle of influence is also important to terrorists, who leverage propaganda, statements from charismatic leaders, various social programs, and other methods to persuade men, women, and children to adopt their ideologies and use violence to bring about change.

The hearts and minds model did not begin in recent centuries among generals and tacticians formulating war plans or terrorist leaders devising propaganda campaigns; rather, the concept reaches far back to spiritual beginnings. The armed conflict plaguing the world throughout the history of mankind is a continuation of a great battle in which we all participated but have since forgotten. In other words, mortal conflict on earth is a likeness and continuation of spiritual warfare past, present, and future. This physical violence fulfills the scriptural truth, "That which is spiritual [is] in the likeness of that which is temporal; and that which is temporal in the likeness of that which is spiritual."[36] Ancient and modern prophets teach us about a spiritual conflict beginning in the pre-mortal existence—a battle between good and evil—and at this conflict's core were the hearts and minds of God's children.

The War in Heaven

The fulcrum of temporal and spiritual warfare balances on the hearts and minds of men. Since the beginning, good and evil actors influenced man's emotions and thoughts. These unseen powers persuade men in the use of their agency, encouraging them to do good or tempting them to do evil. This fundamental principle of agency is central in warfare and has broad applications, such as the war between good and evil, and more scaled applications, including each individual's daily struggle between right and wrong.

Before we came to earth, we lived as spirits in the presence of God. In scripture, we learn of a Grand Council, wherein God the Father presented His Plan of Salvation. When He chose Jesus to become our Savior, rather than Lucifer who sought to destroy the agency of man, Lucifer became "angry," rebelled, and "drew a third of the host of heaven with him."[37] Each of the spirits following Heavenly Father gained the opportunity to come to the earth and have a body and the opportunity to progress, whereas those that followed Lucifer were cast out, never to gain a body or follow a path enabling progression.

Elder Larry R. Lawrence of the Seventy elaborates on the methods of spiritual warfare employed in that pre-mortal war over agency. He explains that as spirits, rather than use weapons like swords or guns, "the premortal war was fought with words, ideas, debate, and persuasion. Satan's strategy was to frighten people."[38] With these weapons, he targeted the hearts and minds of God's individual spirit children. Elder Lawrence states, "the [. . .] advantage that helped Jehovah win the hearts of God's children was the powerful testimonies borne by His supporters, led by Michael, the archangel."[39] Prior to their banishment to outer darkness, Lucifer and his followers are temporarily on the earth to provide opposition during our mortal probation.

The Battle Continues on the Earth Today

The battle for hearts and minds that began in the premortal existence continues today through visible and invisible forces. The prophet Lehi taught, "it must needs be, that there is an opposition in all things," in order to provide man opportunities to make choices and "bring to pass [. . .] good [or] bad."[40] Satan is fully aware of the susceptibility of the hearts and minds of men and masterfully employs time-proven tactics to convince men to misuse their agency.

Positive, godly, noble influences include the Spirit of Christ persuading men to do good works and pursue truth, the Holy Ghost, and the prophets. The Lord taught that revelation involves these good influences acting on these two vital organs. In Doctrine and Covenants, we read, "I will tell you in your *mind* and in your *heart*, by the Holy Ghost, which shall come upon you and which shall dwell in your heart."[41] The Lord also strengthens our resolve and imparts the Gifts of the Spirit through these organs. The Apostle Paul advised the Saints to remain steadfast in Christ, writing to the Philippians, "And the peace of God, which passeth all understanding, shall keep your *hearts* and *minds* through Christ Jesus."[42] He imparts strength and revelation to the hearts and minds of those who are in tune with the Spirit.

Satan and his followers target these vital organs through other means. They understand the impressionability of these core organs representing man's emotions and thoughts. As they target men through temptations of passion, pride, and power, they lay claim to their souls. Satan also influences men through the actions of others. The objective of terrorism, for instance, is to produce fear that prompts change, overriding agency through coercion and threats of violence.

Latter-day Saint Chapel of San Carlos District, Huancayo, Peru

The San Carlos chapel was one particular location with unique manifestations of both good and evil. One morning during the chapel's construction, neighbors notified one of the ward leaders of an explosion. Brother Manuel Moises Sanchez rushed to the site, where he encountered the work supervisor, engineer Julio Cerna. Together, they surveyed the damage, discovering the terrorists had used dynamite, which inflicted little physical damage near the chapel steeple, and finding the perpetrators had left "a red flag with the sickle and hammer, the symbol of the terrorists." The flag belonged to the Shining Path terrorist group, a Communist faction later responsible for the assassinations of two Latter-day Saint missionaries and attacks at other chapels.

The same meetinghouse was the site of spiritual experiences during this era of harsh opposition. One of the ward's bishopric counselors explained that as he approached the chapel one morning, he "heard a choir singing from within the chapel," producing a "beautiful melody." After entering the chapel, the choir ceased, and upon searching every room and the Sacrament Hall and finding no one within the chapel, he felt "joy in his heart," and from thence went forth the saying that "in the San Carlos chapel sang Heavenly Choirs."

On a different occasion, Brother Simeon Bonifacio, who was President of the Huancayo Branch at the time when the stake was a district, was alone one morning cleaning the building on the eve of District Conference. "Suddenly, he had an impression that someone had entered," and upon looking up from where he was standing near the bathroom adjacent to the building entrance, he "saw the Lord." He lowered his eyes and then looked back, but He was gone. Also of note, this same brother later had a dream that he entered a cemetery where people sat upon each gravestone, waiting for someone to do their ordinances vicariously. At the time, there was "much enthusiasm" among members of the District engaged in genealogy work. The opposition presented by the Shining Path and other groups struck during this time of significant spiritual progress.[43]

Forging the Character of the Individual and Society

The repeated application of agency produces habits and character; hence, good and evil forces seek to influence how we use our agency to ultimately transform us into a good or evil person and set the conditions for our eternal fate. Man develops the Christlike attributes, including knowledge, charity, virtue, and faith, through the condition of his heart and mind. Sin and temptation, as well as the emotional and mental drives toward terrorism, also target these vulnerable and susceptible parts of man. The armor of God protects these vital organs.

One Jewish tradition provides a visible reminder of the unseen spiritual battle present within each person. Scripture and oral tradition teach that Jews wore phylacteries, also known as *tefillin*, which were "small leather boxes strapped onto the forehead and left arm to show that their minds and hearts were constantly dedicated to God's law."[44] Each box contained small parchment rolls with text from the Old Testament. Jews wrapped one phylactery around the head, so the box rested on the forehead, and wrapped the other around the left arm, so the box would rest over the heart during prayer. In this way, the phylacteries served to "help them remember to follow God's commandments."[45] The placement of these visible reminders held special significance, symbolic of the battleground between good and evil.

Forces acting on a person's heart and mind help to forge that individual's character. Similarly, these forces collectively forge the ethos, or nature and character, of a society. There may reside within a group of people a mixture of righteous and wicked individuals, but a society can polarize to one extreme or the other. In scripture, the Lord often uses the term Zion to describe the spiritual condition of a group of Saints. The Book of Mormon mentions three Zion societies based on the collective spiritual disposition of the people: Antediluvian Zion (city of Enoch), Nephite Zion (golden Nephite era), and Latter-day Zion (the New Jerusalem).[46]

Individuals may alternatively gravitate toward Satan. When this occurs collectively, that society becomes the antithesis of Zion. The Book of Ether, within the Book of Mormon, recounts the history of a small tribe leaving the Middle East at the time of the Tower of Babel. The Lord spared the group, allowing them to retain their original language and promised to lead them to a choice land. The tribe later occupied the Americas and flourished into a powerful civilization known as the Jaredites. Over hundreds of years of conflict and spiritual decay, the Jaredite society collapsed, culminating in one final battle of epic proportions. Millions were slaughtered, leaving a sole survivor among the corpses of a decimated civilization. The abridger and narrator, a Nephite prophet named Moroni, describes the spiritual condition of the Jaredites just prior to this final battle in one verse of the final chapter. In Ether 15:19, we read,

> "But behold, the Spirit of the Lord had ceased striving with them, and Satan had full power over the *hearts* of the people; for they were given up unto the hardness of their *hearts*, and the blindness of their *minds* that they might be destroyed; wherefore they went again to battle."

All this moral depravity and conflict came back to the condition of their hearts and minds. The verse clearly illustrates the battle between unseen forces acting on the hearts and minds of individuals. Through their agency, they permitted Satan to lay hold on their hearts and minds.

The Heart: Emotions and Feelings

The heart—throughout scripture, history, and literature—symbolizes emotions and passions, or the spiritual core of man. Good and evil actors may target and influence the heart. The "breastplate of righteousness," a critical protection included in the "armour of God," reveals the fragility and potential susceptibility of the heart.[47] This vital organ serves as a key vector through which God refines man, but also a chief target for the fiery darts of Satan.

Several positive and godly actors may influence the heart, including the Holy Ghost. One uplifting influence affecting the heart is the Spirit of Elijah, which "turn[s] the heart of the fathers to the children, and the heart of the children to their fathers."[48] This refers to the important latter-day work of genealogy. Elder David A. Bednar of the Quorum of the Twelve Apostles described the Spirit of Elijah as a "distinctive influence of the Holy Ghost [which] bears powerful witness of the Father's plan of happiness and draws people to search out and cherish their ancestors and family members."[49] Such positive influences inspire godliness and nourish faith, hope, and charity.

Similarly, evil and wickedness can negatively influence the hearts of men in ways that are selfish and cruel. The scriptures mention the spirit of contention, fear, and other negative emotions. The buffetings of Satan can slowly poison the heart with malice and hatred, fomenting violence and acts of terrorism.

The Heart of Cain and the Origins of Terrorism on the Earth

The scriptures teach important principles about Satan's adeptness in appealing to men's emotions and leveraging them to carry out evil works, a necessary skill in promulgating terrorism. A scriptural case study illustrating this strategy of targeting the heart involves the first murder on earth, wherein Cain slew his brother, Abel. Genesis 4:5 provides a brief description of Cain's reaction to God's refusal of his offering, simply stating, "Cain was very wroth, and his countenance fell."[50] This is the only verse summarizing the complex series of thoughts and emotions leading up to the first account of murder on the earth.

Latter-day scripture, however, elaborates on the intricacies of Cain's transformation. Verses in the Pearl of Great Price describe Cain's psychological state prior to, during, and after this murder and Satan's direct role in planting the motive within Cain's heart.

The following account from Moses 5:16–33 (italics added) and commentary describes this murder and analyzes Cain's emotions and thoughts, acknowledging Satan's actions throughout the explanation. Beginning with the initial three verses:

> **16** And Adam and Eve, his wife, ceased not to call upon God. And Adam knew Eve his wife, and she conceived and bare Cain, and said: I have gotten a man from the Lord; wherefore he may not reject his words. *But behold, Cain hearkened not, saying: Who is the Lord that I should know him?*
>
> **17** And she again conceived and bare his brother Abel. And Abel hearkened unto the voice of the Lord. And Abel was a keeper of sheep, but Cain was a tiller of the ground.
>
> **18** And *Cain loved Satan more than God.* And *Satan commanded him, saying: Make an offering unto the Lord.*

Adam and Eve instructed their posterity on the gospel of Christ, but Cain rejected these teachings. When Cain's parents confronted him, Cain responded in a similar manner to how Moses reacted when Satan told Moses to worship him. Moses "looked upon Satan and answered: Who art thou [. . .] and where is thy glory, that I should worship thee?"[51] In both accounts, men were instructed to worship. Moses discerned the evil in Satan's demand and rejected Satan, whereas Cain evidently rejected God early on in his instruction from loving parents. In these first few verses describing Cain's early Gospel and earthly learning and development, we see how his temporal choices mirrored Lucifer's in the pre-existence.

Cain's actions continue:

> **19** And in process of time it came to pass that *Cain brought of the fruit of the ground an offering unto the Lord.*
>
> **20** And Abel, he also brought of the firstlings of his flock, and of the fat thereof. And the Lord had respect unto Abel, and to his offering;

Table 2.1: Comparison between Cain (pre-murder) and Lucifer (pre-rebellion)

Topic	Cain (Moses 5:16–33)	Lucifer (Abraham 3:27–28)
Location/Time	World	Pre-mortal Existence
Knowledge of Gospel	Taught by parents, Adam and Eve	Knew fullness of Plan of Salvation; knew God
Pride; rejected Gospel	Rejected teachings	Rejected Plan of Salvation
Profession/Role	Tiller of the ground (Abel was shepherd of sheep)	Self-proclaimed god of this world (Jesus was shepherd of men)
Loyalty	Loved Satan	Father of Evil; open rebellion against God

> **21** But unto Cain, and to his offering, he had not respect. *Now Satan knew this, and it pleased him. And Cain was very wroth, and his countenance fell.*

One's countenance reflects his or her emotional and mental state. References throughout scripture describe a change in one's countenance worsening after sin or improving during and after repentance. This account states Cain's countenance fell as he surrendered his will to Satan, providing a physical manifestation of his spiritual decay. The account elaborates:

> **22** And the Lord said unto Cain: Why art thou wroth? Why is thy countenance fallen?
>
> **23** If thou doest well, thou shalt be accepted. And if thou doest not well, sin lieth at the door, and *Satan desireth to have thee*; and except thou shalt hearken unto my commandments, I will deliver thee up, and it shall be unto thee according to his desire. And thou shalt rule over him;
>
> **24** For from this time forth thou shalt be the father of his lies; thou shalt be called Perdition; for thou wast also before the world.
>
> **25** And it shall be said in time to come—That *these abominations were had from Cain; for he rejected the greater counsel which was*

> *had from God*; and this is a cursing which I will put upon thee, except thou repent.

Cain's parents, as well as the Lord himself, called Cain to repentance. They explained the gospel of Jesus Christ, emphasizing repentance, and discussed the risks associated with failure in overcoming the natural man. This warning extends to all of us caught in the snares of the natural man and allowing Satan to manipulate us through passions and emotions. Man becomes subject to the will of Satan the more he heeds the spirit of contention, greed, lust, and malice. The following verses outline Cain's actions after failing to heed these warnings.

> **26** And *Cain was wroth, and listened not any more to the voice of the Lord*, neither to Abel, his brother, who walked in holiness before the Lord.
>
> **27** And Adam and his wife mourned before the Lord, because of Cain and his brethren.
>
> **28** And it came to pass that Cain took one of his brothers' daughters to wife, and *they loved Satan more than God.*
>
> **29** And *Satan said unto Cain: Swear unto me by thy throat, and if thou tell it thou shalt die; and swear thy brethren by their heads, and by the living God, that they tell it not; for if they tell it, they shall surely die; and this that thy father may not know it; and this day I will deliver thy brother Abel into thine hands.*
>
> **30** And *Satan sware unto Cain that he would do according to his commands. And all these things were done in secret.*

This secrecy associated with violence has been a chief characteristic among extremist and terrorist organizations since mankind's beginning. Secrecy is a recurring theme in diabolical groups utilizing murder as a weapon for political change or personal gain, evident among the Gadianton Robbers plaguing the Nephite society in the Book of Mormon and modern terrorist factions. Recruits often join such groups relatively easily, but cannot leave under threat of death.

Finally, the final verses of the account reveal the result of Cain's heart turning away from the Lord:

> **31** And Cain said: Truly I am *Mahan, the master of this great secret, that I may murder and get gain*. Wherefore Cain was called Master Mahan, and *he gloried in his wickedness.*
>
> **32** And Cain went into the field, and Cain talked with Abel, his brother. And it came to pass that while they were in the field, *Cain rose up against Abel, his brother, and slew him.*
>
> **33** And *Cain gloried in that which he had done, saying: I am free; surely the flocks of my brother falleth into my hands.*

These verses offer a unique perspective on the mind and heart of a man warped by evil influences. Cain makes a pact with Satan, the Great Imitator, and acquires a new name. Secrecy is an important theme regarding this pact and method of getting gain. Terrorist groups are dependent upon secrecy in their operations and recruiting efforts in similar ways, as their methods go against established and legal forms of acquiring wealth, earning power and influence, and bringing about political change. While Cain's motive involved gain, as opposed to power, change, revenge, and other motives of terrorist groups, Satan's influence on Cain reveals how he targets men's hearts and convinces them to commit violence for unrighteous causes. His acute observation skills enable him to recognize weaknesses, identify the desires of men, and leverage those through his craftiness and cunning to distort perceptions to the convincing of men to commit violent acts, including terrorism.

Transforming Hatred into Action

Multiple adages express the principle that thoughts turn into actions and habits. Ultimately, one of Satan's objectives is to prompt men to commit sin through constant temptation and buffetings, not only claiming their souls by convincing them to spiritually distance themselves from God, but also to harm others in the process. Rather than simply planting hatred in the heart and kindling that flame, he prods men to act on that hatred, often to the detriment of others through physical violence or by imposing their will on others.

Ancient scripture revealed in the latter days provides detailed accounts of historical peoples influenced by Satan's attacks on the heart. Shortly following Adam's death, the spread of violence manifested Satan's influence on men's emotions, as described in the following verse (italics added):

> "And the children of men were numerous upon all the face of the land. And in those days *Satan had great dominion among men*, and *raged in their hearts*; and *from thenceforth came wars and bloodshed*; and a man's hand was against his own brother, in administering death, because of secret works, seeking for power."[52]

The heart served as the root of this deep-seated animosity, springing forth as violence severing the earliest familial ties. This hatred culminated in wars and bloodshed that laid waste to entire civilizations. This Satanic method of infiltrating the heart to bring about violence and terror continues today.

The Book of Mormon is replete with examples of such transformations on the micro (individual) and macro (societal) levels. Latter-day Saint scholar Hugh Nibley commented on the Lamanites' tactics and policies toward their religious Nephite enemies, focusing on the role of emotion. He explained their methods were synonymous with terrorism, driven by hatred and rage. Discussing Mosiah 11:16–17, Nibley commented:

> "Against this rich and apparently strong kingdom, the Lamanites adopt a policy of terrorism—infiltration, but it's terrorism. It's not banditry which is just stealing. Bandits and pirates can be good-natured and even be friendly. These people are animated by hatred and by a policy. They are real terrorists, in other words. They think they are idealists, as it tells us here. Verse 16: 'And it came to pass that the Lamanites began to come in upon his people, upon small numbers, and to slay them in their fields, and while they were tending their flocks.' Then it says in the next verse: 'Thus the Lamanites

> began to destroy them, and to exercise their hatred upon them.' See, they were motivated to exercise their hatred; they were real terrorists. Remember they had the case that they were just freedom fighters for their particular cause, etc. This is terrorism, not just banditry. They didn't just come in to rob them. 'The Lamanites came upon them and killed them, and drove many of their flocks out of the land; thus the Lamanites began to destroy them, and to exercise their hatred upon them.' This is a very bad thing, this terrorism."[53]

The Lamanites held bitter animosity for their brethren, the Nephites, prompting them to commit atrocities and strike fear into the Nephites through their attacks.

Satan continues to target men's hearts in attempts to embroil opposition against the Church, which includes acts of terrorism. In the April 2016 General Conference, Elder Dallin H. Oaks quoted 2 Nephi 28:20 to describe one of the methods Satan uses in the last days to present opposition to the Church, stating Satan will, "rage in the hearts of the children of men, and stir them up to anger against that which is good."[54] Satan will continue to target the heart, warping emotions to drift toward violence and terrorism. As the world darkens preceding the Second Coming, "men will harden their hearts against [the Lord], and they will take up the sword, one against another, and they will kill one another."[55] In recent decades, terrorism rates have risen throughout the world. At times, the Church has been one of the top targets for significant political violence against the US. Groups and lone actors have attacked places of worship, as well as individual members.

The Mind: Thoughts and Perceptions

The mind represents thoughts and decisions. Man's brain is the foundation of logic that manifests itself in the actions of men, who are self-aware and differ from other creations chiefly in the frontal lobe, enabling them to anticipate the consequences of their actions and comprehensively evaluate outcomes of choices before taking action. As Paul describes the components of the "armour of God" to the Corinthians, he lists the "helmet of salvation."[56] This protective guard shields the mind from temptations and evil thoughts leading to sin and spiritual damnation.

Satan and his followers seek to influence the mind and plant seeds of destruction. Regarding this timeless struggle, Elder George Q. Cannon once said the following:

> "We are engaged in the greatest of all warfares [. . .] and it will go on increasing until it will fill the whole earth—until the warfare that has been inaugurated will occupy the thoughts and minds of all the inhabitants of the earth, and until one of these powers will prevail in the earth."[57]

The thought processes culminating in a terrorist attack are one fulfillment of this declaration. Media outlets and storylines sometimes perpetuate perceptions of terrorists as crazed lunatics who illogically wage violence in pursuit of some irrational goal. However, terrorism is deliberate, at least in the sense of the violent action occurring after a thorough mental process of radicalization and moral rationalization for leveraging violence against other humans.

The Perpetrator: Psychology behind Radicalization

Experts seek to understand the psychology behind radicalization and terrorism. A leading scholar in this field is Fathali M. Moghaddam, professor of psychology at Georgetown University and Director of the university's Conflict Resolution Program. Moghaddam explores and describes the process of radicalization in terms of the metaphor of a "narrowing staircase leading to the terrorist act at the top of a building."[58] This metaphor contains a staircase advancing to higher floors, representing more advanced degrees of radicalization. As the individual moves from the ground level to the fifth floor, he or she "see[s] fewer and fewer choices, until the only possible outcome is the destruction of others, or oneself, or both."[59] This model, when viewed through a spiritual lens, reveals aspects of Satan's stratagem in turning the minds of men toward terrorism.

One Book of Mormon account tells of the Nephite traitor Amalickiah, who gained control of the Lamanite armies through a cunning plan. After luring Lehonti down from a mountain camp, "Amalickiah caused that one of his servants should administer poison by degrees to Lehonti, that he died."[60] Similarly, Satan slowly poisons men through these degrees of radicalization. Diverse ideologies counter to the gospel taint the minds and distort logic, helping to justify violence in order to cause political change. Failure to intervene via education on liberty and principles of freedom and agency will result in a distorted perception of reality, tainted by selfishness, a lust for power, and various ideologies. The likelihood of returning to mental normalcy diminishes over time as Satan tightens the chain on captive minds. The Staircase to Terrorism model reveals the systematic process by which sympathizers transition into recruits and become full-fledged terrorists. Through millennia of practice, Satan understands how to subtly take hold of the minds of men and warp rationalization to promote violence and terror.

The Audience: Terrorism's Effects on the Mind

Terrorism is one of the many weapons in Satan's arsenal he employs in attempts to foil God's purposes and man's happiness. Men's hearts and minds play a central role in terrorism, as the general objective through leveraging violence is some form of change resulting from a shift in emotions and thoughts of the target audience. Understanding this concept aids in the study of contemporary terrorism's effects on the Church. For instance, a sudden increase of terrorism in the world's most prolific missionary regions manifests Satan's influence in contending for the souls of men, leveraging terrorism and subsequent fears to counter missionary work. An increase in faith and hope leads Satan to counter by eliciting fear and doubt, which can be attained through terrorism.

CHAPTER 3

IDEOLOGIES AND MOTIVES

"All extremes, except extreme devotion to the Enemy, are to be encouraged."

—Screwtape, in The Screwtape Letters by C. S. Lewis

The Role of Ideology in Terrorism

Ideology is a collection or system of ideals and values of an individual or a group, expressing the shared philosophies and beliefs driving their actions. Oftentimes, extremist groups publish their ideologies clearly in a manifesto, outlining their philosophies and ultimate objective. Some groups distribute propaganda leaflets reflecting their beliefs and motives as they try to recruit like-minded individuals. Many terrorists leave such pamphlets at their attack sites, spray paint symbols or phrases onto nearby walls conveying their demands, or contact media outlets after attacks to claim responsibility and justify attacks. Sometimes, identifying a group's or individual's underlying ideologies may require more analysis. Lone wolves, for instance, may not publicly declare their reasons for carrying out an attack. In such cases, law enforcement may find clues among the circumstances of the attack or evidence. Identifying the ideology behind an attack is essential in understanding why the target became a target and if, when, or how groups or individuals may again attack similar targets.

Studying ideologies serves as a departure point to understand why adherents of a particular extremist faction or terrorist group act in certain ways. Such research can reduce personal bias when analyzing a person or group. Ideologies play a fundamental role in terrorism and grant insights regarding target selection, motive, and the moral justification often necessary to bypass natural inhibitions and carry out violent actions against another human being. The most direct and efficient means to understand why terrorists resort to violence is to study and understand their ideologies.

The Four Waves of Modern Terrorism

Individual and group belief systems and objectives characterized time periods of terrorist attacks in recent history, based on political situations, grievances, methods of communication, and other factors. Terrorism studies expert David Rapoport describes four waves of modern terrorism, categorized based on similar ideologies behind attacks in distinct time periods. He explains most acts of terrorism throughout the world match ideological themes over generational periods, yielding four distinct waves: Anarchist, Nationalist, New Left, and Religious[61] (see Table 3.1).

These waves reflect prevalent themes among terrorist attacks across the globe. They are not necessarily reflective of terrorism themes targeting the Church. The scope of study focuses on contemporary terrorism, dating back to 1979 and the beginning of Rapoport's religious wave. Even so, ancient scripture of the Latter-day Saint canon and Conference talks by General Authorities provide important counsel regarding some of these predominant ideologies fueling terrorism. Also, groups ascribing to various ideologies characterized by these main waves have threatened or attacked the Church within the past forty years.

Lessons on Predominant Ideologies in Religious Context

Anarchist Ideologies

Anarchy, or lawlessness and the lack of political institutions or authority to govern a people, is an extremely inefficient and destructive government situation. Rapoport asserts modern terrorism originated in Russia in the late nineteenth century, beginning with anarchist groups

Table 3.1: Defining Characteristics of Rapoport's Four Waves of Modern Terrorism

Wave	Catalyst	Goals	Targets	Tactics	Reasons for Decline
Anarchist (1870s–1910s)	Slow political reform, declining legitimacies of monarchies	Revolution, eliminate government oppression	Heads of state	Assassinations using dynamite, bank robberies	Aggressive state opposition, beginning of World War I
Nationalist (1920s–1960s)	Versailles Peace Treaty, increased desire for self-determination	Eliminate colonial rule, create new states	Police and military	Guerrilla style hit and run attacks	Achieved goals, colonial rulers withdrew from territories
New Left (1960s–1980s)	Vietnam War, Cold War tensions	Eliminate the capitalist system	Governments, increased focus on US	Hijackings, kidnappings, assassinations	End of Cold War
Religious (1979–2020s) (predicted)	Iranian Revolution, new Islamic century, Soviet invasion of Afghanistan	Creation of global Islamic Caliphate	US, Israel, Europe, mass transportation systems, public venues	Suicide bombings, aircrafts and vehicles as weapons	Unknown

Source: Erin Walls, "Waves of Modern Terrorism: Examining the Past and Predicting the Future" master's thesis, Georgetown University, 2017, https://repository.library.georgetown.edu/bitstream/handle/10822/1043900/Walls_georgetown_0076M_13610.pdf?sequence=1.

fomenting violence aimed at crippling government from the top. He explains that anarchists, dissatisfied with the archaic practice of "traditional revolutionaries [. . .] depend[ing] on pamphlets and leaflets to generate an uprising," attempted to awaken a society with "huge reservoirs of latent ambivalence and hostility" and polarize society through terror.[62] Firearms and dynamite enabled individuals and small groups to strike targets with greater likelihood of success and, in many cases, less risk of interdiction or capture. This spirit of anarchy eventually gave way to anti-colonial motivations precipitating a Nationalist wave beginning in the 1920s, but anarchy persisted as a frequent ideology fueling terrorism throughout several decades.

Ancient and modern revelations provide important counsel regarding anarchy and this ideology's relation to terrorism. Secret combinations of old sought to overthrow governments, operating as anarchist groups intent on getting gain and accumulating power. Anarchist ideologies contributed to the collapse of the Jaredite civilization described in the Book of Mormon. The Jaredites, under the direction of the Lord, left the society of the Tower of Babel before the Lord confounded their language. The group traveled to the coast and constructed boats to cross the ocean, eventually settling in the Americas. The Lord's warning to the civilization regarding anarchists, which eventually contributed to their downfall, is recorded in Ether 8:22–25, where He warns the Jaredites of secret combinations and "seek[ing] to overthrow the freedom of all lands, nations, and countries," which will cause "the destruction of all people, for it is built up by the devil."[63] The scene in ancient America between 279 BC and 130 BC bears similarities to terrorist tactics during the Anarchist Wave of modern terrorism. The downfall of the Jaredite civilization is linked to a secret combination instituted by Akish to assassinate the Jaredite king. The associated oaths of this secret society were ancient practices passed down from Cain, the first murderer, and rooted in guidance from Satan.[64] This secret society intent on assassinating the chief executive persisted for several years and impacted Jaredite culture and politics significantly. Initially, the group overthrew the kingdom of Omer, king of the Jaredites, and then killed the de-facto king, Jared.[65] This secret society and these practices persisted throughout generations. Heth personally assassinated his father, Coriantum, to seize the Jaredite throne years later.[66] Rebellion and assassinations prompted changes to the executive head in subsequent generations, eventually culminating in a civil war destroying the entire civilization.

The Book of Mormon account of the Jaredites is especially relevant to modern-day terrorism, as these actions among the Jaredites parallel terrorism trends during the Anarchist Wave of the 19th century. Assassinations of heads of state became a tactic characterizing both eras, as terrorists sought to overthrow political institutions by attacking those in the highest seats of government. In modern times, this tactic originated in Russia and spread throughout neighboring countries and Europe. Anarchist literature and ideologies extended to the United States, inspiring a second-generation American named Leon Czolgosz to assassinate US President William McKinley in 1893. The aftershock of assassination attempts during the Anarchist Wave, as well as rebellions and attempts to overthrow governments, validate prophetic warnings about anarchism and the Book of Mormon's political teachings for these last days.

Section 134 of the Doctrine and Covenants, recorded on August 17, 1835, is another important segment of doctrine concerning government and anarchy. The entire section outlines the role of government in ruling society, according to God's guidance, but verse 6 is of particular interest, reading as follows (italics added):

> "We believe that every man should be honored in his station, rulers and magistrates as such, being placed for the protection of the innocent and the punishment of the guilty; and that *to the laws all men owe respect and deference, as without them peace and harmony would be supplanted by anarchy and terror*; human laws being instituted for the express purpose of regulating our interests as individuals and nations, between man and man; and divine laws given of heaven, prescribing rules on spiritual concerns, for faith and worship, both to be answered by man to his Maker."

Hence, laws are necessary for the preservation of freedoms and agency. The absence of laws fosters chaos and conditions in which terrorists may operate without restraint.

Nationalist Ideologies

Groups struggling for sovereignty and independence from colonialist ties carried out terrorist attacks throughout the following generation, or wave of modern terrorism. Naturally, much of the terrorism during that era occurred in colonies of powerful empires. Groups like the Basque Homeland/Fatherland and Liberty (ETA) in Spain and the Provisional Irish Republican Army (IRA) waged campaigns of bombings and armed assaults against military and law enforcement targets, attacking the legitimacy of their ruling empires by weakening security.

Terrorists with nationalist ideologies had minimal impacts on the Church during this wave. While imperialism became a commonly cited reason by far-left groups for their attacks against the Church in South America in the late 1980s and early 1990s, these South American groups' main ideologies involved Communist, Maoist, or Socialist philosophies and tenets. They did not attack US-affiliated targets because they were American colonies seeking sovereignty and independence; rather, many claimed to have attacked American businesses and other symbolic targets so as to fend off foreign influences and retain their cultural identities.

New Left Ideologies

Perpetrators of most contemporary terrorism targeting the Church held left ideologies of some form. President Ezra Taft Benson, the prophet during a period of frequent terrorist attacks against the Church, often spoke on the US Constitution and against principles championed under Communism, reflecting a sharp contrast between Communist philosophies and the gospel of Jesus Christ. The culture of the gospel, largely consisting of conservative norms and practices, contrast with those of leftist organizations. These differences sparked tensions in Chile and other South American countries in the 1980s and 1990s, as missionaries sought to convert from the same pool of citizens where leftist factions contented for recruits.

Religious Ideologies

Religion has played a significant role in many instances of terrorism, often providing the necessary reward or spiritual justification to bypass natural inhibitions against violence and murder. Links between religion and violence go back several centuries, as families and tribes grew in size and function to various civilizations with distinct customs, beliefs, and territories. The boundaries where major civilizations met often became regions plagued with war and strife. Members of opposing sides generally practiced different religions. Religion became a key factor of difference and served as another reason to eliminate the opponent.

Man has often misinterpreted the concept of sacrifice and the reasons for justifying war and violence throughout history. Referring to the earliest sacrifices on earth, scripture teaches that "Cain's offering was rejected by the Lord, probably for several reasons, including the fact that it was not done in faith nor in the prescribed and revealed manner."[67] The Lord accepted Abel's offering of the firstlings of his flock, but rejected Cain's offering of fruit he cultivated. In similar manner, Islamist extremists sacrifice themselves in suicide bombings, believing their sacrifice to be the will of Allah and that such violence is justified.

The majority of present-day terrorism involves religious ideologies. Most recent terrorist attacks occurred in the Middle East and involved indiscriminate killings of men, women, and children, often through suicide bombings or other means of self-sacrifice. Fortunately, such terrorism has had limited effects on the Church thus far. Of course, members perished in acts of terrorism such as the attacks on 9/11, but most terrorism targeting the Church or affecting church members involved attacks carried out by leftist factions.

The psychology of terrorism is a continually growing and evolving field of study. Government initiatives seek to identify factors contributing to terrorism and curb exposure to extremist messages, susceptibility to recruitment, and the desire to commit acts of violence. Upbringing, including exposure to prejudices throughout youth, may contribute to one's sense of superiority to other groups, nationalities, and cultures. Likewise, norms in a society help to legitimize and justify certain crimes when targeting select groups. Living conditions, such as poverty, ostracism, and unemployment, may influence individuals' susceptibility to recruitment by extremist organizations. All of these factors contribute to thoughts, intents, and action. The motivations leading men to commit acts of terror spring from their thoughts, intents, perceptions, loyalties, and feelings. In essence, motives develop in their hearts and minds.

Tehrik-e Taliban Pakistan (TTP) Threatens Latter-day Saint Missionaries

In 2001, the United States launched the invasion of Afghanistan to dismantle Al-Qaeda and deny the group safe haven in Afghanistan by ousting the Taliban from power. The Tehrik-e Taliban Pakistan dominated much of the area along the Afghanistan border and posed a significant threat to any nearby Americans. The group, designated a terrorist organization by the US Department of State, is a terrorist faction driven by religious (Islamist) ideologies; the group's characteristics and existence fall in line with David Rapoport's model of the religious wave of modern terrorism.[68] A small number of Latter-day Saint senior missionaries operated in Pakistan at the time, falling under the jurisdiction of the Singapore Mission. They received phone calls from the US Embassy around the time the invasion began, instructing them to flee immediately as the Tehrik-e Taliban would kill any Americans they encountered.[69] Elder G. William Kirby and Sister Joan S. Kirby were serving in an area of Pakistan controlled by the TTP when they received the warning call. They tried to reach their usual taxi driver for a ride to the airport, but they learned the TTP would kill the driver along with the passengers if he transported any white passengers. The Kirby's eventually reached the airport and safely left Pakistan via alternate means.

Ideologies and Motives behind Terrorist Attacks against Latter-day Saint Targets

Although most publicly documented modern terrorism targeting the Church occurred in the late 1980s and early 1990s during Rapoport's Religious Wave, the predominant ideologies fueling attacks against

The Church of Jesus Christ of Latter-day Saints involved far-left ideologies. Most terrorist groups with leftist political ideologies in South America during that period were communist extremist factions, engaging in terrorism in retaliation for US military or political actions or opposing cultural and economic influence of the US. Left wing ideologies are defined as follows in the US Army's field manual on antiterrorism:

> "These groups are usually associated with revolutionary socialism or variants of communism (Maoist, Marxist-Leninist). With the demise of many communist regimes and the gradual liberalization of the remainder toward capitalism, left-wing rhetoric can often move toward and merge with anarchistic thought."[70]

Much of the propaganda disseminated by groups targeting Latter-day Saint chapels conveyed ideals and objectives based on these leftist philosophies, which starkly contrasted with Church doctrine and North American values. Ideologies behind attacks against the Church include: far-left (183 attacks), unknown (119), criminal (4), jihadist (1), and separatist (1).[71] The locations of attacks, displayed in Figure 3.2, provides circumstantial evidence regarding ideologies fueling the attacks. The majority of attacks conducted by groups with unknown ideologies were likely carried out by leftist extremist groups, as most occurred in Chile or other parts of South America during an era dominated by far-left terrorism.

The geographic distribution of these attacks reflects high attack frequency in areas with strong church presence and significant political turmoil associated with terrorism or military dictatorships. Most terrorist attacks targeting the Church occurred in Chile, where leftist groups bombed chapels. Bombings, assassinations, and intimidation took place in Peru during the nation's war on terror, as the Shining Path terrorist group attacked police and military forces, terrorized rural communities and Lima alike, and attacked the Church for suspicions about missionaries' and members' loyalties and affiliations. The vast majority of violence constituting terrorism occurred in South America during a period when that continent experienced a wave of leftist terrorism slightly after the rest of the globe.

Figure 3.1: Geographic Distribution of Terrorist Attacks Targeting the Church

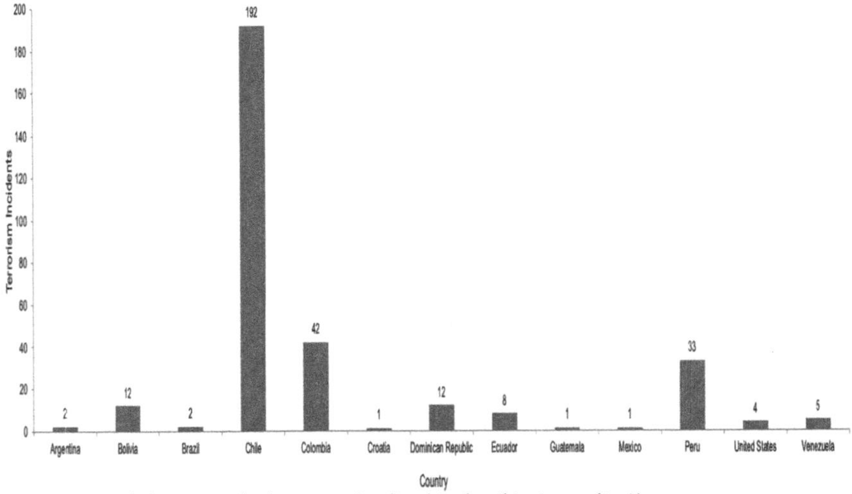

Source: Compiled using multiple sources (outlined in detail in Appendix A).

Far-left terrorism contains several sub-ideologies and motives, many countering imperialism and perceived attacks or influences weakening cultural identity or national sovereignty. Some far-left organizations countered the Church by drawing attention to the contrasting landscape of elegant chapels in less-wealthy communities, some proselyting themes of foreign missionaries, and other facets of Church social dynamics, doctrines, and origins. Suspicions and misperceptions engendered distrust from leftist groups and provided them with a viable target for attacks in protest of US presence and international policies.

Perceptions of American Imperialism

As a whole, citizens of South American countries welcomed North American influences and presence. Many came in contact with Latter-day Saints in their neighborhoods and developed favorable opinions of the Church, seeing the altruism and kindness of these Saints. Those who did not personally know a Latter-day Saint often came in contact with missionaries. Despite a favorable opinion of Saints among most people in South America, extremists viewed Saints as a threat. The most oft-cited reason behind terrorist attacks targeting the Church is the Church's affiliation with the United States. Many of the individuals who conducted bombings, assassinations, or other forms of terrorism against Church facilities or members considered the Church a symbol of the United States. Deputy Director of Central Intelligence Robert M. Gates stated in a 1988 speech that has since been declassified that Chilean terrorists saw the Church as "an extension of American imperialism."[72] Among other attitudes, a perception pervaded South American extremist circles that as the Church grew and trickled into rural areas and among indigenous groups, the influence of the United States replaced local culture and norms with North American culture and norms. Elevated frequencies of terrorism accompanied missionary success and significant membership growth in South America in the late 1980s and early 1990s.

As far back as the 1960s, much of the early Church growth in some South American countries, particularly Bolivia, centered around a small number of US families. Members of the Church serving in the United States Agency for International Development (USAID) or in embassies as military attaches played pivotal roles in Church growth. They experienced challenges, however, as some local nationals failed to distinguish their roles as government representatives or members of the Church; rather, these roles seemed to blend from an outsider's perspective. These Saints' practice of working for the government by day and volunteering for the Church by night or on weekends fostered misconceptions among extremists; they linked the Church to the US Government and political objectives. Rumors spread by word of mouth, strengthening the association between the Church and the US Government in some circles.

Some of these members who served in government capacities later returned to these areas to serve as mission presidents. While local nationals collectively embraced such leaders, this connection between representatives of the US Government and the Church contributed to some extremists' negative perceptions about the Church as an agent of American imperialism. In a few cases, politicians and prominent public figures held suspicions of the Church. In Bolivia, for instance, when populist general Juan José Torres seized control of the government in 1970, "he threatened to ban the LDS Church from Bolivia, precisely because of its relationship with US 'imperialism.'"[73] Hence, conflict resulted due to some church members who had occupied government posts and local authority positions within the Church.

These factors contributing to the perception that the Church was a symbol of the United States, especially as an extension of the US government, led leftist groups to target chapels in South America with bombs and propaganda. A 1985 top secret report of the National Intelligence Council, since declassified, mentions Communist groups' tendency to target the Church in Chile and asserts that the groups were becoming more confident in their tactics due to "increased help from the Soviet Union" in the form of "more central direction and coordination of terrorist activities."[74] In most South American countries, pockets of communist support manifested themselves in the form of terrorism targeting government sites and officials in the late 1980s and early 1990s, especially groups in Chile and neighboring countries targeting the Church. Another declassified CIA report asserts indigenous leftist groups targeted the Church because they viewed the Church's "activities as imperialistic."[75] Propaganda in leaflets and messages published by extremist groups through media outlets consistently claimed the Church served to further US interests in the region on behalf of US imperialism. One terrorist group assassinated a missionary companionship and left a sign next to the missionaries' bodies, reading, "This is how imperialists' supporters die."[76] Throughout these years of more frequent and more intense attacks against Saints, local nationals continued to support Saints in their communities. These rumors and negative perceptions were held by few, but those few managed to strike at vulnerable targets, such as missionaries and chapels.

Several factors contributed to these rumors of the Church's alleged association with US Government interests or furthering imperialistic claims, chief among them being a strong presence of North American missionaries, beautiful chapels in abundance in areas inhabited by the lower and middle classes, and rumors of espionage and subversion. The Church took steps to counteract perceptions regarding missionaries' objectives and the presence of meetinghouses and missionaries in foreign lands. One way leaders attempted to change the image of the Church was to incorporate service hours into missionary schedules, when missionaries would "take off their white shirts and ties and don casual clothes to pick up litter in the plazas, or maybe visit old-folks homes."[77] This visible display of charity likely softened hearts and welcomed discussion between local nationals and young missionaries, helping to curb rumors from spreading or persisting. Leaders published church declarations in South American newspapers outlining the Church's objectives and refuting accusations of imperialism or encroaching on the rights or lands of indigenous peoples.

The Catholic Church's Inability to Keep Pace with Modernization

During the second half of the Twentieth Century, a cultural shift occurred in several historically Catholic countries of South America. In large numbers, people with Catholic roots converted to Protestant faiths. The Church of Jesus Christ of Latter-day Saints grew rapidly, as did the Evangelical church and other denominations with proselyting members. Missionary work contributed to this large-scale transference, as well as many social and cultural conditions.

With this cultural shift came negative perceptions of North America, as most missionaries in South America came from North America with part of their mission to "encourage 'a new liberal, dynamic order like that which Protestantism had inspired historically,' as it was to convert Catholics to their own brand of Christianity."[78] The geographic focuses of this missionary work varied by sect, as Latter-day Saint missionaries mostly proselyted in urban areas, whereas Evangelist missionaries and those of other Protestant faiths labored in rural areas. Multiple anthropologists link the successes of these missionaries to some societal changes, especially the progression of capitalism and modernization, arguing that they "produce[d] the very kinds of social dislocations that make the Protestant religion increasingly attractive to those sectors affected most—the poor."[79] This was typical among Protestant converts in rural areas and some in urban areas converting to The Church of Jesus Christ of Latter-day Saints. Modernization led people to migrate from rural areas to cities throughout South America. Under organizations like the Pentecostal and Latter-day Saint churches, these migrants benefitted from the "new social unit and [. . .] paternalistic authority that [. . .] other organization[s], not even the post-conciliar Catholic Church, could supply."[80] The Church of Jesus Christ of Latter-day Saints, in particular, created a new dynamic in cities. The Church "dr[ew] Chileans from many class positions within urban society into a single organization," breaking down social barriers inhibiting intermingling of classes.[81] Latter-day Saint missionaries also baptized many white-collar workers in places like Santiago. Many of these converts served as local Church leaders shortly after conversion. Emilio Willems, professor of anthropology at Vanderbilt University, contended that the principles of individualism, inherent in Protestant faiths, attracted middle-sector landowners, rather than material attractions.[82] The Church grew rapidly throughout the second half of the twentieth century, as did many other Protestant faiths with missionaries. Toward the close of the 1970s, "a single convert was gained in Chile with 128 hours of proselyting, on average, compared with 480 hours in Argentina."[83] Most South Americans grew to appreciate a Latter-day Saint presence in their communities, admiring members for their selfless service and wholesome lifestyles. Even so, some citizens and governments remained skeptical of the Church and other religious groups. Leftist groups, as well as some scholars and media outlets, planted seeds of suspicion with propaganda attributing the presence of Latter-day Saint and other foreign missionaries to foreign government influence and surveillance, especially the US Government.

As expert anthropologists and sociologists noted, the Catholic Church could not adjust to the drastic cultural and political changes wrought by modernization. In a process uncharacteristic of large-scale religious conversion throughout world history, rather than converting from one major faith group to another (e.g., Islam to Christianity), a continent underwent a sweeping conversion from Catholicism to Protestantism, another religion under the umbrella of Christianity. People clung to these new organizations with social structures and practices aligned with principles and changes emerging from modernization. American political scientist Samuel P. Huntington explained,

> "If traditionally dominant religions do not meet the emotional and social needs of the uprooted, other religious groups move in to do so and in the process greatly expand their memberships

> and the saliency of religion in social and political life. [. . .] The number of Protestants in Latin America increased from roughly 7 million in 1960 to about 50 million in 1990. [. . .] Like the other world religions, Christianity is going through a resurgence connected to modernization, and in Latin America it has taken a Protestant rather than a Catholic form."[84]

In other words, Huntington asserted the Catholic church's inability to keep pace with modernization contributed to a large-scale conversion, as South Americans left Catholicism to join Protestant faiths. The organization and social dynamics within the Church of Jesus Christ of Latter-day Saints contributed to convert retention, as new members gained friends and strengthened relationships and benefited from regular spiritual nourishment through Church activities and the home and visiting teaching programs.

White North American Missionaries Dominated Latter-day Saint Missions

Throughout the various eras of church history, missionaries have always been the predominant image of the Church throughout the world; they are present where the Church is expanding through proselyting efforts. Missionaries are often the first or only contact people have with the Church. During the global era of the Church, as missionaries entered new countries and converts became pioneers and pivotal proselyting forces in their native lands, missionaries played a significant role in the Church's image abroad. Characteristics of the missionary force influenced outsiders' perceptions regarding the nature of the Church.

In the 1980s, most missionaries operating in foreign lands, especially South America, were white North Americans. Aside from clothing and hair style leading some to speculate these missionaries were CIA agents operating on behalf of the US intelligence community, people formulated perceptions about the Church's origins, organization, and objectives based on their limited knowledge of and exposure to the Church. Few temples were operational at the time and there was no internet for searches or educational resources on the religious group. Unless these people lived near a meetinghouse or personally knew a member of the Church, their awareness of the Church and any practices likely stemmed from an interaction with or simply seeing or knowing of missionaries. In foreign countries, citizens generally held favorable opinions of missionaries They admired their wholesome demeanor and nature, appreciated their selfless service, and respected their decision to commit eighteen months or two years in service to God and their fellowman. Despite these widely held favorable perceptions, extremists questioned missionaries' motives in serving abroad for such a long time for no monetary compensation, as well as their appearance mirroring their notions of intelligence agents. These criticisms and suspicions influenced attacks during this era of heightened persecution in the 1980s and 1990s.

Most missions in South America during this period were predominantly composed of white missionaries from North America. Similarly, white North Americans generally led these missions, often with military, government, or business backgrounds. This image led some outsiders to believe the Church was founded in the United States and was affiliated with American principles, such as capitalism. The perception contributed to attacks against the Church carried out by leftist groups protesting American policies or presence in their countries.

As terrorism threats increased in gravity and attack frequency, Church leaders remained mindful of the image portrayed through characteristics of the missionary force. Within months following the 1989 assassination of two North American elders in Bolivia, church leaders adjusted the ratio of local missionaries to Americans to 70:30 and paired each American with a local companion.[85] A chief objective of this change was to alter the image of the Church, believing the adjustment would emphasize the international nature of the Latter-day Saint faith and dissuade similar attacks against North American missionaries. Some missions paired South American missionaries and sent them "into the areas of most risk since they [were] not a target like the [North] Americans."[86] In September 1990, however, Shining Path terrorists killed Elders Christian Ugarte and Manuel Hidalgo in Huancayo, Peru. At the time, the Peru Lima East mission, where they labored, contained 300 missionaries from Peru, 104 North Americans, and 6 from other countries.[87] Elders Ugarte and Hidalgo were both native Peruvians, but the terrorists deliberately targeted them for their membership in the Church and allegedly for their affiliation with the United States, as they perceived the Church to be an American institution at odds with their ideologies.

The demography of the missionary force in parts of South America gradually transformed in the early 1990s from predominantly white North American young men to greater numbers of South Americans. By 1994, "all the missionaries in Peru [were] Peruvians or [were] from other Latin American nations" and "there [were] no North American missionaries in Bolivia."[88] As attacks against the Church subsided and some of the leftist organizations persecuting the Church dissolved, the composition of missionary forces readjusted and white missionaries returned to those South American missions previously vacated.

Elegant Chapels Clashed with Humble Residential Landscapes

The pace of chapel construction throughout South America matched the rapid growth of Church membership. Most chapels in South America are located within residential areas, often surrounded by small, single-story homes. In the United States, chapels may cover a wide geographic area as members can easily commute by vehicle. In South America, however, chapels often cover small geographic areas where members may walk or take a bus to a nearby stop. Few meetinghouses host more than one ward or branch; rather, chapels saturate certain neighborhoods where membership is high and wards meet in buildings that are exclusive to their individual wards.

Rumors increased as the Church increased chapel production in South American cities. In Bolivia, for instance, curiosity grew among some circles about "the Church's purchase of land and construction of Mormon chapels that appeared quickly all over the urban landscape between the 1970s and 1980s."[89] Similarly, chapel construction increased during Pinochet's rule in Chile. Extremists linked the two conditions and speculated about a connection between the dictator and the Church. The architecture of chapels also stood out among small business buildings and humble residences. Throughout South

America, especially in rural areas, the standard chapel was often a juxtaposition among cement one- or two-story homes painted in bright colors. In their host countries, the "elegant [Latter-day Saint] chapels of white cinder block with cast-brass lettering" numbered 1:50,000 Bolivians in 1987, much higher in comparison than the 1:271,000 Brazilians or 1:101,941 Ecuadorians at the time.[90] These chapels became predominant images of the Church, sometimes more so than missionaries or other characteristics of the Latter-day Saint faith.

In some instances, Church buildings resided among other elegant buildings in wealthy areas. The Chile Santiago Temple, for instance, is in the affluent Providencia sector of the city. In cities, some chapels, often within walking distance of members, would appear in neighborhoods of wealthy members of society. Most Chileans respected Saints attending church on Sundays in formal clothes to show respect to the Almighty. Even so, some extremists latched onto this occurrence of elegant chapels appearing in wealthy neighborhoods or poor barrios, which Professor David Knowlton asserted, "established Mormonism as a religious body which made a symbolic offering of formal society and elite status" and contributed to the image of upper-class membership, along with "the preferred Sunday dress for men—suit, white shirt, and tie—with its business associations."[91] These impressive appearances of members and chapels stood out from their modest surroundings, and extremists included this distinction as yet another factor justifying their suspicion.

The growing presence of the Church throughout South America attracted attention and criticism. Some extremists, as well as an occasional citizen or leader, interpreted the increasing number of chapels as efforts by the US to expand and claim territory. A declassified CIA report from 1989 stated that press reports quoted a Bolivian bishop as saying that, "religious sects constitute the spearpoint of Yankee imperialism."[92] Although this was an uncommon opinion, such assertions challenged the legitimacy of Latter-day Saint missionaries and proselyting efforts.

Another factor influencing attack trends dealt with physical presence. Statistics reflect a limited presence of American businesses and other entities in South America for terrorist groups to attack when targeting symbols of the United States. Most incidents involving

American targets involved attacks against facilities belonging to the Church, US embassies and consulates, and American restaurants, specifically McDonalds and Kentucky Fried Chicken. Latter-day Saint chapels constituted a soft target for groups to attack, since chapels had no guards or sentries (with very rare exceptions), as opposed to security forces protecting embassies and consulates. Chapels were thus a stationary long-term target that terrorists could bomb at any hour with low risk.

In the early 1990s, Church leaders directed the modification of chapel design, largely as a way to change the Church's image abroad. In this way, "[Latter-day Saint] architects [developed] a new design that [did] away with the American style, [which were] half the size of the old ones and cost much less to build."[93] Ultimately, most leftist groups disbanded before any real correlation could be drawn from chapel designs and what effects, if any, the modified structural plans had on terrorism statistics.

Doctrine and Social Dynamics Contrasted with Extremist Ideologies

Basic Church doctrine sharply clashed with the mentalities and objectives of extremists, mainly far-left extremists, who sought drastic political change, including aims to overthrow their national governments. Many Church teachings emphasized citizenship and adherence to laws, moving beyond the scriptural guidance to "render to Caesar the things that are Caesar's" to actively participate in civil government and serve in the community.[94] The Twelfth Article of Faith, one of thirteen core Latter-day Saint principles, reads, "We believe in being subject to kings, presidents, rulers, and magistrates, in obeying, honoring, and sustaining the law."[95] As people converted to the Church, far-left extremists perceived a threatening ideological shift as potential recruits joined the opposition—those supporting or submissive to the government—and their support zones dried up. In some cases, this divide even entered homes, as one brother might sympathize with leftist factions and become more active in supporting violent attacks, whereas another brother might join the Church and "become a traitor" in the eyes of any leftist sympathizer family members.[96] Hence, through the lens of these leftist factions, missionaries and chapels became symbols of a growing ideological schism in society.

Educational levels and wealth of Church members also contrasted with membership dynamics of leftist groups. According to the 2002 Chilean Census, 54% of Latter-day Saints completed secondary education and 21% attained higher education.[97] This contrasted with the lack of education and wealth among members of far-left organizations, especially members of the Lautaro Youth Movement (Movimiento Juventil Lautaro, or MJL), which generally consisted of young, uneducated hoodlums. These groups recognized the upward mobility evident among Latter-day Saints, which likely contributed to their aversion to Church members and brandishing them as supporters of American imperialism and capitalism. In the late 1990s, after terrorism targeting the Church waned, "1.5% of Chileans were capitalists, 17% were professionals, and 7.2% were petty entrepreneurs."[98] Such figures are representative of shared ideals among Church members supporting business and basic principles of capitalism. Church members' greater representation in managerial roles and white-collar positions in the workforce provided leftists additional justification for targeting. These elite or upper-class characteristics, as perceived by extremists, likely contributed to groups like the Lautaro Youth Movement targeting the Church in protest of social and wealth disparities, in addition to other grievances.

Right-wing extremist factions, although smaller and less vocal in many cases, also opposed the Church. Following the assassination of two missionaries in Bolivia, a US congressional staffer on the House Foreign Affairs Committee commented:

> "Missionaries agitate both the left and the right: the left because they represent anti-communist America; the right because they proselytize the Indians, and (those on the right) want them left alone and unchanged. The right includes the big landowners and mine owners."[99]

Right-wing groups conducted attacks and spread propaganda in favor of nationalistic ideals, opposing foreign influences. Drug traffickers also supported many right-wing paramilitary groups, leading to increased opposition faced by members of the Church. Left-wing groups, however, were responsible for the majority of terrorism targeting the Church.

Espionage and Conspiracy Theories

Among a handful of inevitable experiences faced by Latter-day Saint missionaries, such as losing a girlfriend or boyfriend or being bitten by a dog, is encountering someone claiming missionaries are members of the US intelligence community. Numerous newspaper articles, as well as memoirs and journals, document locals mistaking missionaries as CIA agents throughout the world, but especially in South America They certainly match the description from books and movies—young, fit, white men with close-cropped hair donning suit and tie—however far from the truth that may be. Many such perceptions, which are still common today, circulated throughout Europe before South America decades ago largely due to Soviet influence.

Material translated by the United States Government's Foreign Broadcast Information Service (FBIS) provides some historical context for this persistent perception about Latter-day Saint missionaries diffused across continents and among various cultures. Propaganda spreading conspiracy theories about the Church's ties to the US Government circulated throughout Europe in the early stages of the Cold War. A November 25, 1953 FBIS translation of a Moscow *Izvestia* article in Danish reveals early indications of propaganda targeting the Church and fabricating an affiliation between genealogical research and intelligence collection efforts. The translation begins by addressing "U.S. secret service activities" in Europe, explaining that "not only in Norway [are] the Mormons [. . .] busily looking up their ancestry," but also in "Sweden, Denmark, West Germany, Holland, Switzerland, England, and Finland."[100] This propaganda message served to raise suspicion about American presence and intentions in parts of Europe following World War II. The article dismisses Latter-day Saint scientific interests in genealogy, asserting that, "it is simply the fact that the FBI wishes to have detailed population information from the West European countries," and that "photographing [. . .] church registers does not serve history; it serves the future."[101] This alarmist tone aims to weaken the legitimacy of family history efforts by Church members and sow concerns about the purpose of collecting microfilms in foreign countries. The article closes, stating Church members conducting family history in Europe are not doing so at the bidding of their leaders in Utah or on behalf of the Lord, but that these efforts result from "the sinister premises of the US FBI in Washington."[102] In other words, Latter-day Saints are agents of the US intelligence community collecting information for some mysterious reason only known to government leaders in the capital.

Suspicions regarding genealogy resurfaced throughout the following years. In Finland, for instance, discussion and media articles in the early 1980s focused on "the Church's microfilming of Finnish Lutheran parish registers three decades previously and the suspicion that these registers were being used for U.S. intelligence purposes."[103] Members of the Church were heavily engaged in genealogy research, which involved careful reviews of newspaper microfiches in search of names and dates. Fortunately, these suspicions of espionage did not incite violence or acts of terrorism in Finland. Soviet propaganda linking the Church to the US Intelligence Community continued throughout the Cold War, especially in Europe, contributing to ideological friction between these influential forces. Despite the charged rhetoric and suspicion contained in Soviet media, however, there is little evidence to suggest the messages incited violence targeting the Church or contributed to any terrorism.

In South America, however, these perceptions gradually spread and likely contributed to terrorism conducted by leftist groups. Broadcasts as early as an October 25, 1975 FBIS translation of an article in Moscow's *Izvestiya* in Russian describes how CIA agents were flooding Latin America, often under the guise of religious preachers or scientists. The article asserts, "frequently [,] espionage is concealed by a religious haze," citing an article from the Peruvian newspaper *Correo*, "which unmasked the activity of the Mormon sect" whose sermons contain "dangerous antinational plans."[104] Few written or broadcasted media outlets overtly alleged that US intelligence agents posed as clergymen, but Soviet broadcasts made this accusation and, on occasion, named the Church as an enabler of intelligence collection or clandestine operations. In a January 6, 1986 article of Moscow's *TASS* in English, the article mentions "a group of Mormon missionaries recently [that] were issued visas to visit the island [Mauritius]," an island east of Madagascar, adding that, "the CIA frequently sends its agents to independent countries under the guise of clergymen."[105] Allegations increasingly focused on Latter-day Saint missionaries serving as CIA agents throughout Latin America and other areas where young men and women preached the gospel.

Church leaders and members consistently denied any connection between the Church and US intelligence services. After Elders Wilson and Ball were killed by a terrorist faction in 1989, Church leaders even participated in a news conference in La Paz, Bolivia "to dispel the myth that the missionaries ha[d] something to do with government agencies."[106] These suspicions among some South Americans did not abruptly begin at the time terrorist attacks against Latter-day Saints spiked in the late 1980s and early 1990s; rather, Soviet broadcasts, South American newspaper and magazine articles and radio broadcasts, perceptions shared by word of mouth, and other factors fostered and enabled these suspicions to grow throughout the 1970s and 1980s.

While news broadcasts citing inflammatory claims led some to question missionaries' intent, some South Americans independently reasoned missionaries were CIA agents due to their appearance and irreconcilable reason for being in their countries simply to teach people about Jesus Christ. Many could not understand the peculiar norm in the Church for young men and women to leave their homes, often learn a foreign language, and serve in the streets of small villages for altruistic reasons. The vast majority of South Americans admired this peculiarity, many inviting missionaries into their homes, but some South Americans remained wary. People easily understood why the CIA or other agencies might recruit Latter-day Saint missionaries as agents. A declassified CIA report stated, "Two Bolivian newspaper articles in May 1988 quoted a US newspaper article that claimed that 'the CIA prefers to recruit Mormon missionaries because of their international experience, ability to speak foreign languages, strict morality, and conservative opinions.'"[107] The CIA has been highly successful in recruiting Latter-day Saints, many of whom are proficient in multiple languages and maintain very high moral standards. In fact, Elder Neal Maxwell, a former member of the Quorum of the Twelve Apostles, conducted "economic analyses for the agency for about a year" as a young man.[108] The CIA and other government entities found Latter-day Saint applicants required little training or vetting before assigning them to various international posts. There were, and are, many Latter-day Saint diplomats because "they know the language and the culture from the missions years ago," where many gained near-native proficiency, as well as geographic and cultural knowledge of certain regions.[109] This trend, however, involves Saints applying to positions or agencies recruiting Saints after their missions; these members did not participate in intelligence gathering during their missionary service. Media alleging ties between the Church and the CIA only served to reinforce these suspicions and weaken legitimacy and present opposition to missionary work where missions were experiencing unprecedented success.

Proselyting missionaries shared concepts with investigators and converts sharply contrasting with philosophies of leftist terrorists in South America. Many leftists accused Latter-day Saint missionaries and other Christian groups of being intelligence agents of the US Government because "these denominations tended to emphasize individual salvation and to de-emphasize social and political issues."[110] As locals joined these denominations, the recruiting pool for leftist factions shriveled. Although these religious groups did not defy or challenge leftist factions, their ideologies clashed with those of leftist groups seeking new members and supporters. Similar to the strict guideline missionaries follow by not discussing politics with locals, church leaders in Chile and other areas tried to adhere to this guideline in meetings and in discussions with other church leaders. Elder Eduardo Ayala, who served as a stake president during this tumultuous time in Chile, stated the following on the matter:

> "We tried not to speak about politics at all. Occasionally, we would meet with leaders who came from Salt Lake City or with the regional representatives and they would not make reference to politics. Nevertheless, someone would say, 'Brothers, how should we confront all this?' They would then provide some

> instruction and would say, 'please apply wisdom, pray often, do the right things, so the members do not leave the path and so you maintain order in the congregations.'"[111]

Members and missionaries sharing democratic principles often witnessed the effects of two distinct ideologies clashing, seeing their chapels bombed or communities harassed by leftists.

While most perceived ties to the US Government's intelligence community concern missionaries active in their proselyting missions, propaganda and rumors also address family history efforts and satellite dishes at chapels. Despite decades of accusations, the Church has consistently denied any affiliation with the CIA or other intelligence organizations. Nevertheless, the Church faced some alarming accusations and criticism relating to this perception, contributing to strong opposition in Europe and some terrorist attacks in South America.

Nationwide Suspicions Close Churches in Ghana

People all over the world have difficulty comprehending why missionaries willingly leave academic programs or other pursuits for eighteen months to two years and commit to lives of celibacy and complete dedication to proselyting. Many also fail to understand why or how missionaries fund their own missions. These peculiarities lead to suspicions about missionaries' intentions and funding sources. These concerns are even more widespread in nations with weak political systems or where perceptions exist of US intelligence agencies influencing national political structures. This was the case in Chile following the coup of 1973, but this mentality also pervaded Ghana in 1989. In early June of that year, the national government accused the Church of "conducting [itself] in a manner that undermine[d] the sovereignty of Ghana," and then "ordered a freeze on all activities of the Mormon church," closing meetinghouses and providing missionaries one week to leave the country.[112] In a nation with a history of colonialism and alleged CIA intervention, a rapidly-growing church with a large foreign missionary presence raised suspicions among some politicians. Media outlets in and around Ghana published critical articles with charged commentary about the Church in the months preceding the freeze. Journalist Ben Ephson wrote the following in the news magazine *West Africa* just two months before the freeze:

> "The proliferation of churches in Ghana—some with dubious, satanic and deleterious doctrines has been of great concern to past and present governments and concerned citizens. The Church of Jesus Christ of Latter-day Saints, headquartered in Salt Lake City, USA is among the new 'Saints' to invade Ghana. Their magnificent, imposing places of worship and offices, coupled with a fleet of posh cars of all kinds and ever-growing membership have earned them many unpleasant tags such as CIA agents, US spies, Unholy saints."[113]

Hence, this alleged association between the Church and CIA, or other intelligence agencies, evolved and existed at different times in certain regions of the world. One key difference between Ghana and parts of South America where rumors persisted, however, is that although these perceptions likely contributed to the Ghanaian government taking actions against the Church, these suspicions did not seem to lead citizens or extremist groups to target the Church through violence and terrorism, as was the case in South America.

The Chilean Coup of 1973 and Church Growth under the Pinochet Regime

Much of the history behind conspiracy theories of North American missionaries working as intelligence operatives is closely associated with the Chilean Coup of 1973, following the Chilean presidential election of 1970. Chileans believed the US Government strongly supported incumbent president Eduardo Frei. At the time, military dictators and Communist heads of state ruled many South American countries, with Chile as a solitary symbol of democracy. Frei could not run for reelection in 1970, as the Constitution of Chile forbid individuals from serving more than two terms as president. Rumors spread that the US's Central Intelligence Agency backed Jorge Alessandri in the presidential election, with the plan he would later resign to enable incumbent president Eduardo Frei to return to power. After socialist Salvador Allende won, he enacted programs benefitting the working class, yielding greater support from their ranks while costing the support of many elites and military officers. Meetings with Fidel Castro and other actions indicated to US leaders Allende's actions would have lasting effects in transitioning the historically democratic country to a socialist or communist nation.

In 1973, political and social conditions worsened. Allende's government did not adequately respond to military grievances and other protests, contributing to changing loyalties and a weakening state. Colonel Roberto Souper surrounded the presidential palace in a failed coup attempt in June 1973, followed shortly thereafter by the Supreme Court issuing a public grievance regarding the government's inability to enforce law. Augusto Pinochet, the Army's General Chief of Staff, became Commander-in-Chief of the Army following the resignation of General Prats. Pinochet and heads of the other military branches then collaborated with the national police force to depose Salvador Allende. On September 11, 1973, the armed forces took action, closing radio and television networks, capturing Valparaíso port, and bombing the presidential palace. Allende allegedly committed suicide after refusing to resign and leave the presidential palace. Pinochet seized control as the head of the Army, leading Chile into a period under military dictatorship that lasted until 1990.

Suspicions of Latter-day Saint missionaries serving as CIA agents or informants for the US intelligence community largely stem from this coup and beliefs that the CIA encouraged and incited it. North American missionaries were often the only Americans that Chilean citizens would see or meet. White young men, dressed in suits and operating throughout the countryside, led some to believe these missionaries gathered intelligence on political and social atmospherics and reported back to the US leading up to the election and during the period preceding the coup. Most citizens supported Latter-day Saints and welcomed their presence, yet some citizens ostracized Saints and some leftist groups targeted meetinghouses, missionaries, and members. Brother Eduardo Lamartine described the conditions and perception of pockets of wary Chileans in the wake of the military coup in the following way:

> "After the military coup [persecution] was more difficult because these groups identified us as though we were a part of the CIA, in fact, there were articles in important magazines saying this and even linking us with the military coup, which was a fallacy. Extremist groups began to arise which wanted to attack something pertaining to the Church, so they attacked chapels, at night they emplaced bombs and on some occasions, they attacked members inside the chapels."[114]

These attacks, symbolic of retribution against the United States for allegedly overthrowing Chile's democratically-elected Salvador Allende in another act of imperialism, waxed until the late 1980s and early 1990s. For a time, the Church was the most common target for anti-US terrorism, with most attacks taking place in Chile.

Some Chileans also perceived a close-nit relationship between The Church of Jesus Christ of Latter-day Saints and General Pinochet for other instances. A couple occasions of Church leaders meeting with or praising General Pinochet may have contributed to this sensitivity. A few years after the coup, Latter-day Saint General Authority Robert Wells, a former banker who had worked in South America, reportedly "paid tribute to the new regime," and called General Pinochet "one of the great leaders of Latin America" who was seeing "the purpose of the Lord."[115] Similarly, President Spencer W. Kimball eventually met with Pinochet. Perhaps rumors regarding an association between The Church of Jesus Christ of Latter-day Saints and the Chilean government would not have been nearly as pervasive had people known the history and circumstances leading to this cordial relationship. David Spencer, a graduate student at Brigham Young University at the time, explained the following:

> "The Chilean government sent a high-level agent to infiltrate the Church and study what the Mormons were all about. In the process, this agent became genuinely converted. Once in the Church, this man turned around and used his contacts to help the Church get recognition among high government circles. Through his contacts, a highly-publicized meeting was set up between the prophet Spencer W. Kimball and General Pinochet, the President of Chile. As a result of the meeting, the

> word was passed out through government circles to collaborate with the Church. It became very easy to acquire property for chapels, obtain permission for missionaries, etcetera."[116]

The Church continued to grow rapidly in Chile, as Latter-day Saint membership steadily increased and new meetinghouses appeared throughout the country.

Second- and third-order effects of contrasts between Church doctrines and leftist ideologies were perhaps most readily apparent in Chile. Leftist groups, frustrated and moved to violence to protest and retaliate against the Pinochet regime, recognized how Latter-day Saint teachings seemingly supported the national government's objectives and opposed their extremist groups' strategic messaging. David Spencer summarized these perceptions as follows:

> "The Church was useful to the Pinochet regime for several reasons. First, the values we taught calmed anti-government sentiment. In fact, many of the values taught by the Church fit right in with the free market economic revolution being put into practice by the Chilean government. Second, the Church was mainly obtaining its converts from among the lower middle-class segments of society. These were also the very segments of society that were most influenced by anti-government agitators. While the Church saw the new symbiotic relationship as an opportunity to grow, the Chilean government saw the relationship as a card it was playing to dampen opposition to the military regime. The Church unconsciously became a tool in Pinochet's policy strategies for internal control. It is perhaps this particular connection that has made the Church more of a target in Chile than elsewhere and why the number of attacks against the Church in that nation have been the greatest in all of Latin America."[117]

Despite this interpretation among leftists of Church doctrines supporting Pinochet's policies and rule, relatively few attacks targeted missionaries teaching these doctrines. Rather, leftist terrorists generally targeted Church buildings through bombings. Leftists bombed chapels and spray-painted propaganda messages on meetinghouse walls when the buildings were unoccupied, so as to not injure citizens and lose legitimacy among supportive locals.

The professions of new converts also likely influenced rumors. Under Pinochet's regime, many educated members of the military and police forces converted and later became local Church leaders.[118] This factor of education, distinguishing white-collar workers from the blue-collar working class, seemed to cast a stigma upon the Church among some circles, labeling the Church as another group segregating society. The upward mobility often experienced by Church members drew suspicions from leftists. Also, to an outsider of the Church who resided in the same community for years, the tendency for educated members of military and police forces and their fulfillment of leadership roles could also potentially be perceived as nepotism, as these converts accepted callings extended by members of this educated social class.

Perceptions of Anti-indigenous Philosophies

Many poor and indigenous people joined Evangelical groups, which saturated the rural landscape, or The Church of Jesus Christ of Latter-day Saints, as many moved to urban centers as a consequence of modernization, where Latter-day Saint missionaries labored. Similar to the trend noted by Alma as he preached to the Zoramites, who, "after much labor among them, began to have success among the poor class of people," many lower-class citizens in South American countries joined the Church.[119] These converts abandoned some of their practices and philosophies as they adopted new ones. According to leftist perceptions, the Protestant wave moving throughout South America in the latter half of the twentieth century threatened their lifestyles and traditions. Leftist factions used these demographic shifts as justification to wage violence against groups or entities sharing philosophies encroaching on indigenous values and norms.

Most of the leftist-bred rumors involving Saints and their purported goal to convert and assimilate natives goes back to notions that the Church furthered American imperialism and pushed American culture and values onto the people of South America. Professor

David Knowlton stated that the perceived US agenda the Church and Evangelical groups allegedly supported included "the domination of Bolivia's Indian masses by 'Euro-Bolivians' those of primary European physical origin and culture."[120] Contributing to this perception or rumor, argued Knowlton, was the Church's established social footing distanced from the lower, native class, due to the fact that the first branch in La Paz, constructed in 1964, resided in "the upper middle-class, white zone of Sopocachi (Branch I), where [. . .] the Church had its headquarters in its own office building, down the block from the Ministry of Defense, and around the corner from the U.S. ambassador's residence."[121] Leftist extremists, including groups and politicians, latched onto such circumstances to allege the Church pursued political objectives.

The Zarate Willka Armed Liberation Front (FAL-ZW), a terrorist group founded on the principles of preserving indigenous culture and resisting foreign influence, strongly opposed Church presence and efforts in Bolivia. In propaganda leaflets and phone calls to local press, group members often expressed scorn for Latter-day Saint missionaries. The FAL-ZW bombed Latter-day Saint chapels in the late 1980s and assassinated two missionaries. Members of the group threatened to kill Mayor Filiberto Cardozo of El Alto de La Paz if he "did not close all Mormon chapels," a demand springing from their opposition to "gringos who come to deceive the poor and humble people."[122] They perceived tithing as a means to rob their countrymen and Church doctrines as a way to brainwash them, replacing local philosophies with conservative teachings. University of Mississippi Professor Chester Quarles, who tracked attacks against Westerners in Project Safe, asserted, "Guerrillas perceive[d] the church's proselyting success as a threat to traditional society."[123] Many of them believed the work of missionaries and members to be supportive of US efforts to assimilate natives and erase indigenous cultures.

Saints attracted negative attention from other groups for their perceived affiliation with the United States. US Army Lieutenant Colonel Alvin D. Cantrell stated the group's assassination of two Latter-day Saint missionaries in May 1989 shared similarities with bombing attempts targeting US Secretary of State George P. Shultz's motorcade and the Bolivian Congress, in that all were linked to the US-sponsored coca crop eradication effort in Bolivia.[124] Crop reduction programs affected the financial stability of the poor native population working the coca fields. Some of the Shining Path's attacks in Peru point back to perceptions of threats to their way of life and culture. Peruvian cultural anthropologists speculated the gruesome tactics of the Shining Path were allusions to tactics used by conquistadores against indigenous leaders, reflecting ideologies closely linked to resisting invading influences threatening their heritage. Group members often beheaded or garroted their victims, similar to how the "Inca emperor Atahualpa was garroted by Pizarro in 1533."[125] Such violence plagued the area around Ayachucho, Peru, where Latter-day Saint members suffered threats causing some families to flee for safety.

Personal Vendettas Mixed with Ideologies—Lone Wolf Terrorism

Analysts often struggle to understand the category of violent acts perpetrated by one individual or a small group of individuals, commonly known as lone wolf terrorism, as perpetrators sometimes fail to divulge their ideologies or motives. Research helps to shed light on these factors, aiding analysts in discerning acts of revenge targeting specific individuals, which would constitute crime, from acts targeting a broader audience with some ideological factor in mind, more characteristic of terrorism. Most lone wolf terrorism in the United States in recent decades falls under far-right or religious ideologies.

Motives behind attacks may be less readily identifiable in attacks conducted by one person or a very small group with no outside contact. Lone wolves "often come up with their own ideologies that combine personal vendettas with religious or political grievances."[126] Hence, assessing the motive can prove challenging, but analysis may identify relevant factors. Occasionally, social media posts, journal entries, or other evidence might indicate motives.

One characteristic of lone wolf terrorism is an increased tendency for hoaxes. Perpetrators acting alone often lack the expertise or logistical support to conduct the type of attack they envision, so they conduct hoax attacks to replicate the fear they hope to incite.

One example includes hoaxes mimicking the 2001 anthrax scare. An inmate in a Georgia prison procured some white powder, wrote letters indicating the substance was anthrax, and sent letters with the powdery substance to two Latter-day Saint temples. Other common hoaxes include bomb scares or other events with biological or chemical agents where lone wolves did not have expertise or logistical support to carry out an attack with actual materials or agents.

The Right People in the Right Places—Responding to the San Bernardino Shooting

On December 2, 2015, married couple Rizwan Farook and Tashfeen Malik entered the San Bernardino County Department of Public Health offices with semi-automatic weapons during a training event and holiday party and killed 14 people and injured 22 others. Investigations revealed the couple became self-radicalized in religious ideologies; their attack became one of many Islamist lone wolf attacks during the same period. Members of The Church of Jesus Christ of Latter-day Saints were present in the building at the time of the attack and one of the injured persons had a sister who attended the Church. In the wake of the tragedy, the Lord facilitated healing and recovery. Brother Kasey Haws witnessed "how the Lord can intervene in things even where agency creates victims like that," especially how the Lord prepared individuals to be in the right place at the right time to serve. Alluding to Mayor Rudy Giuliani's leadership after the 9/11 attacks, Brother Haws stated that when a tragedy occurs, someone needs to rise up and calm the entire community, which is exactly what Mayor Carey Davis did in San Bernardino.

Davis, a devout member of The Church of Jesus Christ of Latter-day Saints, was elected in 2014. Haws described his calm demeanor and described him as a resolute man with kind eyes. His personality provided real healing benefit to the people of San Bernardino after the shooting. Dr. Mohammad Hossain, a prominent Muslim in Redlands, CA and representative of the Muslim community, "reached out to the [Latter-day Saint] Church as a link back into the Christian community" to counter push-back and fears that other Muslims would self-radicalize and possibly conduct similar attacks.[127]

CHAPTER 4

TERRORISTS AND THEIR TACTICS, TECHNIQUES, AND PROCEDURES

"The kingdom will continue to increase, to grow, to spread and prosper more and more. Every time its enemies undertake to overthrow it, it will become more extensive and powerful; instead of its decreasing, it will continue to increase, it will spread the more, become more wonderful and conspicuous to the nations, until it fills the whole earth."

—Brigham Young, in a discourse delivered at the opening of the new tabernacle, Salt Lake City, April 6, 1852

Background and Analytical Focus

Composition, disposition, and strength varied greatly among groups targeting The Church of Jesus Christ of Latter-day Saints. Depending on the origins and predominant ideologies of the group, recruiting efforts may have focused among *campesinos* of rural communities, disenfranchised youth of impoverished *barrios*, or university students in cities. This collection of individuals often lacked expertise in weapons handling and military tactics, but external support from places like Cuba and training provided by nearby paramilitary organizations equipped many cells with rudimentary skills in bomb making and, to a degree, complex attacks involving a bomb and armed assault against a target. Many terrorist groups focused on opposing law enforcement, military, or political entities to weaken security and delegitimize the government. Still, these groups attacked the Church as a perceived agent of American imperialism, cultural influence, or espionage operations. Most groups simply sought to make symbolic attacks against the US, damaging church grounds rather than injuring their countrymen belonging to that congregation. On the other hand, a few groups terrorized local members of the Church and operated by a different litmus in determining what constituted legitimate targets and the appropriate extent of damage or harm. Group strength, or the number of operatives and followers, often varied over time with many groups existing for only a matter of months. Groups range in strength from estimates of fewer than ten members to tens of thousands, depending on factors including leadership, external support, logistics, and resistance from government forces.

Rather than list extensive background information regarding each group, this text focuses on insights and analysis regarding those groups producing the most significant opposition to the Church. Several groups carried out fewer than five attacks against Latter-day Saint meetinghouses, usually targeting the Church in anti-US protests or under suspicions the Church supported US intelligence gathering efforts. Case studies or other detailed analysis of such groups are of little analytical value. Appendix B outlines origins, ideologies, and other chief characteristics of all terrorist groups credited with attacks targeting the Church. These details enhance overall analysis, but do not yield much value in terms of mentality and ideologies behind a fixation on the Church as a target or analysis, propaganda efforts, or tactics.

In addition to understanding the structure of terrorist organizations and the core ideologies propelling individuals and groups to commit violent acts targeting the Church, studying group tactics, techniques, and procedures (TTPs) yields additional information and spurs insights to better understand threats. To distinguish each term, US Army Field Manual 3-90, *Tactics*, defines each one as follows:

"*Tactics* is the employment of units in combat.

Techniques are the general and detailed methods used by troops and commanders to perform assigned missions and functions, specifically the methods of using equipment and personnel.

Procedures are standard and detailed courses of action that describe how to perform tasks."[128]

Adjusting some of these definitions to terrorist groups (e.g., instead of *troops*, use *group members*) adapts these concepts and tailors them for investigation of terrorist organizations and their practices. Groups' patterns of behavior reflect their intent, limitations, support base, weapon preference, and recruiting efforts. Analysis exposes group vulnerabilities for police forces and government agencies to exploit and can aid in predictive analysis.

Relevant Terrorist Groups

Historically, most terrorist groups targeting the Church were leftist factions in Latin America. Characteristics widely varied among groups, explained in detail in Appendix B. Figure 4.1 reflects the total number of attacks attributed to each group, detailed in Appendix A.

Perpetrators often claimed responsibility for attacks by leaving a group flag, spray-painted slogan or group initials, or propaganda pamphlets bearing the group's name at attack sites. Frequently, perpetrators called media outlets to claim responsibility and provide a message justifying the attack for distribution via radio or newspaper. These actions aid in attributing attacks to specific groups for examination and analysis.

Still, the perpetrator remains unknown for several attacks. Such attacks were likely conducted by one of the groups predominantly targeting the Church, such as the Lautaro Youth Movement or Manuel Rodriguez Patriotic Front (FPMR). Evidence facilitates speculation, but to enhance the fidelity and accuracy of statistics and analysis, such incidents remain unattributed without strong evidence regarding modus operandi, timing, location, or other factors yielding compelling indications of a particular group's culpability. There is sufficient information regarding other attacks to identify trends or discern

Figure 4.1: Number of Attacks by Perpetrator Group (1979–2018)

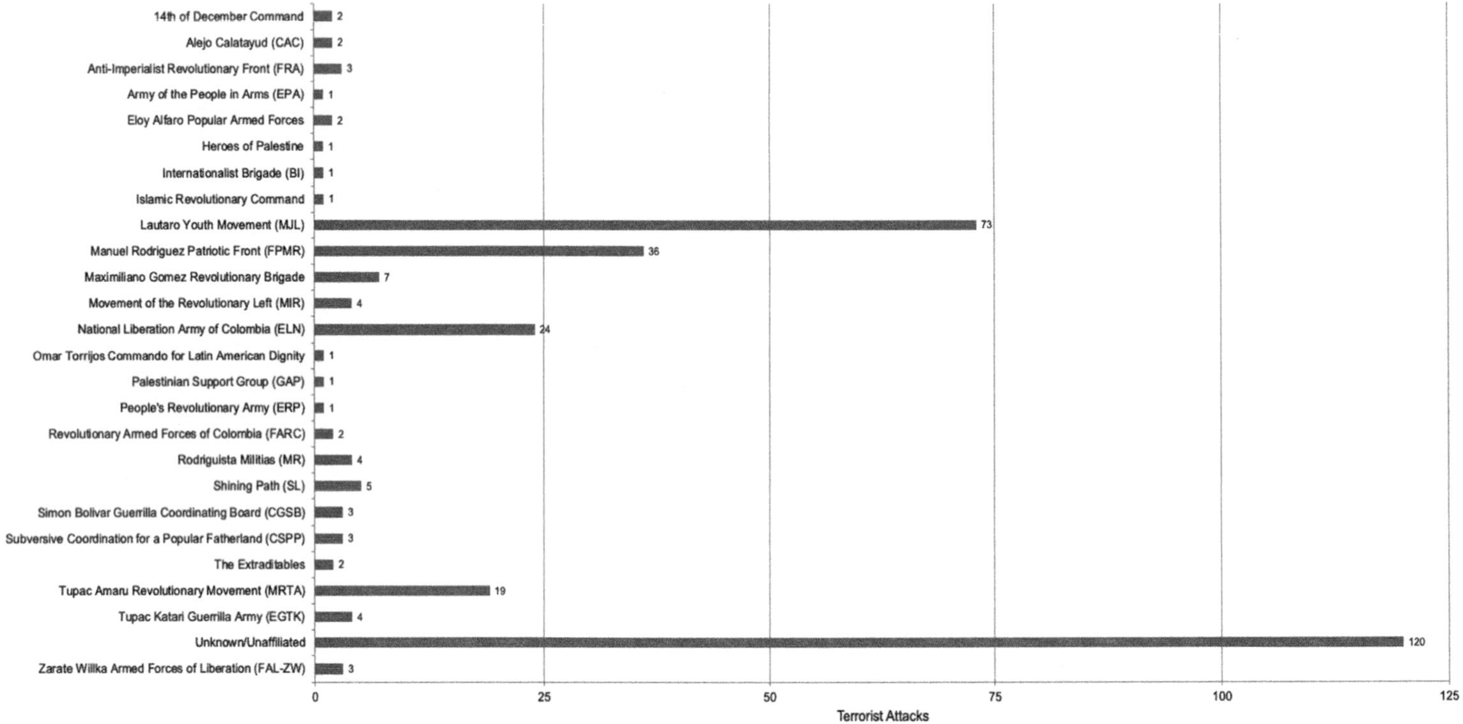

Note: Total value of attacks in this chart exceeds the terrorism incident count in Appendix A of 315; for attacks involving collaboration between two or more groups, all groups involved receive credit for an attack.

Source: Chart based on data compiled from multiple sources, as detailed in Appendix A.

tactics and motives without imposing assumptions, bias, or speculation to the raw dataset; hence, there remains a high number of unattributed attacks to protect the fidelity of data and safeguard the reliability of analysis.

Collaboration between Groups Targeting the Church

Often, members of groups with similar ideologies communicated and cooperated in their attacks and attempts to influence the populace. Media outlets and law enforcement officials credited or suspected collaboration between multiple terrorist organizations in some attacks against the Church. Circumstantial evidence (i.e., timing and location of attacks, shared tactics, and shared leadership) also indicates associations between some groups. Figure 4.2 displays an association matrix including confirmed, suspected, and possible links between various groups that targeted the Church.

Most of the association matrix is blank, reflecting a lack of collaboration between groups. The main contributing factor for this isolation and independence in logistics, planning, and attacks was geographic distance; many groups shared similar ideologies, but there were limited means to communicate and few advantages in doing so. The majority of these groups operated within one country and only in certain urban centers where group members resided and maintained support zones. Differences in ideologies and objectives reduced diffusion between some groups. A third factor involved timing, as some of these groups existed and operated in different time periods, collapsing or disbanding before other listed groups operated. Simultaneous attacks targeting the Church by different groups does not necessarily reflect collaboration and planning; rather, the majority of such instances occurred because of a particular holiday, event, or anniversary serving as a catalyst. The commencement of the Gulf War, for instance, inspired several attacks across multiple countries within a matter of days.

Some of these terrorist groups, however, shared close associations and collaborated in attacks against the Church. Physical

Figure 4.2: Associations between Groups Targeting the Church

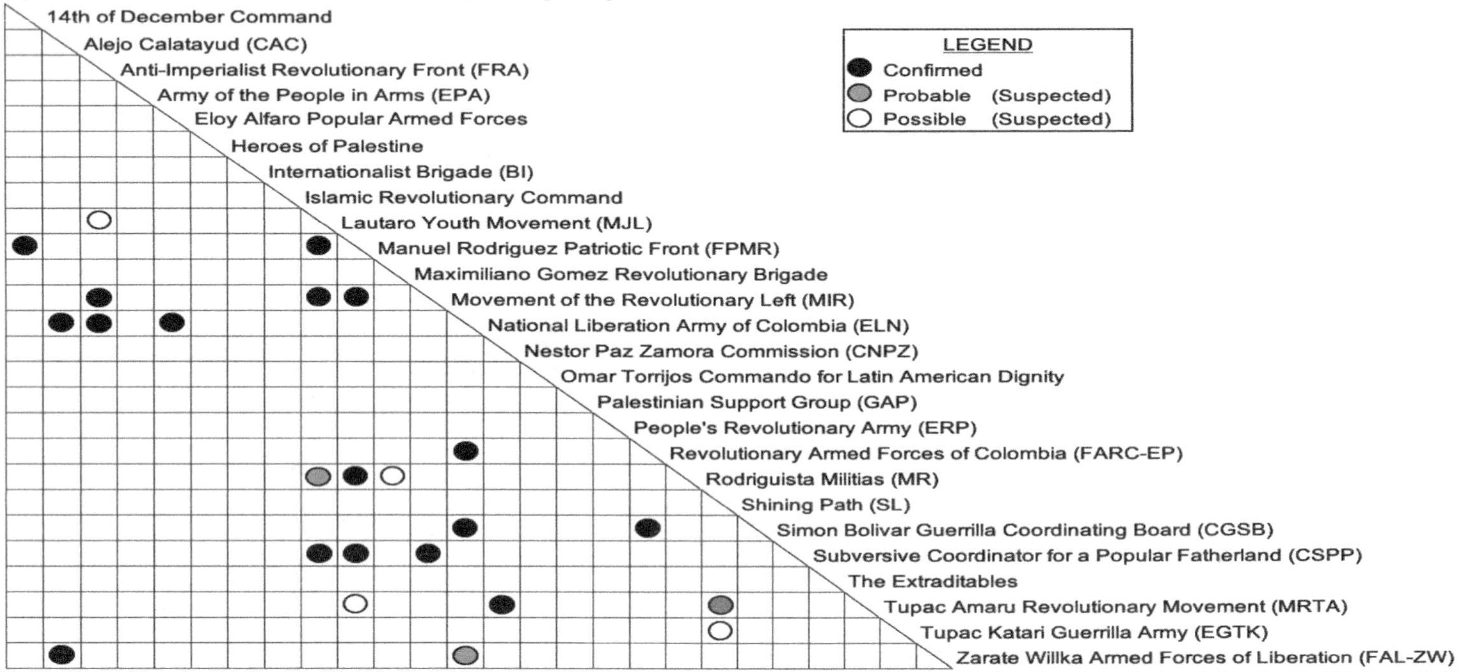

Source: Compiled and generated based on information in Appendix A and independent analysis. Association matrix is based on the analysis tool described in U.S. Army Field Manual 3-24, Counterinsurgency, para. B-53.

Note: This association matrix lists each of the extremist/terrorist factions that targeted the Church since 1980 along the right side of the triangle. Each faction has an assigned row and column within the matrix, revealing links to other organizations. For instance, the Lautaro Youth Movement collaborated with the FPMR, MIR, and CSPP, likely collaborated with the MR, and possibly coordinated with the FRA in targeting the Church.

proximity facilitated cooperation in logistics, recruiting, propaganda, and attacks. Hence, many groups operating in the same locale often shared membership or adhered to similar ideologies. For instance, the National Liberation Army (ELN), Alejo Calatayud Command, and Zarate Willka Armed Forces of Liberation, all operating in Bolivia, contained overlapping membership and leaders.[129] When one group dissolved, new groups emerged, usually containing members originally belonging to the disbanded organization. Two particular groups prevalent in Chile and leading in number of attacks targeting the Church allegedly bear a unique characteristic regarding cooperation and shared interests, as some believe the predominantly adolescent Lautaro Youth Movement's membership consisted of the children of members of the Manuel Rodriguez Patriotic Front.[130] Reporting and evidence suggest that of all the terrorist organizations targeting the Church, the Lautaro Youth Movement and the National Liberation Army of Colombia collaborated the most with other groups. The Lautaro Youth Movement also conducted the majority of terrorist attacks against the Church since 1980. Despite their focus in Santiago, Chile, most collaboration between the Lautaro Youth Movement and other groups occurred in outlying urban centers, including Valdivia, Osorno, and Temuco. In such areas, the group had limited presence and support zones and capitalized on shared ideology and other factors with nearby extremists.

Unique Characteristics of Select Networks

Decentralized Operations of the Lautaro Youth Movement

The Lautaro Youth Movement of the early 1990s mainly consisted of adolescents in Chile carrying out unsophisticated attacks against targets they deemed furthered US imperialism within Chile. Some experts assert members of the Lautaro were the teenage children of members of the Manuel Rodriguez Patriotic Front.[131] The groups followed similar ideologies and operated in the same urban regions of

Chile, principally in Santiago. One basic characteristic differentiating members of these groups was the age cohort, as Lautaros were overwhelmingly adolescents. The Lautaros "regularly recruit[ed] criminals and angry young men from city slums," often affected by poverty and a lack of education and upward social mobility.[132] The Lautaro Youth Movement seemed to lack much operational structure above small teams with leaders in neighborhoods and cities. Some used a vehicle and driver to transport two or three individuals to emplace a bomb at a chapel entrance and spray graffiti. Other attacks involved arson or armed assault with five to seven masked men armed with pistols entering a meetinghouse and setting the building ablaze.

While the Lautaros targeted businesses or other government institutions in a ruthless and violent manner, most of the group's attacks against the Church involved empty buildings and minimal violence. One representative expressed to the *Deseret News* that "the chapel attacks [were] often apparently used as not-too-dangerous training for [Lautaro's] young terrorist recruits."[133] Attacks involved little risk of capture or witnesses; empty chapels provided an ideal location for new members to conduct attacks, as chapels were very accessible and in residential areas where they could easily escape.

Brutality of the Shining Path

The Shining Path is a widely known terrorist group still operating in Peru. Founded and led by Abimael Guzmán, the group began in the rural areas of Peru with the objective of "destroy[ing] existing Peruvian institutions and replac[ing] them with an Indian-based peasant revolutionary regime."[134] Members waged a violent campaign, terrorizing citizens and forcing them to support the group rather than Peruvian military forces. In the beginning, Shining Path operatives mainly targeted Peruvian military facilities and personnel, but the group is notorious for brutal and gruesome punishments inflicted on citizens they identified as supporters of the Peruvian military or government. Whereas many groups practiced discretion and imposed constraints or limits on targets so as to not lose legitimacy in the eyes of locals, Shining Path operatives conducted indiscriminate attacks and killed men, women, and children. Group members tortured and killed Catholic priests, razed villages, killed young men suspected of opposing the Shining Path, and committed other shocking atrocities. They depended on the fear generated through terrorism to force citizens into submission, supporting the group rather than existing Peruvian institutions out of fear of being tortured or killed.

The Shining Path opposed the presence of or interference from foreign powers and outside entities. The group was and remains xenophobic, critical and distrustful of all foreign influences to include China and Russia.[135] This also included foreign influence from the United States in the form of external military support, cultural diffusion, or political actions. The group categorized the Church into this realm of problematic or conflicting foreign influence; group members perceived Latter-day Saint presence and teachings to promote democratic concepts, capitalism, adherence to national laws and supporting government institutions, and other concepts contradicting Shining Path philosophies.

The Shining Path carried out a relatively low number of attacks targeting the Church, considering the group's size and years of activity, opposition to foreign influences, and presence in high-density Latter-day Saint areas. Even so, the attacks they committed were brutal. Adherents struck in Chilca and Huancayo, Peru, assassinating two Latter-day Saint missionaries and bombing chapels. The group also terrorized Church members in Ayacucho through intimidation.

TTP Statistics and Trends

The weapons most frequently employed against the Church included firearms and bombs, characteristic of most terrorist attacks throughout all four waves of modern terrorism. Investigating the preferred tactics of terrorist groups attacking the Church and trends associated with methods of attack reveal indicators of motives, experience levels of those involved, number of perpetrators, ideologies, and group member willingness to accept risk. Table 4.1 displays the number of incidents corresponding to commonly employed attack types targeting the Church in recent decades.

For the purpose of establishing distinct criteria for analysis, armed assault includes attempts to inflict physical harm against persons through the use of firearms or knives. Assassinations involve lethal attacks targeting specific individuals or distinguishable representatives of a group (e.g., missionaries). Biological/chemical attacks involve the use of such weapons or hoaxes. The bombing/explosion attack type includes explosive devices emplaced for the purpose of detonation and inflicting casualties or damage (e.g., sabotage). Facility/infrastructure attacks involve devices other than explosives to cause damage to a structure, as opposed to a person. Hostage taking may involve barricading or kidnapping to achieve a political end state. Overall, attacks aligned with the preferred weapons across all waves of modern terrorism: firearms and bombs. Generally, incidents occurred in South America and reflect attacks conducted by small, risk-averse groups with limited experience. Exploring each type of attack and other trends provides a greater depth of understanding regarding the behavior of each terrorist group or lone wolf.

Table 4.1: Attack Types Targeting The Church of Jesus Christ of Latter-day Saints, 1979–2018

Attack Type	Armed Assault	Assassination	Biological/ Chemical	Bombing/ Explosion	Facility/ Infrastructure	Hostage Taking
Number of Incidents	**8**	**2**	**3**	**255**	**44**	**3**

Source: Statistics reflect data listed in Appendix A, gathered from a variety of open sources.

Particular TTPs

Bombing

Most publicly documented terrorist attacks targeting the Church involve some form of explosives. Interestingly, most of the leftist groups that regularly emplaced bombs beside chapels did so during nightfall in order to, among other reasons associated with risk, reduce the likelihood of casualties. For most groups, their objective was to damage buildings, a visual symbol of damaging the United States. Regarding this characteristic of many bombings in South America, Brother Lamartine remarked on his experience with one such group:

> "It was an extremist group that fixated on the [Latter-day Saint] Church thinking that we had something to do with the CIA, or that we were North Americans. Happily, they never emplaced a bomb in a congregation; they could have done so easily, but people were never attacked. They would say, 'we attack material goods because the people over there are Chilean.' They wanted to attack what they thought were North American interests. So sometimes we would go to the press and explain that the chapels were ours, that they were the result of our sacrifice and that of all the members; that we had nothing to do with the CIA."[136]

Members and Church leaders routinely spoke out after bombing incidents, expressing through media such bombings affected local, indigenous Church members. They tried to convey to extremist groups their perceptions of the Church as a North American church were unfounded and inaccurate. Even so, attacks continued, and terrorists spray-painted anti-US propaganda or left anti-US leaflets at attack sites.

The majority of bombings consisted of rudimentary and slightly sophisticated homemade explosive devices. These bombs contained a small amount of explosive material with a firing train composed of a fuse and mechanical detonator. Such devices produced a small blast radius, often causing superficial, and occasionally, structural damage to buildings. Few explosions produced casualties, mainly due to a lack of personnel nearby, as terrorist groups generally targeted buildings after business hours or religious meetinghouses during non-service hours. Premature detonations occasionally killed unskilled or inexperienced perpetrators emplacing the explosives, due to physical proximity at the time of the blast. For instance, on October 29, 1987, Pedro Cárdenas attempted to emplace a dynamite bomb near a chapel in Sogamoso, Colombia, but a premature detonation gravely injured him.[137] Such instances fulfill the latter-day promise, "That no weapon formed against them shall prosper; that he who diggeth a pit for them shall fall into the same himself."[138] Inexperienced groups often resorted to arson or incendiary devices to damage meetinghouses, avoiding risks associated with emplacing bombs.

Terrorists targeting the Church in South America typically used ammonium nitrate fuel oil, commonly known by the acronym ANFO, or occasionally used dynamite. ANFO was a readily available explosive more stable than many alternatives. Terrorist groups could easily steal the substance from mining or construction sites. Using ANFO in small amounts enabled terrorists to attack more locations, achieving their primary objective of damaging symbolic locations affiliated with the United States while carrying out attacks at a high frequency. This small amount of explosive material would not produce many casualties upon detonation, given the relatively small blast area, but this nested with terrorists' objectives, as few desired to produce casualties. Rather, they wanted to visually inflict damage to American buildings and organizations; they wanted to harm structures symbolizing America but avoid harming their countrymen. Such attacks fostered their influence among leftist sympathizers without losing legitimacy typical among groups conducting indiscriminate attacks. The chemical stability of ANFO reduced risk for novices emplacing or transporting bombs or danger of explosions in caches within groups' support zones in residential areas.

Bombs attracted media hype, granting groups notoriety on news channels and radio broadcasts. Terrorists would often leave propaganda leaflets or flags at attack sites, which enabled reporters and police to attribute attacks with a high degree of confidence to certain factions. Their mention in media provided another means for groups to spread their ideologies and attract like-minded individuals, showing them that attacks against the United States or the local government were feasible and carried little risk.

Latter-day Saint Creator of Ammonium Nitrate Fuel Oil

Melvin A. Cook, a renowned chemist and professor of metallurgy at the University of Utah, developed ammonium nitrate fuel oil (ANFO). Previously, Cook worked for DuPont and the US Government, focusing on explosives research and development. With that background, he tackled the challenge of developing a safe alternative to dynamite and fertilizer after the 1947 disaster in Texas City, Texas when a ship carrying fertilizer exploded, killing approximately 600 people and injuring 5,000 others. Cook developed a more stable alternative by mixing ANFO, developing the first slurry explosives. In 1968, the Swedish Royal Academy of Engineering Science recognized his contributions by awarding Cook the Nitro-Nobel Gold Medal. While ANFO became an invaluable tool for commercial and mining enterprises, terrorists took advantage of the easy-to-make explosive. Most bombings targeting the Church in South America involved ANFO. Reflecting on the harmful uses of ANFO by terrorists and others, Cook once commented, "My objective has always been safety and saving lives."[139] Similar to terrorists' use of other tools, guns and other explosives, for maniacal purposes, terrorists found a way to use ANFO in sinister ways.

Assassination

Throughout human history, extremists attempted to kill political and religious leaders for various reasons. Assassination is "an act whose primary objective is to kill one or more specific, prominent individuals."[140] Terrorist groups often conduct assassinations for the potential high payoff achieved through such attacks, negatively impacting rival groups or governments while influencing the local populace. This tactic quickly produces change and disrupts organizations, especially when the target is the head of that organization. There are often irreparable second- and third-order effects. Assassination is not a new threat to the Lord's Church; rather, zealots and terrorist factions deliberately targeted religious figures in both the Americas and the Holy Land. Latter-day Saint Benjamin George identified this tactic as a key commonality between the Gadianton Robbers of the Book of Mormon and the Sicarii of biblical times, observing:

> "The Gadianton robbers were [. . .] infamous for assassinations. Beginning with Pahoran, [they] assassinated many leaders, including Cezoram and his son, several prophets of the Lord, Lachoneus, and Seezoram. They also attempted to assassinate Helaman. [. . .] The Sicarii were also responsible for killing several people who were involved both politically and religiously in their society. Perhaps the murder for which they were most infamous was that of the high priest Jonathan."[141]

Assassination continues to be an efficient means to cause mass disruption and bring about immediate political change.

Many leftist groups in South America favored assassination as a tactic in the 1980s and 1990s, as assassination presented an efficient method to eliminate political leaders of opposition groups and yielded strong publicity. This tactic also inspired fear in the local populace, which terrorists leveraged for coercion and to retain power and influence. To qualify as terrorism, the purpose of assassination should involve political objectives and a goal to incite fear among a people, as opposed to a personal grievance or revenge-like motives. Terrorist groups, especially leftist factions in Latin America, leveraged this tactic to provoke fear in small villages by killing local leaders to gain notoriety and intimidate locals. The majority of attacks attributed to the Zarate Willka group in Bolivia were assassinations, including that of Latter-day Saint missionaries Jeffrey R. Ball and Todd Ray Wilson on May 24, 1989. The Shining Path in Peru is notorious for the brutality of attacks conducted by group members. Although the Shining Path conducted more bombings and armed assaults than assassinations, the Global Terrorism Database attributes an astounding 834 assassinations to the group.[142] The Shining Path often targeted leaders of different religious faiths, including Catholic nuns and priests.

In rare instances, terrorists also targeted Latter-day Saint leaders. Martin Openshaw and his wife, Idon, explained that while Martin served as a mission president in Peru, men claiming to be members of a local youth group called President Openshaw and asked him to invite the temple president and the rest of the mission presidents in the area to come and speak. They stated the men, likely belonging to a terrorist group possibly in San Martín, attempted to organize a meeting of these Latter-day Saint leaders for sinister reasons. Martin notified the leaders and advised them not to attend such meeting requests, telling the other Latter-day Saint leaders, "They're setting us up."[143] Congregation heads grew wary of such threats during this period of heightened danger.

On occasion, terrorist groups also targeted specific Church members. For instance, President Lloyd Richmond described a Shining Path hit list which included Martin Openshaw's name, who was a well-known leader of the Church serving in Peru as a government liaison in the agriculture sector and as the President of the Peru Lima South Mission. President Richmond explained:

> "He [Openshaw] had been in Peru for eight years [. . . as] the mission president go-between with the embassy. I think the terrorist groups thought he was something other than just a mission president, but he was our go-between. They actually had his name at the top of their hit list. My name was also on the list. [. . .] We know they must have been fairly serious because President Openshaw was evacuated overnight one night [. . .]. They [embassy personnel] then told us we should maintain a low profile [. . . and] they were worried that we would move up to number one on the hit list."[144]

Martin Openshaw and his wife, Idon, expounded upon this assassination threat. President Openshaw explained he had a working relationship with the ambassador and regional security officer (RSO), as he served as warden, in essence, for the Latter-day Saint members in Peru, maintaining accountability and disseminating information from the US Government. Openshaw received all his information from the embassy regarding security threats. He and his family received instruction from the embassy on how to react to terrorist threats, including how to take away a weapon from a perpetrator. Elaborating on this particular threat, Openshaw stated:

> "We had lots of contacts. Everybody knew the car I drove. It was a Suburban. [. . .] The Senderos had just assassinated a priest. They were doing all they could to incite the government and they wanted to target a North American. That's why I got on the list. They wanted the Church—not just North America—they wanted a North American member of the Church on the list. [. . .] They were trying to make a statement. [. . .] The RSO called me one morning and said, 'Hey, we have a strange thing happening, but you're on a list.' He told me what it was. In his lingo, it wasn't sounding right to me because they had set up the hit to be at a temple. Our temple was guarded and you don't go into the temple. I worked in the temple on Saturdays, so that didn't seem right. Then he said where it was. It was a church meetinghouse about ten blocks from the temple.
>
> Then I realized as he was telling me, we'd just been there Sunday to speak at a fireside for the youth. Lots of the kids our kids had grown up with were there. There were two students there who were converts, who'd been students at the university. It was a very leftist university with propaganda, terrorists, Maoists. These two young people would not look at us—would not look us in the eye. We both knew something was wrong. There was just this feeling—something was wrong. When we left, it was a very dark area—very dark. While we visited with friends outside, two men came off of the street and asked for Martin by name. I don't remember what the conversation was, but when they asked for me by name, we wondered about it, but then they left. We were one of the last ones out of the parking lot. We just had this feeling.
>
> We went on home and then we found all this out. I had this intense feeling that something was wrong. Our two Assistants came in, and we sent them on errands to take care of some things so we could go. I told our house help I wanted her to go home and take the rest of the week off. She wasn't a member of the church, but she said, 'Señora, something's wrong, I

> know you're not coming back.' [. . .] Our two Assistants just went around the block, then came back and said, 'President, we have this strong feeling that you and Sister Openshaw need to leave the mission home and that something bad is going to happen.'"[145]

The Openshaws left the mission home and checked into a hotel in Miraflores. They moved again the following evening, after waking up in the middle of the night and feeling a prompting to leave right away. They contacted a friend, an attaché who belonged to the Church, who picked them up and brought the Openshaw family to his home. The next day, the Openshaws returned to the mission home under guard to pick up belongings and identify what belonged to the Church. There were terrorists reconnoitering the home and the neighborhood, monitoring the activity there. The Openshaws were then transported under guard in separate vehicles to the airport, where they boarded an airplane bound for Ecuador.

Church members often felt reassurance and protection from the Holy Ghost during this dangerous period. They believed in God's promises of safeguarding them from danger and they thanked Him "for [His] protecting and watchful care over [His] Saints dwelling far and near."[146] Reflecting on the dangers of that time for members of the Church, Martin Openshaw stated,

> "We were never afraid. [. . .] When I became mission president, we were promised by Elder Ballard we wouldn't have any problems. That kept me going. One of my cities in the mission was Ayacucho, the town next to the town where Sendero Luminoso came from. And I had missionaries in those towns all the time. [. . .] But they didn't attack my missionaries."[147]

Threats and security concerns varied among missions and from year to year, however. A small number of terrorist groups targeted the Church through assassination in certain parts of South America. Those that did drew immediate criticism from local governments, sparking collaboration between American intelligence organizations and local police forces and other entities to track down the killers. The murder of two Latter-day Saint missionaries in Bolivia ultimately led to the downfall of the Zarate Willka group, as the Bolivian government and police forces worked with American officials to root out group members and bring down the terrorist faction. Fears associated with missionary assassinations and threats to Latter-day Saints in various parts of South America influenced the changing demographics of missionaries in certain missions and the reassignment of multiple North American mission presidents and missionaries.

While conditions improved over time, assassination is a threat the Lord's Church faced in ancient times just as in modern times, and this threat will persist throughout the modern era of terrorism. The Church takes precautions in preventing and deterring assassinations. For instance, not all members of the First Presidency and Quorum of the Twelve Apostles attend every session of General Conference, reducing the impact of a mass assassination if a terrorist were to make such an attempt. Historically, many prophets and others received threats or were actually assassinated for calling societies to repentance. Lehi faced this threat in Jerusalem over 2,600 years ago. This reaction to preaching and being called to repentance continues today and will endure as a factor in future terrorism threatening the Church.

Arson

A prevalent tactic among terrorist factions conducting attacks in small groups involves setting fire to targeted facilities. Arson is a low-risk/high-payoff attack which requires little technical knowledge and readily available resources. For these reasons, members of the Lautaro Youth Movement in Chile favored this tactic. The organization generally consisted of young agitated men with limited knowledge or experience of revolutionary tactics. A fundamental Lautaro norm involved *fogueo*, interpreted as "become fired," which was a common concept among revolutionary groups throughout Central and South America describing the progression of recruits from supporting soft missions to more direct operations (e.g., leaflets, sabotage) and eventually operations wherein group members kill targets.[148] Arson suited this hardening of recruits, enabling them to gain experience by attacking empty chapels and sabotaging the facilities through using easily acquired gasoline and matches. Usually hooded, these perpetrators attacked chapels in the evening hours under concealment of the darkness. Such attacks usually caused damage worth thousands of dollars before responders could extinguish the flames.

These low cost/high impact attacks presented quick wins for leftist groups seeking to conduct symbolic attacks against the United States. In other parts of the world, lone wolves and terrorists with little to no training conducted arson attacks targeting chapels in attempts to cause a large amount of property damage despite constraints in equipment, training, and manning. Arson became a leading tactic among small-scale extremist factions targeting Latter-day Saint chapels within the United States in recent decades. This means of swift destruction with limited risk will likely persist as a means of targeting the Church for years to come.

Propaganda

A consistent tactic among terrorist groups throughout history is the spread of lies, misinformation, and claims delegitimizing the government or another target. Propaganda was a bedrock characteristic of anarchist terrorism in the 1920s, polarizing societies and fomenting violence culminating in the assassination of political heads of state. Literature, media reports, pamphlets, and other methods of distributing information produced similar results in South America. Propaganda about the Church surfaced in various countries as a result of suspicion, speculation, and rumor.

Soviet radio transmissions in Spanish throughout South America show that as early as the 1950s Soviets spread disinformation and speculation about Latter-day Saint missionaries serving as agents for North American intelligence agencies.[149] Most propaganda, however, originated internally, produced by leftist factions within these countries. Terrorist groups often left political pamphlets or spray-painted graffiti and group slogans at attack sites. Many terrorists used symbolism, drawing or spray-painting a sickle or leaving a group's flag at sites. These groups thus claimed responsibility for attacks, leaving their mark, but also warned Americans to leave or locals to sever associations with the US or American entities through threatening messages.

Such messaging produced wariness among some locals regarding Latter-day Saint missionaries' intentions and new chapels appearing within their neighborhoods. Propaganda portrayed aspects of the gospel in a negative light, detailing false claims about genealogy efforts as a means to gather intelligence for the US Government or other absurdities. Propaganda served recruiting purposes, further polarizing members of society already harboring negative perceptions of the Church to join in terrorism or provide safe haven to terrorists.

Hoaxes

Hoaxes, activities or threats meant to deceive a target group, provide insight into the ideologies, motives, and possibly resources of terrorists. This distinct tactic does not aim to produce casualties, but effectively leverages minimal resources and experience with circumstances to inspire fear. Hoaxes may reflect a motive to observe reactions and determine response times and other factors, force the target to expend costs in security measures, or simply generate fear in the target audience.

Prevalent terrorist groups in Latin America conducting attacks against the Church in the 1980s and 1990s occasionally used hoaxes. "Terrorist group[s] with established credibility can employ a hoax with considerable success," as the target audience, unable to distinguish hoaxes from genuine threats, anticipates attacks in line with the group's modus operandi.[150] Hoax bombs were often reported at Latter-day Saint chapels in Santiago, Chile during periods and in areas with frequent bombings attributed to the Lautaro Youth Movement and the Manuel Rodriguez Patriotic Front. Such hoaxes, likely carried out by followers of at least one of these two groups, produced fear and prompted responses from law enforcement similar to reactions when members encountered genuine bombs. Terrorists used fewer resources and exposed themselves to less risk by emplacing a hoax bomb but achieved similar results in terms of fear and response.

Hoaxes can also serve as an ideal tactic among lone wolf terrorists. Lone wolves "often come up with their own ideologies that combine personal vendettas with religious or political grievances."[151] Usually lacking expertise had by terrorist groups, such as knowledge of explosives for bomb-making, a lone wolf might employ a hoax. Such a ploy would not inflict casualties but would serve to stimulate fear and cause the target to expend resources the same way the target would respond to a true threat.

A number of anthrax scares since the early 2000s involved hoax attacks. Individuals easily procured a white, grainy substance similar in appearance to anthrax, then used mail services to deliver letters or packages containing the substance to targets. One anthrax hoax targeting the Salt Lake Temple occurred in 1999.[152] In 2008, fake anthrax packages arrived at the Los Angeles and Salt Lake Temples. Suspicions focused on gay rights activists, as the hoax attacks coincided with the Proposition 8 vote in California regarding gay marriage, but a lack of evidence left these claims unsubstantiated.[153] The hoax attacks did not inflict casualties, but generated fear and resulted in significant costs for investigations and security precautions.

In similar fashion, 50-year-old Travis Ball conducted multiple anthrax scares in 2016, one of which targeted the Church. Regarding the case, the US Attorney's Office of the Northern District of Georgia stated the following:

> "Ball sent letters to the State Bar of Georgia, the Atlanta Journal-Constitution, and the Church of Jesus Christ of Latter-day Saints threatening harm to members of each organization. Ball's threatening letters, which contained a substance he claimed was anthrax, were meant to instill fear in the recipients and diverted critical resources from actual emergencies [. . .] On April 7, 2016, while incarcerated in Coffee Correctional Facility in Nicholls, Georgia, Ball mailed [the] letters [. . . , which] stated, 'have some anthrax' and contained a granular substance. [. . .] The letter to the LDS Church threatened to kill Mormons and burn their churches."[154]

Ball's ability to procure a white substance and mail packages containing the substance to intended targets while incarcerated highlights the ease of carrying out a significant hoax attack and vulnerabilities in security systems. Hence, hoaxes present quick-win opportunities for terrorist groups, as hoaxes are often low cost/high impact activities.

Intimidation or Blackmail

Intimidation is an integral aspect of terrorism, as acts of violence categorized as terrorism serve to intimidate or coerce the local populace, members of the targeted organization, or others to act in a certain way. Several instances of intimidation demonstrate how extremists leveraged brutality, hit lists, and other methods to convince North Americans to flee countries or Latter-day Saint members to leave an area for fear of physical harm.

In Peru, the Shining Path was notorious for assassinations and its members' gruesome tactics. Proximity to Shining Path support zones and strongholds posed a serious threat to various Christian sects. In the late 1980s and early 1990s, the frequency of terrorist attacks in Peru led Church leadership to remove North American representatives from the country. Mission President Lloyd Richmond was about six months into his assignment in the Peru Lima North Mission when he and his North American elders were sequestered, going into hiding for a few weeks as President Richmond directed the mission by phone through a Peruvian elder named Juan Pita.[155] Several mission presidents were reassigned, including sending Jerry Cahill from Peru Trujillo to Colombia, Martin Openshaw from Peru Lima South to the Philippines, and Lloyd Richmond from Peru Lima North to the new Argentina Buenos Aires West Mission.[156]

This widespread intimidation and the growth of leftist organizations throughout South America grew to other areas. Garry Flake explained while he served as a mission president in Honduras, he exited a zone conference to participate in a conference call with Church Security and the Area Presidency. He received guidance to keep missionaries indoors due to local threats, and later to pair up North American missionaries with Latin missionaries. Eventually, though, Church leaders withdrew all North American missionaries from the mission and reassigned President Flake to Monterrey, Mexico. President Flake explained the reasons for these movements:

> "Later they told us that what had happened is that there was a group in Honduras that was establishing themselves like the *Sendero Luminoso* in Peru, the Shining Path group, and that there was an infiltrator working with US intelligence sources,

> that I understood was a former Honduran missionary, and he was a Honduran. And he, through the chatter or what had happened, knew that they had a list and that they had killed some people on the list, and they wanted to kill two or more American Mormon missionaries and two or more Peace Corps. And so they battled, following the group and holding us indoors and back and forth. Of course, all of those details didn't come out until later."[157]

The Peace Corps withdrew from Honduras during this period of increased threats. It, along with Latter-day Saint missionaries and chapels, was one of few US-affiliated targets for anti-American attacks.

The Shining Path was responsible for much of this intimidation in Peru. The group was notorious for brutality and targeting peaceful members of society, such as religious leaders of various faiths. President Lloyd Richmond also described an occasion in which Lima Peru Temple President Rudy Mortensen was returning home from a fireside when his car was shot and another in which Richmond was in Mortensen's apartment and "a big bomb exploded and shook the building."[158] Members, although rarely deliberately targeted, were often within close proximity of terrorist attacks. There are countless instances of spiritual promptings guiding these members to safety in the moments prior to such attacks.

While intimidation tactics against the Church often concerned North Americans, some groups threatened South American members for supporting the Church and missionary work and for their perceived affiliation with the United States. In Ayacucho, Peru, the Shining Path maintained enough of a presence that some Saints altered their practices to reduce the chance of being identified as Latter-day Saints. Suspicions of locals wary of the United States and its growing influence in Peru contributed to this secrecy. For instance, new members traveled outside the city to Rio Huatatas to be baptized in the 60-centimeter-deep river rather than hold a service at the chapel.[159] Groups threatened some Latter-day Saint Church leaders and other prominent Christian figures with death. At least three Latter-day Saint families left Ayacucho and emigrated from Peru because of these threats.[160] These threats persisted in other areas of Peru, as well. Brother Manuel Moises Sanchez of Huancayo, Peru received an anonymous letter from a terrorist group "threatening [him] with death."[161] He departed, leaving his family temporarily, acknowledging the terrorists' capability to carry out this threat as, just one month prior, they had assassinated two missionaries in his hometown. Many other Church members who were not directly threatened or targeted, however, remained in their villages or cities, risking continued persecution and attacks.

Terrorists in Bolivia also used intimidation to strike fear into the populace and force Latter-day Saint members, especially North Americans, to leave Bolivia or go into hiding. The Nestor Paz Zamora Commission (CNPZ), a leftist organization in Bolivia, was one such organization, operating chiefly in the Mormon-rich highland region of La Paz. Anthropology professor David Knowlton stated the group "threatened all gringos in Bolivia, including Mormons," and "called the house where one of [his] students, an Anglo-American [. . .] was living, and warned her—warned the family—that they would assassinate her if she didn't get out."[162] Members in Peru and other areas faced similar threats and opposition, forcing some families to leave their homes and occasionally flee the country. During the height of anti-American terrorism in Peru, the MRTA "threaten[ed] to kill any American found on the streets" and the US Department of State issued warnings and travel advisories for Peru and locations with similar threats to American citizens.[163] Such intimidation convinced Church leaders to reassign mission presidents and missionaries, drastically reducing the number of North American Church members in multiple Latin American countries for several months.

Additionally, terrorists occasionally used intimidation tactics to threaten political leaders with physical harm if they would not take action against the Church. After Zarate Willka members assassinated two Latter-day Saint missionaries in Bolivia, group members "threatened to kill the mayor and council members of the suburban city of El Alto de La Paz if they did not drive all 'gringos' out of the city and close its Mormon chapels."[164] The group's reputation for brutality and violence often influenced politicians and other leaders to submit to the group's will. In a similar manner, the group's intimidation tactics allegedly delayed the murder trial of those linked to the murder of the two missionaries. The *Deseret News* cited a report on global terrorism produced by the US Department of State, which stated, "virtually no progress was made (during 1990) in the prosecution of Zarate Willka (a terrorist group) members charged with the 1989 murder of two US Mormon missionaries," as "the government changed prosecutors five times and had not named a judge to hear the case by year's end."[165] Death threats influenced judges to resign from the case and greatly delayed convictions. Properly leveraging intimidation tactics in this way and others targeting fundamental institutions, such as judicial organizations and political groups, enabled terrorists to damage the local government's legitimacy.

Although ransoms may be associated with blackmail and intimidation, incidents involving ransoms generally constitute crime rather than terrorism.[166] In cases like the ransom of Latter-day Saint missionaries kidnapped in Saratov, Russia, perpetrators did not necessarily intend to inspire fear among the general Latter-day Saint population, nor did they kidnap the missionaries to protest US political actions. Such violence transpired on various occasions in Central and South America where terrorist factions hoped to profit from ransom money paid out to guarantee the safety of North American missionaries. The Church's refusal to pay such ransoms is similar to other organizations' practices. Paying a ransom would establish a dangerous precedent, indicating to criminal elements that kidnapping members of the Church would yield ransom money.

Terrorist groups targeting the Church rarely used kidnapping or hostage taking as tactics. Groups frequently kidnapped children of wealthy families and later released them for ransoms; while this tactic commonly occurred in areas where Latter-day Saint families resided, such activities rarely targeted members of the Church.[167] Rather, most leftist groups in Latin America, when targeting the Church, sought to sabotage facilities and minimize collateral damage in the sense of causing bodily harm to Church members. Terrorists generally targeted empty chapels during late evening hours, and if groups encountered members present in chapels at the times of attack, they would most often tie up the members and move them or escort them off the premises before bombing or setting fire to the chapel. Rather than kidnapping or hostage taking, these terrorists held or transported members against their will so as to avoid members' intervening in their attacks or suffering physical harm during attacks. In this way, terrorist groups maintained legitimacy among some support groups willing to sabotage buildings, but not physically harm locals belonging to the Church.

President Howard W. Hunter Interrupted during Multi-Stake Fireside at Brigham Young University

During a 19-stake fireside on February 7, 1993, a man interrupted President Howard W. Hunter of the Quorum of the Twelve Apostles during his address to a crowd of 17,000. 27-year-old Cody Judy walked up to the podium just as President Hunter began speaking on adversity. Cody, "carrying a briefcase and a toy cellular phone wrapped in black tape," instructed those on the stand to step away, "saying he had a bomb and a detonator," which he threatened to detonate. President Hunter stopped speaking, recording ceased, and the fireside halted for about ten minutes as the incident unfolded. All on the stand complied with Cody's instruction, except two Church security officers who refused, remaining with President Hunter. Cody handed a note to President Hunter to read, allegedly calling for the release of the First Presidency and Quorum of the Twelve Apostles, installing Cody as the new prophet of the Church. President Hunter refused to read the letter, and shortly thereafter, the congregation began singing the hymn "We Thank Thee, O God, for a Prophet." Reports then describe a quick succession of events, wherein a man in the audience unsuccessfully tried to distract Cody, a student sprayed Cody with mace, and then the two security guards and 40–50 students "converged on the man" and supported university police in apprehending him. Police investigated the contents of the briefcase, encountering books and a radio, but no explosives. President Hunter, who appeared calm throughout the incident, continued his remarks, telling the crowd, "I want to tell you how good your voices sound." Cody was later charged with kidnapping, among other crimes.[168]

Lone Wolf Attacks

Lone wolf attacks are becoming increasingly common throughout the world. These attacks are difficult to prevent and perpetrators often elude interdiction, as there are few detectable indicators. Mental illness and personal vendettas may mix with extremist ideologies, but authorities often struggle to identify reasons for attacks; lone wolves may not publish their grievances on social media or publish a manifesto, or they might die in an attack, excluding interviews as a potential source of information. Weapons and tactics are often rudimentary with perpetrators using bombs of limited sophistication or basic weapons, such as knives, pistols, or assault rifles. Lone wolves also tend to employ hoax attacks, attempting to incite fear and elicit reactions to fake bombs or biological or chemical agents they cannot procure.

Terrorists acting in isolation, without aid from or in collusion with others, sometimes resort to hoax attacks, especially when they cannot obtain necessary supplies. Travis Ball was already incarcerated and serving time for an arson conviction when he mailed letters to the State Bar of Georgia, Atlanta newspapers, The Church of Jesus Christ of Latter-day Saints, and two local residents in 2016. Within these letters, Ball communicated various threats posing as someone else and included a white substance he stated was anthrax. Given Ball's confinement to a correctional facility at the time he sent these letters, preventing him from conducting arson, he used letters to threaten his targets with physical violence or arson. He leveraged the fear associated with anthrax by mailing a white substance in these letters. The court docket and other evidence provide insight as to why Ball targeted the Church. In his letter (Figure 4.3), he communicates threats reflecting his criminal history as an arsonist.

Rather than send this letter to a local Latter-day Saint meetinghouse or leader, consistent with Georgia addresses for the other letters, Ball sent the letter to Salt Lake City, Utah. He was sentenced to two years in prison followed by three years supervised release and restitution of $10,704.00 to law enforcement, first responders, and others involved in investigation and response efforts.[169]

Figure 4.3: Exhibit 3 in USA v. Ball

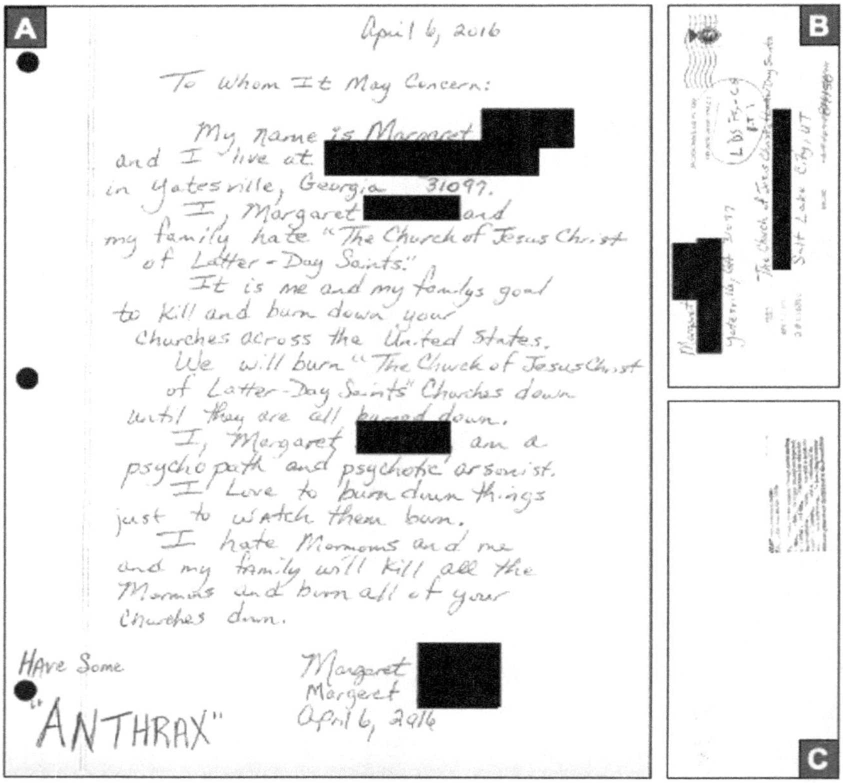
A

April 6, 2016

To Whom It May Concern:

My name is Margaret [redacted]
and I live at [redacted]
in Yatesville, Georgia 31097.
I, Margaret [redacted] and
my family hate "The Church of Jesus Christ
of Latter-Day Saints."
It is me and my familys goal
to Kill and burn down your
Churches across the United States.
We will burn "The Church of Jesus Christ
of Latter-Day Saints" Churches down
until they are all burned down.
I, Margaret [redacted] am a
psychopath and psychotic arsonist.
I Love to burn down things
just to watch them burn.
I hate Mormons and me
and my family will Kill all the
Mormons and burn all of your
Churches down.

Have Some
"ANTHRAX"

Margaret [redacted]
Margaret
April 6, 2016

B

The Church of Jesus Christ of Latter-Day Saints
Salt Lake City, UT

C

Source: United States of America v. Travis Ball, (N.D. Ga 2017).

Note: Exhibit 3, comprised of the letter written by Travis Ball to the Church ("A"), the envelope front ("B"), and the envelope back with stamp of Coffee Correctional Facility in Nicholls, GA ("C").

Timing of Attacks

Terrorists conducted attacks targeting US interests abroad in protest of policies, often relating to political and military activities perceived as imperialistic actions. Various attacks are associated with anniversaries of military occupation or invasion, visits by American political leaders, or American holidays. Propaganda and news summaries reflect a tendency among many far-left groups to attack on specific dates during the year corresponding with political observances or in the wake of a significant political or military event. For instance, the Maximiliano Gomez Revolutionary Brigade, operational within the Dominican Republic, bombed Latter-day Saint chapels in late April 1987 to commemorate the anniversary of the April 24, 1965 US troop invasion of the Dominican Republic.[170] Figure 4.4 includes another example of strategically timed attacks, displaying a time event chart outlining actions taken by the ELN in response to President Bush's participation in a summit on the drug trade.

Most of the terrorism incidents in protest of President Bush's visit, outlined in Figure 4.4, targeted the Church. This trend applies to several attacks against Latter-day Saint chapels in Central and South America in the 1980s and 1990s. Given the heightened security presence around President Bush and difficulty in targeting him, the ELN selected other American targets for their vulnerability and symbolism. The ELN capitalized on targets of opportunity, attacking vulnerable American persons or structures in symbolic attacks against the United States.

The timing of the day at which most terrorists attacked Latter-day Saint meetinghouses was during the late evening or early morning hours, when chapels were empty. This characteristic reflects the objective of most groups to protest political or military events by facility attacks, rather than inflicting casualties and targeting individuals. Small groups, often containing two to seven perpetrators, capitalized on concealment provided by darkness and reduced risk of exposure or reporting due to few or zero witnesses in the area. In conjunction with bomb emplacement and detonation, most groups spray-painted anti-American messages and threats on the sides of chapels or nearby buildings, as darkness granted anonymity and afforded group members adequate time to graffiti propaganda or hate messages.

Analyzing the day of the week on which attacks occurred does not reveal any significant trends. There is no significant correlation between specific days and attacks. Attacks during the weekend (Friday–Sunday) do not reflect any noticeable differences from trends during weekdays. Most perpetrators did not deliberately target Latter-day Saint chapels during worship services on Sunday nights or Tuesday/Wednesday nights during activities. There are no apparent trends with weather conditions or the lunar cycle (the amount of illumination in the night sky providing concealment during operations). Rather, the most significant factor contributing to the timing of attacks involved observances or significant political or military events.

Figure 4.4: Time Event Chart of ELN Activities Protesting President Bush's Visit to Colombia

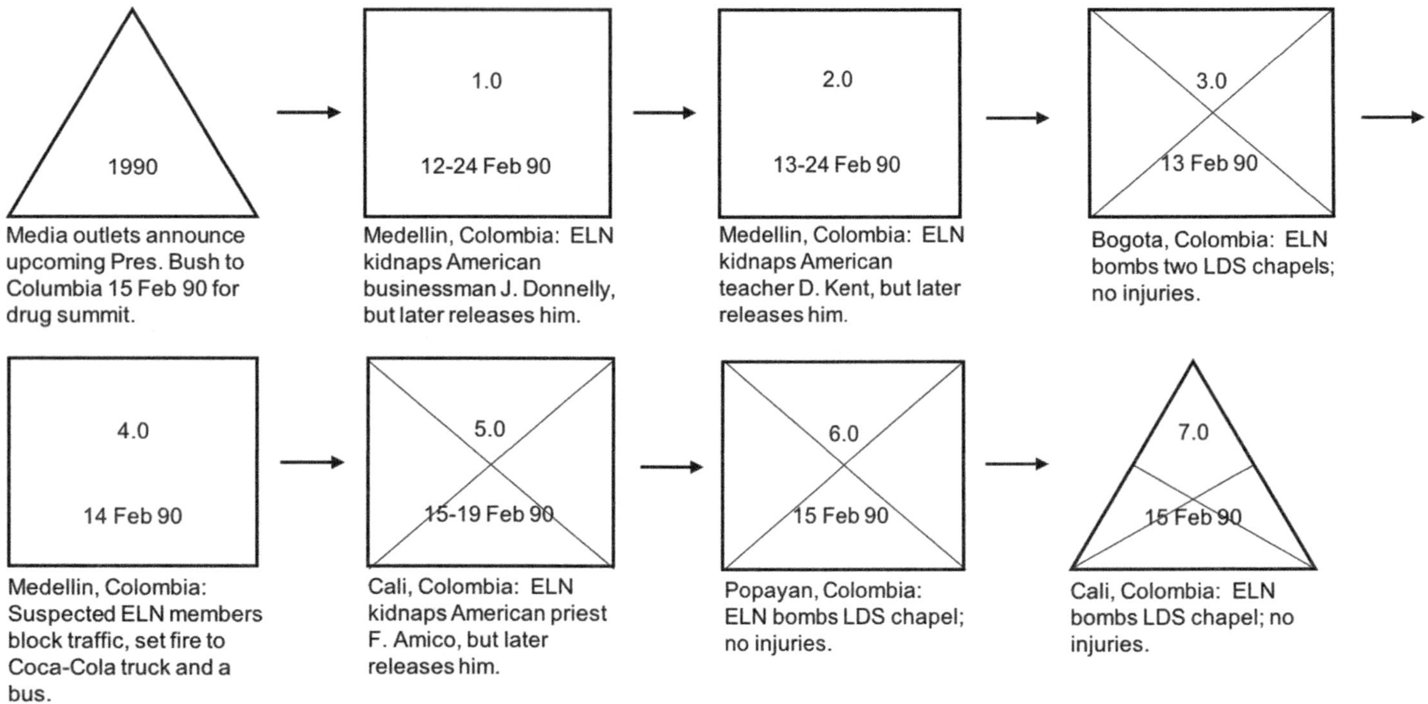

Note: Compiled using incident summaries described in source, Bureau of Diplomatic Security, "Significant Incidents of Political Violence Against Americans: 1987," United States Department of State, 4.

Terrorist Target Selection Criteria

US presence in South America varied in degree and dynamics based on political and economic factors, social characteristics, and several other details. Political presence seemed more permanent with embassies and consulates in highly populated urban centers. Latter-day Saint presence seemed much more pervasive, as missionaries penetrated jungles and forests to reach rural areas populated only by indigenous tribes and chapels sprung up throughout cities and the countryside. US-based businesses varied by country based on population hubs, cultures, natural resources, and more, with restaurants growing in some areas, while mining or production companies boomed in others.

Amidst this diffusion of US culture and increasing presence, extremists encountered a variety of potential targets affiliated with the United States. These included mobile, stationary short-term, and stationary long-term targets, such as those listed in Table 4.2.

Table 4.2: Types of Potential US-linked Targets

	Stationary Long-Term	Stationary Short-Term	Mobile
Government	Embassy, consulate	Conference, summit	Ambassador, motorcade
The Church of Jesus Christ of Latter-day Saints	Chapel (meetinghouse), temple, genealogy center, offices	Religious meeting, seminary session	Missionaries, mission presidents, members
Business	Office building, restaurant	Temporary vendor stand; meeting	CEO, employees

Oftentimes, a significant challenge in antiterrorism efforts is the difficulty in understanding terrorist processes for target selection and prioritization. While infiltrating a terrorist network or seizing documents or media may reveal aspects of target selection, analysts often rely on limited intelligence reporting and models to mitigate bias as they try to determine where an enemy may strike. One method used by Special Operations Forces to evaluate the prioritization of targets from a terrorist's perspective is known as MSHARPP force protection target value analysis. This method helps to "determine the value of the high-risk target to the terrorist attacker" by evaluating targets in terms of seven criteria: mission, symbolism, history, accessibility, recognizability, population, and proximity (MSHARPP).[171] Table 4.3 includes a brief explanation of each of these criteria.

Table 4.3: Description of MSHARPP Criteria

Criteria Factor	Definition
Mission	How critical the target is to an organization's ability to accomplish key tasks.
Symbolism	Symbolic significance of target to attacker and population attacker is terrorizing (Marines – Hezbollah; Statue of Liberty – Americans).
History	History of attacks against this type of target (abortion clinics – right to life groups; federal buildings – militia groups; Jewish centers – neo-Nazi or Palestinian or Arab groups).
Accessibility	How accessible the target is to the public (open posts, building with multiple entrances, no guards or detectors, close to the road).
Recognizability	How well known the target is to the public at large. How easy the value is to recognize without specialized or inside information or explanation of the attack.
Population	How many people are directly affected by the attack. Casualties are a factor for some; embarrassing government drives for others.
Proximity	Whether the target is located near other personnel, facilities, or resources that, because of their intrinsic value or "protected" status and a fear of collateral damage, afford it some form of protection (for example, near national monuments, protected or religious symbols that the enemy holds in high regard).

Source: Christopher M. Schnaubelt, Eric V. Larson, and Matthew E. Boyer, "Vulnerability Assessment Method Pocket Guide," (The Rand Corporation: Washington, DC, 2014), 29; Headquarters, Department of the Army, *Intelligence Analysis*, Training Circular 2-33.4 (Department of the Army: Washington, DC, July 1, 2009), para. D-16.

Analysts evaluate a high-risk target by scoring one to ten for each of the seven criteria, and then determine overall priority of targets through their total scores, the highest score indicating the target of highest priority. Utilizing the MSHARPP model to evaluate and prioritize targets reduces the chance of heuristics, or cognitive biases, interfering with analysis. Western thought, norms, practices, and targeting criteria and prioritization used by friendly forces might negatively influence predictive analysis, framing problems differently than terrorists and contributing to poor analysis. Hence, the MSHARPP method yields a more objective approach in determining terrorists' prioritization of targets.

Applying the MSHARPP model to South American terrorist groups' target selection in the 1980s and 1990s helps to understand why these groups targeted Latter-day Saint chapels and personnel. Table 4.4 displays a MSHARPP Matrix Tool, which includes scores for each of the seven factors, as applied to stationary long-term targets. Common targets in South America included US embassies, Latter-day Saint chapels, and US-based businesses.

Table 4.4: MSHARPP Matrix Tool for Stationary Long-term US-linked Targets in South America

High-risk Target	M	S	H	A	R	P	P	TOTAL
US Embassy	10	8	4	2	9	9	2	44
LDS Chapel	5	3	7	10	4	3	9	41
US Business	2	3	1	6	3	2	5	22

Embassies are clearly high payoff targets for terrorists, given their symbolism housing the US figureheads and key government officials in foreign lands. Even so, statistics for violence targeting US interests show a prominence for attacks against Latter-day Saint chapels for several years in South America, as attacks against meetinghouses carried significantly less risk than those targeting an embassy or consulate.

Mission

Through the lens of a far-left extremist, Latter-day Saint meetinghouses are likely viewed as central to the Church's proselyting mission. These buildings represented the one gathering location for Church members in their neighborhoods. Aside from the homes of members, recent converts, and investigators, most religious instruction and meetings occurred in chapels. Leftists identified these buildings as indoctrination locations, where churchgoers studied the gospel and leaders inculcated followers with values and ideals consistent with national laws and government institutions. Leftists viewed meetinghouses as venues where the United States pushed an imperialist agenda and attempted to propagate cultural influence.

Symbolism

While American culture pervaded Chile and other South American countries through media, physical presence of Americans and American businesses increased slowly. Latter-day Saint missionaries were often the only North Americans some South Americans met. The Church became a symbol of the United States, as the only exposure to North Americans many had involved contact with Latter-day Saint missionaries and many knew the Church Headquarters was located in Salt Lake City. Most attacks targeting the Church during the 1980s and 1990s represented attacks against the United States and American international politics and policies. Mabel Correa, spokeswoman for the Chilean embassy in Washington, DC, remarked, "Most of the attacks were symbolic [as] whatever smell[ed] Yankee, these terrorists put a bomb on that. For them, the chapels [. . .] ma[d]e up a constellation of political symbols."[172] In the absence of multiple physical North American entities, anti-American terrorists targeted Latter-day Saint meetinghouses in hopes of achieving their objectives and harming the United States to affect political change.

History

The trend of attacks against Latter-day Saint meetinghouses did not begin until 1983 with attacks in Colombia. The trend picked up in the late 1980s in various South American countries. As far-left terrorists targeted the Church more frequently, the Church became the most common target for anti-US terrorism. This history of these attacks and the tendency among leftists to target the Church likely influenced new groups or extremists with slightly different ideologies to also attack meetinghouses in their neighborhoods. Hence, history played a significant role in the terrorists' selection of Latter-day Saint meetinghouses as targets, as opposed to embassies or consulates, which extremist groups rarely targeted in successful attacks. Similarly, groups sporadically attacked North American businesses or establishments; the lack of a historical trend to do so likely reduced the likelihood a terrorist group would choose to target such businesses.

Accessibility

In regard to accessibility, Latter-day Saint chapels were vulnerable to physical damage, especially compared to other potential US-affiliated targets in South America. Empty Latter-day Saint chapels became the most frequently targeted sites of anti-US terrorism in South America, largely because they were "seen as a low-risk target for terrorists and a good starting place for apprentice guerrillas wanting to build their confidence."[173] Oftentimes, the greatest threat in targeting such chapels was the terrorists themselves, and the possibility of early detonation of the explosive while still being handled or set by the terrorists.

Latter-day Saint chapels included only one to two factors deterring terrorists and criminals, mainly relying on perimeter fences. Some fashion of a fence, usually six to eight feet high with shattered glass lining the top to deter climbing, protected virtually every home or business in urban and suburban areas with rampant crime. Tall metal fencing lining the perimeter of Latter-day Saint meetinghouses in Chile failed to deter terrorists so much so that President Augusto Pinochet "ordered special vigilance for the property of the Church of Jesus Christ [of] Latter-day Saints in Chile" due to the high frequency of attacks targeting chapels.[174] Usually, meetinghouses were not guarded by personnel. Similarly, the only times people occupied chapels included Sunday meetings, weekly seminary classes, or occasional activities on weeknights. Chilean Latter-day Saint historian Rodolfo Acevedo stated the Church "saturated Chile with chapels," and that, "Many of them [chapels] sat nearly empty, and that made them easier targets."[175] The limited physical security measures protecting Latter-day Saint chapels appealed to terrorists aiming to attack US interests in retaliatory strikes for political reasons. This US-affiliated target containing limited protection offered terrorists the opportunity to attack the US with little risk of harm or capture.

Recognizability

As Latter-day Saint meetinghouses saturated urban centers and also scattered rural landscapes in South American countries, most people recognized chapels and to which religious group they belonged. By the 1980s, missionary work established the Latter-day Saint faith as a prominent minority group in some countries, especially Chile, Bolivia, Ecuador, Peru, and Uruguay. People could generally identify Latter-day Saint missionaries and chapels, both having unique characteristics distinguishing them from other churches, even by those unfamiliar with doctrines and teachings. Those hearing or reading about attacks against chapels readily understood the context and reasons without much information, knowing of the Church's association with the United States.

Population

Leftist terrorists' intent focused on physical damage to buildings in what constituted a symbolic attack against the United States, not on inflicting casualties; rather, they generally sought to avoid killing or injuring Church members in such attacks. Physically harming their countrymen would detract from their message to target the US and would weaken their legitimacy and support among local citizens. Such a tactic would also increase attention from law enforcement and intelligence agencies, limiting their freedom to maneuver and increasing risks to the terrorist group in conducting future attacks.

While most terrorists did not necessarily aim to harm Latter-day Saints for these reasons, many terrorists intended to intimidate them through violence. Propaganda left at attack sites and messages distributed through local media warned members of supporting North American missionaries, participating in what was perceived to be a North American church, and serving as agents to spread capitalism and other principles opposed by leftists. These threats and persecutions led some Church members to leave their homes out of fear of further violence.

Proximity

Proximity is another outlier making Latter-day Saint chapels a viable and attractive target. The layered security of US embassies provides natural standoff from the road and significant protection. Embassies and consulates are also located in urban centers, sometimes at considerable distances from safe havens or support zones of terrorists. Proximity ratings for US businesses may vary substantially, depending on protection gained based on venues. Businesses may include restaurants, surrounded by other stores or residential zones, or corporations whose facilities are in rural areas with abundant natural resources. Latter-day Saint chapels, on the other hand, exist in rural, suburban, and urban areas across countries. Chapels are likely in closer proximity to terrorist groups based on their widely dispersed arrangement, often surrounded by residential zones in South America.

In contrast to the accessibility and vulnerability characteristic of Latter-day Saint chapels, US embassies were the most secure US facilities in foreign countries, integrating layered security to reduce risk. This defense-in-depth concept, including a tiered security system with redundancies (e.g., perimeter fence, entry control point, security cameras, and roving patrol), deters terrorists and reduces the likelihood of a terrorist successfully carrying out an attack. Table 4.5 lists common defense measures at different stationary long-term targets in South America during periods of heightened terrorism targeting The Church of Jesus Christ of Latter-day Saints.

Table 4.5: Typical Defense Measures at US-affiliated Stationary Long-term Targets in South America (c. 1990)

Defensive Measure	Business	Embassy	LDS Chapel
Perimeter Fence	X*	X	X
Full-time Guard(s)		X	
Temporary Guard(s)			X*
Security Cameras	X*	X	
Alarm System	X*	X	
Physical Standoff (>20 ft.)	X*	X	X*
Entry Control Point		X	
24-hr Lighting	X	X	

*Some locations only

Conclusion

Bombings, the most frequent form of attack against Latter-day Saint chapels, involved little risk for perpetrators, a high likelihood to actually cause harm or damage to the target, and probable media exposure. Such attacks required limited planning and flexibility; if perpetrators encountered unsuitable conditions at one chapel (e.g., large group of members gathered outside during intended attack time), they could simply bomb another chapel within a few blocks. Procuring explosives often involved minimal risk of detection, as terrorists could readily obtain ANFO from numerous mining sites or reliable sources. Preparing the bomb required limited expertise and basic components, including blasting caps and fuses. The simplicity of the bomb reduced the amount of time and degree of expertise required for construction. Groups routinely used the same design with minor variations, depending on the amount of available ANFO or dynamite and how many targets the group planned to attack. Most groups utilized small amounts of explosives to cause limited structural damage to chapels, rather than produce a large enough blast to destroy a building or inflict casualties, so groups tended to make more bombs with smaller amounts of explosives. Perpetrators did not need to observe patterns of life of guards (e.g., shift change times or patrol times) and could quickly identify any physical barriers, such as fences, or other deterrents, such as the presence of crowds. Also, the high concentration of chapels in South American urban centers provided perpetrators with flexibility to attack a number of secondary targets—other chapels—within close proximity.

Although most terrorist attacks targeting the Church occurred against stationary long-term targets like chapels, the missionary force has also dealt with the threats and dangers of terrorism. As terrorist groups assessed mobile targets with affiliations to the US, most attacked visiting political officials, while a couple groups targeted Latter-day Saint missionaries. Missionaries are a highly mobile target, as their daily schedule is generally unpredictable to the public, with the exception of when they leave from and return to their residence in the evening, as well as when they attend religious services on Sundays. Groups targeting missionaries generally monitor pattern of life, often conducting surveillance on the companionship for an extended period before attacking. This occurred in the case of a North American missionary companionship assassinated in Bolivia by the Zarate Willka terrorist group. While North American missionaries were generally recognizable as originating from the United States, especially in the 1980s when Caucasian missionaries made up a substantial portion of the missionaries in South American missions, citizens and terrorist groups linked native and Latin American missionaries with the United States by association to the Church. For instance, the Shining Path in Peru assassinated a Peruvian missionary companionship out of hatred for the United States and perceived encroachments on native culture and lifestyle.

Satan's role in terrorism directly and indirectly affecting missionaries is subtle, but evident in the circumstances surrounding attacks. In his book *The Power of Everyday Missionaries*, renowned Latter-day Saint author and businessman Clayton M. Christensen explains that missionaries are on the "front lines in the war against Satan over the souls of men."[176] Hence, physically harming missionaries or causing fear and terror to supplant faith and hope among future missionaries depletes opposition he faces in claiming souls for hell. Missionary assassinations occurred in some of the most successful missions in the world at the most prolific periods of church growth.

South American leftist factions regarded the Church and missionary work as a threat. As columnist Jack Anderson and terrorism expert Dale Van Atta summarized the dilemma, "The bottom line for the leftist groups is frustration in recruiting conservative Christians to their cause. For every convert to the church, there is one less revolutionary to overthrow the government."[177] Preaching gospel principles contradicts ideologies inherent in leftist manifestos and promotes values incompatible with the use of violence to bring about political change.

Government documents and research attribute this motive to several attacks against the Church based on analysis of trends, ideologies of groups conducting attacks, propaganda left at attack scenes and other information. Deputy Director of Central Intelligence, Robert M. Gates, stated in a 1988 speech that has since been declassified that Chilean terrorists saw the Church as "an extension of American imperialism."[178] Indeed, although very few South Americans held this perception, it fueled animosity and violence that put the Church in the crosshairs of several leftist groups.

Islamic State (IS) Publishes Threat to Latter-day Saint Temple in San Diego, California

In late November 2017, images began to pop up across the internet of an armed Jihadist facing the San Diego Latter-day Saint Temple with the threatening statement *Coming Soon* and the tag #San_Diego. Previously, no publicly documented incidents reflected a threat to the Church from the Islamic State. Security responses took effect at the temple, but no attack occurred. The Islamic State used propaganda to intimidate American citizens on previous occasions, such as a published kill list for certain US military personnel and their families and a call for attacks targeting seven US cities. In addition to instilling fear among Americans, another likely objective of the Islamic State involved inspiring lone wolf terrorists to carry out attacks. While some lone wolf attacks in recent years may be attributed to radicalization and recruitment efforts of the Islamic State, the attacks called for in the provided examples of propaganda did not play out.

CHAPTER 5

STRATEGIES AND TACTICS OF SATAN

"It is no secret that Satan wages open war with the truth and all those who live righteous lives."

—Marvin J. Ashton, "A Pattern in All Things," LDS General Conference (October 1990)

Introduction

Many books and journals examine the methods by which men conduct terrorist attacks, but few explore the application of these methods through a spiritual lens to identify and understand Satan's strategies and tactics. Since the beginning, the adversary has sought to supplant the gifts of the Spirit with the disharmony, animosity, and evil produced by the spirit of contention. He continues in modern times to tempt and stir men's hearts and influence men's minds, leading them to carry out his will in opposing all that is good and claiming souls. Terrorism is one weapon in his arsenal he uses to this end.

As a broad strategy, Satan seeks to oppose God's Plan of Happiness and prevent the spiritual progression of men. President James E. Faust remarked that, "Since Satan is the author of all evil in the world, it would therefore be essential to realize that he is the influence behind the opposition to the work of God."[179] While much opposition comes through subtle means, Satan has, on occasion, leveraged terrorism.

After all, the end state of terrorism, according to most descriptions, is to bring about political change through the use of violence. Similarly, Satan "became the devil by seeking glory, power, and dominion by force."[180] Contemporary terrorism is simply a variation of other tactics used by Satan throughout history.

Different aspects of terrorism incidents targeting the Church demonstrate that Satan leverages terrorism as a means to defy the four-fold mission of the Church. He attempts to generate fear through violence and intimidation, maneuvering to prevent and deter members from conducting ordinances and carrying out functions of the Church. Table 5.1 displays some of the methods by which Satan opposes the four-fold mission of the Church.

Table 5.1: Satan's Resistance to the Four-Fold Mission of the Church through Terrorism

Church Mission	Forms of Resistance and Opposition
Perfection of the Saints	Attempts to incite fear among members through bombing campaigns against chapels, deterring them from attending services/activities; challenging faith through doubt and fear
Proclaim the Gospel	Missionaries and converts targeted; killings and threats influenced leaders to relocate missionaries in some cases; intimidation techniques to deter people from investigating and joining the Church
Redeem the Dead	Deter members from temple attendance by targeting temples in threatening propaganda (San Diego Temple by Islamic State) or hoax attacks (Los Angeles and Salt Lake City Temples in anthrax hoax); spread misinformation and suspicions regarding genealogy work
Serve Poor and Needy	Terrorist groups recruit poor, disenfranchised people; isolate and polarize neighborhoods through propaganda and misinformation

Trends reflect a tendency for contemporary terrorism to interfere with proclaiming the gospel, as attacks increased in frequency in those missions with the highest conversion rates and Church leaders extracted North American missionaries from high-threat areas.

Satan's Preference for the Fabian Strategy

The way in which generals choose to direct war depends on several variables, including available resources, popular support, and alliances. Most experts recognize three overall strategies by which one belligerent wages war with other belligerents. These three distinguishable war strategies include attrition, eroding combat power over time; annihilation, the immediate destruction of enemy forces; and exhaustion, the gradual erosion of the enemy's will. Another popular version, however, is a variation of exhaustion known as the Fabian strategy. Satan has employed each of these strategies, depending on time, short-term and long-term objectives, and conditions of the target. The degree of physical resistance and violence to the Church has changed drastically from the persecution faced by Saints and pioneers in the early days of the Church. In terms of spiritual and temporal opposition, contemporary terrorism against the Church reflects Satan's use of elements of the Fabian strategy in recent decades.

As the gospel of Jesus Christ spread throughout the world and the Church experienced drastic growth in areas like South America, Satan focused his resources and introduced physical resistance in areas where other subtle resistance failed. He leveraged terrorism as one means to present opposition and delay Church growth and progress in ways reminiscent of the Fabian strategy. This strategy, named for Roman dictator Quintus Fabius, commonly known as Fabius Cunctatus ("the delayer"), involves "strategies whereby commanders deploy strategically defensive yet tactically offensive methods to forestall a decisive battle—all while marshaling manpower, implements of war, and other resources to right the military imbalance."[181] Oftentimes, a weaker force will employ this strategy against a stronger foe, in hopes of wearing down the enemy through skirmishes and carefully calculated offensive tactics, aimed at forcing the enemy to expend time, efforts, and resources in a prolonged effort to win the war. Throughout history, weaker forces defeated stronger foes not by forcing them to spend more money or exhaust more resources, but by making them spend more than they were willing to afford.[182] This method of war is reminiscent of Mao Zedong's engagement policy for the Red Army, the skirmishes conducted by the Continental Army against British forces, and many other military forces in the history of armed conflict.

In recent decades, most opposition presented by terrorists involved bombings of empty chapels or other small-scale threats and attacks. These tactics reflect a carefully crafted strategy, retaining some legitimacy for citizens to tolerate or even support attacks in the name of defending their country from foreign imperialist influences without attracting too much attention or antagonism from law enforcement or intelligence agencies, which might challenge survival and momentum. These attacks and threats challenged Church leaders to evaluate risks, manage fears and concerns of local members and missionaries, and counter accusations presented in the media. This prolonged series of bombings and other attacks aimed to wear down the momentum of missionary work and Church growth, yet people continued to investigate and join the Church.

When terrorists assassinated a missionary companionship in Bolivia in May 1989, Church leaders implemented a series of security policies for missionaries which involved curfew hours, restricted geographical sectors, and assigning North American missionaries South American companions. Leaders reassigned several North American missionaries to other missions, extracting them from high-risk and unstable areas. In other words, Satan took a calculated risk, foregoing perpetrators' secrecy and limited attention from law enforcement in order to delay missionary work in areas theretofore experiencing rapid growth and conversion. One consequence of this was that law enforcement actions disbanded the Zarate Willka Armed Forces of Liberation, responsible for the missionary assassinations in Bolivia. This assassination and another within about 16 months in Peru, however, disrupted missionary work, influencing Church policies and temporarily impacting missionary assignments.

Opposition

Lucifer, or Satan, plays a central role in the basic principle of opposition, inherent in the nature of the world and earthly life. It was he who presented a counterargument to the Lord's Plan of Salvation, convincing one-third of the spirits present in the Council of Heaven to follow him. Again, in the Garden of Eden, he convinced Eve to eat of the fruit of the Tree of Knowledge of Good and Evil, explaining the importance of knowing opposition in principles such as pleasure and pain. Opposition is pivotal to spiritual development and man's existence. The prophet Lehi taught his son, Jacob, "For it must needs be, that there is an opposition in all things. If not so, [. . .] righteousness could not be brought to pass, neither wickedness, neither holiness nor misery, neither good nor bad. Wherefore, all things must needs be a compound in one."[183] Satan presents many forms of opposition as he contends with the Lord for influence over hearts and minds. The timing of his efforts also reflects a deliberate and refined art in attacking people when they are most vulnerable or susceptible, depending on the situation.

Scriptural accounts reveal aspects of Satan's strategies and tactics regarding the timing of his assaults on Saints. He is an adept strategist, presenting opposition at what he deems the most opportune times. The resistance and opposition he presents may occur before, during, or after times of uplifting spiritual experiences. Following Jesus's baptism, Satan tempted Christ as he lived in the wilderness for forty days. This time of intense Satanic focus on the Savior occurred in the wake of a spiritual experience and ordinance. Satan's resistance is often most evident as spiritual events unfold, such as the persecution faced by Christ's Apostles and the early Saints of the Church following Christ's earthly ministry. In the Book of Mormon, wickedness and moral decay shrouded the early inhabitants of the Americas in spiritual darkness in the days leading up to Christ's visit following His resurrection. Satan continues to carefully time his opposition, especially in the last days as he foments violence countering the Church.

Much evidence suggests Satan leverages terrorism to counter faith through fear and the joys of the gospel with sorrow. One example of opposition in the last days involves Satan's increase in power and influence. This has been a gradual increase throughout the world, but his power and effects of his opposition have been readily apparent in areas where the Church experienced rapid growth. Referring to Brigham Young's prophecy on Satan's power in the last days and Figure 1.1 (comparing key indicators of Church growth and missionary work to terrorism) there is a proportional correlation between these key indicators of good and evil. Generally, there is not a shift in time, along the x-axis, in these proportional changes; rather, as the number of full-time missionaries increased, the number of terrorism attacks and casualties increased at similar rates. The same is generally true for a decrease in these values. This reflects Satan's strategy to oppose missionary work and Church growth as both increase, rather than preceding growth or following the gospel flourishing in foreign lands.

One of the most illuminating pieces of evidence reflecting Satan's tactic of stirring up physical opposition in areas where the gospel flourishes involves the assassinations of missionaries in South America. In Bolivia, missionaries enjoyed great success in proselyting efforts toward the close of the 1980s. For instance, the Bolivia Cochabamba Mission experienced a 66% increase in baptisms between 1987 and 1988 and "the highest retention of members and priesthood leaders" in the area; success continued as the mission achieved 310 baptisms in March 1989.[184] Then, in May 1989, members of the Zarate Willka assassinated Elders Jeffrey Ball and Todd Wilson in Bolivia. Commenting on their deaths, President Harrell Fallis and his wife Beverly Fallis of the Bolivia Cochabamba Mission wrote,

> "We recognize [. . .] that many forces of evil will fight against the truth—we were just beginning our effort to build a temple here in this country and this is a great threat to the powers of darkness. We expect that the greatest progress in the missionary work lies ahead of us, unthwarted by the work of evil men."[185]

Satan sought to deter people from joining the Church by inciting terrorism to provoke fear and doubt.

The general public also opposed Americans for crop eradication efforts, protesting and demanding Americans leave Bolivia. Opposition from the Zarate Willka also persisted in the form of threats to chapels and members' homes, which influenced proselyting operations and even ward activities. In July 1989, for instance, a bomb emplaced at the Santa Cruz chapel led Church leaders to temporarily cease holding meetings or activities in evenings.[186] Despite this persecution, members continued to share the gospel and invite neighbors and acquaintances to the Church, experiencing great success throughout Bolivia. Commenting on a 700% increase in the number of missionaries in the Bolivia Cochabamba mission and an overwhelming number of referrals provided by members, mission president Harrell Fallis and his wife Beverly commented,

> "We hardly have enough missionaries in some areas to handle the people that want to hear the message. [. . .] We feel like it is the time to do miracles here. We want a temple for the people—we have to work harder than Satan is working for the bad—and he is really working HARD here. But we know that we can really make a difference in the future of Bolivia by filling it with priesthood leaders. That is our goal to get wonderful families into the Church that could carry on the work even if North Americans are sent home."[187]

When North American missionaries were, in some cases, removed from South American missions, the members did, indeed, continue proselyting efforts.

Political and economic conditions in neighboring countries also worsened over the following months. President Douglas Earl of the Peru Lima East Mission remarked, "There is no question that there is a lot of terroristic activity [. . .] you hear gunshots, quite a lot in a lot of areas. We feel that things (in Peru) are progressively becoming more chaotic [. . .] because of hyper-inflation, the really awful economy and criminals."[188] Then, in September 1990, Shining Path terrorists assassinated Elders Christian Ugarte and Manuel Hidalgo in Huancayo, Peru. Their deaths marked the second set of Latter-day Saint missionaries assassinated for political reasons, constituting an act of terrorism. At that time, "Huancayo was one of the most productive missionary areas in the Church."[189] Before and after the attack, the gospel flourished throughout the Peru Lima East Mission, which contained Huancayo. Around the time of these assassinations in Bolivia and Peru, most missions sent several North American missionaries home a few weeks early or to other areas for the remainder of their missions. Before being temporarily disbanded, the Peru Lima East Mission ranked fifth among all missions worldwide for number of convert baptisms, and then ranked first in 1989 and 1990.[190]

Hence, opposition severely influenced missionary force composition and disposition, hindering proselyting efforts. Member missionary work, however, drastically improved and bolstered missionary efforts to achieve some of the greatest conversion rates in mission histories and among missions worldwide.

In Chile, opposition came mostly in the form of bombings at empty meetinghouses. The Manuel Rodriguez Patriotic Front and Lautaro Youth Movement were notorious for targeting the Church, bombing sites and causing structural or aesthetic damage and leaving behind propaganda leaflets or spray-painted demands for the Church to leave the country. Opposition mounted into the 1990s with attack frequency increasing as conversion rates increased. Brother Manuel Moises Sanchez expressed remarks on this opposition, sharing the following words:

> "Just as the work of the Lord flourished, opposition also grew. This happened to the [Peruvian] missionaries mistaken as North American missionaries. In the back of the dead missionary was a letter that said, 'Fight the Yankee invasion, Yankees go home.' It was just the beginning in Peru, where the First Presidency opted to withdraw North American missionaries and later on the authorities that directed the Church. This situation started in August '90, in Huancayo where Peruvian missionaries feared leaving [the house] to preach. The stake had stake missionaries [and] I met with them to invigorate them with courage [. . .] to participate in missionary work. Shortly thereafter, I received an anonymous letter with a death threat. I had to leave Huancayo."[191]

While Satan's efforts affected Church risk mitigation policies and practices and prompted the departure of some missionaries and members from high-risk areas, many of his plans backfired. Members rallied in these times of harsh persecution, strengthening wards and stakes. Member missionary work increased and, after Church leaders relocated North American missionaries, the gospel continued to flourish as members invited their neighbors and others to investigate the Church. Publicity surrounding terrorism incidents helped to spread awareness of the Church, especially letters from Church leaders addressing misinformation and rumors about Church presence in foreign lands.

Misinformation

Evidence reveals Satan's reliance on misinformation to influence peoples' hearts and minds. Studying the reasons and justification terrorist groups provided to explain why they bombed meetinghouses or assassinated missionaries sheds light on how Satan leverages propaganda and misinformation to stir up men's hearts against the Lord's Church. Reflecting on Satan's use of words, Latter-day Saint Institute instructor Brother Kevin Bulloch wrote, "History seems to indicate that Satan has very few new strategies but successfully use the same old half-truths packaged a little differently for a particular time or setting."[192] The various claims promulgated by far-left groups in South America in the 1980s and 1990s demonstrate such variations in propaganda and justification for attacks, appealing to indigenous peoples, residents of poor communities, or other sectors of society.

In South America and elsewhere, Satan countered the spread of the gospel with rumors, suspicions, and other types of misinformation. He continues to do so as missionaries enter new lands and people investigate the Church. President George Q. Cannon once spoke on Satan's misinformation campaign to counter the spread of the restored gospel, commenting,

> "The knowledge of this work is being disseminated. With it, however, there goes forth a spirit of falsehood. It would seem as though, with the means of advertising we now have, and with the opportunities that are presented to men to visit us, a better understanding concerning us would be reached by thinking men. Undoubtedly this is the case to a certain extent. But my observation tells me that with the increase of information there is also a proportionate increase of misrepresentation and falsehood. The adversary is more industrious, if possible, in beclouding the minds of the children of men concerning us and concerning this work and the objects we have in view than he ever was. We become more advertised, it is true; but

while we are advertised it is not always in the direction of removing error and giving correct ideas concerning us."[193]

Deception and distortion of truth is a fundamental tactic of Satan. He employs this method to appeal to those who use logic and reason to assess the validity of information. In this way, Soviet news broadcasts and newspaper articles crafted misleading dialogues around the practice of Latter-day Saints conducting genealogy work, claiming they did so to gather intelligence for the US Government. Similarly, leftist groups criticized Latter-day Saint missionaries' proselyting efforts, asserting their objective in teaching locals involved spreading American cultural influence and inculcating people with values supporting government institutions. Misinformation played a key role in helping terrorist groups retain legitimacy in the eyes of locals while targeting the Church, as terrorists justified their actions in behalf of the welfare of their countrymen.

Dehumanization

Satan capitalized on the power of persuasion to desensitize people and lure them into a condition wherein their mental reservations from harming other human beings disappeared. President James E. Faust described Satan as "the world's master in the use of flattery, and he knows the great power of speech."[194] This is evident throughout the scriptures when he personally confronts individuals, such as when he attacks Moses by referring to him as "son of man," in stark contrast to the Lord's referring to Moses as "my son" moments before.[195] Satan's influence is evident in propaganda and the vilification of certain groups of people throughout the earth's history, such as Nazi posters calling or displaying Jews as pigs and other types of animals. He has employed similar tactics against members of the Latter-day Saint faith through libel, slander, propaganda, and other means. One of the themes in such media is the dehumanization of individuals.

Dehumanization is the process of stripping human qualities and characteristics from a group of people. Historically, media campaigns and other forms of persuasive communication led societies to view certain groups as less than human, subjecting members of those groups to prejudice and atrocities by societies at large. In this way, Satan successfully altered peoples' biases and perceptions and manipulated the spiritual condition of people to move "past feeling," similar to the Nephites in the times of Mormon, devoid of spiritual promptings and numb to the voices of the Spirit or reason.[196] Through media and rumors, the power of persuasion led people to develop judgments about missionaries and Saints without having any personal interactions with them.

In similar fashion, however, to other forms of opposition waged against the Church, harsh critics and those employing dehumanization as a means to counter Saints often failed to accomplish their objectives; in some cases, these critics even experienced a change of heart. Such radical repentance and conversion occurred in ancient times, as was the case with Zeezrom in the Book of Mormon, and this type of personal transformation continues in modern times. In the Church's 1885 (annual) General Conference held in the Tabernacle in Logan, Utah, Apostle F. D. Richards made the following statement in his discourse:

> "Inasmuch as the work of God spreads, and its influence and potency are felt among the nations of the earth, so long will this opposition and this antagonism exist, and we must expect it; it cannot be avoided. It is an eternal consequence of our faith. If we reckoned upon anything else, we reckoned wrongly. Every true Saint, when he embraced this Gospel, felt to lay down his good name, his earthly substance, and life itself—all was laid upon the altar. We need not think, however, that although the Lord permits certain things to come upon us, that He will not soften the hearts of the wicked and ungodly. He has told us with a firm decree, that from a time when the Saints commenced to be more faithful they should begin to prevail against their enemies, and they have proved this in the deliverances that have been wrought out in their behalf from time to time. Have we any reason to doubt or lack confidence in the promises of God for the future? Not a particle. Every step of the way affords a greater, a more powerful confirmation and assurance that He is true to His promises, and will carry them out in our behalf."[197]

There are countless examples of individuals who intended to target the Church later having a softening or change of heart, and in some cases, even joining the Church. This process occurred among some publishers and reporters in South America as opposition increased and the Church came under attack in the press. Dale Christensen, a Latter-day Saint mission president serving in Peru in the mid-1980s, described an article within a Chincha newspaper in 1985 wherein Church members were "accused of being *sons of the devil*, spies from the United States, racists, non-Christian, and of having money as [their] God."[198] Christensen explained this particular newspaper profited by publishing libelous articles and then collecting money from the defamed groups or individuals who attempted to counter accusations with retaliatory articles. As the local mission president, Christensen advised members not to contend with enemies and such slander, declaring in a zone conference in Tarma that, "Everyone can change and everyone needs the gospel," and that, "even those who write such things will someday be converted."[199] Christensen, speaking of a personal experience following his declaration, recorded the following:

> "Several months later, at our Monday night farewell dinner, Elder Jorge Olivera, from Cuzco, reminded [me] of the statement [I] had made in Tarma and then described how one of the authors of the article that had been written in Chincha had come to the Church to try to write more bad things and to try to get us to retaliate. Elder Olivera and his companion, Elder Velarde, talked to him and gave him a copy of the Book of Mormon. At first they were a little afraid of him, but later he looked for them and asked to be baptized.
>
> As a result of his conversion, Brother Severiano Francia Alvarez lost his job at the newspaper. This was not a small sacrifice due to the high rate of unemployment in Peru [, but] he couldn't convince his employers that they were doing something terribly wrong. His family and many friends had the discussions and may also have joined the Church."[200]

Even in an area saturated with stigmas regarding Latter-day Saints, a man who produced such messages finally listened to the missionaries and experimented with the Book of Mormon. Elders Jorge Olivera and Cesar Velande were both local native Peruvian missionaries who were transferred sometime later due to "the political unrest and terrorism" that threatened the area in successive months.[201] This man's conversion, however, demonstrates that even where Satan has strong influence, the gospel of Jesus Christ can still penetrate those seemingly most closed off to the truth.

Leveraging Apostates in Secret Combinations and Violent Acts

Across time and cultures, one of Satan's most effective tactics has been leveraging apostates to attack the Church and loyal disciples. The most striking and widely known examples of Satan's successful application of this tactic involve traitors in scriptural accounts and accounts from the early days of the restored Church. In more recent times, this Satanic tactic also manifests itself among those plotting terrorist attacks against the Church.

Personal accounts of members and analysts indicate some people in South America listened to missionary lessons or even joined the Church with ulterior motives, planning to gain insights about Church buildings, leaders, or practices before carrying out an attack. Some assert members who grew distant from the Church through inactivity eventually aligned themselves with revolutionary groups and even participated in attacks. While evidence is generally lacking behind these claims, the background behind one high-profile attack substantiates such accusations. Authorities charged two men and one woman in the 1989 assassinations of Elders Todd Ray Wilson and Jeffrey Ball in La Paz, Bolivia. The woman, Susana Zapana Hanover, was a former member of the Church, her family being one of the first to join what was then known as Branch VIII, near Sopocachi, La Paz.[202] Her family was well known in the area for their history and activity with the Church.

Over time and through increased exposure to revolutionary ideologies, Zapana's loyalties shifted. Johnny Justino Peralta, one of the men detained after the assassinations, testified that, "Susana Zapana [. . .] had participated in different operations" with the Zarata Willka group.[203] This state of spiritual decay likely contributed to her embracing revolutionary values and increasing involvement with the terrorist group. Rather than joining in the more common bombings of empty Church buildings, she participated in one of the few lethal terrorist attacks deliberately targeting Latter-day Saint missionaries.

Zapana's individual situation is reminiscent of that of the Amalekites in the Book of Mormon. This group of dissenters split away from the Nephites because of apostasy and wickedness. They were described as "more hardened than the Lamanites" and having a "more wicked and murderous disposition than the Lamanites."[204] In other words, the group of apostates became more wicked than nonmembers, which constituted the main and persistent opposition to the Nephites. Similarly, Zapana's affiliation to the Zarate Willka and dedication to resistance seemingly overpowered and supplanted the loyalty to family and traditional values she developed through Church attendance in her youth.

The Traditions of their Fathers

Satan adeptly perpetuates misconceptions, grievances, and other falsehoods through generations as parents pass on philosophies to their children. This is an oft-repeated pattern throughout the Book of Mormon and other scriptures, where generations of men wallowed in evil practices because of the traditions of their fathers, which they carried on and continued to practice and pass down.

Circumstantial evidence from David Rapoport's theories on modern terrorism also supports this notion that passing down traditions and philosophies plays a role in terrorism targeting the Church. Terrorism carried out by leftist factions dominated the globe during the period between 1960 and 1980, later replaced by a wave of religious terrorism. However, terrorism incidents targeting the Church do not follow this model; rather, there is a slight delay, as attacks by leftist extremists dominated the persecution faced by the Church in the 1980s and 1990s. While communist and far-left philosophies existed in South America in previous decades, terrorism plaguing the Church in the fourth wave of modern terrorism was actually conducted by groups following ideologies characteristic of the third wave, the prior generation.

A more specific example of evidence involves the alleged connection between the Manuel Rodriguez Patriotic Front and the Lautaro Youth Movement. Some believe the predominantly adolescent Lautaro Youth Movement's membership consisted of the children of members of the Manuel Rodriguez Patriotic Front, another far-left terrorist organization operating in generally the same areas.[205] These two groups conducted most of the recorded attacks targeting the Church in recent decades, accusing the Church of being an agent of American imperialism and committing various wrongs against their countrymen. These conditions echoed circumstances among the Lamanites, who were "a wild, and ferocious, and a blood-thirsty people, believing in the tradition of their fathers, [. . .] believing that they were [. . .] wronged [. . .] by their brethren."[206] These parallels reflect Satan's employment of a similar tactic in a different time under other pretenses.

Satan's *Schwerpunkt* Remains the Souls of Men

Satan continues to focus his efforts in spiritual combat, fighting for the souls of men rather than mortal combat and a rising body count. This concept can best be described in military terms as *schwerpunkt* in the German lexicon, meaning in a conflict the "weight (or focus) of effort," a principle that "deal[s] almost exclusively with the strategic level of war."[207] In other words, Satan leverages all available assets at his disposal to the end of claiming the souls of men and dragging them down to hell with him. In *The Screwtape Letters*, C. S. Lewis has Screwtape succinctly summarize this effort as follows in his explanation to Wormwood:

> "In the long run either Our Father or the Enemy will say 'Mine' of each thing that exists, and specially of each man.

> They will find out in the end, never fear, to whom their time, their souls, and their bodies really belong—certainly not to them, whatever happens."[208]

Incidents of terrorism and other tactics targeting the Church or affecting perceptions of Saints serve to resist the gospel of Jesus Christ and present opposition, but ultimately, Satan is after our souls.

While media outlets and household conversations focus on violence and threats associated with terrorism, those seeking to understand Satan's tactics should maintain perspective and view these events in the last days through a more eternal lens. Terrorism can certainly claim lives and inflict permanent physical wounds, but terrorism can also damage faith and hope. While terrorism is one mechanism by which Satan can achieve these objectives, he focuses on more subtle and crafty tactics targeting men's spiritual condition and souls. Concerning perspective, Dale Van Atta, a Latter-day Saint expert on terrorism, stated the following in an interview with *Meridian Magazine* one month after the 9/11 attacks:

> "While we are horrified at the events, as Latter-day Saints we know that terrorist attacks alone are not the issue. We have a different war to fight. It is a war against Satan, a war against sin. The people that we have lost and are losing in increasing numbers is more to a tide of evil and temptation than to terrorist attacks. Any good LDS parent who has lost a child to sin is as much the walking wounded as those who have lost loved ones in New York or Washington, because in our eternal perspective, the second death is the truly bad one. [. . .] This war of terrorism pales in comparison with the war we fought in heaven."[209]

Modern society is more apt to identify and condemn acts of terrorism than other evils, such as sins associated with immorality. The First Presidency once described Satan by stating that, "He is working under such perfect disguise that many do not recognize either him or his methods."[210] Such is the case with moral decay in a society, as standards worsen by almost imperceptible degrees over time. Terrorism, however, is generally recognized as evil; hence, Satan prefers more subtle tactics involving spiritual matters. This modus operandi explains such strong opposition against the Saints in early days of the Church's restoration, when spiritual buffetings in large part failed to slow down missionary work and the growth of the Church. In 1881, Elder John Morgan delivered a discourse in the Assembly Hall in Salt Lake City in which he said, "We find that the spirit of opposition that we have to meet, as a rule, culminates in violence; and that the more success we have in baptizing people, the more bitter the feeling manifested toward us by our opponents."[211] Again, this tendency to resort to violence and terrorism may not be an initial response prompted by Satan, but comes as a later resort behind spiritual attacks. This is most evident in the late 1980s and early 1990s as terrorism spiked in missions in Peru and Chile, which were among the most successful missions in the world.

CHAPTER 6

THE CHURCH

"It is the validity which draws the fire of the adversary. Combine validity and visibility, as in our time, and there is even more reaction. The adversary would scarcely pay any attention to a still numerically obscure Church unless he recognized what is underway for just what it is."

—Elder Neal A. Maxwell in a devotional at Brigham Young University, 1977

Introduction

Since Joseph Smith's First Vision in 1820, Satan has sought to interfere in the affairs of the Lord's restored church. In addition to the many spiritual wiles and darts of the adversary, Satan's arsenal includes weapons meant to inflict physical harm. While on Patmos, John recorded a vision wherein he saw a woman, symbolic of the Lord's church, give birth to a child, representing the "kingdom of our God and his Christ."[212] The prophecy describes Satan's opposition to the Church throughout time, beginning in the premortal existence. This persecution drove the woman into the wilderness, "symbolic of Satan driving the ancient church into the period of the Great Apostasy, when the authority of the priesthood was taken from the earth."[213]

After the Church was restored in the latter days through the prophet Joseph Smith, Satan continued to oppose the Saints. The final verse in Revelation chapter 12 describes this resistance, stating, "The dragon was wroth with the woman, and went to make war with the remnant of her seed, which keep the commandments of God, and have the testimony of Jesus Christ."[214] Various acts of terrorism targeting the Church and faithful members are one form of fulfillment of this prophecy. The New Testament Institute Student Manual states, "the remnant of the woman's seed that Satan and his followers war against includes the latter-day Church restored through the Prophet Joseph Smith," and that, "Satan wages his fiercest battles against the Saints of the true and living Church."[215] While this often involves spiritual warfare of sorts, terrorism is an extremely tangible and perceptible form of this fierce opposition.

The forms of persecution faced by the Church vary throughout history, but terrorism is one form with heightened activity in recent decades. Since 1979, there have been over 300 incidents of terrorism directly targeting The Church of Jesus Christ of Latter-day Saints. This does not include incidents not reported to law enforcement, media outlets, or otherwise annotated in private or restricted Church records, nor does this include planned attacks foiled or interdicted by law enforcement. Figure 6.1 displays the number of attacks targeting the Church by year in recent decades.

The Spirit has guided Church leaders and members in how to appropriately respond. At various times, Church leaders issued statements concerning terrorism. They have also invoked blessings of protection for structures and people. They have followed the Spirit in determining appropriate responses to threats and violence associated with civil strife.

Persecution in Ayacucho, Peru

The Shining Path, which began in Ayacucho, maintained a stronghold there. Latter-day Saints residing in "the city of churches" faced intimidation that led them to conduct baptisms away from the chapel for fear of observation by terrorist groups.[216] José Maria Gonzalez, an early convert and pioneer of the Church in Ayacucho, stated that while he served as district president in the 1980s, "the revolutionaries had their spies watching members at the church [meetinghouses]. Rather than being baptized in the chapel, people were baptized [in other places] outside the chapel, near Ayacucho, like the Río Muyurín [river passing through Muyurina, a small town to the northeast of Ayacucho] and Río Huatatas."[217] People wanted to avoid detection, preventing Shining Path spies from identifying them as Latter-day Saint converts. Gonzalez stated the depth of the Huatatas was only 60 centimeters, just high enough for members to be fully submerged if they laid on their backs in the water.[218] These baptisms represented the shift among some of the populace in Ayacucho toward what was perceived as a right-wing philosophy counter to the principles advocated by the Shining Path; a group of citizens compliant with the rule of law and opposed to the group's revolutionary beliefs. Violence and persecution increased to the point where three or four Latter-day Saint families left Ayacucho. Gonzalez explained that missionaries also suffered persecution, such as one incident in which "two revolutionaries took away missionaries' church items and gave them pamphlets with the hammer and sickle to distribute."[219] Despite these trials, the faith of the members remained strong and the branch grew to become a stake shortly thereafter.

Figure 6.1: Chronological Distribution of Terrorism Incidents Targeting the Church

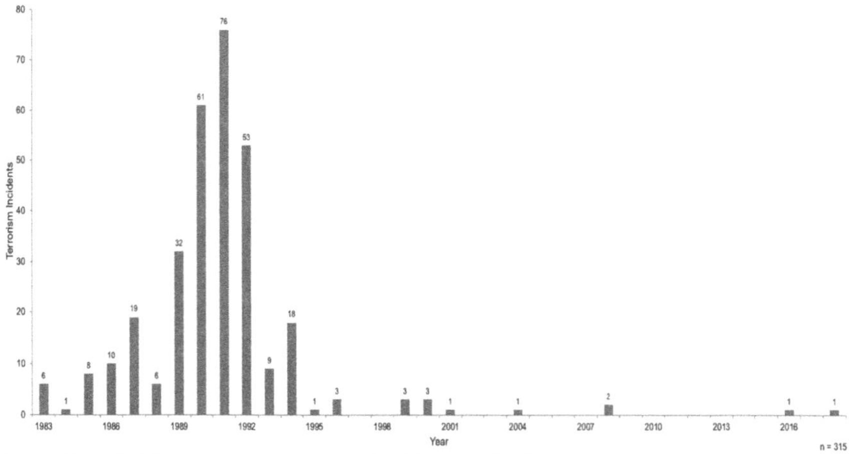

Source: Compiled from various sources, as outlined in Appendix A.

Church Statement on Terrorism

Several months before the onset of a series of terrorist attacks targeting the Church in Latin America, Church leaders addressed terrorism and crime. At the end of 1981, the First Presidency released a statement wherein leaders stated, "Peace, order, and dignity cannot long survive in society when hatred, intolerance, and suspicion motivate human behavior."[220] This statement, addressing leftist terrorism throughout South America and other forms of violence throughout the world, preceded a slew of attacks directly targeting the Church in 1983. Opposition, mainly in the form of bombings, steadily increased over the following years. The Church received support from local governments and law enforcement. On August 14, 1985, Humberto Barrientos, official Church spokesman in Chile, reported the military government of Augusto Pinochet "ordered special vigilance for the property of the Church of Jesus Christ of Latter-day Saints in Chile," due to the high frequency of terrorism targeting chapels.[221] While the Church suffered from the greatest number of attacks in Chile, Latter-day Saints also received government and law enforcement support when assassinations of missionary companionships occurred in other countries in the late 1980s.

Fierce opposition in South America persisted into the early 1990s. In March 1994, the *Ensign* interviewed the South America North Area Presidency about Church growth and challenges. When asked about some of the challenges the Church faced in South America, these leaders provided the following response:

> "Even though our greatest challenge is violence and terrorism, with some attacks on buildings in Peru, and similar problems in Bolivia, the Church has not suffered too much. And Church members are helping the people in these nations to change. The principles of prayer and scripture study have helped change the countenance of our people in these countries. For example, we have fifty-two stakes in Peru now, and the change in Colombia has been marvelous. People are anticipating construction of the temples there and in Ecuador, and their feelings about their situation have improved. The local Saints

> are assuming responsibilities. They are a leavening influence in these nations. There is a new spirit of optimism and a spirit of hope. We're excited with what we're seeing. We attribute it to the impact of the gospel and the Church."[222]

Despite persecution, the Church flourished in these countries. Missionary work and Church growth gained momentum and temples eventually appeared in the land.

Dedicatory Prayers for Church Buildings

Leaders of the Church invoke a blessing upon many buildings belonging to the Church through a dedicatory prayer. The speech and themes within dedicatory prayers often echo themes of General Conferences of the same period and include blessings tailored to the needs of local people and situations. Temple dedicatory prayers generally include some phrase referencing protection for the edifice and temple grounds, but oftentimes, these references directly or indirectly refer to prominent threats during that period. In the early and mid-1980s, for instance, many temple dedicatory prayers referenced war, contention, and annihilation, as the Cold War occupied the worried minds of many Americans. One common theme in recent decades is protection from the elements, such as natural disasters.

Another theme among dedicatory prayers is a reference to and invoked protection from the evil designs of men, which includes terrorism. General Authorities list components of the temple and temple grounds, which sometimes include adjacent buildings. One slight variance among prayers is the extent to which Church leaders invoke physical protection of the temple from various threats. There are no significant trends or correlations in the degree of physical protections invoked and region, time, or current events. None of the analyzed 141 temple dedication and rededication prayers mention *terror* or *terrorism* verbatim; rather, prayers include phrases encompassing such threats to varying degrees. The most apparent trend is the prevalence of at least mentioning protection from harm caused by men and their misuse of agency, most evident in similar wording and degrees of invoked protections in dedicatory prayers between 1996 and 2018. A few clusters of prayers with similar degrees of invoked protections may be associated with high-visibility terrorist attacks occurring around the same time. After multiple bombings of chapels in Colombia in late 1983, the series of temples dedicated over the following 24 months generally included stronger invoked blessings regarding physical threats. Similarly, shortly after the attacks of September 11, 2001, President Hinckley's dedicatory prayers for two North American temples included multiple invoked blessings of protection concerning evil plots. Few publicly-known threats, plots, or attacks in recent history targeted Latter-day Saint temples, but some notable instances in public records include anthrax hoaxes targeting the Salt Lake City Temple in 1999, another anthrax hoax targeting the Salt Lake City and Los Angeles Temples in 2008, and the Islamic State propaganda threatening an attack against the San Diego Temple in 2017.

Despite the fact that most contemporary terrorism targeting The Church of Jesus Christ of Latter-day Saints occurred in Latin America, dedicatory prayers for temples on that continent do not trend toward using vocabulary reflecting greater threats. Likewise, a rise in frequency of terrorism incidents across the globe throughout recent decades did not lead to an upward trend line for threat values reflected in dedicatory prayer vocabulary. Likewise, other notable terrorist attacks did not cause general shifts or clusters of references to physical harm in dedicatory prayers offered shortly after those attacks. Overall, temple dedicatory prayers do not reflect dramatic correlations or readily discernible connections to contemporary terrorism.

General Authorities Receive Bomb Threat during Dedication of BYU Jerusalem Center

The Brigham Young University extension center in Jerusalem roused suspicions and contention among residents of Jerusalem and Jews in other parts of the world, especially during construction and around the time of the dedication. The mayor of Jerusalem, Teddy Kollek, contended, "the fight [was] not over the Mormon Center but over the character of Israel," yet Orthodox rallies took place in the United States and Latter-day Saint meetinghouses in Washington, DC and New York received bomb threats.[223] Opposition subsided as Church leaders asserted the Church would not use the BYU Jerusalem Center for proselyting purposes, but opposition again arose in 1989, when President Howard W. Hunter traveled to Jerusalem with other Church leaders to dedicate the center. Elder Boyd K. Packer of the Quorum of the Twelve Apostles spoke at the dedication and later described the following incident:

> "As I was speaking, there was some excitement in the back of the hall. Men in military uniforms had entered the room. They sent a note to President Hunter. I turned and asked for instructions. He said, 'There's been a bomb threat. Are you afraid?' I said, 'No.' He said, 'Neither am I; finish your talk.' The dedication services proceeded without incident; there was no bomb."[224]

Intimidation and terrorism threatened leaders as they carried out the Lord's work, but the Lord protected His servants. Such divine protection is partial fulfillment of the two most recent dedications of the Holy Land, one in Haifa and one in Jerusalem in May 1933, wherein John A. Widtsoe of the Quorum of the Twelve Apostles "prayed that the enemies of the Church would be confounded."[225] The Lord has continued to watch over the Saints assembled in Jerusalem.

Conference Center Dedicatory Prayer

On October 8, 2000, President Gordon B. Hinckley performed the dedication of the Conference Center in Salt Lake City, Utah. This was to be the new location for all General Conferences conducted semi-annually by the Church, seating 21,000 to see and hear General Authorities. Within the dedicatory prayer, President Hinckley implored, "Protect it [the Conference Center] from the storms of nature and the desecrating hand of the vandal and destroyer. Preserve it from conflict and acts of terrorism."[226] While the prayer included allusions to harm caused by men or inspired by Satan, President Hinckley specifically mentioned *terrorism*, distinguishing this prayer from those offered for temples. Indeed, the setting seems suitable as a very likely target among those seeking to inflict harm against the

Church—the site hosts a dense concentration of members and high-level Church leaders at predictable times each year. Since President Hinckley dedicated the Conference Center, the site has hosted hundreds of thousands of visitors. Even so, visitors, members, and General Authorities alike have remained under the Lord's protection while at the site.

Removing Missionaries from Areas of Conflict

On occasion, dangers stemming from terrorism, most often associated with coups and armed conflict, spurred the evacuation of missionaries. In recent decades, this occurred in Iran, Ukraine, and Venezuela, among other countries. Such instances do not necessary reflect divine inspiration to remove missionaries from an area immediately before some civil uprising or large-scale act of violence, taking action before the issuance of US Department of State advisories or other warning signs of pending danger. Instead, Church leaders, including area authorities and mission presidents, act under the divine guidance of the Holy Ghost and follow security protocol to assess risk and make decisions. This is not to say that missionary evacuations are completely reactionary; rather, evacuation timing varies from instance to instance based on many circumstances and promptings.

Missionaries Evacuated from Haiti, 1991

The Church evacuated missionaries assigned to Haiti after the September 28–30, 1991 coup ousting President Jean-Bertrand Aristide. Aristide, elected just eight months earlier, was regarded as Haiti's first democratically elected leader. His platform, focused largely on improving conditions for the poverty-stricken people of Haiti, threatened Haitian elites. Under the direction of Army General Raoul Cédras and with the support of several military officers and police officials, the Haitian Army seized control of the government.

Instances of terrorism increased over the following months, combating the harsh rule of the military. Human rights activists and others accused the ruling regime of atrocities and murders, all of which fomented civil strife and conflict. Much of the terrorism following the coup targeted the police, government, and military.

The circumstances surrounding the 1991 missionary evacuation from Haiti reflect an aspect of Church leaders assessing a situation and taking appropriate steps to mitigate risk. As conditions worsened immediately following the coup, Church leaders followed the guidance of the US Department of State advisory to evacuate the country. Fifty-six missionaries and Port-au-Prince Mission President Robert O. Hickman were reassigned or granted early releases.[227] The frequency of terrorist attacks increased following the missionary evacuation.

Missionaries Protected during Civil Unrest in Haiti, 1991

At the end of September 1991, tensions rose and threatened Saints in Haiti. Four elders had been serving in Jeremie, the site of one of nine Church units in Haiti. Attempts to evacuate these elders failed, as the airport shut down, they lacked assistance from the embassy, and even phone service was unreliable. The elders contacted the mission home to report that "their apartment was surrounded by about twenty to thirty in a mob shouting about getting the Mormons and the Blanc[o]s," and that this mob returned later that day "with about fifty people." The modus operandi of mobs involved burning buildings and people. Mission president Robert O. Hickman stated that the elders moved to the apartment's second story to "form a circle, and pray." Unbeknownst to them, an inactive member of the Church was among the mob assembled outside, and he decided to climb the outside of the building to a balcony. The elders saw the man reach the balcony, so they backed into a bedroom and continued praying. When they finished their prayer, "they could not hear anymore shouting," and after returning downstairs, "they saw that the iron bars protecting the entrance to their apartment had been torn off, but the mob had not entered the apartment." President Hickman learned that the inactive member was so impressed by the divine protections he witnessed there that day that he became an active member of his branch again, and he shared his account with the members of the Jeremie Branch.[228]

Missionaries Evacuated from Turkey, 2016

More recently, a group of Latter-day Saint missionaries operated in Turkey in 2016, when an unexpected coup attempt took place. Elements of the Turkish military attempted to take control of the Turkish government on July 15, 2016. Several deaths and injuries were associated with skirmishes, but ultimately, the Turkish government quelled the rebellion and defeated those involved in the uprising. Latter-day Saint missionaries left the country within the following two weeks. The frequency of terrorism activities in Turkey increased after the missionaries departed.

This sequence of events reflects missionaries did not flee the country prior to the coup or during the events that ensued surrounding the coup attempt. Missionaries departed, however, before casualties spiked weeks later. The Holy Ghost likely played a significant role in directing Church leaders when to evacuate them and how to best manage risk and keep them safe.

As political turmoil erupts in various parts of the world in the coming decades, missionaries will likely need to evacuate from areas to avoid danger. The Church Security Department will continue to assess threats and help Church leaders manage risk and make decisions. Church leaders will continue to heed advisories of the US Department of State. While missionaries cannot reasonably avoid all dangers associated with terrorism, the Spirit will guide them and their leaders to properly navigate the turbulent political environments of the world.

Response to Terrorism

Ancient and modern scriptures contain teachings on preserving personal righteousness, maintaining perspective, and dispelling myths and lies by sharing truth. Personal revelation plays a pivotal role in navigating among persecutions of the last days. On multiple occasions, Church members, acting on spiritual promptings, benefitted from physical protection in the midst of harm. The Lord and His servants instruct members to keep covenants. Still, however, righteous people suffer due to others' misuse of agency. A strong testimony of the Plan of Salvation helps in coping with suffering associated with terrorism. Elder Bradford of the First Quorum of the Seventy elaborated on the importance of personal righteousness, saying,

> "In a world where transgression, corruption, and terrorism strike fear into men and women, where can we turn for safety and security? There is no safety and security except in righteousness. There is no place to hide. There are no walls to keep out the adversary and his campaign of opposition. There is no defense against the uncertain and unknown except righteousness. Fear in the hearts and minds of men and women can be turned to peace only by replacing that fear with an understanding of God's plan of happiness and the knowledge that they are doing all they can do to become righteous and worthy to qualify for eternal salvation."[229]

There are many external influences at play, beyond the power or control of those opposed to terrorism. In these circumstances, leaders highlight the role of personal accountability. Elder Hales of the Quorum of the Twelve Apostles affirmed, "We boldly declare that the answer to the terror, destruction, and even genocide of these last days is found in the scriptures. [. . .] We must remember that we have control over who we are no matter how difficult the world becomes."[230] Scripture study, prayer, and following spiritual promptings are critical individual responsibilities in this time of persecution and opposition.

As terrorists spread rumors and lies as they justify attacks and seek to embolden like-minded extremists to wage violence, Church members must counter such falsehoods by sharing truth. Similar to the War in Heaven, countering evil influences includes the testimony of the gospel, a key instrument of spiritual warfare. Appropriate responses also include media statements from Church leaders, refuting false claims of terrorists and explaining the role of The Church of Jesus Christ of Latter-day Saints and proselyting efforts of members and missionaries.

CHAPTER 7

PROTECTION AND MIRACLES

"For I am God, and mine arm is not shortened; and I will show miracles, signs, and wonders, unto all those who believe on my name."

—Doctrine and Covenants 35:8

Introduction

God's works are manifest in all varieties of circumstances, including experiences involving terrorism. Such violence is an outward expression and fulfillment of some of the most heinous and evil intentions of man, yet some of God's greatest mercies are often revealed as these events unfold. Divine protections afforded to Saints surviving acts of terrorism are a modern fulfillment of many ancient promises. While Appendix A lists attacks specifically targeting The Church of Jesus Christ of Latter-day Saints (i.e., members, buildings, or missionaries), this chapter also contains accounts of Saints affected by terrorism not necessarily targeting the Church. Some accounts describe experiences of Latter-day Saints affected by attacks indiscriminately targeting people or attacking groups or organizations other than the Church. For instance, some testimonies recount Islamist attacks in Europe against airports.

Although such attacks do not factor into analysis regarding terrorism attacks targeting the Church, which is the focus of this work, investigating these accounts reveals God's awareness of His Saints and how terrorism, on a broader scale, may affect Church members. This is obviously not a complete list of miracles associated with terrorism incidents. Open sources and interviews include additional accounts, but they are not included in this recounting and analysis due to permissions or other factors. The accounts which are discussed herein, however, reveal terrorism as an occurrence of increasing frequency pervading even the most secure countries and cities. Such instances reflect that Saints may be subject to dangers associated with terrorism even though they are adhering to gospel principles and afforded certain divine protections by covenant, similar to vulnerabilities and possibilities associated with natural disasters.

Protection from Car Bomb in Miraflores, Peru

Idon Openshaw explained that while her family lived in Peru, they once had a visitor, a young woman, who was very independent and wanted to go out in the evenings during her stay. Idon and her husband, Martin, warned this young woman about the dangers associated with visiting sites where tourists would commonly gather, as terrorists targeted these large groups with car bombs and other types of explosives. Despite their warnings, she was persistent and wanted to visit the town square in Miraflores, where groups often gathered on the weekends. The Openshaws eventually relented, sending one of their daughters with the visitor so she would not be alone. Idon explained, "While they [her daughter and their visitor] were at a little creperia there, there was a car bomb just a block away while they were there."[231] The family recognized the Lord preserved both young women, keeping them out of harm's way.

Protection in the Altiplano of Peru

Elders Jorge Olivera and Cesar Velande, Peruvian missionaries serving in the Cuzco area, were transferred away from their assigned area due to "the political unrest and terrorism" threatening their safety.[232] The Elders opened up a new area in the altiplano. Despite violence and ill perceptions of Latter-day Saints in the area, the Elders preached fearlessly under the protecting hand of the Lord. One wrote the following describing an experience of divine protection and their success in preaching the restored gospel:

> "It was a great opportunity and challenge to be able to open the marvelous program at Huancavelica. We spent Christmas getting the necessary luggage ready for a few days to see the program, because missionaries had never gone there to open it. We got to Huancavelica at 5:30 p.m. We retrieved our luggage, and we went to look for a place to spend the night. We walked down the street and we entered a hotel. There weren't any vacancies. And likewise in the second and third hotels. Finally we found a hotel. We paid and entered, but as soon as we walked in the door of the room I said to my companion, "Let's get out of here!" My companion agreed with me, and we made the excuse that there wasn't any showers or hot water, and they gave us back our money and we left. We arrived at another hotel and we stayed there. It was a lot better and we felt tranquil. We were there for a week looking for a room, but there wasn't one.
>
> There were a lot of policemen that were protecting the city from the 'Sendero Luminoso,' more commonly known as terrorists. Three days after we left from the hotel where we paid and left it was blown up by dynamite. We went to look at it. The room where we would have stayed was totally destroyed. Then we understood that the feeling that we had was not our imagination, but that it was the spirit of the Lord that was protecting us and watching over us. At first, it didn't seem like anything serious to us, but when we thought about it again, we understood better. The protection that we all have is like a glove. When the hand goes into the glove, the glove can do what it needs to do, but without the hand, it lays there motionless. The Spirit is the same. When we have the Spirit we do what is right, but when it goes away from us, it is better to try to obtain it.
>
> There were a lot of explosions and one was only a block away from where we were staying. The days went by in that

manner. I had never used a package tricycle instead of a taxi to move the things. We traveled to Huancayo many times, and we spent many nights traveling in the bus. Because when the sun came up, we had to cross a hanging bridge to the other side to the bus that was waiting for us on the other side of the river to take us to Huancavelica. We had to do that because the terrorists blew up the bridge that the buses went across on. Those nights were really cold, and me and my companion felt happy to experience all of this being in the service of the Lord.

One day there was a curfew, but we didn't know anything about it. My companion had a change and didn't know anything about the curfew, because one morning we walked to our room and nothing happened to us. Another time we were coming from the fallen bridge to the city. It was a half an hour walk. Maybe there were terrorists or policemen in the mountains, but nevertheless, we came laughing and joking, happy to be alive. My companion's brother, who is a policeman, said that the motto of the policemen there is 'We prefer suspicious people dead before alive.' And that is the way that the policemen were there. We were happy to find a member of the Church who was there because of work reasons. Through him we found the room where we lived and at the same time was our chapel for our sacrament meetings of three people.

When we finally started to work, after all of this, we had a family of 12 people. Father, mother, and the children. They wanted to get baptized, and the words they said were of great satisfaction to us because another family of 8 were progressing also. These two families were a total of 20 people. They told us that since we had come into their lives they had more work, and that they weren't lacking anything. Another family of 6 was almost impossible helping them to understand the true gospel. We gave a Book of Mormon to them, which bore testimony of itself, until they asked for their baptisms. The week that I left we were going to have 17 baptisms. My testimony has grown a lot."[233]

This account reflects the sheer amount of opposition in areas of abundant spiritual conversion. Satan is aware of the diligent work of missionaries and members faithfully sharing the gospel. He is a master at leveraging fear associated with violence to deter people from conversion. He has also sought to impede the work from going forward by targeting those spreading the restored gospel through spiritual and physical attacks. As the account reflects, terrorists indirectly interfered with missionary work by bombing infrastructure, impeding travel. Even so, these missionaries found joy in these trials as they continued to labor diligently in the work of the Lord. Despite violence and opposition, people joined the Church in vast quantities.

This Elder noted an important principle of divine communication by acknowledging that the prompting received to leave the hotel was not simply a personal thought or feeling, but a warning from the Holy Ghost. This concern about distinguishing personal thoughts from promptings of the Holy Ghost is a common topic in General Conference talks, as well as sacrament and testimony meetings. This account reflects the importance of quickly heeding such promptings, believing they are divine communications. Countless instances of missionaries heeding such warnings demonstrate protection provided through the Holy Ghost by acting in faith.

Early Morning Seminary Student Discovers Bomb

On July 8, 1988, an early morning seminary student discovered a package at a Latter-day Saint chapel in the Alto San Pedro section of La Paz, Bolivia. He took the package home and showed the package to his father, who immediately called the police. The bomb, contained within the package, miraculously did not explode and the father and son turned the bomb over to the police when they arrived.[234] No group claimed responsibility for emplacing the bomb. Among other scriptures, this account is a manifestation of the Lord's promise, "there is no weapon that is formed against you shall prosper."[235] He protected this young man from physical danger, despite all likelihood that the bomb should have exploded when handled.

An Instrument in God's Hands: Prepared by Experience

On the evening of Tuesday, July 4, 1989, armed assailants entered the Javiera Carrera Branch's meetinghouse, abruptly interrupting a seminary class in the Latter-day Saint chapel at 9531 Santa Raquel Street in the La Florida district of Santiago, Chile. The group of seven masked individuals, armed with revolvers, held the 19 seminary students and two North American missionaries hostage. This tactic was in line with the modus operandi of the Lautaro Youth Movement, the terrorist group tallying the most incidents of contemporary terrorism against the Church. Lautaro members physically harmed and threatened members of the Church in nearby districts of Santiago within months of this incident; the potential for violence was high.

One of the missionaries present had previously served as a Green Beret, or member of the Special Forces, in the US Army. Hence, this elder embarked on missionary service at an age beyond that of a typical 19-year-old young man entering the missionary field. This military background contributed to his advanced maturity and his ability to maintain composure as the incident unfolded. Additionally, this missionary had received training in hostage negotiation as a member of the Special Forces, which played a pivotal role in how the event played out.[236] The elder leveraged this training to successfully convince the terrorists to release all hostages.

The assailants then forced the missionaries to strip, and then used their clothes to set the building ablaze. As the perpetrators fled, they left propaganda and literature similar to that left at other attack sites. The fire caused approximately $2.5 million (modern value) in damages, destroying the entire building and prompting a complete rebuild. However, due to the intervention of this trained and inspired missionary, there were zero casualties.

This incident attests to the Lord's intimate knowledge of each of His children and the revelation associated with missionary assignments. The Lord directed the elder's assignment to a mission in Chile rife with violence and terrorism threatening the Church. A mission president, following guidance from the Holy Ghost, assigned the elder to an area where the Lord would leverage his unique skill set from military service in a critical moment when young Church members encountered an incident with high probability for violence and physical harm. This elder's background armed him with the proper and rare skill set to negotiate with the terrorists, but there is no doubt the Holy Ghost guided him in what to say, fulfilling in an interesting way the promise, "For it shall be given you in the very hour, yea, in the very moment, what ye shall say."[237] The Lord used this young man as an instrument in His hands and enabled him to successfully convince the terrorists to release their hostages unharmed.

Elder W. Craig Zwick, emeritus member of the First Quorum of the Seventy, shared some reflections on the incident and the ward's reaction in *More to Your Story*, a book he coauthored with his wife, Jan. The incident occurred on his first day serving as mission president of the Chile Santiago South Mission, where the incident occurred. He and his two sons visited the site less than twenty-four hours following the attack, finding that of the chapel and contents, only three charred paintings, some chairs from the cultural hall, and the piano remained, having been transported by members at great personal risk.[238] There, they met with the branch president Patricio G. Latorre Orellana and his Branch Council in what remained of a mechanical equipment room, which meant partially destroyed walls with some steel material showing where a roof used to be. That Sunday, Elder Zwick, his wife, and one of their sons attended the ward's sacrament meeting, which they held outside with the chairs that remained from the destroyed meetinghouse. He stated that "more than two hundred people were there for the fast and testimony meeting," and that as members administered the sacrament, he and those present "felt a sublime reverence that [they] will never forget."[239] Love and faith emanated from the members and those who attended the meeting to support and comfort them.

Elder Zwick also described Elder Richard G. Scott's visit to the ward weeks later. During his visit, he gave this branch, which generally consisted of fewer than thirty-five members consistently attending services each Sabbath, an apostolic blessing, wherein he, "promised them in the name of Jesus Christ that they would grow to be multiple strong units in the Church and would become an 'ensign to [their] nation."[240] Actions quickly played out, fulfilling this promise in the following months. Elder Zwick wrote:

> "The ensuing weeks and months did bring growth to the Javiera Carrera Branch. By the first month of 1990, only six months after the fire, the branch had grown by convert baptisms and member reactivations into a solid ward. In fulfillment of Elder Scott's blessing, the ward grew from one to two. Eventually, the two wards expanded to three wards and a branch. By May 1992, less than three years after that memorable night in July 1989, papers were submitted for the creation of the Javiera Carrera Chile Stake. Miraculously, an entire stake was created from approximately the same geographic area of the original Javiera Carrera Branch."[241]

Similar to other wards and areas targeted by terrorists, the Javiera Carrera Branch prospered spiritually to a great degree in the months that followed. This pattern of blessings following trials and persecution is reminiscent of trials faced by pioneers and early Saints elsewhere and at other times in history, "For after much tribulation, [. . .] cometh the blessing."[242] This scriptural truth is manifest in the repeated occurrence of missionary work and conversion growing fastest in areas of South America plagued by terrorism in the 1980s and 1990s.

Protection and Resiliency in the Face of Threats

In the evening of August 26, 1990, two missionaries met with their mission leader at their chapel in western Santiago, Chile. In addition to holding a meeting to discuss missionary work in the ward, the elders had coordinated to meet with the mission leader there so afterwards they could all remain at the chapel to teach a young woman who expressed interest in the Church, since male missionary companionships could not teach young women without someone else present. Describing what happened next, Elder Scott Earl wrote the following account in his journal:

> "At 7:15 pm, we [he and his companion] were in the chapel with Omar Zañatu having Correlation Meeting when the doorbell rang. Before that, we had been talking [...] about the killings of two missionaries in Peru. [...] Omar left to open the gate to the church.
>
> And then all of a sudden, two [masked] guys entered with guns [a pistol and a rifle]. As one entered, he pointed a gun at my face. The barrel was about a foot from my face, and he said, 'Stay where you are and nothing will happen to you.' The other guy entered and walked behind me, and as he did so, he hit me in the head with the butt of his pistol, saying, 'Shut up, Yankee.' So now I have a lump on my head. Then, the first guy said, 'Now, we don't have anything against the Mormons. It's the blankety-blank [signifying expletive] Yankees.' And at this time, I knew I was dead, and I could practically feel the bullet enter my head. I was so nervous that the only thing I thought about was what I was going to do once I was dead."

One man walked around Elder Earl and pointed a gun at his companion. Elder Earl explained how the event unfolded as follows:

> "As [one] was looking me in the eyes with the pistol pointed at my head, I said 'Please, don't shoot, don't shoot.' Then my companion asked, 'I have a question. What are you going to do with us?' And I wanted to kill him for saying that. Then, another guy entered the room with a camera and started taking pictures of us in the chapel while they were throwing gasoline around getting ready to burn the chapel."

The assailants took the missionaries' backpacks and added them to a pile of items they had made and doused with gasoline. There was gasoline spread all across the tile floor. Elder Earl stated that one of the men lit a match and, "turning to the elders, said as he threw the match, 'If I ever see you here again, I'll kill you.' [...] They took off running, and we sat there watching the chapel burn until it was safe enough to go look for a phone to call a fireman."

Reflecting on the experience hours later in the safety of the mission home, Elder Earl wrote the following in his journal at 2:40 am:

> "The terrorists said if they saw us walking those parts again, they would kill us. [...] I can't go to sleep, I'm so nervous. I know the Lord protected us and my testimony has really grown tonight through this experience. [...] And I know the Lord's watching over his servants, the missionaries."

Elder Earl suspected the young woman was involved in the terrorist group that attacked him that night. When later granted the option to return home, transfer to another mission, or remain in his mission, Elder Earl prayerfully decided to remain in his mission.[243]

Missionaries and Family Absent during Small Arms Attack

During the evening hours of December 1, 1990, a small group of Lautaro Youth Movement members in a Chevrolet LUV truck pulled up to the private residence of Luis Enrique Sandoval. His family and two North American missionaries resided in the home. The terrorists called for the "gringos" to come outside, and then they fired several shots at the home and one of the youth spray-painted "Fuera Yankees de Chile M.J.L." on the front wall of the residence before they all sped off in the truck.[244] Witnesses stated the individuals were no more than 25 years old, dressed in regular clothes and unmasked. Neighbors explained a woman carrying a larger firearm than the other group members directed their actions on site. The attack preceded a visit to Chile by US President George H. W. Bush.

The Lord protected the family and missionaries from harm. Luis Sandoval said, "It had been a miracle that there were no wounded and that coincidentally, the house was empty at the moment the unknown [perpetrators] fired."[245] He and his wife and child had left for the supermarket, and Elders Charles Gaber (19) and Brandon Page (20) had also left the home moments before the attack. Bullets damaged the large front windows and main entrance door, as well as interior walls and furniture within the residence. Luis Sandoval explained,

> "This is not an isolated event, as there had been various days in which it seemed that there was something in the works against them [the missionaries]. [. . .] Through phone calls, they were summoned to two orientation meetings [initial discussions with investigators], but at the arranged locations, the missionaries did not encounter those who supposedly requested to meet with them. Now we understand these were ambushes that for some reason failed."[246]

He closed the interview explaining he was not intimidated and that he and his wife would continue hosting the North American missionaries.

A Quick Resolution

During the evening of Wednesday, December 5, 1990, Brother Roberto Alejandro del Rio Troncoso attended a bishopric meeting for his ward. He served as the First Counselor in the ward bishopric and met with five other brethren to discuss the needs of members and upcoming events. A group of youths, some men and women leaders, and two North American missionaries were also present for meetings at the chapel, located at 714 Los Lirios in the Puente Alto sector of Santiago, Chile. Abruptly, an unexpected visitor interrupted the Bishopric Meeting. As Roberto recounted:

> "A man—a young man—entered the room, his face covered by a black mask. He carried a revolver in his hand. He instructed us to stay put while his companions proceeded throughout the chapel. We then heard people in the hallways pouring gasoline and lighting it on fire—about four other young men. There was a group of youth gathered at the entrance of the chapel. The assailants held them there, threatening them, together with two missionaries from North America that were assigned to the ward at the time."[247]

As the attack unfolded, Roberto and others silently prayed that the attack would quickly pass and for the assailants to leave. Sisters in the building were very nervous. The members present were worried the attackers would destroy the whole building or harm the North American missionaries.

After about two minutes, the men fled. Church members quickly organized themselves to put out the various fires in different rooms throughout the building. The cultural hall and sacrament hall contained fires but suffered little damage. The remainder of the building, however, suffered significant damage in the two or so minutes that transpired. The assailants conducted the attack in retaliation for President George H. W. Bush's visit to Chile that month. Bishop Manuel Morales provided a statement to the local police, but the Church members never heard anything else about the assailants or if the police captured them.

Despite the danger faced by these Church members, the Spirit reassured individuals the Lord would protect them. Roberto stated that "the protection [of God] strengthened the testimonies of each person involved," with the event only intensifying his belief that, "God always accompanies us."[248] Reflecting on the challenges faced by Latter-day Saints in Chile, Roberto felt that the period of persecution in Chile was similar to the conditions surrounding the pioneers. He shared the following:

> "We were totally vulnerable. In that time [in Chile], attacks against Mormon chapels were constantly occurring. They were very frequent. I felt defenseless, because really, you could not do anything. There was a sense of vulnerability, above all. We were vulnerable to an attack by anyone. It reminds me of the time of the pioneers of the Church—the way we suffered was, in many ways, the same way they suffered, but our sufferings were very minimal in comparison."[249]

Perceptions about the Latter-day Saint faith and Church leaders incited the creation of mobs targeting the pioneers and members in the early days of the Church. While persecution in Chile resulted less from ideological differences between leftist philosophies and Church doctrine and more from perceptions about Church affiliations with the US Government and American imperialism, intolerance among members of society manifested itself similarly nearly 150 years after the persecution faced by early Saints in the US through violence and destruction.

On the Lord's Errand

Rodolfo "Rudy" Mortensen, who served as President of the Lima Peru Temple, served in a dangerous time in the early 1990s when terrorist groups targeted members of the Church, especially local and North American leaders. As he drove home one evening from a fireside, terrorists stopped his vehicle and shot his window.[250] Martin and Idon Openshaw knew President Mortensen and his chauffeur well. They elaborated on this account by sharing the following:

> "Somehow, they stopped him, and the guy shot point blank at President Mortensen. The window was up. The window shattered, but the bullet never penetrated. They were both scared to death. Rudy's brother-in-law, [Richard T.] Bretzing, was the head of Church security. Rudy didn't want to leave when he was asked to leave, but he said, 'Okay, I'll go.'"[251]

Logic cannot explain this occurrence of events. For all accounts, the bullet fired by this assailant should have killed President Mortensen. In scripture, however, the Lord declared, "In righteousness shalt thou be established: thou shalt be far from [. . .] terror; for it shall not come near thee. [. . .] No weapon that is formed against thee shall prosper. [. . .] This is the heritage of the servants of the Lord."[252] His intervention miraculously protected President Mortensen as he was about his Lord's work.

Honoring the Garment Invites Physical Protection from Evil

May 16, 1992 began as a typical Saturday for the Medina family. José Medina, along with his sister and seven-year-old nephew, went to clean the chapel located at 1661 Huelén Street in the Cerro Navia section of Santiago, Chile. The family habitually cleaned the building each Saturday to prepare the sacrament hall and other rooms for Sunday services. José had returned from serving a full-time mission less than a year prior and was then serving as the ward executive secretary. His father, José Medina Apablaza, served as the bishop and planned to join the family at the chapel later that morning to help clean.

Some time passed as José cleaned before he heard a knock at the building entrance doors. He and his sister sent José's nephew to open the door, anticipating that the bishop had arrived to assist. The following is José's personal account of what happened next:

> "Suddenly, there was noise and running footsteps, and then I felt a pistol behind my head. They dragged me, shouting threats with vulgar language, and threw me to the floor. They also did this to my sister, who, just prior, had left to go use the bathroom. They poured gasoline on me and began to pour gasoline throughout the building, in each room that had carpet. They told me not to move and they would set the chapel on fire."[253]

José explained that he had no idea of the ages of these five men, as they wore masks to hide their faces. Reports and media later alleged they were members of the Lautaro Youth Movement. Characteristics of the attack matched the group's modus operandi, including the use of masks and pistols, entering occupied chapels in small groups, and using gasoline to light chapels on fire. Members of the Lautaro routinely targeted the Church and committed several acts of terrorism in Santiago in the previous months.

José explained that he was silently praying as the men carried out the attack. He knew that if he fought with them, they would have killed him. The men set fire to the Primary room, sacrament hall, and cultural hall as they went throughout the building. They held his sister at gunpoint, too, but both remained calm. He offered prayers in silence that God would protect his family and that the men would leave the chapel.

After igniting the gasoline, the men began leaving the building. The one guarding José grabbed him and dragged him across the floor toward the entrance doors, and then left him by the entrance to join the other men gathered outside the building. José rose and rushed toward the fire to extinguish the flames. He then heard a gunshot. He headed toward the entrance again to see what happened. His father had arrived and encountered the men outside, near the building entrance, and had tried to fend them off with a hammer. One of the men shot him in the leg. The group fled, fearing an immediate response from the local police.

As the Medina family reunited around the bishop, they quickly checked him to assess his injuries and provide aid. In his own words, José explained:

> "They shot him in one leg—near the knee. There was a hole in his pant leg. There was a hole in his garment, but his leg, the flesh, had no trace of a bullet. For us, it was truly a miracle of God.
>
> God protected us because we kept our covenants. It was a strong, traumatic experience, but just as all things are, with God, all things happen for a reason. This experience did not distance us from the Church, but rather strengthened us even more in the gospel. I know God was there, that he protected my father and protected me. I was doused in gasoline, all my clothes—they would have set me on fire, but God was there to protect us. I testify that God watches over us."[254]

The Medina family and firefighters put out the remaining flames. The chapel did not suffer significant damage.

As José stated, his father's faithfulness and adherence to standards regarding the garment invited divine protection. Bishop Medina's experience is one manifestation and fulfillment of the following statement made by President Spencer W. Kimball on May 31, 1948:

> "Temple garments afford protection. [. . .] Generally I think our protection is a mental, spiritual, moral one, yet I am convinced that there could be and undoubtedly have been many cases where there has been, through faith, an actual physical protection."[255]

There are also many parallels between this attack and scriptural accounts of faithful disciples. Reflecting on the event, José said he considered his family's experience like, "the time when Daniel was thrown into the den of lions and the Lord watched over him."[256] Indeed, this particular account shares striking resemblances with the account contained in scripture. Daniel was thrown into the den because others observed him engaged in prayer, a routine form of daily worship he practiced in a time when such practices were outlawed. Similarly, the Medina family was cleaning the chapel, a weekly occurrence for them, when they were subjected to violence. In Daniel's account, after God intervened by sending an angel to "shut the lion's mouths," Daniel was delivered from the den, and "no manner of hurt was found upon him, because he believed in his God."[257] Similarly, as José described the condition of his father's leg, no manner of hurt was found upon him, a blessing José credited to his father's faithfulness in keeping his covenants.

Protection During the Oklahoma City Bombing

On April 19, 1995, American right-wing terrorist Timothy McVeigh bombed the Alfred P. Murrah building in Oklahoma City, Oklahoma. At 9:02 a.m., the 4,800-pound bomb contained in a Ryder truck detonated beside the building, killing 168. At the time, Brother William Bonebreak of the Midwest City Second Ward, Oklahoma City South Stake, was on the fourth floor of the federal building. Sergeant Bonebreak was serving as the Reserve Operations Non-commissioned Officer (NCO) for the Oklahoma City Recruiting Battalion, headquartered in the Murrah building.[258] Members of the unit were preparing to relocate the headquarters to a different office downtown. Moments prior to the explosion, Sergeant Bonebreak was sitting at his desk and talking with his supervisor, Captain Henderson Baker. He explained:

> "My office faced out the side that blew up. All of a sudden, the world went black. There was a loud explosion. I got under my desk. There was debris falling around. After a little bit of time, I got out from under my desk. I went to take a step and there was no floor. The floor stopped about two feet from my desk. My chair was in the rubble four stories below."[259]

After miraculously surviving the explosion and falling debris, Sergeant Bonebreak set out to provide aid to others in the building. He and three coworkers dug through rubble and found others "buried under filing cabinets, collapsed ceiling, debris and glass."[260] All four were awarded the Soldier's Medal for "voluntarily risking their lives to save others."[261] Two-and-a-half hours after the explosion, Brother Bonebreak was able to call home and speak with his wife, Yvonne Bonebreak, the Ward Relief Society President. Medical personnel treated him for lacerations and abrasions on his back, arms, legs, and ankles. In the wake of the attack, Brother and Sister Bonebreak expressed gratitude for the comfort of the restored gospel.

Madrid Train Bombings

Brother Bitin Uema, a 44-year-old physician and convert to the Church, sat on a train during his regular 40-minute commute to his office in Madrid when a detonation rocked the train car. His was one of four train cars blown apart by explosives in a terrorist attack that claimed 201 lives and injured 1,400 individuals on March 11, 2004. The blast propelled Brother Uema into the air and he lost consciousness but was fortunate to have avoided knocking into the train car ceiling. As he regained consciousness, he realized "everybody around him was dead [. . . and] he found he could not move."[262] Rescue workers initially counted Brother Uema among the dead, but quickly saw he was alive and rushed him to the Madrid hospital. The blast rendered him nearly deaf and inflicted severe chest pain, but Brother Uema was fortunate to have survived. He explained, "Although I was very [shaken] by the nightmare that I was going through, . . . I broke into tears and thanked Heavenly Father that I was still alive."[263] He expressed sorrow in being unable to render aid to other victims. The experience profoundly affected him, and during his recovery, he explained to his bishop that he was "going to put many things in order now," having previously been a less active member.[264] Brother Uema's experience was one of several miracles among Church members in Madrid that day.

The attack occurred within the boundaries of the Madrid Spain East Stake. Many Saints routinely used these trains as part of their daily commute to and from work, but on the day of the bombings, several "missed the trains because of many 'coincidences.'"[265] Some members were aboard the targeted train, but in different carriages from those that exploded, and suffered only emotional trauma and some ear problems due to the blasts. Many local Saints donated blood and offered assistance in other ways.

Elder Mason Wells at the Boston Marathon and Bombings of Paris and Brussels

Throughout recent decades, missionaries have encountered various forms of danger. The prophet Mormon observed that, "those who were faithful in keeping the commandments of the Lord were delivered at all times."[266] Perhaps one of the most compelling modern manifestations of this declaration is the experience of Elder Wells. Wells survived three significant terrorist attacks: the Boston Marathon Bombing, the Paris Bombings, and the Brussels Bombings. Wells describes these events and his personal growth as a result of these attacks in intimate detail within his coauthored work, *Left Standing: The Miraculous Story of How Mason Wells's Faith Survived the Boston, Paris, and Brussels Terror Attacks*. Elder Dallin H. Oaks referenced the Brussels bombing as he described God's involvement and intervention in terror attacks, declaring the following:

> "God rarely infringes on the agency of any of His children by intervening against some for the relief of others. But He does ease the burdens of our afflictions and strengthen us to bear them, as He did for Alma's people in the land of Helam (see Mosiah 24:13–15). He does not prevent all disasters, but He does [. . .] blunt their effects, as He did with the terrorist bombing that took so many lives in the Brussels airport but only injured our four missionaries."[267]

The Lord preserved Wells, despite the odds of surviving three separate terrorism incidents where the perpetrators carried out indiscriminate attacks with ruthless tactics. These miracles manifest the truthfulness of the gospel of Jesus Christ and the Lord's promises contained in the scriptures. They also demonstrate God's love and the tender mercies He brings to pass for those who believe in Him.

CHAPTER 8

SOLACE IN THE WAKE OF TRAGEDY

"For my thoughts are not your thoughts, neither are your ways my ways, saith the Lord. For as the heavens are higher than the earth, so are my ways higher than your ways, and my thoughts than your thoughts."

—Isaiah 55:8–9

Introduction

In recent decades, acts of terrorism—those deliberately targeting the Church and others where Saints were injured or affected—inflicted casualties and led to tragedies. Even so, such occurrences often include accounts of divine comfort, direction, explanations for events, or even encounters between those who passed beyond the veil and their loved ones left behind. Shortly after the assassinations of Latter-day Saint missionaries in 1990, Elder Ballard commented,

> "We are doing and will continue to do all within our power to reduce any risks that could harm our missionaries. However, in today's world of violence, the church cannot eliminate all risk nor guarantee absolutely that a missionary never will be ill, or injured, or harmed. [. . .] Today, Satan is stirring in the hearts of wicked men and women all over the world."[268]

Scriptural accounts of hardships demonstrate purpose in sufferings and afflictions. The scriptures are replete with examples of prophets who endured trials with patience. While the Lord eventually delivered many of these Saints from their trials, some, like the Book of Mormon prophet Abinadi, gave their lives in holding true to their convictions.

On occasion, faithful Church members suffer as a result of man's misuse of agency. Elder Neal A. Maxwell of the Quorum of the Twelve Apostles stated that, "the faithful will not be totally immune from the events on this planet," which includes terrorism.[269] In addition to meetinghouses, members and missionaries alike have been targeted by terrorists in recent years. The likelihood that a Church member will be targeted or harmed in a terrorist attack remains very low, but the possibility exists.

The spiritual welfare of men takes priority over their temporal welfare, as reflected in the efforts of the Church and the overall strategy and subtle tactics of the adversary. Reiterating Clayton M. Christensen's remarks, missionaries serve on "the front lines in the war against Satan over the souls of men," so it is logical and sound to anticipate significant opposition—even terrorism—in new missionary focus areas in the last days.[270] Elder M. Russell Ballard made a similar allusion to the premortal war between good and evil and relevance to members today on the earth when he wrote, "The members of the Church hold a frontline position in the contest for the souls of men."[271] Satan has contended for the souls of men since he first incited rebellion in the hearts of the children of God in the premortal existence, and he will continue to fight viciously to lay claim to more souls. Some of the weapons he uses in this fight involve violence and temporal harm, leveraging fear and other negative emotions linked to terrorism. Similar to other violent and heinous acts perpetrated by men, God patiently allows men to misuse their agency, which often affects others' physical well-being.

Despite the inherent dangers associated with service on the front line, missionaries and members involved in missionary efforts have rarely been killed or permanently injured as a result of terrorism, or even due to other causes. In 1989, when many terrorist groups in South America targeted the Church, Elder Ballard explained the following:

> "The death rate of young male missionaries from the United States serving worldwide is one-fifth the rate of young males of comparable age in the general population of the United States [. . . and] missionaries obviously have a much lower risk of death than others of comparable age."[272]

These statistics have not worsened since, despite an increasing number of conflicts and natural disasters. Faithful missionaries remain under the constant watch-care of a loving Heavenly Father protecting them from harm and guiding them through the Holy Ghost.

Called to Stand as a Witness Against Wickedness at the Judgment Bar

God permits certain faithful and righteous men, women, and children to die at the hands of the wicked for them to stand as witnesses against wickedness and guilty parties. In the Book of Mormon, Alma and Amulek learned this powerful truth through the Holy Ghost as they witnessed evil and felt compelled not to intervene. Alma 14:8–11 reads:

> **8** And they brought their wives and children together, and whosoever believed or had been taught to believe in the word of God they caused that they should be cast into the fire; and they also brought forth their records which contained the holy scriptures, and cast them into the fire also, that they might be burned and destroyed by fire.
>
> **9** And it came to pass that they took Alma and Amulek, and carried them forth to *the place of martyrdom*, that they might witness the destruction of those who were consumed by fire.
>
> **10** And when Amulek saw the pains of the women and children who were consuming in the fire, he also was pained; and he said unto Alma: *How can we witness this awful scene? Therefore let us stretch forth our hands, and exercise the power of God which is in us, and save them from the flames.*

> **11** But Alma said unto him: *The Spirit constraineth me that I must not stretch forth mine hand; for behold the Lord receiveth them up unto himself, in glory; and he doth suffer that they may do this thing, or that the people may do this thing unto them, according to the hardness of their hearts, that the judgments which he shall exercise upon them in his wrath may be just; and the blood of the innocent shall stand as a witness against them, yea, and cry mightily against them at the last day.*

Both leaders learned this painful truth as the Lamanites burned women and children in front of them. These men knew they could call upon divine assistance and control the elements to deliver these women and children, but the Spirit directed Alma not to interfere.

Lessons set forth in the Book of Mormon offer insight into the Lord's purpose in permitting obedient and faithful disciples to suffer pain and death inflicted by evil men. The Lord is mindful of the righteous men, women, and children who pass away due to circumstances resulting from terrorism or other evils. He assures us that such disciples will have rest and that He will mete out justice. The prophet Moroni explained, "For the Lord suffereth the righteous to be slain that his justice and judgment may come upon the wicked; therefore ye need not suppose that the righteous are lost because they are slain; but behold, they do enter into the rest of the Lord their God."[273] This explanation for deaths of righteous Saints at the hands of evildoers still holds true today.

Missionaries Assassinated in Bolivia

In early 1989, distrust grew among some Bolivians wary of US intentions in their country. American officials pressured Bolivian leaders to curtail coca crops and the rampant production of cocaine, which often made its way into the United States for distribution. Rumors circulated that the United States considered building an airport in La Paz to launch an invasion of Bolivia to eradicate cocaine crops.[274] In a very literal sense, such discussion threatened the livelihood of the poor, indigenous working class. Through the lens of the average Bolivian farmer whose annual income totaled four hundred American dollars, a bushel of coca leaves raking in ten dollars was preferable to a bushel of corn yielding only one dollar.[275] The working class was overwhelmingly dependent on the high revenues of coca farming.

During this phase of internal strife in the late 1980s, a terrorist group emerged known as the Zarate Willka Armed Forces of Liberation, named after a peasant farmer who led an Indian uprising in 1890. The Zarate Willka conducted a handful of attacks against US Government targets, as these extremists considered North American efforts to eradicate coca a threat to their lifestyle and that of their countrymen. They came to associate the Church with the United States and considered the Saints a viable target.

Missionary work excelled in Bolivia in the late 1980s, especially toward the end of that decade. In 1989, as the Church faced strong opposition from groups like Zarate Willka, "the Church in Bolivia had grown by a stunning 37.5 percent in a brief two-year period."[276] As spiritual opposition to Church growth was seemingly failing, the Church encountered new forms of opposition. After a day of proselyting, Elders Jeffrey Ball and Todd Wilson returned to their residence around 10:20 p.m.. Members of the Zarate Willka Armed Forces Liberation had been monitoring the elders leading up to the attack that evening. Both died nearly instantly, with one victim sustaining four 9.65 mm bullet wounds, likely caused by an Uzi submachine gun.[277] The attack shook the community and reverberated to Saints throughout the world.

While the Church suffered from many terrorist attacks during this era, this attack greatly deviated from the norm of minor bombings of empty chapels. The assassination of these two elders constituted "the first politically motivated slayings in the history of Mormon missionary work."[278] About thirty minutes following the assassination, group members delivered a handwritten manifesto to media outlets. The message read,

> "The violation of our national sovereignty cannot remain unpunished. The Yankee invaders who come to massacre our peasant brothers are warned the same as their internal lackeys. The poor have no other path than to rise up in arms.

> 'Our hatred is implacable and our war is to death.' Zarate Willka Armed Liberation Front."[279]

This statement manifests the political motive behind the attack, as the terrorists sought to protest what they perceived to be imperialism and encroachment on their sovereignty. Judging by the manifesto, Zarate Willka members seemingly targeted the Church's North American missionaries in protest of US coca crop eradication efforts, which negatively impacted indigenous peoples. Members of the Zarate Willka claimed the Church was involved in violent acts targeting these native persons and alleged the Church was somehow trying to seize land belonging to these individuals. These assassinations also "coincided with the arrival in Bolivia of the first contingent of US military engineers, technicians, and troops, charged with leveling Patti-Patti Hill to construct an airport for the city of Potosi."[280] The Zarate Willka clearly despised the United States and wanted to send a message by attacking vulnerable North Americans in their community.

The Church issued a declaration following the assassination, published in Spanish in newspapers throughout Bolivia, wherein Church leaders refuted the assassins' accusations that the Church was responsible for killing farmers or involved in efforts to take over lands belonging to indigenous people.[281] Local members also attempted to clarify the role and objectives of missionaries and the Church as a whole through word of mouth. Those of other faiths even published favorable commentaries supporting the Church. Catholic leaders published articles in newspapers explaining "how good the Mormons are and not to turn them away," and one newspaper editor who often wrote articles criticizing the Church "wrote a very positive article about the Church with favorable comments more than [he] ha[d] ever before done."[282] The community rallied behind the Saints.

A somber mood prevailed in the neighborhood of the missionaries' apartment following their assassination. The community immediately acknowledged the evil nature of the attack, as no reasonable person could understand why someone would gun down missionaries. One neighbor of the missionaries, Rosario de Davalos, commented, "The devil attacked us that night."[283] The Bolivian people responded.

Bolivian intelligence and law enforcement painstakingly investigated the murders, inviting the FBI to collaborate.

Church members and missionaries mourned but carried on missionary work with even more resolve. Elder M. Russell Ballard of the Church's Quorum of the Twelve Apostles visited local Church leaders in Bolivia to discuss security threats and feasible plans for proceeding with missionary work. In one meeting, an elderly Bolivian stake president addressed the Apostle in the midst of local leaders, saying, "Elder Ballard, we have decided that we cannot allow anything to ever happen again like what has happened to our North American brethren. We will begin taking more of this missionary work into our own hands."[284] The Bolivian members did just that. President Steven R. Wright, the mission president presiding over the two assassinated elders, described how the public became more sympathetic and receptive to the Church and how members rallied to share the restored gospel. He stated a significant change occurred "in the way members [were] cooperating with the missionaries. There [was] more friendshipping and fellowshipping, and members [. . .] increased their efforts in finding investigators. Members [gained] courage to talk to their friends about the gospel."[285] This energy spread throughout neighboring countries and grew. Shortly thereafter, Elder M. Russell Ballard remarked, "The Spirit of the Lord is really hovering over the northern South America countries. We've never before experienced such a momentum of people looking to the Church as we are now."[286] Member missionary work reached new bounds in the wake of tragedy.

The US Government quickly collaborated with national officials to find the perpetrators responsible for the shootings and issued a $500,000 reward for information leading to arrests.[287] The timing of the group's manifesto delivery to media outlets reflects the deliberate planning and coordination behind the assassinations. Authorities knew the assailants conducted surveillance and identified the missionaries' residence as a choke point. They investigated how the assailants could have known the missionaries' routine and daily schedule, well enough to predict when they would arrive home in the evening.

After the Bolivian Police committed all available resources to identify and capture the assailants, subsequent investigations revealed "the elders that were assassinated had let their assassins into their apartment before when they had inquired about the church, and a map of their apartment was found in the custody of the killers."[288] Eventually, police detained four suspects directly related to the attack. Authorities charged Zarate Willka members Johnny Justino Peralta-Espinoza, Victor Eduardo Prieto-Encinas, Simon Mamani Quispe, and Susana Zapana Hannover with the assassinations of Elders Todd Ray Wilson and Jeffrey Ball. Hannover, a medical student, was a former member of the Church, her family being one of the first to join what was then known as Branch VIII, near Sopocachi, La Paz.[289] She filled the reconnaissance function the evening of the murders, acting as a lookout and signaling to the armed assassins when the missionaries approached their residence after a day of proselyting. One of four FBI agents sent to Bolivia to investigate the assassinations, Latter-day Saint Mike McPheters, learned Hannover "apparently became a member for the express purpose of collaborating with the Zarate Willka organization."[290] This attack deviated from the modus operandi of the Zarate Willka, targeting religious personnel rather than strictly government or political targets. Previous to this assassination, group attacks included bombing a political motorcade in an assassination attempt and bombing the US embassy.

In the wake of these assassinations, many spiritual events unfolded. During Elder Ball's funeral service, President Thomas S. Monson spoke. President Monson declared, "He's gone home on a missionary transfer. He is still on his mission; he has not been released. He carries on in the spirit of missionary work."[291] After the assassinations, President Steven B. Wright of the Bolivia La Paz Mission, to which both young men pertained, had the following dream, which he shared with Elder M. Russell Ballard:

> "I saw these two elders dressed in white, standing at the doors of a beautiful building. They were greeting numerous people, who also were dressed in white as they entered the building. It was obvious from their dress that those who entered were Bolivians. I envisioned the temple that will someday be built in Bolivia. Elders Wilson and Ball were ushering those they had prepared to receive the gospel in the spirit world into the temple to witness the vicarious ordinances being performed in

> their behalf. This dream has been a great comfort to me and has helped me to understand and accept their deaths."[292]

Elder Ballard explained this dream is consistent with a heavenly vision on the work of redemption in the afterlife that President Joseph F. Smith experienced and recorded. President Smith's vision is contained in the Doctrine and Covenants, which reads, "I beheld that the faithful elders of this dispensation, when they depart from mortal life, continue their labors in the preaching of the gospel [. . .] in the great world of the spirits."[293] In partial fulfillment of President Wright's dream, President Gordon B. Hinckley dedicated the Cochabamba Bolivia Temple, currently the only Latter-day Saint temple in that country, on April 30, 2000.

Another series of events following the missionaries' assassinations reveals how their deaths played a pivotal role in three convert baptisms. The following paraphrases the account, described within a *Church News* article:

> Around 1975, Oscar and Olga Lobo, a Bolivian couple, attended Brigham Young University in Provo, Utah. They attended English courses taught by Steven R. Wright. During their studies, the young couple expressed their desire that Oscar's parents join the Church, which Oscar and his brother Luis had done. Oscar's parents, Jorge and Elena Lobo, met several Church members over the following years, including President Grant Faucett, former president of the Argentina Buenos Aires North Mission, and his wife, Betty.
>
> When Elders Wilson and Ball were assassinated, Faucett Mortuary, owned by Grant Faucett, made the funeral arrangements for Elder Wilson in Wellington, Utah. During the funeral, Sister Faucett sat beside Sister Marsha Bryner, whose son, Bill, was serving in the La Paz mission office when the two elders died. As the two women conversed, Sister Faucett mentioned the non-member Lobo family in Bolivia. Sister Bryner then sent a letter to her son, mentioning the Lobo couple who lived in La Paz, a city of over 1.5 million inhabitants.
>
> Within a week, Elder Bryner was invited to the home of a recent convert named Jorge Vidovic. Vidovic's mother, Celfa,

> was investigating the Church and had invited two friends to listen to the missionaries. The two friends were Jorge and Elena Lobo. Shortly thereafter, Celfa Vidovic and Jorge and Elena Lobo were baptized on August 2, 1989 by Luis Lobo, who was visiting Bolivia on a business trip, and confirmed by President Wright.[294]

These assassinations shocked the community where they occurred, as well as wards worldwide, but blessings also resulted from these events as Saints exercised faith and hope.

Missionaries Assassinated in Huancayo, Peru

On Wednesday, August 22, 1990, members of the Shining Path (Sendero Luminoso, SL) assassinated Elder Christian Andreani Ugarte, 21, of Trujillo, Peru, and Elder Manuel Antonio Hidalgo, 22, of Arequipa, Peru. The two elders were en route to the home of members for lunch when they were ambushed and shot at 1:30 p.m. in Batanyacui, in the district of El Tambo.[295] The Shining Path, known for brutal attacks against the innocent, did not normally attack members of The Church of Jesus Christ of Latter-day Saints, but they did so in this instance, not deviating from their modus operandi in terms of tactics. The elders were beaten, each shot once in the head, and one was stabbed in the throat.[296] Elder Ugarte would have completed his mission approximately two weeks after his death, whereas Elder Hidalgo had only begun his mission about four months prior to his death.[297] This marked the second assassination incident of Latter-day Saint missionaries by terrorists in this era of contemporary terrorism.

Circumstances and inspiration felt by each of the two elders preceding their deaths reflect the Lord's awareness of this pending event and His knowledge of their fate, casting doubt on the opinion among some that their deaths were a coincidence or arbitrary act. In the final months of his mission, Elder Ugarte asked the Mission President, President Douglas Earl, if he and his companion, Elder Hidalgo, could be transferred together to Huancayo, where Elder Ugarte had previously served.[298] President Earl felt inspired to act on that request and transferred the elders to Huancayo in June 1990. Such a request by a missionary and the granting of a request by the mission president is not a common occurrence.

Following the assassination, mission authorities visited the missionaries' room and reviewed their belongings. In doing so, they discovered that the elders "were aware that they were under surveillance."[299] Nevertheless, the missionaries fearlessly continued to share the gospel. They found among the writings of Elder Hidalgo repeated references to his favorite scriptures, Doctrine and Covenants 101:32–38, with special emphasis on verses 35 and 36:

> **35** And all they who suffer persecution for my name, and endure in faith, though they are called to lay down their lives for my sake yet shall they partake of all this glory.
>
> **36** Wherefore, fear not even unto death; for in this world your joy is not full, but in me your joy is full.[300]

In his final interview with his mission president, Elder Hidalgo had shared his beliefs regarding this scriptural promise.[301] Elder Hidalgo's writings and testimony preceding his death hint at the inspiration he received from the Lord and reassurances he felt in the face of danger.

Experiences and testimonies shared by the elders' family members provide additional examples of tender mercies and evidence of the Lord's involvement in this tragedy. President José Andres Neyra of the Trujillo Stake stated that Ugarte's mother, "had premonitions that her son was going to be killed on his mission," and so "when [President Neyra] called, she knew."[302] She experienced a divine premonition of the pending loss. Gladys Ines Ayaviri de Ugarte, a member by birth in one of the Church's first families in Trujillo, said that, "[her son] had come to her in a dream a couple of nights before [his death] and had told her that he would die."[303] A tender mercy prepared her for the tragedy.

The families of the slain elders expressed their determination to support missionary work and preaching the gospel following the incident. In a meeting one week after the assassinations, Elder Ugarte's father, Justo Tito Ugarte, conveyed to Church members that the Lord blessed his family with peace. Elder M. Russell Ballard, who attended the meeting, reported, "He said he knew his son is doing the work of the Lord on the other side," and that Brother Ugarte, "encouraged other missionaries not to fear and not to give up because of this unfortunate incident in the quest to take the gospel to the honest in heart in Peru."[304] These missionaries acted on this message of hope, laboring until Church leaders transferred some to other missions.

Elder Hidalgo's parents, Manuel Francisco Hidalgo and Virginia Pella de Hidalgo, struggled with the news of their son's death. Both recent converts at the time, they struggled to grasp the purpose behind the assassination and felt for a time that hope was forlorn. The Lord, however, comforted them and provided solace. Both of Elder Hidalgo's parents expressed a resolute and firm belief in God's purposes in the weeks following their son's death. In a letter to President Ezra Taft Benson, Brother Hidalgo shared the following:

> "With profound sadness we received word of the death of our son. [. . .] We know that this separation is temporary and that soon we will be reunited with him for all eternity. [. . .] Our Father in Heaven wanted to have [him] at his side to continue as a missionary preaching his gospel in the spirit world, and we understand that and feel joy and gladness that he is continuing his work.
>
> Moreover, nothing or no one can stop my wife and me—when the time comes—from being ready for a call from the Lord to follow our son's example in going forward to preach the gospel."[305]

Elder Hidalgo's mother also received strength and comfort through a spiritual experience shortly after her son's death. Elder Hartman Rector Jr., of the South America North Area Presidency, told Virginia she would see her son in dreams that week.[306] Indeed, Sister Hidalgo explained that later that week, her son, dressed in a white tunic, came to her in the night and told her things that calmed her, saying "Mother, don't worry, I am fine. Take care of Father and my brothers. And never stop attending church."[307] Elder Ballard also met with Brother and Sister Hidalgo after their son's death. Learning of their intention to be sealed in the temple, he encouraged them to do so in January.[308] The Hidalgo family acted on this invitation, despite some opposition up to the day of the sealing, as their transportation plans fell through. Eventually, through the help of a taxi driver who was a member of the Church, the Hidalgo family was sealed in January 1991 with Elder Hidalgo's first mission companion, Dana Nottinghim, serving as his proxy.[309] Those closest to these elders, their parents, found peace in the Lord and an assurance that the Plan of Salvation enables them to live with their sons again. Their testimonies about the spirit world and God's purposes in trials grew in a way only gained through such a profound tragedy.

Loss in the Oklahoma City Bombing

Paul Broxterman awoke and followed his standard morning routine in the early morning hours. He kissed his wife, Cammy, before departing for the Alfred P. Murrah Federal Building in downtown Oklahoma City, Oklahoma. Most mornings, Paul would peck her softly so as not to wake her, but that Wednesday morning of April 19, 1995, Paul gave a more affectionate farewell, kissing Cammy and saying, "Goodbye, my Love."[310] He then headed to work, in a position he started just three weeks prior as an investigator with the Department of Housing and Urban Development.

Broxterman embraced the recent opportunity to move from Arizona to Oklahoma. He "felt like he was going home" and "would be close to his ancestral roots," given the close proximity to the Potawatomi Nation's home of Shawnee, Oklahoma.[311] Over the years, Paul studied his Native American heritage, researching his pedigree and Potawatomi culture through a lens of Latter-day Saint beliefs and temple work.

Paul converted and was baptized and confirmed as a member of the Church after serving as a radioman in the Navy during Vietnam. His mother, Peggy, explained that Paul was "mischievous and unsettled—until he joined the LDS Church and married his wife, Cammy."[312] Early on in his membership and into his later life, Paul was fascinated with genealogy. He dedicated countless hours to research. Since converting, Paul felt a pull to perform temple work for deceased family members and he sought out every opportunity to do so. Within one week of their marriage and sealing ceremony in the Manti, Utah

Temple, Paul and Cammy visited six other temples and spent three hours at the Family History Library in Salt Lake City.[313] After various assignments in western states with the Internal Revenue Service, the Bureau of Indian Affairs, and the Department of Agriculture, Paul accepted an assignment as an investigator with the Department of Housing and Urban Development. He and his family relocated from Arizona to Oklahoma City, Oklahoma. There, the Broxtermans joined the Oklahoma City Oklahoma North Stake of the Church.[314] Their new residence placed the family approximately forty-five minutes from the center of the Potawatomi Nation in Shawnee, Oklahoma.

As Paul settled into his new assignment on the fifth floor of the Murrah Federal Building, he continued to set up his workspace. One of the secretaries brought a plate of cookies to the different offices around 8:30 a.m., visiting Paul and seeing him at his desk setting up his computer system.[315] Then, at 9:02 a.m., an explosion rocked the building. A Ryder rental truck containing over 4,800 pounds of ammonium nitrate fertilizer, nitromethane, and diesel fuel exploded beside the building, killing 168 people and injuring over 680 others. The explosion decimated the offices occupied by the Department of Housing and Urban Development. As rescue workers and volunteers began searching through the rubble, there was no sign of Paul Broxterman.

In the aftermath of the attack and as Paul remained a missing person, the community served the Broxterman family. Cammy's new ward family rallied to her aid as several members demonstrated true discipleship, "willing to mourn with those that mourn [and] comfort those that stand in need of comfort."[316] Cammy's appreciation for the ward and her account of their efforts reflects the charity and empathy of Christ-like men and women. She explained,

> "We had just been to that ward one time, and then a few days later, [Paul] was killed. Our visiting teachers were right there, and they took care of my kids for me while I was at the crisis shelter. One of the ward members loaned me her phone—cell phones weren't common, but I really needed to have one. I never knew who it was that loaned me the phone. Then, after I moved up to Frenchtown, Montana, I was serving as Relief Society President and I introduced myself during

> Relief Society, since we had a visitor. She shared that she was visiting from the Edmonton, Oklahoma Ward. I told her what happened, and I told her I was never able to find the person who loaned me a phone, and she said it was her."[317]

Gary Newman, President of the Oklahoma City Stake, shared a touching account about a warm gesture days after the attack. He stated that during a stake priesthood meeting Sunday evening, four days after the attack, an announcement was made about the missing Church member. "We had a visitor just passing through [. . . who] came up and gave $200 to my counselor for the family. We don't even know who he was."[318] This sense of community unity quickly spread throughout Oklahoma City.

Workers discovered Paul's body in the rubble thirteen days after the attack, on what would have been his 43rd birthday. Paul's body was shipped to Topeka, Kansas. Two years earlier, Paul had taken his family on a seven-state trip "identical to one his grandfather had taken him on as a boy," and when they visited Paul's grandmother's grave in Topeka, "the experience moved [him] to buy his own plot there."[319] Paul was buried beside his grandmother.

The Broxterman family's experiences reflect God's method of enabling His children to serve those in need and answer their prayers. President Spencer W. Kimball once said, "God does notice us, and he watches over us. But it is usually through another person that he meets our needs."[320] People in the community carried out this function provided temporal relief for Cammy and her family. The Lord also worked through Cammy's relatives to bring her emotional and spiritual comfort and peace.

Bonds of Love Endure in the Wake of Sandy Hook

The early death of little children because of one's misuse of agency is a particularly tragic condition of mortality and the ability to make choices that affect others. The Sandy Hood Elementary School mass shooting, which occurred on December 14, 2012, dominated headlines for months. Twenty-year-old Adam Lanza entered the school in Newtown, Connecticut and fatally shot 27 individuals, including 20 children between six and seven years old and six adults, before taking his own life. Although some questions remain unanswered about what precipitated the attack and the perpetrator's mental and emotional state, spiritual experiences in the wake of the tragedy brought comfort and understanding to many of those affected.

Alissa Parker, a member of the Church, wrote *An Unseen Angel* about her journey of healing and hope after losing her six-year-old daughter, Emilie, in the shooting. Her moving account includes her feelings of despair and utter sadness in searching for meaning, confused why she or God could not intervene that day. She describes visiting the temple and receiving divine guidance to contact and speak with Lanza's father about his son. She explains how she came to know of Emilie's proximity and her mission of comfort to her family and others. Victims' families experienced an outpouring of love and compassion from people throughout the country in the form of prayers, care baskets stacked to storage office ceilings, and reverence in honoring and remembering the departed. Alissa describes how many people, including strangers, comforted her by listening when she wanted to open up and reaching out to share memories of Emilie or ways Emilie inspired or touched them. In addition to these messengers of God's love, Alissa tells of unseen forces, including her deceased father and daughter, which comforted her and helped her gain a deeper understanding of this event.

In her book, Alissa included one such instance of Emilie's new mission when she discussed an unexpected letter she received from Cici, the mother of Emilie's friend Arianna from the school she previously attended in Albuquerque, New Mexico. In the letter, Cici described Arianna's devastation in learning of Emilie's death and the difficult time she had in coping. Alissa describes what came next in the letter as follows:

> "One afternoon, Arianna's father went to check on her as she was playing in the backyard. She was alone, but he heard her speaking. It didn't sound like the normal prattle of imaginative play. It sounded like she was in animated conversation with someone. When her dad asked Arianna who she was talking

> to, she looked up and excitedly said, 'It's Emilie! She is here with me! She is okay!'
>
> Cici and her husband were caught completely off guard, but Arianna spoke with such surety that their hearts were touched. In the following weeks, the same thing happened several more times. Once Cici came into the room where Arianna was playing and asked who she was talking with.
>
> Ariana said again, 'It's Emilie, Mom. Can you feel her? Sit here and be quiet. Can you feel her here with us?'"[321]

Arianna transformed into her former happy self. Her parents grew closer and returned to church as they worked on their spiritual goals. Alissa's experiences after this tragedy strengthened her testimony of the eternal nature of families and the love of Heavenly Father. Hearing the dreams and spiritual experiences of others confirmed to her the active role Emilie played on the other side of the veil in comforting and teaching others. She gained new insights about scriptures referring to angels and their comforting role.

CHAPTER 9

PREDICTIVE ANALYSIS REGARDING THEORIES

"The devil has the world so perfectly at his disposal that it requires few devils to keep it in subjection [. . .] the whole legion of devils has nothing to do but look after the 'Mormons' and stir up the hearts of the children of men to destroy them."

—Elder George A. Smith, Journal of Discourses, 5:364

Introduction

The fields of study relating to terrorism have grown over time, especially since the 9/11 attacks. Terrorism threats are likely to become a growing concern for religious institutions as religious liberty comes under attack. Even so, predictive analysis relating to potential risks faced by the Church remains within the Church Security Department with few, if any, insights offered by students, professors, government agencies, or others speculating on pending threats. Fortunately, a drastic increase in funding and dedicated resources in academic circles and government agencies contributed to a vast increase in literature on terrorism studies within the past twenty years. While much of this literature investigates past incidents and trends, some provides analysis and contains beliefs about future terrorist threats and trends on a global and regional scale. Experts develop theories grounded in evidence from statistics and extensive research, presenting analysis on how terrorism may evolve in the future. Predictive analysis, grounded in tried and tested analytical methods, loses fidelity beyond five to ten years due to unforeseeable conditions and circumstances. Studying theories for the next wave of modern terrorism, anticipated to begin within the next decade, is worth investigating to forecast possible implications for The Church of Jesus Christ of Latter-day Saints within the next generation.

The Fifth Wave of Modern Terrorism: Exploring Implications for the Church

An objective method to frame future terrorism threatening the Church is to explore possibilities developed by theories for the predominant ideologies and characteristics dominating the next wave of terrorism. Professor David Rapoport's framework for modern terrorism includes four distinct waves categorizing time periods of terrorism activities based on principal themes. This model generally holds true to characterize terrorism trends across the globe throughout recent history. Based on the duration of former waves, Rapoport and other experts predict the religious wave, which began in 1979, will endure until the 2020s before a fifth wave replaces the religious wave.[322] Researchers have speculated on the characteristics and leading ideology of this anticipated fifth wave. The most oft-conjectured and supported themes for this fifth wave include new tribalism, jihadist terror groups, technology, and anti-globalization, all of which pose unique implications for Church expansion and distinct threats to Church facilities and members.

New Tribalism Wave

Jeffrey Kaplan, Associate Professor of Religion at the University of Wisconsin-Oshkosh, proposed a fifth wave called New Tribalism. In this wave, terrorists seek "a utopian vision to create a perfected society in their local regions."[323] Genocide and rape provide the means to bring this goal to fruition and transform society within one generation; adherents kidnap young men to turn into soldiers and young women to become child brides.[324] The apocalyptic nature of groups' ideologies and visions is also characteristic of this wave. Kaplan consistently refers to the Khmer Rouge of Cambodia as the group initiating this fifth wave, along with the Lord's Resistance Army in Uganda as a paradigmatic standard.[325]

Based on the limited geographic scope characterizing groups in this wave, using violence in their local regions to bring about changes in society, threats to the Church would exist mainly in regions already rife with terrorism. Parts of Africa, southeast Asia, and the Middle East seem to be more vulnerable to the emergence of these types of terror groups. Statistics suggest these groups do not deliberately target religious institutions regularly; rather, they attack security forces to gain freedom of maneuver, and private property and citizens on a large scale, in line with their characteristic tactic of genocide and ethnic cleansing. For instance, the Khmer Rouge conducted only two attacks targeting religious figures/institutions of 160 registered incidents of terrorism and the Lord's Resistance Army attacked 13 religious targets of 305 total incidents of terrorism.[326] In this theoretical wave, terrorist groups would likely target foreign missionaries for their race. Rather than single out the Church, groups would target members similar to the rest of society, kidnapping youth and killing those not meeting ethnic criteria to procreate and yield the next generation.

Wave Dominated by Jihadist Terror Groups

Dr. Anthony Celso, Associate Professor at Angelo State University, proposed a fifth wave characterized by Jihadist groups. In this theoretical wave, notions against apostate Muslims and non-Muslims continue to inspire attacks. An "overarching desire for isolation from society" distinguishes groups like Boko Haram and the Islamic State from other Islamist extremist groups dominating the fourth wave, or religious wave, of modern terrorism.[327] These groups reject man-made governments and social constructs in pursuit of creating a society based on practices instituted in the times of the Prophet Muhammad in a new Caliphate. Tactics in this wave would likely include unrestrained violence targeting ethnic groups and communities of other religious denominations, as well as attacks against Muslims perceived to be corrupt or deemed apostates for their acceptance or tolerance of worldly institutions, as opposed to strict interpretation of the Qur'an. Jihadist terrorist groups may inflict severe damage to communities and wage brutal campaigns in pursuit of their goal, but ultimately, their objective of a utopian society based on strict interpretations of Islamic doctrine is irrational and unattainable.

According to publicly available information, jihadist groups have not typically targeted The Church of Jesus Christ of Latter-day Saints. The Islamic State's threat published online in late 2017 depicted an armed jihadist facing the San Diego Temple, but few jihadist groups have threatened the Church. Granted, there is a very limited Latter-day Saint presence in the Middle East and North Africa, where senior service missionaries labor and Church members meet in small groups. Due to limited presence and the lack of proselyting, among other reasons, few jihadists in those regions know or care about the Church.

A noteworthy possibility regarding jihadist terror groups' posture toward the Church involves inherent threats stemming from differences in Latter-day Saint and Islamic doctrine. The Islamic faith's *shehadah* is the basis for the first of five Pillars of Islam, which are basic tenets all Muslims should follow. The *shehadah* is a testimony or declaration of faith, which reads as follows: "There is no God but God. Muhammad is the Messenger of God."[328] This declaration contains two direct avowals and an implied third: first, that there is no God but Allah; second, that Muhammad is his prophet (meaning the final prophet, or seal of the prophets); and third (by inference), the Qur'an is Allah's final revelation to man. A Jihadist group inductee, such as one pledging allegiance to Al-Qaeda, must also make this pledge.

The Church of Jesus Christ of Latter-day Saints is the only institution on earth confronting and contradicting all three components of the Islamic *shahadah*. In stark contrast to Islam, multiple Gods; ancient, modern, and future prophets; and continuing recorded revelation are all doctrinal elements of The Church of Jesus Christ of

Latter-day Saints. As was noted in previous chapters, perpetrators of terrorism targeting the Church did not do so following Islamist or religious ideologies, even though that was characteristic of most terrorism throughout the world since 1979. This can largely be attributed to the fact that the Church still has a small footprint in the Middle East and many predominantly Islamic nations. This, however, will change in the future as the restored gospel enters new lands. When this takes place, the Mullahs and Imams to whom jihadists pledge allegiance through *bay'a* and to whom group leaders go seeking strategic guidance will perceive threats associated with Latter-day Saint doctrines. This clash of ideologies will provoke opposition, which, given the last 40 years of terrorism dominated by Islamist ideologies, will mostly likely take the form of terrorism.

If jihadist ideologies continue to grow and come to dominate terrorism in what becomes the fifth wave of modern terrorism, the Church's interactions with such groups will greatly depend on the expansion of the Church to new areas of the Middle East or cultural clashes in areas of Church presence outside the Middle East. As missionaries enter African nations, for instance, white and local missionaries may enter or encounter support zones or battle zones of jihadist groups like Boko Haram. Such groups deeply imbed tenets of *jahiliyyah* in their ideologies and justification for violence, "using *takfir* to ex-communicate and legitimize violence against other Muslims."[329] As locals receive missionaries and join the Church through baptism and confirmation, they abandon their Muslim faith and become targets of violence by jihadist groups, increasing the likelihood of violence and threats against missionaries, members, and facilities. Unrestrained violence and brutality characterize such groups, which often use public executions to coerce the populace to comply with their demands at the risk of death. Such groups would not practice the restraint exercised by leftist factions in Chile in the late 1980s and early 1990s, which often targeted empty chapels or forced members out of chapels prior to bombing them, deliberately targeting objects and minimizing collateral death and injuries. Rather, jihadist groups would likely kill missionaries for preaching to and converting Muslims and kill converts for abandoning their faith. In areas where jihadist groups flourish, Church leaders would remove missionaries and reassign them to neighboring countries with greater security, similar to events that transpired in South America after the Zarate Willka terrorist group assassinated US missionaries.

Although religious extremist groups have rarely targeted the Church throughout the religious wave, there is a possibility jihadist groups may target the Church in a fifth wave characterized by jihadist ideologies. Investigating this possibility through the application of contrarian techniques aids predictive analysis by "challeng[ing] ongoing assumptions and broaden[ing] possible outcomes."[330] One such technique, known as high impact/low probability analysis, investigates an event with a low likelihood of transpiring, but if the event were to occur, the effects would be devastating.

High Impact/Low Probability Analysis: Jihadists in Nigeria

A sample high impact/low probability analysis regarding jihadist terrorism in Nigeria targeting the Church reveals characteristics and circumstances of a feasible, albeit unlikely, threat. In recent years, Nigeria boasted some of the strongest Church growth in the world, despite missionaries entering the country only forty years ago. In 2018, Nigeria contained over 150,000 members, 361 wards, 246 branches, 6 missions, and 1 temple.[331] Retention of new converts is also generally greater than other regions experiencing rapid Church growth.

Jihadist factions, such as Boko Haram, might target the Church in a wave dominated by such terrorist groups for their overlapping in regions of the world and their starkly differing philosophies or for the Church's perceived affiliation with the United States, a chief enemy of Jihadist groups. Terrorism experts describe the organization formerly known as Boko Haram (before the group aligned with the Islamic State and changed their name) as a jihadist organization. Boko Haram, commonly interpreted to mean "Western education is a sin," is a militant Islamic faction which waged violence throughout western Africa, mainly in Nigeria.[332] The group's Islamist ideology is dominated by the concept of *takfir*, or meting out punishment to apostate Muslims and others who are impure for non-Muslim practices. This fundamental tenet is a chief reason the group aligned with the Islamic State and changed their name to reflect the union. While adherents conducted a majority of attacks against private citizens and property, a large percentage of their targets were religious figures and institutions. While Boko Haram mostly targeted private citizens and property between 2009 and 2016 (constituting 931/2,077 attacks), the group also frequently targeted religious figures/institutions (153 attacks).[333] Studying Boko Haram's ideology, tactics, target selection, and other facets may aid in assessing how Christian groups like the Latter-day Saint Church may face persecution and terrorism in a fifth wave dominated by such groups. Army Techniques Publication (ATP) 2-33.4, *Intelligence Analysis*, sets forth six steps for effective high impact/low probability analysis, applied to a scenario in the following paragraphs to explore possible implications for the church based on terrorism conducted by jihadist groups in Nigeria.

Step 1: Define high-impact outcome

Terrorism in Nigeria during a fifth wave characterized by jihadist groups could involve mass casualty attacks against Latter-day Saint chapels, as well as attacks against other religious groups. Several of Boko Haram's attacks against religious targets since 2009 have included significant casualty counts, with one resulting in 122 killed and 270 wounded.[334] In such attacks, Jihadists often employ suicide bombers and complex attacks with explosives and gunfire indiscriminately targeting men, women, and children. A mass casualty attack against a Latter-day Saint target would mark the first such attack in several decades. Targeting a congregation during worship hours or just prior to or after a service would likely yield a high number of casualties, due to high member concentration in a small area. Second- and third-order effects of such an incident would include teaching restrictions and possible evacuation of missionaries, increased security measures to protect chapels and members, and fear among local members for their affiliation with the Church. While the event is unlikely, one of such consequence merits further investigation.

Step 2: List plausible pathways to the low probability outcome

A review of terrorism incidents reveals a myriad of methods to achieve a high casualty count through a terrorist attack. Historically, terrorists throughout the age of modern terrorism preferred firearms and explosives. This jihadist group also preferred firearms and explosives; 48 percent of attacks against religious targets between 2009 and 2016 involved bombings, while 36 percent involved armed assault.[335] Hence, in generating a predictive assessment regarding the type of attack and methods employed in a mass casualty attack against a Latter-day Saint target in Nigeria, applying statistics and trends of existing jihadist groups in the area suggest such an attack would likely involve firearms, explosives, and possibly suicide bombers.

One plausible pathway is a complex attack targeting a sole Latter-day Saint chapel during religious services. A jihadist terror group would likely incorporate this attack into a campaign plan targeting Christian denominations in general, grouping in the Church and targeting only one Latter-day Saint chapel based on proportionality among viable Christian targets. Initially, reconnaissance through physical or electronic means would lead jihadists to plan the location and time of the attack, identifying worship hours, viable Latter-day Saint chapels to attack, and even anticipated attendance levels. The group would then employ a suicide bomber to access the meetinghouse during services and detonate the explosive among worshipers. Gunmen outside the chapel gates would then target those evacuating the meetinghouse. Such a complex attack, involving multiple methods to inflict casualties (i.e., bombing/explosion, armed assault, facility/infrastructure attack), is unlikely, but is worth investigating due to the potential devastating impact. Another plausible pathway is a series of bombings against Latter-day Saint chapels. The jihadist group would identify chapels to target, and then resource the explosives and manufacture bombs. The group would likely emplace the bombs during or near worship hours with some sort of delay or remote detonator. Alternatively, perpetrators could emplace a victim-activated anti-personnel mine or explosive device. This attack would reduce risk for the jihadist group, in terms of operatives at the site when law enforcement responds, as they could emplace the devices and leave the scene.

Step 3: Determine possible triggers for changes in momentum

A possible trigger influencing momentum of attacks could involve the increased presence of Latter-day Saint missionaries in jihadist support zones. Missionary work in areas of jihadist recruitment and other support may generate a cultural clash, due to starkly contrasting philosophies among the Latter-day Saint and jihadist adherents. This could lead jihadists to attack Church members or facilities in order to force out the invaders and dissuade locals from joining or supporting the Church. Changes in jihadist groups' resources and supplies might also change the momentum of attacks or threats, as a lack of explosives due to seized caches or frozen financial accounts might lead terrorists to use their limited supplies to attack a prioritized list of targets, with security personnel near the top and the Church lower in priority.

Step 4: Identify plausible, but unpredictable triggers of sudden change

US Government involvement in political or military operations may trigger an abrupt focus in targeting the Church for its perceived affiliation to the US. Due to the sensitive nature of such operations, only those in small political and military circles would have prior knowledge of impending military actions, making such a trigger unpredictable to outsiders. If American forces train and assist, or directly target, jihadist groups in Nigeria, the groups might attack vulnerable symbols of the US like Latter-day Saint meetinghouses. Such attacks would avoid the risk and inherent dangers of confronting superior US military forces, while still conducting symbolic attacks against the United States by attacking vulnerable targets of opportunity. Another possible trigger could be Latter-day Saint support for and sheltering of refugees displaced by the jihadist groups. The groups might then associate the Church with their prioritized targets, increasing focus against the Church.

Step 5: Identify indicators for each pathway

Attacks against other Christian denominations would serve as a reliable indicator of either pathway. Such attacks would identify jihadist targets and increase the risk for incidents against members or a meetinghouse. Characteristics of attacks might also reveal aspects of a group's objectives, helping leaders to determine how to reduce risk. Propaganda may also serve as an indicator for either terrorist attack pathway. An ideological clash may take place as Latter-day Saint missionaries encroach upon jihadist support zones, where Islamists recruit adherents through radicalization. Latter-day Saint values contrast with religious extremist philosophies, deterring Latter-day Saint converts or investigators from supporting or joining jihadist groups. Such a clash of cultures in certain communities might lead jihadists to disseminate propaganda against the Church or target Church members or meetinghouses directly.

Step 6: Identify factors deflecting a bad outcome or encouraging a good outcome

A security-in-depth approach for physical security measures at Latter-day Saint meetinghouses can reduce vulnerability and deter terrorists from conducting certain types of attacks. Fences surrounding chapels in South America, for instance, led terrorists to bomb the fence entrance in an attempt to gain access to the chapel and conduct further sabotage attacks, whereas some terrorists used Molotov cocktails, which they could throw over the fence to cause minimal damage to the meetinghouse. Fences around chapels in Nigeria would reduce some of the risk associated with terrorist attacks by jihadist organizations. Additional security measures to deflect a bad outcome could involve Latter-day Saint missionaries. Aside from instituting curfew hours for personal safety, mission leaders could forbid missionaries from entering areas identified as jihadist support zones, reducing the chance of a clash resulting from missionaries converting those in a potential jihadist recruiting pool. Such a restriction would limit Latter-day Saint exposure to jihadist groups and reduce Latter-day Saint presence in areas of concern. Proactive practices by Church leaders in anticipating danger and threats can also deflect a bad outcome. An example would be temporarily closing the Latter-day Saint temple if violence and civil unrest increase due to political issues.

Technological Wave

Dr. Jeffrey Simon, president of Political Risk Assessment Company, Inc. and a former RAND Corporation analyst, offers an alternative theory for a fifth wave. He theorizes a wave wherein "there will be no single type of terrorist ideology [. . .] in the same way anarchism, anti-colonialism, new left/Marxism, and religious fundamentalism dominated the preceding four waves."[336] Rather, he suggests methods by which terrorists conduct their missions will more accurately reflect global terrorism trends than ideology. He believes "the influential role of technology will be the defining characteristic of the Fifth Wave," set in motion by the Internet, which acts as a force multiplier for individuals and small groups attempting to influence a large body or harm a more formidable target.[337] In addition to relying on the Internet for recruitment, logistics, planning, and other aspects of preparation, terrorists in this wave would leverage the Internet to conduct more large-scale and dangerous attacks. Simon explains two characteristic tactics employed by terrorist groups in the technological wave include accessing critical information (i.e. maps, blueprints, and security measures) online for use in planning attacks and waging successful cyber-attacks targeting critical infrastructure, financial systems, and vulnerable aspects of government and business.[338] In these circumstances, terrorists might use the cyberspace domain to target the Church in various ways.

Threats to the Church during the Technological Wave

Aspects of this theorized wave characterized by terrorists leveraging technology pose threats to the Church. Theorized characteristics of this wave do not limit extremists and groups to cyber attacks; rather, groups will likely leverage technology in mission planning, enhancing reconnaissance, logistics, weapons, and training to reduce risk and increase likelihood of mission success.

Table 9.1: Morphological Analysis of Technological Factors in Targeting the Church

Motives	Targets	Methods
• Blackmailing • Damaging the reputation • Identify theft • Industrial sabotage • Surveillance and exposure of temple activities • Propaganda • Espionage (finances, investments, agricultural stores, future building plans, security details for temples) • Counter-ideology • Protest US Government actions	• General Authorities • Church websites • Social media accounts of General Authorities and influential Saints • Family history sites • Family history databases • Church Headquarters • Church tithing archives/databases • Church membership records • Church History Library files • Church employees with access • Temples/ meetinghouses • General Conference	• A "Genius Hacker" • An "Inside Man" • Botnets • Mass attack by thousands of computer users • Social engineering • Honeypots • Syntactic attacks (i.e., virus, worm, trojan horse, malware, spyware) • Semantic attacks (i.e., brute-force, denial-of-service attacks, spoofing, phishing) • Open source intelligence-gathering

Table 9.1 facilitates analysis of possible scenarios by linking together one factor under each heading for a unique scenario in the process, *Plausible Scenario = Motive + Target + Method.* Some plausible scenarios follow.

> *Scenario A:* An Islamist terrorist group intending to bomb Latter-day Saint chapels in protest of US Government intervention in the Middle East uses open sources to locate addresses of Latter-day Saint chapels, identify meeting times, and study map and traffic data to plan attack.
>
> *Scenario B:* A left-wing domestic terrorist cell intending to bomb the Conference Center during General Conference.
>
> *Scenario C:* A right-wing extremist faction recruits a hacker to conduct a phishing attempt against Church employees at the

Church Headquarters to obtain personal information about a General Authority to plan a kidnapping.

Scenario D: A technologically savvy leftist faction attempts to sabotage Church genealogy files through a virus.

There is an extremely small amount of publicly available information on cyber activities targeting the Church or investigations detailing terrorists' use of the Internet to plan and conduct attacks against the Church. Theoretically, actors could target the Church's financial systems, historical databases, and other vital records or systems. Additionally, actors may target Church websites and online material by modifying site content or redirecting searches to other sites with misinformation or distorted content. Government actors in recent conflicts have demonstrated the utility of such attacks for waging propaganda campaigns. This is an increasingly common tactic among tech-savvy terrorist and extremist groups. As group ideologies drift further down extremism scales and farther from Church culture and religious tenets, groups will likely target Church sites opposing their viewpoints.

Anti-Globalization Wave

An additional theory for the fifth wave centers on far-right populist ideology and strict nationalist stances often perceived as xenophobia. According to this theory, factors including the Syrian civil war, the United Kingdom's referendum to leave the European Union (known as "Brexit"), and the United States 2016 presidential election manifested a transition from religious extremism to ideologies based on xenophobia and nationalism characterizing terrorism across the world.[339] A variety of groups would engage in terrorism across a wide range of political and social issues. Other characteristics of the anti-globalization wave include a surge in lone operators conducting independent or sponsored attacks, often engaging in repeated attacks against a target due to reduced personal risk in the absence of direct contact.[340] Individuals and groups would likely capitalize on free speech policies and online anonymity, generating hype and controversial online content to polarize societies. Another characteristic of this wave involves domestic terror groups "designing targeted violence campaigns to weaken the institutional weight of the world's largest international alliances and organizations like the European Union, United Nations, North Atlantic Treaty Organization (NATO), and World Trade Organization."[341] Rather than attack government institutions or law enforcement, terrorist groups would target international organizations and institutions supporting practices they hope to abolish. Terrorist factions will "fight against the increasingly liberal world order led by US hegemony," adhering to far-right populist ideologies.[342] Such characteristics of terrorists and their ideologies present implications and potential security concerns for the Church.

According to these characteristics, groups might target the Church for doctrines perceived as supporting immigration and toleration, but such attacks are unlikely. The Church has a reputation for service, especially for providing food and material support to refugees in recent years. The Church's great missionary efforts and the diversity of members reflect the universal nature of the Church, largely based on acceptance and tolerance. Such cultural norms contrast the xenophobic mentalities of terrorists dominating this proposed wave, which might engage in propaganda or attacks targeting the Church. Foreign groups might target the Church for perceived links to the United States, a chief target of terrorism for the country's liberal philosophies spreading throughout the world, as meetinghouses and missionaries are vulnerable, yet symbolic, targets. Even so, such attacks are unlikely. Historically, mainly leftist factions adhering to communist ideologies targeted the Church with minimal threats from far-right groups.

CHAPTER 10

PREDICTIVE ANALYSIS REGARDING PROPHECIES

"Treachery and terrorism began with [Satan . . .] and they will continue until the Son of God returns to rule and reign with peace and righteousness among the sons and daughters of God."

—Gordon B. Hinckley, "The Times in Which We Live"

Introduction

Prophecies of pending events often present an ominous picture of the future. Interpretations of some scriptures suggest terrorism serves to call this generation to repentance. Natural disasters, wars and rumors of wars, terrorism, and other events contribute to the picture described by President Ezra Taft Benson when, speaking on the last days, he stated, "The world will present a scene of conflict such as has never been experienced before. Still, men's hearts will be hardened to the revelations from heaven."[343] Despite the turmoil throughout the world, society remains distant from God and largely spiritually dormant.

General trends and characteristics of terrorism have changed over time, as reflected by David Rapoport's model of the four waves of modern terrorism and other frameworks and models analyzing terrorism. There has been a wax and wane of violence, attack frequency, brutality, and other facets of terror, but despite counterterrorism efforts, terrorism will persist as the restored gospel goes forth to every land in the coming years. When asked if terrorism is a threat that will ever go away, Dale Van Atta, an investigative reporter and a Latter-day Saint expert on terrorism, replied that, "in some ways, it's a war that will never end until Christ comes again."[344] Lone wolves are growing in abundance, radicalized through the Internet and equipped with weapons or components by a vast network of possible suppliers.

The frequency and intensity of terrorism, in general, continues to rise. Elder M. Russell Ballard said, "The prophecies of the last days lead me to believe that the intensity of the battle for the souls of men will increase and the risks will become greater as we draw closer to the second coming of the Lord."[345] While Satan continues to focus on spiritual warfare, he will continue to incite violence against the Church. Elder Neal A. Maxwell, describing Satan's approaches in resisting the building up of the kingdom, stated that, "Everything in the arsenal of the adversary will eventually be used."[346] This certainly includes terrorism.

Multiple prophecies about the spread of the restored gospel, war, and other topics will likely involve terrorism of some form. Historical evidence and other circumstances aid in assessing how terrorism might affect the Church in conditions set by prophecies coming to pass. Assessments generated through predictive analysis lose fidelity and reliability the more distant the time period, as terrorism trends and other circumstances may drastically change five to ten years beyond the present. Even so, establishing assumptions based on prophesied changes and situations sets conditions to use relevant evidence when generating assessments for future events with greater fidelity than some theories developed by terrorism experts.

Gospel Preached unto Every Nation

In these times of wars and rumors of wars, armed conflict severely limits proselyting, sometimes even closing off countries to missionary work where the Church already had a presence after new violence and threats arose. War, however, often presents possibilities for the expansion of the Church and preaching of the restored gospel. The condition of wars and rumors of wars in the last days seems prerequisite to latter-day prophecies stating, "this gospel shall be preached unto every nation, and kindred, and tongue, and people" and "every man shall hear the fullness of the gospel in his own tongue, and in his own language."[347] Recent decades are replete with examples of how war preceded proselyting, and this characteristic of Church growth will likely continue throughout this period of wars and rumors of wars.

Previous conflicts demonstrate how Soldier-missionaries or government employees can serve as instruments in the hands of God in bringing the gospel to new lands. Willard Call and George Seaman, two Latter-day Saint servicemen in the Spanish-American War who were set apart as missionaries before leaving Utah to embark on military service, made the first attempt to introduce the gospel in the Philippines in 1898.[348] Church members again attempted to proselyte during World War II and held meetings throughout that country. Some remained after the war ended, and despite restrictions on baptisms due to the lack of permanent Church units in the country, these servicemen's proselyting led to the first baptism in the Philippines, with Elder Harold B. Lee's approval.[349] Latter-day Saint servicemen continued to play a pivotal role in Church growth throughout the following years. Following World War II, "Church groups were organized at two US military bases—Clark Air Base and Subic Bay Naval Base—as Latter-day Saint service members looked forward to the establishment of a more formal Church presence" in the country.[350] War enabled Latter-day Saint servicemen to proselyte to the people of the Philippines in times when missionaries were not permitted to enter the country. Their assignments to bases fostered early Church presence following the war and prepared the people for missionaries and chapels in the coming years.

Other circumstances of conflict may affect Church growth and perceptions of the Church influencing a propensity among groups to directly target the Church. In Chile, for instance, many Chileans linked the 1973 coup wherein General Augusto Pinochet seized power to covert efforts of the CIA to overthrow Salvador Allende's leftist regime. Pinochet's policies, including economic reforms, influenced social structures and many perceived that they "widened the gap between rich and poor—sending the rich to the bank and leaving the poor to proselytes."[351] Some became suspicious and distrustful of the Church's successes during the period of rapid Church growth following the coup and under Pinochet's regime, including construction of new chapels in rural areas. Rumors of missionaries acting as US intelligence agents—reporting on sectors of the Chilean population and preaching tenets contradictory to leftist revolutionary philosophies—also contributed to extremist groups in Chile attacking Latter-day Saint targets. This characteristic of terrorism against the Church may emerge in other regions in the future as Latter-day Saint servicemen and government officials introduce the Church in countries affected by war or areas presenting opposition to US presence.

War will likely open more countries to the gospel in coming years. Conflict in the Middle East will likely prepare the way for further expansion of the Church through newly gained religious freedoms in lands where despots previously ruled for centuries. In enduring conflicts, servicemen will likely play an important role in establishing the Church, given their presence in areas otherwise prohibited to civilians and Latter-day Saint missionaries and their access to the indigenous population. Latter-day Saint members of the United States and other governments, such as embassy workers, will also likely serve in this capacity of introducing the Church to leaders and citizens of other countries.

Terrorism is more common than previous decades, however, and may accompany Church expansion in various regions, especially as missionaries enter areas following a period of war. The prophecy contained in Isaiah 19 outlines a civil war, a period of tyranny, and severe drought in Egypt preceding the gospel's entry into that country, where it will flourish. The circumstances of these trials apparently humble Egyptians prior to missionary work commencing and lead to political changes to formally recognize the Church. Civil wars and other conflicts tend to contribute to increases in the frequency of terrorism, such as nationalist groups rising up and using violence to coerce imperialists to leave and grant them independence after World War II. Such conflicts may affect nearby Latter-day Saints or Church representatives, such as missionaries, simply given their physical presence near hot spots for terrorism. Extremist groups may not directly target the Church, but in the course of terrorism attacks targeting military or police targets to delegitimize the local government, Church members may become collateral in such attacks due to proximity.

Religion often plays a central role in conflict, especially due to religious motivations and ideologies fueling powerful Islamist groups in recent years. Historically, however, terrorism targeting the Church is more attributable to anti-US sentiments and leftist ideologies than religious ideologies. In Nigeria, for instance, the Church has a strong presence with over 150,000 members, 6 missions, and 1 temple.[352] Despite conflicts like the Second Nigeria Christian-Muslim War of 2004 and religious terrorism waged by the Boko Haram insurgency, databases and open sources do not register any terrorism incidents directly targeting the Church. Throughout the post-1979 stage of global terrorism, dominated by religious ideologies, the Church suffered minimal threats or acts of terrorism attributable to terrorists acting on religious ideologies.

As war opens countries to the Church, a trend likely to continue involves the first Saints in these countries serving in the Armed Forces or government. Missionaries arriving to these countries may also face higher threats of terrorism. Reiterating Clayton M. Christensen's remarks, missionaries serve on "the front lines in the war against Satan over the souls of men," so it is logical and sound to anticipate significant opposition, even terrorism, in new areas opening to the restored gospel in the last days.[353] Proselyting may involve a phased approach to teaching investigators, wherein missionaries may meet in private with investigators in the homes of members, and eventually be able to preach in public. Depending on cultural norms in the region, new converts may also face persecution or terrorism.

Gospel Flourishing in Egypt

Throughout recent decades, Middle Eastern countries generally contained the highest frequency of terrorism incidents and the most catastrophic casualty counts. Motivations largely stemmed from Islamist ideologies, hence Rapoport's categorizing the post-1979 era as a wave characterized by religious-inspired terrorist attacks. Despite this trending characteristic of global terrorism, few incidents targeting Church facilities or members in this era resulted from radical religious ideologies. As the restored gospel continues to enter new countries, however, religiously motivated terrorism and the tumultuous conditions in the Middle East will likely impact the Church in more direct ways. Isaiah 19 contains a prophecy regarding the growth of the Church in the Middle East, particularly in Egypt. As outlined in Table 10.1, Isaiah foresaw political events that would prepare Egypt to receive the restored gospel, providing descriptions of a series of concrete events preparatory to Egyptians joining the Church and making eternal covenants.

Table 10.1: Prophecies in Isaiah 19 and Common Interpretations

2: And I will set the Egyptians against the Egyptians: and they shall fight every one against his brother, and every one against his neighbor; city against city, and kingdom against kingdom.	Civil war/internal turmoil erupts in Egypt. The possibility for this could be an event like the Arab Spring in 2011 or some significant political upheaval yet to occur in Egypt.
4: And the Egyptians will I give over into the hand of a cruel lord; and a fierce king shall rule over them, saith the Lord, the Lord of hosts.	A powerful and oppressive regime and leader will overtake the Egyptian government and rule in tyranny.
5: And the waters shall fail from the sea, and the river shall be wasted and dried up. **6:** And they shall turn the rivers far away; and the brooks of defence shall be emptied and dried up: the reeds and flags shall wither.	A drought will strike Egypt, severely damaging fishing and other major industries.
8: The fishers also shall mourn and all they that cast angle into the brooks shall lament, and they that spread nets upon the waters shall languish. **9:** Moreover they that work in fine flax, and they that weave networks, shall be confounded.	The fishing, fine flax, and weaving represent Egypt's major industries (fishing, linens, and cotton), and "to have all three fail would be a national calamity."[354]

11: Surely the princes of Zoan are fools, the counsel of the wise counsellors of Pharaoh is become brutish: how say ye unto Pharaoh, I am the son of the wise, the son of ancient kings? **12:** Where are they? Where are thy wise men? And let them tell thee now, and let them know what the Lord of hosts hath purposed upon Egypt. **13:** The princes of Zoan are become fools, the princes of Noph are deceived; they have also seduced Egypt, even they that are the stay of the tribes thereof. **14:** The Lord hath mingled a perverse spirit in the midst thereof: and they have caused Egypt to err in every work thereof, as a drunken man staggereth in his vomit.	This section "clearly promises that the leaders of Egypt's major centers would be as fools and unable to save their nation. Zoan was Tanis, Noph was Memphis, and No was Thebes."[355]
17: And the land of Judah shall be a terror unto Egypt, every one that maketh mention thereof shall be afraid in himself, because of the counsel of the Lord of hosts, which he hath determined against it.	This echoes fears experienced by Egyptians during conflicts with Israel in 1948, 1967, and 1973. Future conflicts may incite these conditions and feelings yet again.
18: In that day shall five cities in the land of Egypt speak the language of Canaan, and swear to the Lord of hosts; one shall be called, The city of destruction.	Relations between Egypt and Israel will improve. The act of swearing, as manifested by etymology of words in Semitic languages, is associated with oaths and covenants. The verse describes a time in the last days when Egyptians covenant with Jesus Christ, meaning that they practice the restored gospel. The "city of destruction" may be Heliopolis.[356]
19: In that day shall there be an altar to the Lord in the midst of the land of Egypt, and a pillar at the border thereof to the Lord. **20:** And it shall be for a sign and for a witness unto the Lord of hosts in the land of Egypt: for they shall cry unto the Lord because of the oppressors, and he shall send them a saviour, and a great one, and he shall deliver them. **21:** And the Lord shall be known to Egypt, and the Egyptians shall know the Lord in that day, and shall do sacrifice and oblation; yea, they shall vow a vow unto the Lord, and perform it.	The gospel will be preached in Egypt. The altar represents a temple. The pillar is often associated with the temple, as during the exodus, a pillar of cloud hovered over the camp by day, and at night it transformed into a pillar of fire over the tabernacle. Egyptians will pray unto God because of the tyrannical regime and they will be delivered, similar to other historical occurrences wherein the Lord humbled a group of people and later delivered them. The Egyptians will make covenants and faithfully keep them.

22: And the Lord shall smite Egypt: he shall smite and heal it: and they shall return even to the Lord, and he shall be entreated of them, and shall heal them.	
23: In that day shall there be a highway out of Egypt to Assyria, and the Assyrian shall come into Egypt, and the Egyptian into Assyria, and the Egyptians shall serve with the Assyrians.	There is no clear interpretation on this verse or the following verses. The described interactivity and exchange, though, reflects an alliance or strong association between "Egypt and Assyria (or the nations that inhabit those ancient territories)."[357]
24: In that day shall Israel be the third with Egypt and with Assyria, even a blessing in the midst of the land: **25:** Whom the Lord of hosts shall bless, saying, Blessed be Egypt my people, and Assyria the work of my hands, and Israel mine inheritance.	These final verses are "of particular interest to Latter-day Saints, for they promise that Egypt and other nations of that part of the world will embrace the restored gospel."[358] Egypt, Assyria, and Israel will form an alliance and the Egyptians will accept the restored gospel.

Throughout Isaiah 19, the author repeatedly uses the phrase "in that day" to "signal to the reader the parts of his vision that pertained to the last days," as that phrase "suggests future fulfillment."[359] These verses describe the construction and use of a temple within Egypt, wherein Egyptian Saints gather to make covenants with the Lord. Opposition will likely strike in various forms, as Satan is not the type to stand idly by as the gospel enters and flourishes in a country filled with people recently humbled by civil war, tyranny, and famine. Analyzing terrorism trends in Egypt and Satan's strategies in other areas where the gospel flourished provides insights about how terrorism may affect the Church in Egypt as events fulfill this prophecy.

Analysis of Competing Hypotheses to Assess Possible Terrorist Threats to the Church

One approach to analyze terrorism trends and determine how terrorism will most likely affect the Church's growth in Egypt is to apply the Analysis of Competing Hypotheses (ACH) tool. This methodology, developed by the Central Intelligence Agency in the 1970s, is a "procedure grounded in basic insights from cognitive psychology, decision analysis, and the scientific method," and helps to limit bias and remain objective when investigating a complex problem and trying to predict likely outcomes.[360] By developing a series of hypotheses and evaluating available evidence in terms of each hypotheses, one may assess which hypotheses are most likely to occur based on which ones have the most supporting evidence. In assessing future terrorism impacts on the Church in Egypt, the following hypotheses are included in the ACH model:

H1: Islamist groups will attempt to bomb the Latter-day Saint temple.

H2: Islamist groups will attempt to bomb Latter-day Saint chapels.

H3: Islamist groups will attempt to assassinate Latter-day Saint missionaries.

H4: Islamist groups will attempt to assassinate Latter-day Saint leaders (e.g., mission president, general authorities).

H5: Islamist groups will attempt to assault local (Egyptian) Latter-day Saint converts.

H6: Islamist groups will not target the Church.

While these hypotheses are not necessarily mutually exclusive, as terrorists could pursue multiple forms of targeting the Church, the ACH methodology aids in assessing the overall likelihood of each hypotheses occurring based on a series of assumptions and available evidence. One key assumption is that with the emergence and acceptance of the restored gospel in Egypt, Satan will resort to stirring rage in the hearts of men and fuel terrorism against the Church. This overt form of opposition is a shift from his usual subtle tactics in hindering conversion, but he resorted to violence and tactics commonly characterized as evil when missionaries enjoyed unprecedented success in Latin America in the late 1980s and early 1990s. Another key assumption is that despite a series of humbling experiences, including civil war, tyranny, and drought, terrorism tactics and trends attributable to Islamist groups in Egypt will continue at similar rates. Deep-seated extremist ideologies would likely persist through drastic political and economic changes, as Egypt is the birthplace of groups like the Muslim Brotherhood and where writers like Sayyid Qutb spread charged and divisive doctrines on *jahiliyyah* and other socially polarizing concepts. These assumptions posit that certain characteristics of terrorism will persist through regime changes and cultural transformations taking place among Egyptians in the future. Investigating prophecies and historical trends and contextual circumstances aids in assessing the likelihood of each hypothesis. Evidence relating to these hypotheses follows.

E1: Less than 3% of terrorism incidents in Egypt in the past nearly 50 years targeted religious figures/institutions.

Historically, most terrorism within Egypt targeted the military or facets of the public security apparatus, especially police forces. Such forms of terrorism grew with the Arab Spring, as citizens revolted against their oppressive governments throughout North Africa, including Egypt. Terror and intimidation against Christian groups, such as adherents of Coptic faiths, exists in relatively small amounts. Of the 2,214 terrorism attacks in Egypt between 1970 and 2016, only 58 targeted religious figures/institutions.[361]

The distribution of attacks against religious figures and institutions over time was generally constant until around 2013, when a marked increase occurred and held steady for the following three years. This increase mirrors similar proportional increases of attacks against other forms of targets during the same period, attributable to civil war conditions during the Arab Spring. Although data from recent decades suggests relatively few occurrences of terrorism targeting religious figures and institutions occurred, those conducting such attacks often employed brutal methods with high death tolls, intentionally targeting religious facilities during times of high concentration to inflict more casualties. Also, the emergence of a new Christian sect within Egypt may incite more attacks to drive out the new religion and intimidate locals not to join the group. While Satan focuses on inflicting spiritual damage to men and women through subtle means, he will break from character and incite openly destructive physical attacks through terrorism when necessary, as was evident in spikes of terrorism in certain missions and districts of Peru, Bolivia, and Chile, which were some of the most successful missions in the late 1980s. Since his crafty tactics targeting spiritual matters failed, he resorted to other means to disrupt the flourishing missionary work. Terrorism is just one weapon in his arsenal, and not a primary weapon, due to the ease of identifying terrorism as evil, lacking the ambiguity among some spiritual matters that societies may condone or permit. When the gospel flourishes in Egypt, though, as the prophecy states with the faithful covenant-keeping membership and a frequented temple, Satan will likely resort to terrorism in an attempt to thwart missionary work and oppose the spread of the restored gospel.

E2: The frequency of terrorism incidents in Egypt tends to increase during and after significant political change.

Incidents of terrorism in Egypt rose in early 2011, as the revolutionary wave originating in Tunisia and sweeping across North Africa known as the Arab Spring struck Egypt. Terrorism continued to rise and spiked during this phase of lawlessness as various leaders occupied the executive seat of the Egyptian government. Figure 10.1 displays the distribution of the 2,165 incidents of terrorism in Egypt between 1970 and 2016, as registered in the Global Terrorism Database.

Figure 10.1: Distribution of Terrorism Incidents in Egypt by Year (1970–2016)

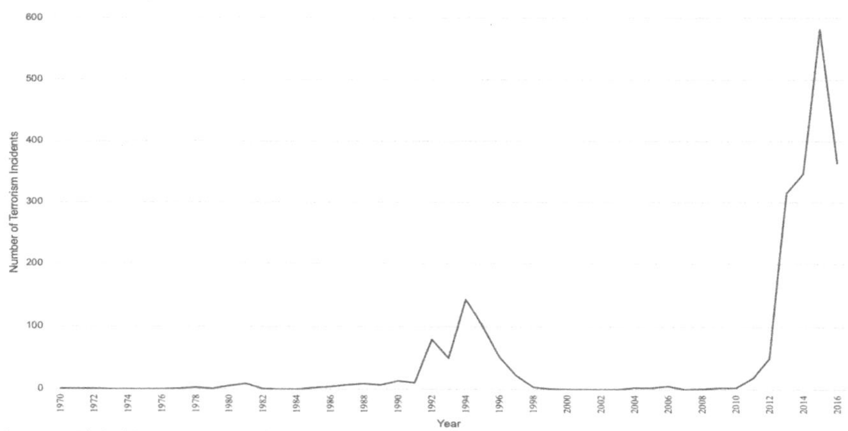

Source: Global Terrorism Database.

According to Isaiah 19:2, a civil war or significant internal strife will precede the Egyptians' acceptance of the gospel. The Egyptian crisis between 2011 and 2014 included regime changes between Hosni Mubarak, Mohamed Morsi, and Abdel Fattah el-Sisi, resulting from protests, a coup d' etat, and elections. Such political upheaval could mirror conditions of or partially fulfill this prophesy.

Significant political changes are necessary to help beckon the gospel and foster a political climate in Egypt within which the Church may emerge and grow. In 1980, Brother Thomas Parker, an attorney, "was appointed agent for the Church to pursue a petition with the Egyptian government to grant legal recognition of the Church."[362] The government permits Latter-day Saint members to congregate in homes and hold meetings, but members are not allowed to proselyte and the Church is not officially recognized. Despite these freedoms, Egyptian citizens who converted overseas and later returned to Egypt voiced concerns regarding the Egyptian government and attention from State Security. The US Department of State reported, "according to credible sources in the LDS community, citizen members sometimes avoid meetings out of fear of harassment from State Security."[363] A small Latter-day Saint presence in the country for over thirty years maintains one active branch in the entire country, generally consisting of foreigners who work in capacities as representatives of their foreign governments for political and business entities. The Egyptian government's formal recognition of the Church is a prerequisite for the fulfillment of prophecies of Egyptians accepting the gospel and constructing a temple, as described in Isaiah 19.

E3: Slightly more than 1% of terrorism incidents in Egypt in nearly the past 50 years targeted tourists.

Attacks targeting tourists are generally consistent and evenly distributed going back to 1970; there are no spikes or recent increases. This data is relevant because most Church members in Egypt are foreigners and as the Church enters and grows in Egypt, the demographics of membership will mostly reflect foreign members operating within Egypt, especially as missionaries enter the country. These demographics will change and become more balanced over time as convert baptisms increase, but initially, foreigners will dominate Church membership in Egypt. These circumstances following formal recognition of the Church would necessitate foreign missionaries being responsible for proselyting, similar to early Church growth in Latin America. Historically, North American missionaries in several Latin American countries were targeted for their affiliation to the United States, based on their race and recognizable uniform of a church headquartered in the United States. This low percentage of attacks targeting tourists, however, is inconsistent with hypotheses involving attacks against Latter-day Saint leadership and missionaries and does not suggest a strong threat to such members based on race or foreign status.

E4: Bombs and small arms are the most commonly used weapons in terrorist attacks within Egypt, accounting for the weapon type in over 90% of terrorism incidents.

Bombs and small arms have been the preferred weapons of choice among terrorists since the days of anarchists in Russia in the late 1800s. This trend continues in Egypt, where the vast majority of perpetrators used bombs or firearms. Between 1970 and 2016, 50 percent of the 2,214 terrorist attacks in Egypt involved explosives and 40 percent involved firearms.[364] These will likely remain the preferred weapon types in the era when the Church grows in Egypt. This evidence is very consistent with hypotheses involving bombings of structures or assassinations of leaders and missionaries (H1, H2, H3, and H4).

E5: In recent decades, few incidents of anti-US political violence occurred in Egypt.

Annual US Department of State reports reflect a relatively small number of anti-US political violence incidents in Egypt throughout recent decades. Most of the incidents targeted the US Embassy in Cairo, oftentimes beginning as protests and erupting into physical altercations with guards. Radical Islamists attempted to assassinate embassy personnel on other occasions and some bombed American restaurant chains and banks in protest of US Government actions. Individuals and groups carrying out this political violence against Americans

Figure 10.2: Number of Anti-US Political Violence Incidents in Egypt by Year

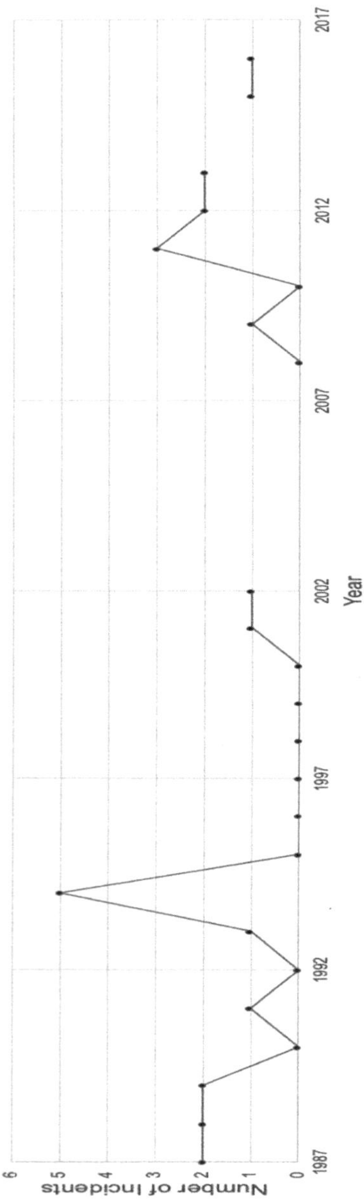

Source: Calculated using data from U.S. Department of State's annual "Significant Incidents of Political Violence Against Americans" between 1987 and 2016. There is no information available for years depicted on the graph lacking a data point.

preferred bombs and small arms, consistent with most other terrorism incidents in Egypt throughout recent decades. On multiple occasions, terrorists did not deliberately attack Americans; rather, some Americans affected by terrorism and accounted for in statistics were collateral damage of indiscriminate attacks. Figure 10.2 displays the frequency of anti-American political violence over time, as documented in annual reports by the US Department of State.

Information and circumstances of attacks indicate Egyptians conducting protests and attacks against the United States most often targeted the US Embassy due to symbolism associated with the prominent government facility. Occasionally, groups targeted American restaurants or other businesses due to accessibility and vulnerability. This characteristic of terrorism would suggest a Latter-day Saint temple might pose a new type of symbolic target against the United States, due to the Church's affiliation to the West and a temple's prominence among other buildings in an urban area like Cairo. Similarly, Latter-day Saint chapels marked with the common plaque in the native language announcing the building's religious purpose and might attract anti-US violence.

Alternatively, historical trends might suggest an inclination among Egyptian terrorists to target American missionaries. Of the American individuals targeted in violent attacks, several were in close proximity to the US Embassy when attacked, linking them to the United States, or were utilizing an embassy vehicle for transportation when attacked. Terrorists planning an attack against the United States for reasons of political protest might target American missionaries for their vulnerability and accessibility, as well as the ease of obtaining positive identification of targets by their appearance, including race, name tag, suit, and other distinct characteristics.

E6: Historically, monotheistic religions with missionaries tend to generate friction with other religions.

The inherent nature of missionary religions clashes with other faiths, as missionaries seek to convert atheists and adherents of other religions to save them from spiritual destruction. Adherents are often less tolerant than non-missionary or polytheistic faiths. In outlining concerns with missionary monotheistic religions and their likelihood of generating conflicts, terrorism studies expert Dr. Jeffrey Bale stated the following:

> "Missionary monotheistic religions insist that it is the duty of their followers to spread their faith throughout the world, whether by means of proselytizing and/or by having recourse to the sword, since they believe that it is meant for all of mankind rather than only a select ethno-cultural community. This attitude is almost guaranteed to generate friction or bring them into outright conflict with the adherents of other religions."[365]

Hence, Latter-day Saint proselyting in Egypt would likely clash with a culture dominated by Islam. Copts (another missionary monotheistic religion) are able to practice their religion in Egypt, but incidents of terrorism attest to the friction between these two faiths. These fundamentals of missionary religions and their inherent challenges to coexist are very consistent with hypotheses involving violence targeting the Church.

E7: Over 60% of religious targets in terrorism incidents in Egypt are Christian figures/institutions.

An Islamist aversion to Christianity accounts for the high percentage of attacks against Coptic and other Christian people and buildings. Nearly 65% of terrorist attacks against religious figures/institutions in Egypt targeted Christian persons or buildings.[366] These attacks mostly targeted Copts, a predominant Christian minority in Egypt, but also targeted Catholic and Evangelical churches.

Islamist groups have a strong presence within Egypt. These groups leverage preexisting sectarianism and further polarize society through propaganda. Even if such extremist factions do not endure some of the turbulent times ahead for Egypt, their ideologies will likely persist into the post-civil war and tyranny period to again incite violence against Christians. Cultural norms and practices contribute to this characteristic of terrorism targeting Christians. While some prejudice and intolerance may subside with new laws, Christian targets will likely remain the majority of religious targets for the foreseeable future. This evidence is very consistent with hypotheses of future terrorism targeting Latter-day Saints, missionaries, and Church facilities in Egypt.

E8: Egyptians targeted American businesses in protest of US Government policies based solely on their US affiliation.

Reports of terrorist attacks targeting American banks and restaurants in Egypt attribute violence to those institutions' affiliations with the United States. Similar trends occurred in other countries and on other continents, as perpetrators with anti-US sentiments targeted such buildings and businesses as symbols of the US on their soil—vulnerable targets they could attack in protest of US Government actions or policies. Chapels, missionaries, and members of the Church fall into this category of facilities and representatives under the umbrella of the US.

Despite the fact that the name of the Church does not list affiliation to the United States, people around the world know the Church was established and is headquartered in the United States. The majority of members live outside of the United States, yet perceptions link the Church to the United States. Rumors and conspiracy theories about missionaries serving as agents of the Intelligence Community and satellite dishes at stake centers sending and receiving intelligence reports only perpetuate misconceptions. With the prophesied emergence of the Church in Egypt, extremists with anti-US sentiments might attack Church buildings and representatives in similar symbolic attacks against the United States. In Latin America in the late 1980s, terrorists assassinated indigenous missionaries; even though they were not white North American missionaries, terrorists deemed them guilty by association to the United States as missionaries of a perceived North American church. Similarly, albeit less likely, terrorists in Egypt might even target local converts in addition to Latter-day Saint facilities and missionaries for this perceived link to the United States.

E9: Less than 10% of terrorism incidents in Egypt against religious targets involved assassination attempts of leaders.

Most attacks against religious institutions consisted of bombing buildings or shooting congregations, but a small number involved assassination attempts of specific religious figures. Victims in three of the five such attacks, described in Table 10.2, were Christians. Most terrorism against religious targets in Egypt is indiscriminate, using religion as a sole criterion, rather than age, gender, social status, or prominence within the church. Rarely did terrorists deliberately intend to kill a figurehead or specific member of the church or congregation.

These limited statistics reflect the mentality among extremists in Egypt to cause fear by indiscriminate attacks, wherein all adherents of a particular faith share equal likelihood of being targeted. This evidence suggests in future periods of increased Latter-day Saint presence in Egypt, terrorists would likely target members at chapels during services rather than plan and carry out an assassination attempt against a General Authority or local leader.

Table 10.2: Assassination Attempts Targeting Religious Figures in Egypt

Date	City	Target	Perpetrator	Motive	Success?	Description
25-Jul-92	Dayrut	Guard at church	Unknown	Unknown	Unknown	None.
13-Feb-97	Abu Qurqas	Coptic Christians	Al-Gama'at al-Islamiyya (IG)	Unknown	Unknown	None.
30-Sep-13	Abu Qorqas	Coptic Bishop: Anba Makarios	Muslim extremists	Speculated sectarian violence	No	Terrorists opened fire on target's vehicle
5-Aug-16	Sixth of October	Former Grand Mufti: Sheikh Ali Gomaa	Hasam Movement	Targeted for supporting the government	No	Terrorists opened fire on target, injuring body guard
6-Nov-16	Arish	Cleric: Shaykh Sulayman Abu Hiraz	Sinai Province of the Islamic State	Group believed target practiced witchcraft	Yes	Assailants abducted 100-yr old target and beheaded him

Source: Global Terrorism Database.

E10: Deliberate attacks against Americans generally involved those easily identifiable as Americans.

Most Americans involved in terrorism incidents within Egypt were not tourists or businessmen, but individuals easily identified as Americans by their employment at the US embassy. On multiple occasions, extremists conducted assassination attempts targeting embassy workers near the embassy or traveling in government vans.[367] Proximity to the embassy at the time of attacks attests to this conjecture that individuals were deliberately targeted for their affiliation to the United States, as some involved melee attacks against those standing in line to enter the embassy during work hours. In another instance, a man targeted the US defense attaché on a high-traffic road, trying to cut him off in traffic and hitting his vehicle with a club.[368] Although there is a small pool of incidents involving American victims, such data illustrates a trend among perpetrators to attack easily identifiable Americans, either as targets of opportunity or through detailed reconnaissance and establishing pattern of life for a specific target. The small number of American tourist victims of terrorism further substantiates this apparent tactic. This evidence suggests terrorists would target easily distinguishable Latter-day Saint missionaries in Egypt, wearing suits and name tags, and likely from a pool of white North American males. There is also a greater likelihood of an attack at constructed Latter-day Saint chapels or a temple, as opposed to a local shop doubling as a meetinghouse for religious services, which would better blend in and present a less distinguishable target.

E11: Apostasy in Islam is a punishable offense (sometimes, death) and perceived as *jahiliyyah*, deserving worse disgrace than that of non-believers.

Many Islamic governments in the Middle East incorporate some form of negative reinforcement into laws to deter Muslims from abandoning their faith or joining a different religion. In recent times, Egyptians punished converts under Egypt's Penal Code. Article 98(f) of Egypt's Penal Code, as amended by law 147, states, "whoever makes use of religion in propagating, either by words, in writing, or in any other means, extreme ideas for the purpose of incident strife, ridiculing or insulting a heavenly religion or a sect following it, or damaging national unity" is punishable with imprisonment or a hefty fine.[369] While the law does not list death as a punishment, interpretation of Article 2 of the Egyptian Constitution, enshrining Sharia law, may permit death. Under Sharia law, non-governmental groups or elders often mete out punishments under strict interpretation of the Qur'an, generally much more draconian in interpretation and brutal in punishment, especially for apostasy. The *Hisbah* doctrine, referring to accountability, is another facet of Islamic practices influencing conversion to the Church. This principle establishes the charge of governments and rulers to intervene and forcefully keep peace and good order under Sharia law, fulfilling the divine guidance of "enjoining what is right, forbidding what is wrong."[370] Hence, interpretation follows that leaders should enforce Sharia law and may coerce subjects to comply through punishment.

While the laws and policies regarding religion and proselyting must inevitably change in Egypt to permit the Church to officially enter and grow, culture may present challenges in assimilation and adjusting to the presence of a new Christian sect. These laws are based on deep-seated ideologies and norms, with extremist interpretations of *jahiliyyah* widely accepted and condoned within Egypt. Despite political changes in laws permitting church practices, and even humbling experiences like civil war and suffering under tyranny, some extremists would likely target the Church in the early period of formal recognition by the Egyptian government and growth in the following years.

Although missionaries have entered parts of the Middle East in past decades, including Iran and Lebanon, few people in that region have heard the restored gospel. There are inherent risks associated with conversion due to cultural norms, explaining why in Iran, for instance, "few Iranians embraced Mormonism (about 15 altogether)" for the potential backlash of "ostracism, unemployment, disinheritance, and even threat of death."[371] Egyptian investigators would undoubtedly face similar dilemmas in converting to the Church. Even so, Muslims in Western countries still face risks in joining the Church if they associate with other Muslims. Such is the case in Germany, the European country with the greatest number of modern-day refugees from war-torn countries like Syria, Iraq, and Afghanistan.

E12: To date, there are no publicly documented instances of terrorism against the Church in Egypt.

The Egyptian government has not yet formally recognized The Church of Jesus Christ of Latter-day Saints, despite Church efforts over multiple decades. There remains only one branch in Egypt, consisting mainly of foreigners and occasional converts who joined the Church in another country and later returned to Egypt.[372] This small group of members has not fallen victim to terrorism, according to publicly available information. While this constitutes a very small sample pool, this evidence suggests the member body present in Egypt may not have been easily identifiable as Latter-day Saint members by not meeting in a chapel constructed by the Church with a visible label on the side of the building. Likewise, there is no proselyting missionary presence. A circumstantial factor worth consideration is the lack of terrorism in Latin America in periods of early Church presence. Terrorism did not strike areas like Chile until times of drastic growth. The subsequent terrorism associated with Church growth and construction of chapels became known as the "boom years," in multiple senses of the word.[373] Hence, the lack of terrorism targeting the Church in Egypt is likely attributable to a very small physical and symbolic presence; this will surely change and the Church will likely encounter opposition during periods of prophesied growth.

Analysis: Analysis of Competing Hypotheses suggests H2 is the most likely scenario for terrorism targeting the Church in Egypt in the future.

Applying the ACH methodology is one way to mitigate bias and generate objective analysis regarding future attacks. Each sampling of evidence supports or refutes each hypothesis in varying degrees, ranging from evidence inconsistent with a hypothesis, refuting the likelihood of certain attacks, to evidence very consistent with a hypothesis, strongly supporting the likelihood of other attacks.

According to evidence from available data, the most likely hypothesis on future terror threats to The Church of Jesus Christ of Latter-day Saints in Egypt is H2, involving terrorist groups attempting to bomb Latter-day Saint chapels. These religious structures are easily identifiable as Christian worship centers, with the visible label on the outside of the chapel including the name Jesus Christ and the architectural style being clearly distinct and different from minarets of mosques or architectural features of other religious groups. Chapels are a hub for

Table 10.3: ACH for Possible Terrorist Threats to the Church in Egypt

NA	Not Applicable
I	Inconsistent
N	Neutral
C	Consistent
VC	Very Consistent

	H1	H2	H3	H4	H5	H6
E1	I	I	I	I	I	C
E2	VC	VC	VC	VC	VC	I
E3	NA	NA	I	I	NA	N
E4	C	VC	VC	C	VC	I
E5	I	I	I	I	N	C
E6	C	C	VC	C	N	I
E7	VC	VC	VC	VC	VC	I
E8	VC	VC	VC	VC	C	I
E9	NA	NA	I	I	NA	C
E10	VC	VC	VC	C	N	I
E11	C	VC	C	N	VC	I
E12	N	N	N	I	I	C

religious activity during activities and worship services. This makes these structures a high payoff target, as terrorists can achieve high mortality rates in an attack due to higher concentrations of worshippers. Bombing chapels poses fewer risks to perpetrators, who may emplace a bomb and achieve adequate standoff prior to detonation to avoid injury and evade capture. Terrorists may bomb these structures in symbolic attacks against the US Government for unpopular policies, due to the Church's perceived affiliation with the United States.

All Missionaries Withdrawn from Assignments Abroad

A separate prophecy indicates there will come a time when missionaries will be called home from service abroad, as the Times of the Gentiles closes and the Lord transitions from a warning voice of preaching to meting out punishments prior to the Second Coming. Concerning this topic, the Prophet Brigham Young once said the following (italics added):

> "Do you think there is calamity abroad now among the people? Not much. All we have yet heard and all we have experienced is scarcely a preface to the sermon that is going to be preached. *When the testimony of the Elders ceases to be given, and the Lord says to them, 'Come home; I will now preach my own sermons to the nations of the earth,'* all you now know can scarcely be called a preface to the sermon that will be preached with fire and sword, tempests, earthquakes, hail, rain, thunders and lightnings, and fearful destruction. What matters the destruction of a few railway cars? You will hear of magnificent cities, now idolized by the people, sinking in the earth, entombing the inhabitants. The sea will heave itself beyond its bounds, engulfing mighty cities. Famine will spread over the nations, and *nation will rise up against nation, kingdom against kingdom, and states against states, in our own country and in foreign lands; and they will destroy each other, caring not for the blood and lives of their neighbors, of their families, or for their own lives.* They will be like the Jaredites who preceded the Nephites upon this continent, and will destroy each other to the last man, through the anger that the Devil will place in their hearts, because they have rejected the words of life and are given over to Satan to do whatever he listeth to do with them. You may think that the little you hear of now is grievous; yet the faithful of God's people will see days that will cause them to close their eyes because of the sorrow that will come upon the wicked nations. The hearts of the faithful will be filled with pain and anguish for them."[374]

This recall of all missionaries will safeguard them from much of the pending destruction, removing them from areas affected by several calamities described by Brigham Young following this suspense of missionary work. Even so, war and other destructive forces will likely increase in the period leading up to this missionary withdrawal, probably affecting missionaries and members throughout the world in various ways. Another prophecy concerning this time period, shared by Heber C. Kimball, is as follows:

> "The judgments of God will be poured out upon the wicked to the extent that our elders from far and near will be called home. Or, in other words, the gospel will be taken from the Gentiles and later on will be carried to the Jews."[375]

This second prophecy elaborates on Brigham Young's words, suggesting the severity and extent of destruction will require missionaries return home so as to avoid harm. Throughout recent history, terrorism has played an increasingly prominent role in contributing to death tolls worldwide. In many senses, terrorism is imbedded with other forms of conventional warfare, leading US Army training centers and doctrine to move away from force-on-force battles of conventional armies and focus on hybrid warfare, a blend of both conventional and unconventional threats, such as terrorist groups. Worldwide statistics for incidents meeting criteria to be defined as acts of terrorism reflect a rise in terrorism incident frequency over time. The frequency of terrorism incidents and associated death tolls will likely remain high or continue to generally rise over time as governments collapse, nations engage in war or suffer from internal strife, economies fail, natural disasters plunge communities into chaos, and other calamities strike. While missionaries and members will likely not escape all the physical harm associated with terrorism during this period, time lines revealed in relevant prophecies indicate missionaries will avoid most of these calamities during their foreign assignments.

Israel and the Two Witnesses

The Holy Land has been a hot spot for dedicatory prayers throughout this dispensation. Orson Hyde pronounced the first dedicatory prayer over the Holy Land on October 24, 1841, focused on the gathering of Israel. Of the eleven apostolic blessings pronounced over the Holy Land since the restoration of the gospel, John A. Widtsoe of the Quorum of the Twelve Apostles performed the two most recent blessings in 1933 in Haifa and Jerusalem, wherein he "prayed that the enemies of the Church would be confounded."[376] The Lord honored this petition for protection on many occasions.

In recent decades, the Church has had a small presence in the Holy Land. That presence has encountered opposition. For instance, two policemen and two policewomen were injured on August 8, 1985 while dispersing a demonstration of nearly 200 Jewish zealots that gathered to protest a Latter-day Saint delegation visiting Israel to discuss the construction of a Brigham Young University center in Jerusalem.[377] When General Authorities dedicated the BYU Jerusalem Center, opposition developed again, and a bomb threat surfaced. Despite the concentrated Latter-day Saint presence associated with the BYU Jerusalem Center, there is no proselyting, as there are strict policies in place to prohibit proselyting. When Israel permits the preaching of the restored gospel once again, General Authorities may rededicate the land for missionary work. As each of these historical dedications contained petitions specific to the challenges of those times, such as the welfare of the Church and confounding the Church's enemies, future dedicatory prayers might address terrorism in some way and staying the hand of Satan from the Lord's representatives in the Holy Land.

There is a possibility that the prophesied martyrdom of the two witnesses mentioned in Revelation 11 will be the result of an act of terrorism. In a land where small arms attacks and stabbings by lone wolf terrorists and small groups is routine, this is a feasible possibility. The ministry of these two witnesses equates to nearly three-and-a-half years, comparable to Christ's formal ministry in the Holy Land according to scripture, estimated by most experts to be slightly over three years.

Elder Bruce R. McConkie remarked that the aforementioned witnesses are,

> "Followers of that humble man Joseph Smith, through whom the Lord of Heaven restored the fullness of his everlasting gospel in this final dispensation of grace. No doubt they will be members of the Council of the Twelve or of the First Presidency of the Church."[378]

Based on interpretation of the relevant prophecy in scripture, these modern leaders of the Church will succumb to physical opposition resulting in martyrdom while in Israel, and, given the commonplace nature of violence, lone wolf and small group attacks, and unsophisticated weapons, terrorism may be the cause of their martyrdom.

Conclusion

Saints will inevitably encounter terrorism in the future, whether through indiscriminate attacks or as targets of those with ill will toward the United States or the Church itself. This form of violence has become commonplace as people seek to uproot institutional foundations and supplant the government with their own political constructs. As we approach the Second Coming, terrorism is but one of the many aspects of turmoil expected to increase in magnitude and frequency.

Due to the nature of predicting future events, analysis can only yield likely threats to anticipate based on limited available evidence, constructing an incomplete and blurry picture of what may actually play out. Thinktanks, intelligence agencies, and other government entities—even those employing machine learning and computer simulations to mitigate bias and human error—have failed to anticipate terrorist attacks or actions by rival governments due to the complexities of human nature and factors influencing an enemy's actions. Luckily, however, a prophet of God and personal revelation provide reliable and unerring guidance in these perilous times. The Lord has consistently guided church leaders—the prophet, mission presidents and local leaders—to take actions to prevent or respond to terrorism. Obeying the Lord's instruction and striving for personal worthiness are the best defenses against whatever Satan may try to incite in the hearts of men.

APPENDIX A

CHRONOLOGICAL LIST OF TERRORISM INCIDENTS TARGETING THE CHURCH OF JESUS CHRIST OF LATTER-DAY SAINTS

Note: This list contains events targeting The Church of Jesus Christ of Latter-day Saints deemed terrorist incidents based on available evidence. Events are those for which there is strong evidence about a specific date or range of days, as well as details regarding location (at least city or village, if not a specific address or neighborhood). Categorization is based on consistency with definitions used by the National Consortium for the Study of Terrorism and Responses to Terrorism (START), the US Department of State, and facets of definitions used by other organizations and entities (refer to Introduction for more information on criteria and other considerations). Most incidents are included in the Global Terrorism Database (GTD) and/or the RAND Database of Worldwide Terrorism Incidents (RDWTI), but this appendix also includes additional events based on evidence in favor of categorization as terrorism incidents.

June 30, 1983—Bucaramanga, Colombia

The ELN claimed responsibility for three bombings of targets linked to the United States, including the Church. Pamphlets at the scenes stated the purpose of the attacks was to "support the heroic struggle of the ELN's Central American brothers against Yankee imperialism," coming in the wake of American intervention in nearby conflicts. The dynamite attacks caused damages upwards of three million pesos but did not cause any casualties.[379]

November 28, 1983—Bucaramanga, Colombia

The ELN bombed a Latter-day Saint chapel as part of a series of five bombings targeting Latter-day Saint chapels with eight bombs during dawn. There were no casualties, but the explosion caused a fire with damages totaling around $110,000. According to police, the assailants gagged the watchmen in the chapel, painted slogans on the walls, and left behind an ELN flag.[380]

November 28, 1983—Bucaramanga, Colombia (second attack)

The ELN bombed a Latter-day Saint chapel as part of a series of five bombings targeting Latter-day Saint chapels with eight bombs during dawn. There were no casualties, but the explosion caused a fire with damages totaling around $110,000. The assailants painted slogans on church walls and left behind an ELN flag.[381]

November 28, 1983—Bucaramanga, Colombia (third attack)

The ELN bombed a Latter-day Saint chapel as part of a series of five bombings targeting Latter-day Saint chapels with eight bombs during dawn. There were no casualties, but the explosion caused a fire with damages totaling around $110,000. The assailants painted slogans on church walls and left behind an ELN flag.[382]

November 28, 1983—Bucaramanga, Colombia (fourth attack)

The ELN bombed the Diamante meetinghouse as part of a series of five bombings targeting Latter-day Saint chapels with eight bombs during dawn. There were no casualties, but the explosion caused a fire with damages totaling around $80,000, including damaged classrooms, restrooms, and the main chapel. The assailants painted slogans on church walls and left behind an ELN flag.[383]

November 28, 1983—Bucaramanga, Colombia (fifth attack)

The ELN bombed the Canaveral meetinghouse as part of a series of five bombings targeting Latter-day Saint chapels with eight bombs during dawn. There were no casualties, but the explosion caused a fire with damages totaling around $60,000, including a damaged bathroom and office area and a collapsed roof. The assailants painted slogans on church walls and left behind an ELN flag.[384]

December 21, 1984—Medellin, Colombia

An explosive (unknown substance) detonated at a Latter-day Saint chapel, causing one injury and property damage (unknown extent and value).[385]

July 4, 1985—Santiago, Chile

A bomb detonated at a Latter-day Saint chapel, causing zero injuries. The FPMR claimed responsibility for other bombings that week targeting five nearby Latter-day Saint churches, regarding these chapels as spearheads for the US secret service. No one was injured. Pamphlets left at scenes and slogans written on walls read, "Yanks out of Chile" and "Easter Island, Chilean territory," referencing a US plan to use the Pacific island as an emergency landing site for a space shuttle."[386]

July 4, 1985—Santiago, Chile (second attack)

A bomb detonated at a Latter-day Saint chapel, causing zero injuries. The FPMR claimed responsibility for other bombings that week targeting five nearby Latter-day Saint churches, regarding these chapels as spearheads for the US Secret Service. No one was injured. Pamphlets left at scenes and slogans written on walls read, "Yanks out of Chile" and "Easter Island, Chilean territory," referencing a US plan to use the Pacific island as an emergency landing site for a space shuttle.[387]

July 4, 1985—Santiago, Chile (third attack)

A bomb detonated at a Latter-day Saint chapel, causing zero injuries. The FPMR claimed responsibility for other bombings that week targeting five nearby Latter-day Saint churches, regarding these chapels as spearheads for the US Secret Service. No one was injured. Pamphlets left at scenes and slogans written on walls read, "Yanks out of Chile" and "Easter Island, Chilean territory," referencing a US plan to use the Pacific island as an emergency landing site for a space shuttle.[388]

July 4, 1985—Santiago, Chile (fourth attack)

A bomb detonated at a Latter-day Saint chapel, causing zero injuries. The FPMR claimed responsibility for other bombings that week targeting five nearby Latter-day Saint churches, regarding these chapels as spearheads for the US Secret Service. No one was injured. Pamphlets left at scenes and slogans written on walls read, "Yanks out of Chile" and "Easter Island, Chilean territory," referencing a US plan to use the Pacific island as an emergency landing site for a space shuttle.[389]

July 4, 1985—Coronel, Chile

One to four explosions took place at a Latter-day Saint chapel. The FPMR claimed responsibility for other bombings that week targeting five nearby Latter-day Saint churches, regarding these chapels as spearheads for the US Secret Service. No one was injured. Pamphlets left at scenes and slogans written on walls read, "Yanks out of Chile" and "Easter Island, Chilean territory," referencing a US plan to use the Pacific island as an emergency landing site for a space shuttle.[390]

July 4, 1985—Lota, Chile

A bomb detonated at a Latter-day Saint chapel, causing zero injuries. The FPMR claimed responsibility for other bombings that week targeting five nearby Latter-day Saint churches, regarding these chapels as spearheads for the US Secret Service. No one was injured. Pamphlets left at scenes and slogans written on walls read, "Yanks out of Chile" and "Easter Island, Chilean territory," referencing a US plan to use the Pacific island as an emergency landing site for a space shuttle.[391]

July 4, 1985—Concepcion, Chile

A bomb detonated near the front entrance of a Latter-day Saint chapel. The blast blew windows out of adjoining buildings and caused an estimated $5,000 in damages. No one was injured.[392]

July 4, 1985—Antofagasta, Chile

A bomb detonated at a Latter-day Saint chapel. The FPMR claimed responsibility for bombings during the same week targeting five other Latter-day Saint churches in other areas, regarding these chapels as spearheads for the US Secret Service. No one was injured. Pamphlets left at scenes and slogans written on walls read, "Yanks out of Chile" and "Easter Island, Chilean territory," referencing a US plan to use the Pacific island as an emergency landing site for a space shuttle.[393]

March 27–28, 1986—Santiago, Chile

A bomb detonated in a Latter-day Saint chapel, starting a fire that caused moderate damage (unknown extent or value) before firefighters put out the fire.[394]

April 19, 1986—Caracas, Venezuela

An explosive (unknown substance) detonated at a Latter-day Saint chapel in Puerto Ordaz, in southeast Venezuela. The detonation caused property damage (unknown extent and value) and zero casualties, but the terrorist who carried out the attack was seriously injured. The assessed motive was to protest US attacks on two Libyan cities.[395]

April 22, 1986—Santiago, Chile

A gelignite bomb detonated outside a Latter-day Saint chapel (one of four different Latter-day Saint chapels bombed that day), totaling $18,000 in damages to entrances and windows across all chapels.

Explosions caused zero casualties. The suspected motive was to protest against the United States.[396]

April 22, 1986—Santiago, Chile (second attack)

A gelignite bomb detonated outside a Latter-day Saint chapel (one of four different Latter-day Saint chapels bombed that day), totaling $18,000 in damages to entrances and windows across all chapels. Explosions caused zero casualties. The suspected motive was to protest against the United States.[397]

April 22, 1986—Santiago, Chile (third attack)

A gelignite bomb detonated outside a Latter-day Saint chapel (one of four different Latter-day Saint chapels bombed that day), totaling $18,000 in damages to entrances and windows across all chapels. Explosions caused zero casualties. The suspected motive was to protest against the United States.[398]

April 22, 1986—Santiago, Chile (fourth attack)

A gelignite bomb detonated outside a Latter-day Saint chapel (one of four different Latter-day Saint chapels bombed that day), totaling $18,000 in damages to entrances and windows across all chapels. Explosions caused zero casualties. The suspected motive was to protest against the United States.[399]

April 22, 1986—Santiago, Chile (fifth attack)

A gelignite bomb detonated outside a Latter-day Saint chapel (one of four different Latter-day Saint chapels bombed that day), totaling $18,000 in damages to entrances and windows across all chapels. Explosions caused zero casualties. The suspected motive was to protest against the United States.[400]

June 26, 1986—Pereira, Colombia

The ELN and the Eloy Alfaro Popular Armed Forces (members of the self-styled America Battalion) claimed responsibility for bombing a Latter-day Saint chapel in Pereira. The attack caused costly property damage and zero casualties. The attack was in conjunction with another bombing targeting a different Latter-day Saint chapel and government targets in nearby cities.[401]

June 26, 1986—Calarca, Colombia

The ELN and the Eloy Alfaro Popular Armed Forces (members of the self-styled America Battalion) claimed responsibility for bombing a Latter-day Saint chapel in Calarca. The attack caused costly property damage and zero casualties. The attack was in conjunction with another bombing targeting a different Latter-day Saint chapel and government targets in nearby cities.[402]

December 16-23, 1986—Santiago, Chile

The FPMR bombed (unknown substance) a Latter-day Saint chapel, causing property damage (extent and value unknown) and zero causalities.[403]

April 28, 1987—Santiago, Dominican Republic

The Maximiliano Gomez Revolutionary Brigade claimed responsibility for one to three homemade bombs thrown at a Latter-day Saint chapel, causing property damage. The attack coincided with a bombing of a separate Latter-day Saint chapel and commemorated the anniversary of the April 28, 1965 US troop invasion of the Dominican Republic.[404]

April 28, 1987—Santiago, Dominican Republic (second attack)

The Maximiliano Gomez Revolutionary Brigade claimed responsibility for one to three homemade bombs thrown at a Latter-day Saint building, causing property damage. The attack coincided with a bombing of a separate Latter-day Saint chapel and commemorated the anniversary of the April 28, 1965 US troop invasion of the Dominican Republic.[405]

April 28, 1987—San Francisco de Macoris, Dominican Republic

The Maximiliano Gomez Revolutionary Brigade claimed responsibility for a bomb thrown from a motorcycle at a Latter-day Saint chapel, damaging a wall and windows. The attack commemorated the 12th anniversary of the April 24, 1965 US troop invasion of the Dominican Republic.[406]

April 28, 1987—Barahona, Dominican Republic

The Maximiliano Gomez Revolutionary Brigade claimed responsibility for an explosion at a Latter-day Saint chapel. The attack commemorated the anniversary of the April 28, 1965 US troop invasion of the Dominican Republic.[407]

April 28, 1987—Azua, Dominican Republic

The Maximiliano Gomez Revolutionary Brigade claimed responsibility for smashing the car of a Latter-day Saint missionary while the car was parked in front of a Latter-day Saint chapel, commemorating the anniversary of the April 28, 1965 US troop invasion of the Dominican Republic.[408]

April 28, 1987—Santo Domingo, Dominican Republic

Youths of the Maximiliano Gomez Revolutionary Brigade claimed responsibility for vandalizing a Latter-day Saint chapel in a working-class neighborhood. The attack commemorated the 12th anniversary of the April 24, 1965 US troop invasion of the Dominican Republic.[409]

April 29, 1987—Santo Domingo, Dominican Republic

In an anonymous phone call to the evening newspaper ULTIMA HORA, the Maximiliano Gomez Revolutionary Brigade claimed responsibility for an attack against a Latter-day Saint chapel in La Vega, commemorating the anniversary of the April 28, 1965 US troop invasion of the Dominican Republic.[410]

June 24, 1987—Santiago, Chile

A bomb, believed to be 400 grams of ammonium gel, exploded in front of a Latter-day Saint chapel, breaking windows within a 100-meter radius of the blast, but causing zero casualties. No group claimed responsibility.[411]

June 27-29, 1987—Santiago, Chile

A bomb exploded at the perimeter gate of a Latter-day Saint chapel, causing limited damage to the gate and zero casualties. No group claimed responsibility for the attack.[412]

July 9, 1987—Concepcion, Chile

A powerful bomb exploded at the entrance of a Latter-day Saint chapel, causing extensive property damage to the chapel and six houses nearby, but inflicting zero casualties.[413]

July 12, 1987—Santiago, Chile

A Molotov cocktail was thrown against a Latter-day Saint chapel's front wall in Puente Alto, causing minimal property damage and no casualties. On the chapel's wall was written, "Out of the common peoples' territories Yankee invaders." No group claimed responsibility.[414]

July 29, 1987—Santiago, Chile

Five Molotov cocktails were thrown at a Latter-day Saint chapel, and then the assailants broke into the chapel through one of the windows and threw incendiary devices throughout the building, destroying five rooms by fire and causing approximately $25,000 in damage and zero casualties. No group claimed responsibility for the attack.[415]

October 29, 1987—Tunja, Colombia

At 8:30 a.m., members of the ELN utilized dynamite to bomb a Latter-day Saint church at the intersection of Calle 12 with Carrera 10 in the Aquimin neighborhood. The explosion could be heard throughout a large portion of the city and damaged the electrical energy system and part of the Latter-day Saint chapel (extent and value unknown). One woman was slightly injured. The attack occurred in conjunction with two other attacks. The perpetrators left ELN propaganda at the site.[416]

October 29, 1987—Duitama, Colombia

Slightly after 8:30 a.m., members of the ELN bombed a Latter-day Saint church with dynamite. The perpetrators hid the bomb beneath rags or cloths near the building entrance. The detonation destroyed the windows and two entrance doors nearby, but none of the 17 parishioners within the chapel were injured. The attack occurred in conjunction with two other attacks. The perpetrators left ELN propaganda at the site.[417]

October 29, 1987—Sogamoso, Colombia

Sometime after 8:30 a.m., a bomb containing dynamite detonated near a Latter-day Saint chapel. The explosion gravely injured Pedro Cárdenas, a worker at the Acerias Paz del Rio steel mill, who attempted to emplace the bomb near the chapel. The ELN claimed responsibility for the attack, as well as two others that occurred in conjunction with this bombing.[418]

November 6, 1987—Santiago, Chile

Three members of the MJL claimed responsibility for multiple incendiary devices thrown at the perimeter wall of a Latter-day Saint chapel in Puente Alto, causing minor property damage and zero casualties.

On one of the chapel walls, the assailants wrote, "Fuera Yankis America Rebelde Vencera Juventud Lautaro" (Yankees Out! Rebel America Will Win, Signed Lautaro Youth).[419]

November 18, 1987—Santiago, Chile

An unspecified number of individuals threw a Molotov cocktail inside a Latter-day Saint chapel in La Florida, causing minor property damage and zero casualties. Three unignited Molotov cocktails and pamphlets were discovered near the chapel. Leaflets found in the area were signed by the MJL and contained the slogans, "Yankees Out" and "Che Lives."[420]

December 8–9, 1987—Copiapo, Chile

Unknown assailants detonated a bomb on the front lawn of a Latter-day Saint chapel at the intersection of Mendez and Rodriguez Street, breaking at least 16 panels in the building and seriously damaging the chapel's flagpole. The bomb consisted of about 400 grams of ammonium gelignite. The explosion did not cause any injuries.[421]

December 10, 1987—Santiago, Chile

Four men threw Molotov cocktails and a burning tire at a Latter-day Saint chapel at the intersection of Vicente Valdes and Juan Pineda Streets in La Florida. Pamphlets at the attack site read, "Rebel youth for victory and a plentiful life, Lautaro Youth Movement's 5th Anniversary."[422]

January 15, 1988—Avellaneda, Argentina

A bomb detonated at a Latter-day Saint chapel at approximately 3:30 a.m., causing property damage (extent and value unknown) and zero casualties. No group claimed responsibility for the attack.[423]

July 8, 1988—La Paz, Bolivia

A bomb exploded at a Latter-day Saint chapel located in the Victoria. The assailants cut through the metal perimeter gate to plant the bomb at the chapel entrance. They also threw paint-filled balloons against the building and spray-painted "Yankees Out of Bolivia" and "CIA agents" on the chapel walls. The explosion damaged the front doors and 15 windows but caused zero injuries. No group claimed responsibility.[424]

July 8, 1988—La Paz, Bolivia (second attack)

An early morning seminary student discovered a package at a Latter-day Saint chapel in the Alto San Pedro section of La Paz. He took the package home where his father immediately called the police. The bomb, contained within the package, miraculously did not explode and the father and son turned the bomb over to the police. There were no injuries. No group claimed responsibility.[425]

July 19, 1988—Valparaiso, Chile

A bomb detonated near the rear entrance of a Latter-day Saint chapel at 485 Admiral Montt in the Cerro Alegre neighborhood of Valparaiso. The bomb consisted of 800 grams of ammonium gelignite. The bomb caused extensive damage to the building's walls and windows. Additionally, the explosion injured three minors who were inside the building when the detonation occurred. Luis Herrera, 15, and Miguel Salazar, 16, sustained minor injuries to their legs and rested at home on the following days. The other minor, Nelson Perez, 13, suffered a broken arm and received medical care at the Valparaiso first aid clinic. No group claimed responsibility for the attack.[426]

August 23, 1988—Concepcion, Chile

A bomb detonated at the Latter-day Saint chapel at 3856 Gomez Carreno Street in Talcahuano, causing property damage valued at approximately 50,000 pesos, which included the destruction of a wall, the roof, and the windows of the church. The explosion did not cause any injuries. Local police determined that the bomb contained 50 grams of ANFO blasting agents and a slow fuse.[427]

November 25, 1988—Coquimbo, Chile

Two individuals wearing ski masks, likely members of the FPMR, threw two Molotov cocktails inside a Latter-day Saint chapel at 526 Manuel Jesus Rivera Street of San Juan, causing little property damage and zero casualties.[428]

March 23, 1989—Tarija, Bolivia

At about 1:30 a.m., a bomb containing dynamite detonated on the windowsill of a Latter-day Saint chapel on Abaroa Street, Villa Fatima. The explosion caused property damage (extent and value unknown) and zero casualties. The Zarate Willka Armed Forces Liberation was likely responsible.[429]

May 24, 1989—La Paz, Bolivia

At about 10:20 p.m., members of the Zarate Willka Armed Forces Liberation assassinated two Latter-day Saint missionaries, Elder Jeffrey Ball and Elder Todd Wilson, as the missionaries entered their residence. Both died almost instantly. Autopsies revealed that one of the victims sustained four 9.65 mm bullet wounds, meaning the terrorists likely used Uzi submachine guns. Thirty minutes after the attack, two La Paz newspapers received a note from the Zarate Willka Armed Forces Liberation, in which the group claimed responsibility, conducting the attack in protest of US violation of political sovereignty. The attack coincided with the arrival in Bolivia of the first contingent of US military engineers, technicians, and troops, charged with leveling Patti-Patti Hill to construct an airport for the city of Potosi. A Church spokesman stated that the previous year, a dynamite bomb was placed at a Latter-day Saint chapel in the same area as the assassination, but the perpetrators were never found. The assassinations prompted an emergency meeting of the Bolivian Police high command, who, less than 40 hours after the assassinations, declared an emergency state for all cadre in an effort to capture the assailants.[430]

July 2, 1989—Santiago, Chile

Unknown perpetrators (suspected to be members of the MJL) attacked a Latter-day Saint chapel with an explosive device and guns.[431]

July 4, 1989—Santiago, Chile

Members of the MJL conducted an attack targeting a Latter-day Saint chapel at 9531 Santa Raquel Street in the La Florida district of Santiago. Seven unmasked youths carrying revolvers invaded the chapel and encountered two missionaries teaching seminary. The armed group took hostages, holding 14 people at gunpoint. One of the missionaries was older and had been trained in hostage negotiation. He was able to convince the assailants to release the hostages. The group then forced the missionaries to strip, one of which was an American missionary named Balart. They used the missionaries' clothing to set the building on fire, dousing the cultural hall with gasoline and setting it aflame. The missionaries then called the mission president to report the incident. The fire destroyed stage curtains, a sound system, and damaged some ceiling tiles, causing around $12,000 worth of damages. The terrorists also left a bomb, which police later defused. They left subversive leaflets in which they claimed responsibility for the attack and then fled. Subsequently, the Fifth Santiago Appellate Court indicted Marco Antonio Mardones Villarroel (28) and Jorge Leandro ("Omar") Escobar Diaz (24) for violating Article 1, Paragraph 6, of the Antiterrorist Law that punishes those involved in arson or who plant explosive devices. Police apprehended a third perpetrator, who was under age 17 and considered a juvenile.[432]

July 10, 1989—Santa Cruz, Bolivia

At about 10:15 p.m., a powerful bomb containing dynamite exploded inside a Latter-day Saint chapel on Aleman Avenue of Santa Cruz de la Sierra belonging to the Hamacas Ward, Paraiso Stake. Media reports in La Paz stated the bomb was activated electronically. The detonation shook the concrete foundations of the building, causing extensive property damage, ripping eight doors off the hinges, destroying the front entrance, and breaking windows. President Erwin Birnbaumer of the Santa Cruz Paraiso Stake estimated damages at around $16,000, and also reported that a guard force was hired to watch that meetinghouse and others in the area. Edgar Rada, spokesman for the Church in La Paz, stated there were zero casualties. Parishioners and neighbors speculated the bomb was placed inside the chapel earlier that night during a service. Some neighbors said they saw a white car trying to escape following the detonation, but it crashed into a wall and a person exited and boarded a bus. A La Paz newspaper reported that at 5:00 p.m. the following day, the press office of the Santa Cruz Government center received a call wherein the Zarate Willka Armed Forces Liberation claimed responsibility. The group had voiced their plan to attack the Church one week prior to the bombing, threatening to attack unless four jailed group members were released from prison. Rada stated that the Santa Cruz church received no warning of the bomb. Police guards were hired to watch the chapel and other buildings in the city.[433]

July 14–15, 1989—Santiago, Chile

Unknown perpetrators threw an incendiary bomb at a Latter-day Saint chapel on the corner of Vicuna Mackenna and Mirador Azul Streets, in front of bus stop no. 10. The fire department of the Nunoa District brought the fire under control, but the bomb destroyed the entire meeting hall and part of the school operating at the site. There were no casualties.[434]

July 15, 1989—Santiago, Chile

Around 8:15 a.m., two armed men of the Lautaro Youth Movement set a Latter-day Saint chapel in La Florida on fire. It is possible the men were already hiding within the chapel when a custodian opened the building. The men used flammable liquids to set the arson, causing extensive property damage and zero casualties. The entire roof and a large room were burned. The men left several Popular Rebellion Front Lautaro propaganda leaflets in the chapel.[435]

July 20, 1989—Osorno, Chile

At about 8:00 p.m., an unknown number of individuals belonging to the FPMR bombed a Latter-day Saint chapel at 875 Manuel Antonio Mata Street in downtown Osorno, causing minimal damage to the chapel's façade. Approximately 34 parishioners, including eight US Citizens, were within the chapel during the detonation, which they described as a large firecracker. A man claiming to be a member of the FPMR called a radio station to claim responsibility, stating the attack commemorated the 10th anniversary of the Sandinista Revolution in Nicaragua. Local residents stated recent bombings in the area were only noise bombs causing minor damage, matching the effects of two nearby bombings that evening.[436]

July 20, 1989—Valparaiso, Chile

Members of the FPMR strafed a Latter-day Saint chapel in the La Esperanza section of Valparaiso with machine gun fire, causing property damage (extent and value unknown) and zero casualties.[437]

July 20, 1989—Quilpue, Chile

A bomb detonated at a Latter-day Saint chapel entrance, causing property damage (extent and value unknown) and zero casualties. The Movement of the Revolutionary Left (MIR) claimed responsibility.[438]

August 23, 1989—Osorno, Chile

At 8:10 p.m., a bomb containing approximately 200 grams of ammonium gelignite exploded at the entrance of the Latter-day Saint chapel at 1624 Avenida Pacífico in the Rahue Alto sector. The explosion, heard within a large radius, caused property damage to the chapel's windows and front entrance. Ten children between 12 and 16 years old were in the building studying the scriptures with their instructor, Monica Oyozon Vazquez, when the bomb detonated. Alejandro

Mauricio Aribel Manque, 16, living in Osorno, suffered a cut on his right leg, but the others escaped unharmed. The FPMR claimed responsibility, leaving pamphlets at the scene.[439]

September 6, 1989—Santiago, Chile

In the evening, a bomb exploded at the Latter-day Saint chapel at 2320 La Rioja Street in Quinta Normal. The explosion broke several windows and caused zero casualties. According to the local police, the bomb contained no more than 100 grams of explosives. No group claimed responsibility.[440]

November 1, 1989—Bogota, Colombia

A bomb exploded at the entrance of a Latter-day Saint chapel during the evening, causing minor property damage and zero casualties.[441]

November 17, 1989—Bogota, Colombia

Suspected leftist guerrillas utilized two bombs containing up to five pounds of dynamite total to damage the rear side of a Latter-day Saint chapel in southern Bogota. The blasts caused minor property damage to windows and doors of the chapel, but yielded zero casualties.[442]

November 22, 1989—Santiago, Chile

A bomb exploded at a Latter-day Saint chapel in the Conchali district. The bomb tore a man, unofficially identified as Alejandro Benegas, to pieces. The explosion also injured another man (unidentified), who was treated at the J. J. Aguirre Hospital. Both men were reportedly trying to set the bomb at the chapel when it detonated. Local police searched for other perpetrators, who allegedly escaped in a purple Volkswagen station wagon. The bomb reportedly contained 2 kilograms of ANFO. Members of the FPMR claimed responsibility for the attack.[443]

December 20, 1989—Santiago, Dominican Republic

A small homemade bomb exploded at the entrance of a Latter-day Saint chapel, causing property damage (extent and value unknown) and zero casualties.[444]

December 21, 1989—Santo Domingo, Dominican Republic

At 9:10 p.m., two gunmen riding a motorcycle shot at Latter-day Saint missionary David Hadley Read, injuring his leg with one of three bullets fired. The bullet went through his knee. A passerby transported Elder Read and his companion to a local hospital to treat the injury. The attack was apparently fueled by anti-American sentiment following the US invasion of Panama.[445]

December 21, 1989—Bani, Dominican Republic

A Latter-day Saint missionary reported that an unknown assailant threw a Molotov cocktail at another missionary, missing the missionary but hitting a Dominican child.[446]

December 23, 1989—Quilpue, Chile

A bomb exploded at the entrance of a Latter-day Saint chapel, causing minor property damage to the façade of the chapel and zero casualties. A mechanical detonator with a slow-burning fuse detonated the bomb, which had a blast radius of approximately 50 meters.[447]

December 24, 1989—Rancagua, Chile

A bomb exploded at a Latter-day Saint chapel entrance, causing minor property damage and zero casualties. A sign found near the chapel read, in Spanish, "Yankees out of Panama."[448]

December 24, 1989—Santiago, Chile

A bomb exploded at a Latter-day Saint chapel entrance in the El Bosque suburb of Santiago, causing minor property damage and zero casualties. "Yankees out of Panama" was painted near the chapel.[449]

December 24, 1989—Santa Marta, Colombia

Unknown perpetrators bombed a chapel in retaliation for the US invasion of Panama. The explosion caused property damage (extent and value unknown) and zero casualties.[450]

December 25, 1989—Chiclayo, Peru

Members of the MRTA planted a bomb after dark at a Latter-day Saint chapel in retaliation of the US invasion of Panama. The detonation caused significant property damage, but zero casualties.[451]

December 25, 1989—Chiclayo, Peru (second attack)

Members of the MRTA bombed the front of a Latter-day Saint chapel after dark, causing significant property damage, but zero casualties. The MRTA left leaflets at the scene, stating the group conducted the attack in retaliation of the US invasion of Panama.[452]

December 27, 1989—Loja, Ecuador

Unknown perpetrators bombed a Latter-day Saint chapel, causing property damage (extent and value unknown) and zero casualties.[453]

December 27, 1989—Quilpue, Chile

Members of the FPMR bombed the front of a Latter-day Saint chapel in retaliation for the US invasion of Panama. The bomb consisted of 150 grams of explosive material detonated by a mechanical blasting cap. The explosion broke three windows and caused zero casualties. A sign near the incident read, "Yankees get out of Panama Frente

Patriotico Manuel Rodriguez." Messages on Church walls read, "Yankees, out of Panama," and "No more intervention in Panama."[454]

December 28, 1989—Tarapoto, Peru

Members of the Tupac Amaru Revolutionary Movement (MRTA) bombed a Latter-day Saint chapel, utilizing an unknown amount of dynamite. The blast caused property damage (extent and value unknown) and zero casualties.[455]

December 28, 1989—Santiago, Chile

In the evening, members of the MJL threw flaming gasoline-soaked rags at the Latter-day Saint chapel at 1141 Espectadores Street in the Frei suburb of Santiago. The attack caused no damage or casualties. The MJL conducted the attack, leaving pamphlets at the scene.[456]

December 29, 1989—Santiago, Chile

Six members of the FPMR, described as four young men and two young women, poured gasoline around the entrance of a Latter-day Saint chapel, lit the gasoline on fire, and then fled. The attack caused minimal damage to the chapel and zero casualties. The group left MJL pamphlets at the scene.[457]

December 29, 1989—Santiago, Chile

At 1:15 a.m., unknown perpetrators threw incendiary bombs at a Latter-day Saint chapel in the Nunoa district, causing minor damage and zero casualties. The assailants painted the walls and left Lautaro Youth Front pamphlets at the scene.[458]

December 29, 1989—Tarapoto, Peru

Unknown perpetrators bombed the entrance of a Latter-day Saint chapel. Pamphlets left at the scene stated that all "Mormons and DEA agents" must leave San Martin Department in the Upper Huallaga

Valley in the next 30 days 'or face the consequences.'" Officials believed MRTA to be responsible for the attack.[459]

December 31, 1989—Santiago, Chile

Individuals suspected to be members of the FPMR bombed a Latter-day Saint chapel entrance, causing light damage. Police estimated the bomb had 150 grams of explosive material and stated it contained a mechanical detonator. No group claimed responsibility.[460]

January 1, 1990—Cochabamba, Bolivia

Members of the CAC bombed a Latter-day Saint chapel, causing property damage (extent and value unknown) and zero casualties.[461]

January 1, 1990—La Paz, Bolivia

A bomb detonated at the entrance of a Latter-day Saint chapel, damaging the entrance doors and destroying about 60% of the chapel's windows, but inflicting zero casualties. Leaflets signed by CAC were found near the chapel.[462]

January 1, 1990—Calama, Chile

A bomb detonated at the entrance of a Latter-day Saint chapel, damaging the entrance doors and several windows, but inflicting zero casualties. No group claimed responsibility.[463]

January 2, 1990—Cabudare, Venezuela

Members of the Omar Torrijos Cammando for Latin American Dignity (anti-intervention group) threw six Molotov cocktails at a Latter-day Saint chapel on the outskirts of Barquisimeto, causing little property damage and zero casualties. Only three of the cocktails exploded. Local media reported that the group attacked the chapel to protest the invasion of religious sects into Venezuela, stating that the Latter-day Saint are "agents of the CIA.[464]

January 2-3, 1990—Santiago, Chile

Perpetrators firebombed a Latter-day Saint chapel, causing moderate property damage (extent and value unknown) and zero casualties. Pamphlets from the MJL were found at the scene.[465]

February 13, 1990—Bogota, Colombia

Suspected members of the ELN bombed a Latter-day Saint chapel with dynamite during the early evening, causing minor property damage and zero casualties. Latter-day Saint Bishop Alberto Cadena told the press he had recently received anonymous threats over the phone warning him that bombs would be emplaced in his chapels because they represented US interests and were a means to protest the presence of President Bush at the drug summit in Cartagena on February 15th.[466]

February 13, 1990—Bogota, Colombia (second attack)

Suspected members of the ELN bombed a Latter-day Saint chapel with dynamite during the early evening, causing minor property damage and zero casualties. Latter-day Saint Bishop Alberto Cadena told the press he had recently received anonymous threats over the phone warning him that bombs would be emplaced in his chapels because they represented US interests and were a means to protest the presence of President Bush at the drug summit in Cartagena on February 15th.[467]

February 13, 1990—Popayan, Colombia

Members of the ELN bombed a Latter-day Saint chapel, causing minor property damage and zero casualties. The ELN conducted the attack to protest President Bush's visit to Cartagena.[468]

February 14–15, 1990—Cali, Colombia

Members of the ELN bombed a Latter-day Saint chapel with low-level explosives, causing minimal damage and zero casualties. The group stated the attack protested President Bush's imminent arrival for the Cartagena drug summit.[469]

February 15, 1990—El Recuerdo, Colombia

Members of the ELN attacked a Latter-day Saint chapel with incendiary devices, causing zero casualties and property damage (extent and value unknown).[470]

March 1, 1990—Loja, Ecuador

Unknown perpetrators bombed a Latter-day Saint chapel, causing property damage (extent and value unknown) and zero casualties.[471]

March 1, 1990—Loja, Ecuador (second attack)

Unknown perpetrators bombed a Latter-day Saint chapel, causing property damage (extent and value unknown) and zero casualties.[472]

March 9, 1990—Santiago, Chile

At 10:30 p.m., a bomb detonated at the Latter-day Saint chapel at 4540 Juan Griego Street in San Joaquin. The explosion caused minor property damage and zero casualties. Members of the FPMR claimed responsibility. This explosion was one of seven that occurred in Santiago that night.[473]

March 11, 1990—Santiago, Chile

Unknown perpetrators bombed a Latter-day Saint chapel in the Nunoa section of Santiago, causing minor property damage and zero casualties.[474]

March 14, 1990—Santiago, Chile

Unknown perpetrators bombed the Latter-day Saint "church" (unclear whether this was the temple or chapel located at the site, as they are directly beside each other) at the intersection of Pedro de Valdivia and

Pocuro Streets in southeast Santiago, causing minor property damage and zero casualties.[475]

May 14, 1990—Santiago, Chile

A bomb detonated at a Latter-day Saint chapel at 11 p.m., causing extensive property damage to the entrance door and to windows of nearby homes. The explosion caused zero casualties, despite the presence of 30 parishioners in the chapel at the time of the explosion. Several FPMR pamphlets were found at the scene. During the same evening, terrorists bombed the US Consular Annex, another Latter-day Saint chapel, and seven other locations within Santiago. While no group claimed responsibility, the Global Terrorism Database credits the 14th of December Command with the attack, but the FPMR may have also been involved.[476]

May 14, 1990—Santiago, Chile (second attack)

A bomb detonated at a Latter-day Saint chapel in Las Condes around midnight, causing property damage (extent and value unknown) and zero casualties. During the same evening, terrorists bombed the US Consular Annex, another Latter-day Saint chapel, and seven other locations within Santiago. While no group claimed responsibility, the Global Terrorism Database credits the 14th of December Command with the attack, but the FPMR may have also been involved.[477]

May 21, 1990—Santiago, Chile

Unknown perpetrators detonated a small improvised explosive device in front of the Latter-day Saint chapel at 8579 Manuel Errazuriz Street in the San Miguel section of Santiago, causing minor property damage and zero casualties.[478]

May 22, 1990—Ovalle, Chile

Unknown perpetrators detonated an explosive device at a Latter-day Saint chapel, causing property damage (extent and value unknown) and zero casualties.[479]

May 24, 1990—Talca, Chile

Unknown perpetrators detonated an explosive device at a Latter-day Saint chapel, causing property damage (extent and value unknown) and zero casualties. That same day, terrorists bombed another Latter-day Saint chapel and the Binational Center.[480]

May 24, 1990—Talca, Chile (second attack)

Unknown perpetrators detonated an explosive device at a Latter-day Saint chapel, causing property damage (extent and value unknown) and zero casualties. That same day, terrorists bombed another Latter-day Saint chapel and the Binational Center.[481]

May 24, 1990—Curico, Chile

Members of the FPMR called a local radio station and claimed responsibility for a bombing at a Latter-day Saint chapel. The bomb contained approximately 200 grams of explosive gelatin. The explosion caused property damage (extent and value unknown) and zero casualties.[482]

May 26, 1990—Santiago, Chile

Unknown perpetrators bombed the front of a Latter-day Saint chapel located at 4540 Juan Griego. The explosion caused moderate property damage and zero casualties. Police reported that the bomb contained 250 grams of explosive gelatin.[483]

May 27, 1990—Santiago, Chile

Unknown perpetrators, likely belonging to Milicias Rodriguistas, bombed a Latter-day Saint chapel, causing minor to moderate property damage. The explosive device contained 300 to 500 grams of explosive gelatin. This was one of three attacks against separate Latter-day Saint chapels that day.[484]

May 27, 1990—Santiago, Chile (second attack)

Unknown perpetrators, likely belonging to Milicias Rodriguistas, bombed a Latter-day Saint chapel, causing minor to moderate property damage. The explosive device contained 300 to 500 grams of explosive gelatin. This was one of three attacks against separate Latter-day Saint chapels that day.[485]

May 27, 1990—Santiago, Chile (third attack)

Unknown perpetrators, likely belonging to Milicias Rodriguistas, bombed a Latter-day Saint chapel, causing minor to moderate property damage. The explosive device contained 300 to 500 grams of explosive gelatin. This was one of three attacks against separate Latter-day Saint chapels that day.[486]

May 28, 1990—Santiago, Chile

Unknown perpetrators, likely members of the Milicias Rodriguistas, bombed a Latter-day Saint chapel, causing moderate property damage and zero casualties.[487]

May 30, 1990—Santiago, Chile

Unknown perpetrators bombed a Latter-day Saint chapel in the La Cisterna region of Santiago, destroying 27 windows and zero injuries. The explosive device contained about 50 grams of TNT.[488]

June 26, 1990—Santiago, Chile

Unknown perpetrators threw an explosive device against the front of a Latter-day Saint chapel in the Maipu neighborhood, resulting in extensive glass breakage and minor structural damage, but zero casualties. There were FPMR/D pamphlets at the scene. The bomb seemed to have consisted of 100 grams of explosive gelatin with a firing train composed of a fuse and mechanical detonator. The attack occurred on the birthday of former President Salvador Allende, which included several other bombings throughout Chile.[489]

July 26, 1990—Santiago, Chile

Unknown perpetrators, likely members of the FPMR/D, bombed a Latter-day Saint chapel with a explosive device containing 100 grams of explosive gelatin. The detonation caused light property damage and zero casualties. A man claiming to be a spokesman for the FPMR told a Santiago newspaper the attack was in protest of the impending visit of President Bush.[490]

July 26, 1990—Chillan, Chile

Unknown perpetrators, likely members of the FPMR/D, bombed a Latter-day Saint chapel in Zañartu around 10:45 p.m., causing only light property damage and zero casualties. The bomb consisted of 200–300 grams of compressed homemade powder and a fuse. This was one of three bombings against Latter-day Saint chapels that night.[491]

July 26, 1990—Chillan, Chile (second attack)

Unknown perpetrators, likely members of the FPMR/D, bombed the Latter-day Saint chapel at the intersection of Avenida O'Higgins and Santa Blanca around 10:45 p.m., causing light property damage and zero casualties. The bomb consisted of 200-300 grams of compressed homemade powder and a fuse. This was one of three bombings against Latter-day Saint chapels that night.[492]

July 26, 1990—Chillan, Chile (third attack)

Unknown perpetrators, likely members of the FPMR/D, bombed a Latter-day Saint chapel in Francisco Ramírez, near the local hospital, around 10:45 p.m., causing only light property damage and zero casualties. The bomb consisted of 200-300 grams of compressed homemade powder and a fuse. This was one of three bombings against Latter-day Saint chapels that night.[493]

July 27, 1990—Santiago, Chile

In the evening hours, five armed assailants entered a Latter-day Saint chapel at the corner of Centro América and Carlos Dávila, in San Ramón. They encountered a Latter-day Saint leader and various children in the building, whom they forced to leave the site. They detonated an explosive device and poured flammable liquid around the second floor of the building, and then set the building ablaze. The fire destroyed the entire building but caused zero casualties. There were anti-US/pro-Cuban pamphlets found at the scene. The US Department of State assessed the MJL conducted the attack, even though it took place the night after the Autonomous FPMR made 12 threats against targets linked to transnational threats.[494]

July 28, 1990—Santiago, Chile

Members of the MJL threw a Molotov cocktail at a Latter-day Saint chapel in the La Florida section of Santiago at approximately 9:40 p.m., causing light damage and zero casualties. They spray-painted a slogan in Spanish nearby that said, "Yankees out of Chile—MJL."[495]

August 22, 1990—Santiago, Chile

Members of the Roberto Nordenflycht Commando of the FPMR bombed the front of the Latter-day Saint chapel at 1141 Los Salvavidas Street in the Nunoa section of Santiago around 11:55 p.m.. The detonation broke windows of the chapel and nearby homes and damaged furniture. There were zero casualties. The bomb seemed to have been composed of 200 grams of Tronex, with a firing train consisting of a fuse and a mechanical detonator.[496]

August 22, 1990—Huancayo, Peru

Members of the Shining Path assassinated two Latter-day Saint missionaries. A handwritten note left on one of the bodies read, "Struggle for the people's war. Yankees out. Long live the People's war. Communist party of Peru." Police stated the missionaries, like other Latter-day Saint in the area, had previously received death threats.[497]

August 26, 1990—Santiago, Chile

Five men and one woman, all members of the MJL, entered a Latter-day Saint chapel in La Florida and threw a Molovov cocktail into the occupied chapel. Parishioners quickly put out the fire. MJL pamphlets were found at the scene. This was one of three MJL attacks targeting Latter-day Saint chapels that same night. An individual claiming to be a member of the MJL, in an anonymous call to the UPI news agency, said the attacks were staged as a tribute to terrorist Julio Jacinto Eyzaguierre, alias Roberto, who died on August 24 after being wounded by a Carabineros noncommissioned officer during an attack by the Lautaros targeting a supermarket in Conchali. The individual said the group targeted Latter-day Saint chapels because the religion was founded in the United States and is considered a symbol of imperialism in Chile.[498]

August 26, 1990—Santiago, Chile (second attack)

Three masked and armed members of the MJL entered a Latter-day Saint chapel in western Santiago (La Cisterna/San Miguel area). One struck a US missionary on the head with a pistol. Another took photographs of the missionaries with guns pointed at their heads. The men covered the tile floor with gasoline and lit the chapel on fire before fleeing. This was one of three MJL attacks targeting Latter-day Saint chapels that same night.[499]

August 26, 1990—Santiago, Chile (third attack)

Members of the MJL threw Molotov cocktails at a Latter-day Saint chapel in the Ochagavia section of Santiago, causing property damage (extent and value unknown) and zero casualties. This was one of three MJL attacks targeting Latter-day Saint chapels that same night.[500]

September 4, 1990—Copiapo, Chile

At approximately 1 a.m., a bomb with 300 grams of ammongel and activated by a slow-burning fuse detonated in front of a Latter-day Saint chapel on Rodriguez Street, damaging the building façade and windows, but inflicting zero casualties. There were FPMR/D and MJL pamphlets at the scene.[501]

September 4, 1990—Curico, Chile

At approximately 9:55 p.m., a bomb detonated in front of a Latter-day Saint chapel on Merced Street, causing minimal damage and zero casualties. The device contained about 200 grams of Tronex activated by a slow-burning fuse. No group claimed responsibility.[502]

September 11, 1990—Valdivia, Chile

At approximately 9:45 p.m., a bomb detonated in front of the Latter-day Saint chapel at 292 Riquelme Street. The bomb contained 1 kilogram of ANFO, a mechanical detonator and a slow-burning fuse. The explosion broke one window and caused zero casualties. No group claimed responsibility.[503]

October 5, 1990—Santiago, Chile

Four armed individuals approached a Latter-day Saint chapel at the 16th block of Vicuna Mackenna Avenue and, after threatening the watchman, entered the building and detonated a powerful bomb, causing substantial damage to the building. The group left leaflets at the church and fled. They intercepted a bus, firebombing it after ordering the passengers to exit, destroying the bus interior. An anonymous caller then called an international news agency, claiming responsibility for the attacks that marked the third anniversary of the Lautaro Rebel Forces. An investigation revealed the bomb at the Latter-day Saint chapel contained about 2 kilograms of explosive gelatin.[504]

October 31, 1990—Concepcion, Chile

A bomb exploded in front of a Latter-day Saint chapel in Penco at approximately 5:45 a.m., causing light property damage to the building wall and the windows of two adjacent houses. There were zero casualties. The bomb consisted of 100 grams of ANFO blasting agents and a slow fuse. FPMR leaflets were found at the site.[505]

November 13, 1990—Santiago, Chile

At 10:45 p.m., four unknown assailants broke the front window of a Latter-day Saint chapel in Conchali and tossed a firebomb inside, causing light damage and zero casualties. They spray-painted MJL propaganda on the building.[506]

December 1, 1990—Santiago, Chile

At about 10:40 p.m., four individuals in a pickup truck threw an explosive device that detonated in front of the Latter-day Saint chapel at 150 Muñoz Gamero in Conchali, seriously damaging the windows and causing zero casualties. The bomb contained 150 grams of explosive Tronex, set off by a blasting cap with a fuse. An individual claiming to be a member of the MJL later called UPI and claimed responsibility. It is likely the perpetrators conducted the other attack that evening targeting members of the Church.[507]

December 1, 1990—Santiago, Chile

In the evening hours, four members of the MJL drove up to 2573 Avenida Las Torres, a private residence in the Salto sector of Conchali, and began shooting and yelling for the "Gringos" to come outside. Two Latter-day Saint missionaries, Charles Gaber and Brandon Page, resided at the residence with a Chilean Latter-day Saint family. Bullets damaged windows, the main entrance door, interior walls, and furniture at the residence. The perpetrators drove a Chevrolet LUV truck. The perpetrators wrote "Fuera Yankees de Chile MJL" in black spray paint on the front wall of the residence. An individual claiming to be a member of the MJL later called UPI and claimed responsibility. There were no injuries associated with the attack. In an interview with a local newspaper, Luis Enrique Sandoval, the owner of the residence, stated the perpetrators conducted the attack against the North American missionaries in protest of the pending visit of President Bush. It is likely the perpetrators conducted the other attack that evening targeting the Church.[508]

December 5, 1990—Santiago, Chile

At 9:07 p.m., a bomb detonated in front of the Latter-day Saint chapel at 185 Mirador Azul Street in La Florida, causing minor property damage and zero casualties. No group claimed responsibility.[509]

December 5, 1990—Santiago, Chile

At 10:15 p.m., a bomb detonated in front of the Latter-day Saint chapel at 872 Vicente Valdez Street in La Florida, causing minor property damage and zero casualties. No group claimed responsibility.[510]

December 5, 1990—Santiago, Chile

Late in the evening, five masked individuals entered the Latter-day Saint chapel at 714 Los Lirios Street in the Puente Alto section of Santiago. They encountered 26 people inside the church. As one of the masked individuals held six men at gunpoint in the Bishop's office, interrupting a Bishopric meeting, the others sprinkled gasoline throughout the building and set it on fire. The Church members were unharmed. Prior to fleeing, the assailants left statements protesting President Bush's visit to Santiago on the building.[511]

December 5, 1990—Santiago, Chile

At 10:59 p.m., a bomb detonated in the Latter-day Saint chapel at 5200 Transito Street in Pudahuel, causing significant property damage and a fire, but no casualties. No group claimed responsibility.[512]

December 6, 1990—Santiago, Chile

Around 10:50 p.m., unknown perpetrators threw a Molotov cocktail in front of a Latter-day Saint chapel in Lo Prado, causing no damage and zero casualties. No group claimed responsibility.[513]

December 6, 1990—Osorno, Chile

Unknown perpetrators threw a firebomb inside a Latter-day Saint chapel, causing minor damage and zero casualties. The MJL claimed responsibility.[514]

December 7, 1990—Santiago, Chile

At 12:05 a.m., unknown perpetrators threw a firebomb at the Latter-day Saint chapel at 5245 Baron de Juras Reales in Conchali, causing no damage and zero casualties. No group claimed responsibility.[515]

December 7, 1990—Santiago, Chile

At 12:10 a.m., unknown perpetrators detonated a bomb containing 300 grams of explosive gelatin in front of a Latter-day Saint chapel at 6004 Independencia in Santiago, damaging doors and windows, but causing zero casualties. No group claimed responsibility.[516]

December 7, 1990—Santiago, Chile

At 12:20 a.m., ten members of the FPMR threw three firebombs inside a Latter-day Saint meetinghouse in La Cisterna, causing moderate property damage and zero injuries. The FPMR/D claimed responsibility.[517]

December 7, 1990—Concepcion, Chile

At 12:45 a.m., unknown perpetrators detonated a bomb containing 1.5 kilograms of dynamite or ANFO in front of the Latter-day Saint chapel at 99 Membrillar in the Penco region of Concepcion, causing moderate damage and zero casualties. No group claimed responsibility.[518]

December 14, 1990—Santiago, Chile

At 11:30 p.m., unknown perpetrators detonated a bomb in front of the Latter-day Saint chapel at 5245 Baron de Juras Reales Street in Conchali, causing light damage and zero casualties. The bomb had 0.3 kilograms of ammonium gelignite. No group claimed responsibility.

On March 6, 1991, local press reported a suspect, Pedro Ortiz, had been arrested in connection with the attack.[519]

December 16, 1990—Santiago, Chile

Two men and two women threw several incendiary bombs at a Latter-day Saint church in Conchali. They fired shots in the air and left leaflets from the MJL prior to fleeing. Local police stated the church was completely destroyed by fire.[520]

December 16, 1990—Santiago, Chile (second attack)

Ten members of the MJL entered the La Pincoyan Latter-day Saint chapel while 28 Saints (including one American citizen) were attending a Sunday school class. The assailants forced the evacuation of the building at gunpoint and then poured flammable liquid around the interior of the building, setting the church on fire. The fire gutted the chapel and completely destroyed the inside but caused zero casualties. Prior to fleeing, the assailants spray-painted Lautaro slogans and "Yankees out of Chile" on the outside wall of the chapel.[521]

January 16, 1991—Guayaquil, Ecuador

At approximately 2 a.m., a dynamite bomb detonated at a Latter-day Saint chapel, causing damage to the chapel's windows and walls, but inflicting zero casualties. No group claimed responsibility.[522]

January 16, 1991—Quilpue, Chile

Unknown perpetrators bombed a Latter-day Saint chapel in Quilpue to protest Operation Desert Storm, causing property damage (extent and value unknown) and zero casualties. No group claimed responsibility, but the Anti-Imperialist Revolutionary Front (Frente Revolucionario Antimperialista) seemed responsible, as members of the group recently stated that they would carry out selective attacks against 15 US targets in Chile if the US military did not stop the attack against Iraq immediately.[523]

January 16, 1991—La Serena, Chile

At about 11 p.m., a bomb containing 300 grams of dynamite exploded at the rear of the Latter-day Saint chapel located at 1935 Nicaragua, causing heavy damage and zero casualties. The explosion destroyed the entrance door and some windows. No group claimed responsibility, but the Anti-Imperialist Revolutionary Front (Frente Revolucionario Antimperialista) seemed responsible, as members of the group recently stated that they would carry out selective attacks against 15 US targets in Chile if the US military did not stop the attack against Iraq immediately.[524]

January 16, 1991—Quilpue, Chile

At about 11 p.m., a bomb containing 400 grams of explosive gelatin exploded in front of a Latter-day Saint meetinghouse along Camino Troncal. Police sources indicated the chapel was half destroyed by the resulting fire. There were no casualties. No group claimed responsibility, but the Anti-Imperialist Revolutionary Front (Frente Revolucionario Antimperialista) seemed responsible, as members of the group recently stated that they would carry out selective attacks against 15 US targets in Chile if the US military did not stop the attack against Iraq immediately.[525]

January 17, 1991—Santiago, Chile

At about 2 a.m., unknown perpetrators left a hoax bomb in front of a Latter-day Saint chapel in Conchali.[526]

January 18, 1991—Barquisimeto, Venezuela

At dawn, members of the Internationalist Brigade threw a Molotov cocktail at a Latter-day Saint chapel entrance, causing minor property damage and zero casualties. Captain Ali Gomez, a spokesman for the Internationalist Brigade, called EFE at dawn to declare that the attack was aimed at a US concern in Venezuela in retaliation for US actions against Iraq. He stated, "the Mormons serve as US spies in Venezuela," and that Latter-day Saint chapels would be targeted in future attacks.[527]

January 18, 1991—Anapolis, Brazil

Members of the "Grupo de Apoyo a Palestina" (GAP), or "Palestinian Support Group," threw five Molotov cocktails at a Latter-day Saint chapel, causing property damage (extent and value unknown) and zero casualties. The group claimed responsibility in calls to radio stations and left an anti-US message written on a poster in front of the chapel, which read, "Death to the Americans, long live the Palestinians." PLO officials in Brazil disclaimed any responsibility for the attack.[528]

January 19, 1991—Vina del Mar, Chile

At about 10:30 p.m., a bomb containing about 400 grams of ammonia gelatin and activated by a mechanical system exploded at the Latter-day Saint chapel at the intersection of Las Torres and Pasaje Dos, damaging the door and several windows, but causing zero casualties. No group claimed responsibility, but officials suspected the attack was in protest of Operation Desert Storm.[529]

January 21, 1991—Valparaiso, Chile

A bomb containing about 300 grams of ammonia gelatin exploded in the back of a Latter-day Saint chapel, damaging the chapel's back door and several windows. The explosion caused zero casualties. No group claimed responsibility.[530]

January 22, 1991—Iquique, Chile

At about 6 p.m., local police defused a bomb in front of a Latter-day Saint chapel after receiving an anonymous phone call tipping them off to the location. No group claimed responsibility.[531]

January 22, 1991—Portoviejo, Ecuador

A bomb detonated at a Latter-day Saint chapel, causing over $2,000 worth of damage to exterior doors and adjoining windows. The explosion caused zero casualties. No group claimed responsibility.[532]

January 22, 1991—Guayaquil, Ecuador

A bomb detonated at a Latter-day Saint chapel, causing over $1,400 worth of damage to windows near the chapel's entry. The explosion caused zero casualties. No group claimed responsibility.[533]

January 25, 1991—Chimbote, Peru

Seven armed members of the group Sendero Luminoso (SL) interrupted an evening meeting in a Latter-day Saint chapel and threatened to blow up the building. The parishioners reportedly convinced the terrorists not to do so. The SL members left the building after writing, "Yankees go home," and drawing a hammer and sickle on the blackboard.[534]

January 26, 1991—Copiapo, Chile

A bomb containing 300 grams of ANFO and a slow-burning fuse exploded in front of a Latter-day Saint chapel. The explosion produced a blast radius of approximately 80 meters and caused considerable damage to the chapel entrance and front door. Police discovered another bomb at the building and successfully defused the bomb. No group claimed responsibility.[535]

January 27, 1991—Santiago, Chile

A bomb containing 50 grams of ANFO detonated at the Latter-day Saint chapel at 1791 Central America Street in the San Ramon district. The explosion caused minor property damage, including two broken windows, and zero casualties. No group claimed responsibility.[536]

January 27, 1991—Santiago, Chile (second attack)

At approximately 11:05 p.m., a bomb containing 100 grams of ANFO fired by a slow-burning fuse detonated in front of the Latter-day Saint chapel at 95 Fernandez Albano Street in La Cisterna. The explosion damaged two windows at the back of the church. There were zero casualties. No group claimed responsibility.[537]

February 1, 1991—Huaraz, Peru

At about 8:15 p.m., unknown assailants emplaced four sticks of dynamite at the gate of the perimeter fence of a Latter-day Saint chapel. Only one stick exploded, causing moderate damage to the gate and zero casualties. No group claimed responsibility.[538]

February 2, 1991—Santiago, Chile

Members of the dissident faction of the Manuel Rodriguez Patriotic Front (FPMR/D) bombed a Latter-day Saint chapel in the Renca district of Santiago. The bomb consisted of 300 grams of dynamite and destroyed over 60 windows but caused zero injuries. A FPMR/D spokesman called local media to claim responsibility for the attack, stating the attack occurred in retaliation of US military actions in the Persian Gulf.[539]

February 3, 1991—Medellin, Colombia

Members of a group called Heroes of Palestine claimed responsibility for bombing a Latter-day Saint chapel, causing property damage (extent and value unknown) and zero casualties.[540]

February 3, 1991—Itagui, Colombia

Members of the ELN bombed a Latter-day Saint chapel, causing minor property damage and zero casualties. The ELN claimed responsibility for the attack and another bombing of an Israeli-owned leather manufacturing plant, stating the group stood, "in solidarity with the heroes of Palestine" and protested US involvement in the Persian Gulf conflict.[541]

February 4, 1991—Huacho, Peru

Students from a local university stoned a Latter-day Saint chapel to protest the war in the Persian Gulf, breaking some windows but causing zero casualties. Students also burned an effigy of President Bush. The presence of Church members prevented further damage.[542]

February 9, 1991—Pisco, Peru

A bomb detonated at a Latter-day Saint chapel, causing minimal property damage and zero casualties. The MRTA claimed responsibility, with leaflets at the scene stating the attack was, "in reprisal for one of the most bloody and inhumane wars by which Yankee imperialism displays its contempt for Iraq and all the Arab peoples." Police found and deactivated a second bomb at the scene.[543]

February 10, 1991—Huancayo, Peru

At about 8:30 p.m., members of the MRTA threw a bomb over the perimeter wall of a Latter-day Saint chapel in the Manti district, damaging an exterior door and breaking windows. The individuals also spray-painted, "Yankees go home" and "Yankees out of the Gulf" on the church and perimeter wall. There were no reported injuries.[544]

February 10, 1991—Huancayo, Peru (second attack)

Members of the MRTA bombed the perimeter fence of a Latter-day Saint chapel in the Mantaro district. The explosion blew off the fence gate and broke several windows. MRTA graffiti and group flyers were left at the scene. There were no reported injuries.[545]

February 11, 1991—Huancayo, Peru

At around 9:30 p.m., a bomb detonated at the entrance of a Latter-day Saint chapel in the San Carlos district. The explosion caused extensive damage to the chapel's windows, pews, and light fixtures. The MRTA claimed responsibility and left pamphlets at the scene, as well as anti-American graffiti on the building's wall and perimeter fence.[546]

February 13, 1991—Santiago, Chile

At about 12:50 a.m., a small bomb detonated in front of a Latter-day Saint chapel in the Estacion Central district. Police did not provide a description of the exact composition of the bomb, but they stated the bomb was designed mostly for noise than damage. The explosion caused minimal damage to the church and zero casualties. No group claimed responsibility.[547]

February 13, 1991—Santiago, Chile (second attack)

At about 11:30 p.m., a bomb detonated at a Latter-day Saint chapel in the Maipu district, causing moderate damage and zero casualties. There were pamphlets of the MIR at the scene saying, "No to the imperialist war."[548]

February 13, 1991—Huancayo, Peru

A bomb detonated at a Latter-day Saint chapel in the Chilca district, causing moderate damage and zero casualties. Local press reports credited the MRTA with the attack, as well as three other bombings of Latter-day Saint chapels in the city that same day.[549]

February 13, 1991—Huancayo, Peru (second attack)

A bomb detonated at another Latter-day Saint chapel in the Chilca district, causing moderate damage and zero casualties. Local press reports credited the MRTA with the attack, as well as three other bombings of Latter-day Saint chapels in the city that same day.[550]

February 13, 1991—Huancayo, Peru

A bomb detonated at a Latter-day Saint chapel in the Tres Esquinas district, causing moderate damage and zero casualties. Local press reports credited the MRTA with the attack, as well as three other bombings of Latter-day Saint chapels in the city that same day.[551]

February 13, 1991—Huancayo, Peru

A bomb detonated at a Latter-day Saint chapel in the Sanos Chicos district, causing moderate damage and zero casualties. Local press reports credited the MRTA with the attack, as well as three other bombings of Latter-day Saint chapels in the city that same day.[552]

February 14, 1991—Caracas, Venezuela

At about 4:30 a.m., a pipe bomb detonated in front of a Latter-day Saint chapel, causing moderate property damage, including damage to the chapel's glass door and windows. Local media reported that the bomb did not explode fully due to poor construction. A witness reported seeing individuals throw the bomb at the chapel from a passing vehicle. The explosion caused zero casualties. No group claimed responsibility.[553]

February 14, 1991—Buenos Aires, Argentina

A maintenance worker discovered a hoax bomb at a Latter-day Saint chapel. A handwritten note in Spanish was near the hoax bomb, written by a group known as the "Islamic Revolutionary Command." They emplaced the hoax device to protest US involvement in the Persian Gulf.[554]

February 14, 1991—Huancayo, Peru

During the early evening hours, a bomb detonated at a Latter-day Saint chapel in the Chilca district. The chapel suffered structural damage, but the explosion did not inflict any casualties. Authorities credited the MRTA with the attack.[555]

February 16, 1991—Santiago, Chile

At about 8 a.m., members of the Lautaro Youth Movement (MJL) poured gasoline on chairs and the carpet before setting fire to a Latter-day Saint chapel, causing extensive property damage. The group subdued a guard to gain access to the chapel, but there were zero reported injuries. The group left pamphlets protesting the US-led war against Iraq. Members of the MJL called the local offices of United Press International (UPI) to claim responsibility.[556]

February 18, 1991—Huancayo, Peru

A bomb detonated near the front door of a Latter-day Saint chapel in the San Carlos district. The explosion blew out several of the chapel's glass windows and damaged the entrance door and sewage pipes. No group claimed responsibility.[557]

February 18, 1991—Esmeraldas, Ecuador

A bomb detonated at a Latter-day Saint chapel, causing nearly $400 in damage to the roof and a wall of the building. The explosion caused zero casualties. No group claimed responsibility.[558]

February 23, 1991—Ica, Peru

Around 10:30 p.m., a bomb placed by a side glass door of a Latter-day Saint chapel detonated, causing damage to the building doors, the interior of the building, and about 20 windows. There were MRTA flyers protesting Operation Desert Storm at the site. MRTA members also called a local radio station to take credit for the attack and one other targeting a Latter-day Saint chapel that evening.[559]

February 23, 1991—Ica, Peru (second attack)

Around 10:30 p.m., individuals tossed dynamite at a Latter-day Saint chapel. Detonation damaged the chapel's vaulted ceilings and broke over 25 windows. There were MRTA flyers protesting Operation Desert Storm at the site. MRTA members also called a local radio station to take credit for the attack and one other targeting a Latter-day Saint chapel that evening.[560]

February 23, 1991—Huancayo, Peru

A bomb detonated near the front of a Latter-day Saint chapel in the Chilca district, damaging the entrance door and some windows. The blast caused zero casualties. No group claimed responsibility.[561]

February 25, 1991—Riobamba, Ecuador

A bomb detonated at a Latter-day Saint chapel, causing nearly $250 in damage to the building windows and walls. Zero casualties were reported. No group claimed responsibility.[562]

March 2, 1991—Chiclayo, Peru

Around 8:30 p.m., members of the MRTA emplaced dynamite at a Latter-day Saint chapel, one of four Latter-day Saint chapels targeted that same evening. The bomb exploded, causing minimal property damage and zero casualties. There were lengthy MRTA flyers found at the site, some of which included the demand for all North American missionaries to exit Peru within the next 15 days. Flyers also demanded that the chapels be turned over to the Peruvian Ministry of Education.[563]

March 2, 1991—Chiclayo, Peru (second attack)

Around 8:30 p.m., members of the MRTA emplaced dynamite at a Latter-day Saint chapel, one of four Latter-day Saint chapels targeted that same evening. The bomb exploded while people were attending religious services in the chapel, causing minor injury to one Peruvian Latter-day Saint leader and significant damage to the interior of the building. There were lengthy MRTA flyers found at the site, some of which included the demand for all North American missionaries to exit Peru within the next 15 days. Flyers also demanded that the chapels be turned over to the Peruvian Ministry of Education.[564]

March 2, 1991—Chiclayo, Peru (third attack)

Around 8:30 p.m., members of the MRTA emplaced dynamite at a Latter-day Saint chapel, one of four Latter-day Saint chapels targeted that same evening. Police found and deactivated the device. There were lengthy MRTA flyers found at the site, some of which included the demand for all North American missionaries to exit Peru within the next 15 days. Flyers also demanded that the chapels be turned over to the Peruvian Ministry of Education.[565]

March 2, 1991—Chiclayo, Peru (fourth attack)

Around 8:30 p.m., members of the MRTA emplaced dynamite at a Latter-day Saint chapel, one of four Latter-day Saint chapels targeted that same evening. Police found and deactivated the device. There were lengthy MRTA flyers found at the site, some of which included the demand for all North American missionaries to exit Peru within the next 15 days. Flyers also demanded that the chapels be turned over to the Peruvian Ministry of Education.[566]

March 3, 1991—Santiago, Chile

At about 8:40 a.m., two young men and a woman entered a Latter-day Saint chapel during services and forced the congregation to evacuate the building at gunpoint. The group then poured flammable liquid around the interior of the building and set the contents on fire, causing property damage (extent and value unknown) and zero casualties. They shouted anti-American slogans as the fled. They left MJL literature at the scene. This was one of three attacks conducted by MJL members that day targeting Latter-day Saint chapels in Santiago.[567]

March 3, 1991—Santiago, Chile (second attack)

At about 10:15 p.m., a bomb detonated beside a Latter-day Saint chapel in the Lo Prado section of Santiago, causing moderate damage to the exterior door and several windows. The perpetrators also spray-painted anti-American slogans relating to the Gulf War and MJL graffiti on the front of the chapel. There were zero casualties. This was one of three attacks conducted by MJL members that day targeting Latter-day Saint chapels in Santiago.[568]

March 3, 1991—Santiago, Chile (third attack)

At about 11:00 p.m., a bomb detonated in front of a Latter-day Saint chapel in the Renca district of Santiago, breaking several windows and causing zero casualties. The perpetrators spray-painted anti-Desert Storm and MJL graffiti on a nearby wall. There were zero casualties. This was one of three attacks conducted by MJL members that day targeting Latter-day Saint chapels in Santiago.[569]

March 13, 1991—Valparaiso, Chile

At about 10:45 p.m., unknown perpetrators threw two Molotov cocktails inside a Latter-day Saint chapel, causing light property damage and zero casualties. No group claimed responsibility.[570]

April 11, 1991—Chimbote, Peru

At about 8:10 p.m., a bomb detonated at a Latter-day Saint chapel, causing property damage (extent and value unknown) and zero casualties. This was one of two attacks targeting a Latter-day Saint chapel in Chimbote that evening. No group claimed responsibility.[571]

April 11, 1991—Chimbote, Peru (second attack)

At about 8:10 p.m., a bomb detonated at a Latter-day Saint chapel, causing property damage (extent and value unknown) and zero casualties. This was one of two attacks targeting a Latter-day Saint chapel in Chimbote that evening. No group claimed responsibility.[572]

April 14–15, 1991—Santiago, Chile

Members of the MJL threw one or more Molotov cocktails into a Latter-day Saint chapel in Penalolen, starting a fire that caused extensive damage to furniture inside the building. There were MJL pamphlets at the scene calling for "Yankees out of Chile." There were zero casualties.[573]

April 17, 1991—Chimbote, Peru

A bomb detonated near the entrance door of the Latter-day Saint chapel, damaging the door and windows. One Church member was injured by flying glass. No group claimed responsibility.[574]

May 2, 1991—Manti, Peru

At about 8:00 p.m., unknown perpetrators emplaced a bomb between two wings of a Latter-day Saint chapel. The explosion damaged doors, windows, and the ceiling of the church, totaling over $4,000 in damages. There were no casualties. No group claimed responsibility.[575]

May 2, 1991—Chilca, Peru

At about 8:00 p.m., a bomb detonated in front of the main door of a Latter-day Saint chapel, damaging the doors and nearby windows. There were no casualties. No group claimed responsibility.[576]

July 7, 1991—Santiago, Chile

At about 7:15 p.m., assailants threw an incendiary device and fired several shots at a Latter-day Saint chapel in the Penalolen section of Santiago, causing one injury and breaking several windows. The ward's bishop and four members were within the chapel at the time of the attack. The assailants wore masks with the symbol of the Movement of the Revolutionary Left. They shouted FPMR/D slogans and left a US flag at the scene, fleeing on foot.[577]

July 8, 1991—Coquimbo, Chile

Unknown perpetrators threw a bomb, composed of 150 grams of anfo, onto the soccer field adjacent to a Latter-day Saint chapel. The explosion broke several chapel windows and caused zero casualties. No group claimed responsibility.[578]

July 8, 1991—Santiago, Chile

Three individuals wearing handkerchiefs printed with the acronym "MIR" on their faces left a bomb hidden in a detergent box in the Latter-day Saint chapel at 9200 Las Parcelas Street in the Penalolen district of Santiago. The explosion broke several windows but caused zero casualties. The assailants reportedly fired their weapons into the air as they fled the scene.[579]

July 27, 1991—San Cristobal, Dominican Republic

A bomb detonated at a Latter-day Saint chapel during the late evening hours, causing little property damage and zero casualties. No group claimed responsibility, but local police officials suspected the terrorists also bombed the San Cristobal Governor's home and Police Station that same week.[580]

August 18, 1991—Santiago, Chile

At about 10:00 p.m., a bomb detonated in front of a Latter-day Saint chapel in the Poblacion José Maria Caro neighborhood. The bomb contained 250 grams of dynamite with the firing train consisting of a fuse and a mechanical detonator. The explosion caused moderate property damage and zero casualties. The perpetrators spray-painted MJL slogans on the church prior to fleeing.[581]

September 11, 1991—Ovalle, Chile

At about 10:30 p.m., a small bomb detonated in front of a Latter-day Saint chapel, causing minor damage and zero casualties. No group claimed responsibility.[582]

September 11, 1991—Santiago, Chile

At about 11:30 p.m., unknown perpetrators detonated a bomb in front of a Latter-day Saint chapel in San Joaquin, causing light property damage and zero casualties. No group claimed responsibility.[583]

September 17, 1991—Santiago, Chile

At about 9:00 p.m., three assailants armed with short-barreled firearms and wearing masks bearing the logo of the FPMR/D entered the Latter-day Saint chapel at 9460 Los Andes Street in the Quinta Normal district. They forced four individuals inside the building to leave and then threw an explosive device inside the building. The bomb failed to detonate, and local police removed the bomb. Leaflets found at the scene stated the Lautaro group was joining Chile's

Independence Day celebration, which marked the country's 181st year of independence.[584]

October 5, 1991—Santiago, Chile

At about 11:35 p.m., unknown perpetrators bombed the Latter-day Saint chapel on 5 April Avenue in the Estacion Central district. According to local police, the small bomb contained approximately 100 grams of ammonium gelignite and the firing train consisted of a fuse and a detonator. The explosion caused light property damage and zero casualties. No group claimed responsibility.[585]

October 8, 1991—Temuco, Chile

At about 10:50 p.m., two unknown perpetrators detonated a bomb in front of a Latter-day Saint chapel. The explosion caused moderate property damage and zero casualties. The explosion also destroyed some windows of nearby buildings. According to local police, the bomb contained 500 grams of tronex ignited by a fuse connected to a detonator. No group claimed responsibility.[586]

October 10, 1991—Santiago, Chile

At 8:00 p.m., four armed assailants entered a Latter-day Saint chapel in the San Miguel district and forced seven individuals inside to leave. The group spray-painted walls with slogans, including one reading, "Yankees out—MJL." The group detonated a bomb containing 200 grams of blasting powder, causing moderate property damage that included destroying several windows. There were zero casualties. In a phone call to the UPI news agency, a member of the MJL claimed responsibility and stated the attacks had an anti-US Government objective.[587]

October 11, 1991—Santiago, Chile

At 9:20 p.m., a bomb detonated in front of a Latter-day Saint church in the Lo Espejo district, causing minor property damage and zero injuries. The bomb contained about 100 grams of dynamite. The perpetrators spray-painted MJL and anti-American graffiti on the chapel walls. In a phone call to the UPI news agency, a member of the MJL claimed responsibility and stated the attacks had an anti-US Government objective.[588]

October 11, 1991—Santiago, Chile (second attack)

At 10:45 p.m., a bomb detonated at the Latter-day Saint church at the intersection of Carmen Mena Street and Las Industrias Avenue in the San Miguel district, causing minor property damage and zero injuries. The bomb contained about 100 grams of dynamite. The perpetrators spray-painted MJL and anti-American graffiti on the chapel walls. In a phone call to the UPI news agency, a member of the MJL claimed responsibility and stated the attacks had an anti-US Government objective.[589]

November 16, 1991—Santiago, Chile

At about 9:10 p.m., unknown perpetrators threw a homemade bomb into the front garden of a Latter-day Saint chapel in Lo Espejo. The bomb did not detonate, and local police successfully removed the device, which consisted of a metallic tube containing 300 grams of ammonium nitrate, water, and oil, with a mechanical detonator and a slow fuse. No group claimed responsibility.[590]

November 23, 1991—Santiago, Chile

At 7:45 a.m., a bomb detonated near the entrance of a Latter-day Saint chapel in the La Florida district, breaking several windows and damaging the entrance door. There were no casualties. There were MAPU-Lautaro pamphlets at the scene. This was one of four attacks targeting Latter-day Saint chapels that day in Santiago.[591]

November 23, 1991—Santiago, Chile (second attack)

At 7:50 a.m., a bomb detonated at a Latter-day Saint chapel in San Joaquin, damaging the entrance door and breaking several windows. There were no casualties. There were MAPU-Lautaro pamphlets at the scene. This was one of four attacks targeting Latter-day Saint chapels that day in Santiago.[592]

November 23, 1991—Santiago, Chile (third attack)

At 9:15 p.m., a bomb detonated at a Latter-day Saint chapel in La Cisterna. The device contained screws and nuts packed around 150 grams of ANFO activated by a mechanical detonator and burning fuse. The church was empty at the time of the explosion, but 10 children were walking past the building when the bomb detonated. Three suffered injuries requiring hospitalization and seven suffered acoustic trauma. The US Department of State noted that it was believed this was the first instance of a shrapnel bomb used to target the Church in Chile. This was one of four attacks targeting Latter-day Saint chapels that day in Santiago.[593]

November 23, 1991—Santiago, Chile (fourth attack)

At 10:05 p.m., local police deactivated a bomb placed in front of a Latter-day Saint chapel in the Lo Espejo district. This was one of four attacks targeting Latter-day Saint chapels that day in Santiago.[594]

December 10–11, 1991—Temuco, Chile

A bomb detonated at the entrance of a Latter-day Saint chapel in the southwest area of Temuco. The device contained 3 kilograms of Tronex. The explosion caused nearly $10,000 in damages, destroying the entrance door and several windows, but causing zero casualties. Members of the Ejército Revolucionaria del Pueblo (ERP) (Argentina) (the "Pelantaro" faction of the Revolutionary Army of the People/Patria Libre) claimed responsibility in phone calls to local radio stations. The Montoneros (Argentina) may have also been responsible.[595]

December 22, 1991—Santiago, Chile

In the late evening, a bomb detonated at a Latter-day Saint chapel, causing minor property damage and zero injuries. No group claimed responsibility, yet members of the MJL likely conducted the attack.

This was one of two bombings that evening targeting different Latter-day Saint chapels.[596]

December 22, 1991—Santiago, Chile

In the late evening, a bomb detonated at a Latter-day Saint chapel, causing minor property damage and zero injuries. No group claimed responsibility, yet members of the MJL likely conducted the attack. This was one of two bombings that evening targeting different Latter-day Saint chapels.[597]

January 25, 1992—Santiago, Chile

At 10:50 p.m., a bomb detonated at a Latter-day Saint chapel entrance in the Quinta Normal district, causing property damage (extent and value unknown) and zero casualties. The MJL was responsible.[598]

January 25, 1992—Santiago, Chile (second attack)

At 10:55 p.m., a bomb detonated in front of a Latter-day Saint chapel in the La Florida district, causing property damage (extent and value unknown) and zero casualties. Pamphlets from the MAPU-Lautaro group were found at the scene.[599]

March 11, 1992—Santiago, Chile

At 11:30 p.m., a bomb detonated in front of a Latter-day Saint chapel in the San Miguel district, causing minor property damage and zero injuries. No group claimed responsibility.[600]

March 12, 1992—Santiago, Chile

At about 1 a.m., a bomb detonated on the window ledge of a Latter-day Saint chapel in the Nunoa district, causing minor property damage and zero casualties. No group claimed responsibility.[601]

March 26, 1992—Santiago, Chile

Members of the MAPU-Lautaro group bombed a Latter-day Saint chapel in the San Miguel district, causing minor property damage and zero casualties. There were pamphlets calling for, "Yankees out of Chile" at the scene. This was one of three attacks targeting Latter-day Saint chapels in Santiago that evening.[602]

March 26, 1992—Santiago, Chile (second attack)

Members of the MAPU-Lautaro group bombed a Latter-day Saint chapel in the San Miguel district, causing minor property damage and zero casualties. There were pamphlets calling for, "Yankees out of Chile" at the scene. This was one of three attacks targeting Latter-day Saint chapels in Santiago that evening.[603]

March 26, 1992—Santiago, Chile (third attack)

Members of the MAPU-Lautaro group bombed a Latter-day Saint chapel in the La Victoria district, shattering all the building's windows and damaging the ceiling. There were zero casualties.[604]

March 26, 1992—Calama, Chile

A bomb detonated at a Latter-day Saint chapel, shattering window glass and damaging the roof, but inflicting zero casualties. The perpetrators left MJL pamphlets at the scene.[605]

March 26, 1992—La Serena, Chile

At about 10:15 p.m., a bomb was discovered in front of a Latter-day Saint chapel. The fuse malfunctioned and local police deactivated the device. No group claimed responsibility.[606]

March 31, 1992—Santiago, Chile

At 10:50 p.m., a bomb detonated in front of a Latter-day Saint chapel in the Renca district, causing minor property damage and zero injuries.

There were pamphlets signed by the dissident faction of the Manuel Rodriguez Patriotic Front (FPMR/D) and the MAPU-Lautaro group at the scene.[607]

May 14, 1992—Santiago, Chile

Members of the MAPU-Lautaro organization entered the Latter-day Saint chapel near Varas Mena Street in the San Miguel district and interrupted a religious class. Individuals in the group verbally insulted the American missionary leading the class and struck a 19-year-old Chilean woman in the head when she attempted to defend the missionary. Then, at about 9:15 p.m., a bomb detonated within the building, causing minor property damage and zero casualties. The group left pamphlets belonging to the MAPU-Lautaro group at the scene. Local media reported that this was the third time that the same Latter-day Saint chapel was bombed.[608]

May 15, 1992—Santiago, Chile

At about 9:40 p.m., a group of individuals entered the Latter-day Saint chapel at the intersection of Carmen Mena Street and Las Industrias Avenue in the San Miguel district and poured a flammable liquid in one of the rooms. They ignited the liquid, which caused a fire that burned several furniture items. The group carried out a subversive propaganda action at the site with slogans mentioning the 24th anniversary of the MAPU. There were zero casualties. No group claimed responsibility, but perpetrators likely belonged to the MAPU-Lautaro organization, which conducted a separate attack that same evening.[609]

May 15, 1992—Santiago, Chile (second attack)

After 9:40 p.m., a bomb detonated inside a Latter-day Saint chapel in the Pedro Aguirre Cerda district, damaging several chapel windows and doors, but causing zero casualties. There were MAPU-Lautaro pamphlets reading "Yankees out of Chile" at the site.[610]

May 16, 1992—Santiago, Chile

At around 6:40 p.m., five masked members of the MJL entered the Latter-day Saint chapel at 1661 Huelen Street in the Cerro Navia section. They encountered a man, his sister, and the man's nephew cleaning the chapel prior to services the following day. They doused the man in gasoline and spread gasoline throughout the building, in every room with carpet. They threatened the man and his sister, holding them at gunpoint as the other members of the group ignited the gasoline. As the men gathered to leave the building, the bishop, José Medina Apablaza, entered the scene and grabbed a hammer to fend off the assailants. One of them shot the bishop in the leg and the group fled, fearing an immediate response from local police. The bishop miraculously sustained no injury and there was no significant damage to the building. Local media reported that this was the fourth bomb/fuel attack against that particular Latter-day Saint chapel in recent days.[611]

May 16, 1992—La Serena, Chile

At about 10 p.m., a bomb detonated in front of a Latter-day Saint chapel, damaging the building's windows and doors. There were no casualties. There were MAPU-Lautaro pamphlets at the scene.[612]

May 24, 1992—Santiago, Chile

At about 7:45 p.m., four men and one woman entered a Latter-day Saint chapel in the La Florida district. They forced 70 parishioners to leave the building. Then, the group poured flammable liquid on furniture and rugs and set the building on fire, burning several furniture items but causing zero casualties. The perpetrators left MAPU-Lautaro pamphlets at the scene.[613]

June 23, 1992—La Paz, Bolivia

At around 10:00 p.m., a bomb detonated near a Latter-day Saint chapel, damaging the building's wall, doors, and windows. There were zero casualties. The scene contained a hat labeled with EGTK letters—the acronym for the Tupac Katari Guerrilla Army—and group pamphlets.[614]

June 26, 1992—La Paz, Bolivia

A bomb detonated at the Latter-day Saint chapel at Avenida Bautista 1142 in the Zona Cementerio of La Paz. People had left the cemetery opposite the chapel a few minutes before the attack. The detonation made a hole in the building floor and damaged the ceiling and also broke windows of nearby buildings. Local media reported this was the second time the chapel was targeted, referencing a similar attack that occurred in either 1987 or 1988. There were zero casualties. Local authorities suspected the EGTK was responsible.[615]

July 5, 1992—Santiago, Chile

A bomb detonated in front of the Latter-day Saint chapel at 150 Munoz Gamero Street in La Recoleta district. The explosion caused property damage (extent and value unknown) and zero casualties. Police found MAPU-Lautaro pamphlets at the site. The group also claimed responsibility through a phone call to the UPI news agency.[616]

July 5, 1992—Santiago, Chile (second attack)

A bomb detonated inside the Latter-day Saint chapel at 4767 Santo Domingo Street in the Quinta Normal district. The explosion caused property damage (extent and value unknown) and zero casualties. Police found MAPU-Lautaro pamphlets at the site. The group also claimed responsibility through a phone call to the UPI news agency.[617]

July 5, 1992—Santiago, Chile (third attack)

A bomb detonated in the Latter-day Saint chapel at the intersection of Santa Maria and Concepcion Streets in the Renca district. The explosion caused property damage (extent and value unknown) and zero casualties. Police found MAPU-Lautaro pamphlets at the site. The group also claimed responsibility through a phone call to the UPI news agency.[618]

July 16, 1992—Paipote, Chile

At around 9:30 p.m., a bomb detonated at the entrance of a Latter-day Saint chapel, damaging part of the building's structure and shattering several windows. The approximate value of the property damage totaled 2 million pesos. There were no casualties. Local police determined the bomb consisted of 300 grams of industrial ANFO blasting agents and was activated by a fuse. Another similar charge planted on the side of the church failed to detonate. An individual claiming to be a member of the MJL called a local media outlet to claim responsibility in repudiation of "Yankee imperialism."[619]

July 21, 1992—Valdivia, Chile

At dawn, a bomb detonated at the entrance of the Latter-day Saint chapel in Valdivia. The bomb contained approximately 100 grams of ANFO blasting agents and was activated by a mechanical device with a slow fuse. The explosion caused property damage (extent and value unknown) and zero casualties. Pamphlets from the Subversive Coordinating Board for a Free Fatherland (Coordinadora Subversiva por Una Patria Libre) were found at the site, but later on, the MJL claimed responsibility for the attack through a phone call to a press agency, stating the attack was in memory of those who died and were arrested during the past few days by the police.[620]

July 21, 1992—Temuco, Chile

At about 11:45 p.m., a bomb detonated in front of a Latter-day Saint chapel, shattering at least 19 window glasses. There were zero casualties. There were pamphlets from the "Subversive Coordination for a Popular Fatherland" found at the scene, discussing the struggle of the Mapuche Indians. Police suspected the MJL was responsible for the attack.[621]

July 23, 1992—Santiago, Chile

Unknown perpetrators bombed the Latter-day Saint chapel at 1290 Magdalena Vicuña in San Miguel district. The bomb contained

200 grams of ammonium gelignite and caused significant property damage and zero casualties.[622]

July 23, 1992—Santiago, Chile

Unknown perpetrators bombed the Latter-day Saint chapel on Sergio Chepi in the La Cisterna district of Santiago. The bomb consisted of 200 grams of ANFO blasting agents. The detonation caused considerable property damage and zero casualties. There were subversive pamphlets found at the site.[623]

July 23, 1992—Araucania, Chile

Members of the MJL bombed a Latter-day Saint chapel, causing property damage (extent and value unknown) and zero casualties.[624]

July 23, 1992—Concepcion, Chile

Unknown perpetrators bombed a Latter-day Saint chapel in the Chiguayante district of Concepcion, causing property damage (extent and value unknown) and zero casualties.[625]

July 25, 1992—Oruro, Bolivia

At about 5:20 a.m., a bomb detonated at a Latter-day Saint chapel, shattering several windows and leaving a crater in the middle of the chapel's courtyard. There were no casualties. EGTK pamphlets were found at the scene.[626]

July 26, 1992—Santiago, Chile

Unknown perpetrators bombed a Latter-day Saint chapel, causing property damage (extent and value unknown) and zero casualties.[627]

July 27, 1992—Santiago, Chile

At about 12:10 a.m., a bomb detonated in front of a Latter-day Saint chapel in the Maipu district, damaging the two main entrance doors and shattering several windows. No group claimed responsibility, but Chilean police credited the MJL.[628]

July 28, 1992—Santiago, Chile

A bomb detonated near the rear of the Latter-day Saint chapel at 1681 Huelin Street in the Cerro Navia district. The detonation caused considerable property damage to the chapel and neighboring residences, including shattered windows. The bomb consisted of ANFO blasting agents, activated by a safety fuse. Pamphlets from the FPMR/D were found at the scene.[629]

August 3, 1992—Coquimbo, Chile

Local police deactivated a bomb discovered inside a Latter-day Saint chapel. There were pamphlets with MJL slogans found at the scene.[630]

August 5, 1992—Santiago, Chile

Members of the MJL bombed a Latter-day Saint chapel in the Renca district, causing property damage (extent and value unknown) and zero casualties.[631]

August 5, 1992—Santiago, Chile (second attack)

Members of the MAPU bombed a Latter-day Saint chapel in the Quinta Normal MJL, causing property damage (extent and value unknown) and zero casualties.[632]

August 5, 1992—Santiago, Chile (third attack)

Members of the MJL bombed a Latter-day Saint chapel in the La Recoleta district, causing property damage (extent and value unknown) and zero casualties.[633]

September 11, 1992—Santiago, Chile

Unknown perpetrators bombed a Latter-day Saint chapel, causing property damage (extent and value unknown) and zero casualties.[634]

September 12, 1992—Coquimbo, Chile

Unknown perpetrators bombed a Latter-day Saint chapel, causing property damage (extent and value unknown) and zero casualties.[635]

October 7, 1992—Santiago, Chile

Unknown perpetrators bombed a Latter-day Saint chapel, causing property damage (extent and value unknown) and zero casualties.[636]

October 7, 1992—Santiago, Chile (second attack)

Unknown perpetrators bombed Latter-day Saint chapel, causing property damage (extent and value unknown) and zero casualties.[637]

October 11, 1992—Santiago, Chile

A bomb detonated at a Latter-day Saint chapel in the San Miguel district. The explosion caused property damage (extent and value unknown) and zero casualties. The assailants presumably belonged to the MJL. The group likely conducted the attack to protest the 500th anniversary of the discovery of the Americas on October 12.[638]

October 11, 1992—Talcahuano, Chile

Local press reports credited the MJL with planting a bomb at a Latter-day Saint chapel. The detonation caused property damage and zero casualties. Pamphlets found at the scene included slogans protesting the Columbus Day anniversary.[639]

October 11, 1992—Talcahuano, Chile (second attack)

Local press reports credited the MJL with planting a bomb at a Latter-day Saint chapel. The detonation caused property damage and zero casualties. Pamphlets found at the scene included slogans protesting the Columbus Day anniversary.[640]

October 12, 1992—Santiago, Chile

Unknown perpetrators bombed a Latter-day Saint chapel in Conchali, causing property damage (extent and value unknown) and zero casualties. The attack was one of three targeting Latter-day Saint chapels that day, presumably by the MJL in protest of the 500th anniversary of the discovery of the Americas.[641]

October 12, 1992—Santiago, Chile (second attack)

Unknown perpetrators bombed a Latter-day Saint chapel in Puente Alto, causing property damage (extent and value unknown) and zero casualties. The attack was one of three targeting Latter-day Saint chapels that day, presumably by the MJL in protest of the 500th anniversary of the discovery of the Americas.[642]

October 12, 1992—Santiago, Chile (third attack)

Unknown perpetrators bombed a Latter-day Saint chapel in the Quinta Normal, causing property damage (extent and value unknown) and zero casualties. The attack was one of three targeting Latter-day Saint chapels that day, presumably by the MJL in protest of the 500th anniversary of the discovery of the Americas.[643]

November 11, 1992—Valparaiso, Chile

Local police deactivated a bomb discovered near a Latter-day Saint chapel. No group claimed responsibility.[644]

November 25, 1992—Bogota, Colombia

Colombian guerrillas detonated a bomb at a Latter-day Saint chapel, causing property damage (extent and value unknown) and zero casualties. This was part of a series of attacks including another bomb targeting a separate Latter-day Saint chapel and eight other bombs targeting other US-affiliated buildings.[645]

November 25, 1992—Bogota, Colombia (second attack)

Colombian guerrillas detonated a bomb at a Latter-day Saint chapel, causing property damage (extent and value unknown) and zero casualties. This was part of a series of attacks including another bomb targeting a separate Latter-day Saint chapel and eight other bombs targeting other US-affiliated buildings.[646]

December 14, 1992—Santiago, Chile

Unknown perpetrators bombed a Latter-day Saint chapel, causing property damage (extent and value unknown) and zero casualties.[647]

December 17, 1992—Santiago, Chile

Members of the FPMR bombed an unoccupied Latter-day Saint chapel in the Renca district, causing property damage (extent and value unknown) and zero casualties.[648]

December 19, 1992—Talca, Chile

Members of the MJL bombed a Latter-day Saint chapel, causing property damage (extent and value unknown) and zero casualties.[649]

December 23, 1992—Penco, Chile

Members of the MJL bombed a Latter-day Saint chapel, causing property damage (extent and value unknown) and zero casualties.[650]

February 5, 1993—Cuzco, Peru

At about 7:55 p.m., a small explosive device detonated at a Latter-day Saint chapel, causing moderate property damage. There were 20 parishioners within the chapel when the bomb exploded, but there were zero reported injuries. Sendero Luminoso was likely responsible for the attack.[651]

March 22, 1993—La Paz, Bolivia

At about 9:00 p.m., a dynamite charge detonated near a Latter-day Saint chapel in El Alto, causing minor property damage and zero casualties. Several EGTK pamphlets found at the scene read, "the struggle begins." A cloth banner displaying the group's acronym was also found at the scene.[652]

May 13, 1993—Santiago, Chile

At about 9:00 p.m., two men and one woman wearing ski masks and dark glasses and belonging to the MJL entered a Latter-day Saint chapel in the Quinta Normal district. They hit and overpowered the Chilean Latter-day Saint bishop, then sprayed the entire building with fuel and set the fuel on fire. This destroyed the building but caused zero deaths. The group fled via taxi after leaving pamphlets at the scene.[653]

May 27-28, 1993—Santiago, Chile

A bomb detonated at a Latter-day Saint chapel in the Conchali district, which was one of nine targets of bomb attacks throughout Santiago. The explosion caused property damage (extent and value unknown) and zero casualties. No group claimed responsibility, but the bombings were attributed to the FPMR Autonomous Faction, as several FPMR pamphlets were found at the scene.[654]

July 26, 1993—Talcahuano, Chile

At about 8:00 p.m., three men and one woman entered a Latter-day Saint chapel in the Villa Acero district, carrying a Cuban flag and a cardboard box they claimed contained a bomb. All were armed. They doused the building with gasoline, which they then set on fire, causing extensive damage. The eight Americans and four Chileans present in the chapel at the time of the attack were unharmed. The assailants left pamphlets belonging to the "Coordinadora Subversiva Por Un Patria Popular" (Subversive Coordinator for a Popular Fatherland), a group consisting of elements of the Lautaro group, the MIR, and the dissident faction of the Manuel Rodriguez Patriotic Front (FPMR/D). The group then fled in a stolen taxi. Local police later inspected the cardboard box, which revealed no traces of a bomb.[655]

September 10, 1993—Santiago, Chile

During evening hours, a medium-sized bomb detonated in front of a Latter-day Saint chapel in La Florida, causing zero injuries. No group claimed responsibility, but the detonation took place a few hours before the 20th anniversary of the military coup ousting the Salvador Allende government in 1973. Local media reported the same chapel was targeted at least twice previously.[656]

September 11, 1993—Santiago, Chile

Unknown perpetrators bombed a Latter-day Saint chapel in Conchali, causing minor property damage and zero casualties. The bombing marked the anniversary of the coup against Allende in 1973.[657]

October 7, 1993—Osorno, Chile

A bomb detonated near a Latter-day Saint chapel in Rahue Alto, shattering windows and damaging the building's back entrance door, but causing zero casualties. There were pamphlets belonging to the MJL and the Manuel Rodriguez Patriotic Front/Dissident Faction (FPMR/D) at the scene.[658]

November 27, 1993—Punta Arenas, Chile

Three youths (unknown affiliation to terrorist groups, possibly MJL) attacked a Latter-day Saint chapel by arson, causing property damage (extent and value unknown) and zero casualties.[659]

January 23, 1994—Medellin, Colombia

At about 9:30 a.m., four or five armed and masked Colombians entered the El Prado Chapel, interrupting a talk delivered by Church member Hugo Tobón, and asked if any "gringos" were present. After parishioners stated there were no Americans, the group told the 120–130 parishioners to leave the building, and then detonated explosives that destroyed the sacrament hall and a large portion of the building. There were zero casualties. The assailants allegedly belonged to the Simon Bolivar Guerrilla Coordinating Board (CGSB) and apparently conducted the attack to protest the presence of US Soldiers in Colombia participating in Fuertes Caminos (Strong Roads), a series of engineer-oriented exercises throughout South America involving US Army National Guard Soldiers.[660]

January 23, 1994—Bucaramanga, Colombia

Members of the ELN bombed a Latter-day Saint chapel during the evening hours when no one was present in the building, virtually destroying the chapel and inflicting zero casualties. The two devices used contained 2 kilograms of dynamite and the damage value totaled an estimated 7 million pesos. The group conducted the attack to protest the presence of US Soldiers in Colombia participating in Fuertes Caminos (Strong Roads), a series of engineer-oriented exercises throughout South America involving US Army National Guard Soldiers.[661]

February 15, 1994—Cali, Colombia

The ELN took credit for bombing the Almendros Latter-day Saint chapel, causing nearly $1,000 in property damage and zero casualties. The bombing was in protest the presence of 150 US Soldiers in Juanchaco, Colombia participating in Fuertes Caminos (Strong Roads), a series of engineer-oriented exercises throughout South America involving US Army National Guard Soldiers.[662]

March 4, 1994—Barranquilla, Colombia

Unknown perpetrators planted a bomb at a Latter-day Saint chapel, which was found and defused before detonation. No group claimed responsibility.[663]

March 4, 1994—Manizales, Colombia

Unknown perpetrators planted a bomb at a Latter-day Saint chapel, which was found and defused before detonation. No group claimed responsibility.[664]

March 6, 1994—Chinchina, Colombia

Unknown perpetrators planted a bomb at a Latter-day Saint chapel, which was found and defused before detonation.[665]

March 10, 1994—Buga, Colombia

Unknown perpetrators attacked a Latter-day Saint facility with gunfire. There were zero casualties.[666]

June 15, 1994—Chilca, Peru

Shining Path members bombed a Latter-day Saint chapel, causing property damage (extent and value unknown) and zero casualties.[667]

June 17, 1994—Huancayo, Peru

Shining Path members bombed a Latter-day Saint chapel, causing property damage (extent and value unknown) and zero casualties.[668]

June 27, 1994—San Andres Cholula, Mexico

Unknown perpetrators conducted an attack against Latter-day Saints involving hostage taking (kidnapping) and firearms.[669]

July 25, 1994—Guatemala City, Guatemala

Unknown perpetrators conducted an attack against Latter-day Saints involving hostage taking (kidnapping) and firearms.[670]

August 2, 1994—Cali, Colombia

The Revolutionary Armed Forces of Colombia (FARC) claimed responsibility for bombing a Latter-day Saint chapel. The bomb contained a half kilogram of dynamite placed in a can. The explosion caused property damage (extent and value unknown) and injured two people nearby. FARC flyers left at the site protested US intervention in Haiti.[671]

August 2, 1994—Cali, Colombia (second attack)

The FARC claimed responsibility for bombing a Latter-day Saint chapel. The bomb contained a half kilogram of dynamite placed in a can. The explosion caused property damage (extent and value unknown) and zero casualties. FARC flyers left at the site protested US intervention in Haiti.[672]

September 10–11, 1994—Santiago, Chile

Unknown perpetrators targeted a Latter-day Saint chapel with a bomb, causing zero casualties.[673]

September 10–11, 1994—Santiago, Chile (second attack)

Unknown perpetrators targeted a Latter-day Saint chapel with a bomb, causing zero casualties.[674]

September 30, 1994—La Paz, Bolivia

Unknown perpetrators threw a 1/4 stick of dynamite into a Latter-day Saint chapel, causing minor property damage and zero casualties. No group claimed responsibility.[675]

October 22, 1994—Neiva, Colombia

Members of the CGSB bombed a Latter-day Saint chapel, causing minor property damage and zero casualties.[676]

October 22, 1994—Neiva, Colombia (second attack)

Members of the CGSB bombed a Latter-day Saint chapel, causing minor property damage and zero casualties.[677]

April 28, 1995—Barahona, Dominican Republic

Two or three armed men entered the front entrance area of a Latter-day Saint chapel during a dance sponsored by the church and attended by about 50 people, most of whom were Dominican. The men tossed two improvised explosive devices contained in soup cans. Only one of the devices exploded, injuring a female guest in the arm. As the men fled, they fired five or six gunshots in the air. No group claimed responsibility, but the event was likely related to the anniversary of the 1965 US invasion of the Dominican Republic.[678]

September 20–21, 1996—Barrancabermeja, Colombia

A Latter-day Saint chapel under construction suffered significant structural damage. Five bombs had been placed in the construction area by unknown perpetrators, but only two detonated. The explosions blew the roof off the building and destroyed all the installed doors and windows. There were no casualties. Workers at the site had previously been threatened by the FARC, ELN, the Popular Liberation Army, and the Jaime Bateman Front, but the Global Terrorism Database credits the ELN with this attack. There were also reports that possible guerrillas had surveilled the site during construction and groups attempted to force the construction company to hire local workers at twice the normal rate. Guerrillas also tried to prevent the construction of the building's steeple, which they thought was an antenna for transmitting messages to the CIA.[679]

November 7, 1996—Tulua, Colombia

Members of the ELN threw two small improvised incendiary devices at a Latter-day Saint chapel during the early morning hours, causing minor property damage and zero casualties. Anti-US propaganda belonging to the ELN was found at the scene, which condemned the US Government efforts to reinstate extradition and denounced US elections.[680]

November 8, 1996—Santiago, Chile

Six hooded individuals threw five Molotov cocktails at a Latter-day Saint chapel in the Cerro Navia area, two of which failed to ignite. The attack caused property damage (extent and value unknown) and zero casualties. A hoax bomb was also found outside the chapel.[681]

March 3, 1999—Salt Lake City, United States

A worker in the mail room of the Church Office Building opened an envelope at about 9:57 a.m. The envelope contained a letter claiming, "Congratulations, you've been exposed to anthrax." Three employees were decontaminated at the scene and taken to University Hospital for medical treatment. The letter was taken to the University of Utah for testing, where officials declared the letter a hoax. At the time, anthrax threats were a daily occurrence throughout the United States. Several packages appeared throughout the Salt Lake Valley in weeks preceding this event, consisting of similar packaging and lettering, and postmarked from Lexington, KY.[682]

March 7, 1999—Cali, Colombia

Members of The Extraditables bombed a Latter-day Saint chapel, causing property damage (extent and value unknown) and zero casualties.

This was one of two attacks targeting Latter-day Saint chapels in east Cali. Combined, the attacks involved four bombs, two of which were dynamite charges. Inconsistencies in reporting exist with regard to casualties, but the Global Terrorism Database lists zero.[683]

March 7, 1999—Cali, Colombia (second attack)

Members of The Extraditables bombed a Latter-day Saint chapel, causing property damage (extent and value unknown) and zero casualties. This was one of two attacks targeting Latter-day Saint chapels in east Cali. Combined, the attacks involved four bombs, two of which were dynamite charges. Inconsistencies in reporting exist with regard to casualties, but the Global Terrorism Database lists zero.[684]

April 11, 2000—Cali, Colombia

At around dawn, a bomb (mostly comprised of gunpowder) detonated at a Latter-day Saint chapel. This was one of three attacks targeting separate Latter-day Saint chapels that morning with property damage ranging from minimal to severe. There were no casualties. In one incident (unclear which), witnesses observed an unidentified man on a motorcycle throwing a bomb at one of the churches. In one incident (unclear which), the chapel was targeted with two bombs, but law enforcement authorities diffused one unexploded bomb at one of the chapels. A missionary in the Colombia Cali Mission stated two of the bombs were tossed from cars and one was placed at a gate, which blew the gate off. No group claimed responsibility, but locals suspected the ELN.[685]

April 11, 2000—Cali, Colombia (second attack)

At around dawn, a bomb (mostly comprised of gunpowder) detonated at a Latter-day Saint chapel. This was one of three attacks targeting separate Latter-day Saint chapels that morning with property damage ranging from minimal to severe. There were no casualties. In one incident (unclear which), witnesses observed an unidentified man on a motorcycle throwing a bomb at one of the churches. In one incident (unclear which), the chapel was targeted with two bombs, but law enforcement authorities diffused one unexploded bomb at one of the chapels. A missionary in the Colombia Cali Mission stated two of the bombs were tossed from cars and one was placed at a gate, which blew the gate off. No group claimed responsibility, but locals suspected the ELN.[686]

April 11, 2000—Cali, Colombia (third attack)

At around dawn, a bomb (mostly comprised of gunpowder) detonated at a Latter-day Saint chapel. This was one of three attacks targeting separate Latter-day Saint chapels that morning with property damage ranging from minimal to severe. There were no casualties. In one incident (unclear which), witnesses observed an unidentified man on a motorcycle throwing a bomb at one of the churches. In one incident (unclear which), the chapel was targeted with two bombs, but law enforcement authorities diffused one unexploded bomb at one of the chapels. A missionary in the Colombia Cali Mission stated two of the bombs were tossed from cars and one was placed at a gate, which blew the gate off. No group claimed responsibility, but locals suspected the ELN.[687]

September 15, 2001—Varazdin, Croatia

An unknown perpetrator threw a grenade into a Latter-day Saint chapel, causing property damage (extent and value unknown) and zero casualties. The perpetrator committed the attack in a political statement to protest US military involvement in foreign lands, attacking the Church due to connections to the US. There were no members in the chapel at the time of the attack because they were attending a conference in Zagreb.[688]

May 27, 2004—Valencia, Venezuela

Unknown assailants detonated a fragmentary grenade in front of a Latter-day Saint chapel entrance at 5:45 a.m. Several pamphlets found at the scene belonged to a subversive group called the Army of the People in Arms (EPA). The pamphlets denounced Yankee imperialism around the world, particularly in Venezuela. They identified

Latter-day Saint chapels as an interest of Yankee imperialism, claiming they were religious strongholds for political penetration and a front for covert intelligence operations. The explosion caused minimal property damage and zero casualties.[689]

November 13, 2008—Los Angeles, United States

An envelope containing a white powdery substance appeared in the mail arriving at the Latter-day Saint temple in Los Angeles, California. Testing revealed the powdery substance was not anthrax. The hoax came shortly after a November 4 vote in California that narrowly passed Proposition 8, but the FBI did not identify links between the perpetrator(s) and the Latter-day Saint Church, whose members attracted attention for supporting Proposition 8 to ban same-sex marriage.[690]

November 13, 2008—Salt Lake City, United States

An envelope containing a white powdery substance appeared in the mail arriving at the Latter-day Saint temple in Salt Lake City, Utah. An employee in the recorder's office within the temple annex (separate from the temple) opened a manila envelope, finding within it, another white envelope with a white powdery substance inside. Testing revealed the substance was not anthrax. The hoax came shortly after a November 4 vote in California that narrowly passed Proposition 8. Even so, the FBI did not identify links between the perpetrator(s) and the Church, whose members attracted attention for supporting Proposition 8 to ban same-sex marriage.[691]

July 25, 2016—Las Vegas, United States

Unknown perpetrators conducted an incendiary attack against a Latter-day Saint chapel, causing property damage (extent and value unknown) and zero casualties.[692]

December 2, 2018—Goiânia, Brazil

Uilker Alves (28) entered the Latter-day Saint chapel located in the Colina Azul Sector of Goiânia during Sunday worship service and threatened members with two butcher knives. Witnesses stated he entered the chapel and told the crowd everyone was going to die. The attacker cut two members of the congregation and hit two others before he was injured and arrested. Alves later stated he carried out the attack because he was upset that Church representatives never followed through on a promise to visit him after meeting him in the street in 2013.[693]

APPENDIX B

ALPHABETICAL LIST OF RELEVANT TERRORIST GROUPS

14th of December Command

Founded: c. 1990
Disbanded: c. 1991
Ideology: Isolationist
Location: Chile
Tactics: Bombings, hijacking
Targets: Transportation, religious
AKA: N/A

Description: A small group which operated in Chile for a matter of months. The group targeted businesses and religious institutions, most likely operating under an isolationist ideology to expel foreigners.[694]

Alejo Calatayud Command (CAC)

Founded: c. 1987
Disbanded: c. 1989
Ideology: Isolationist, Marxist/Leninist
Location: Bolivia
Tactics: Bombings, narcotics trafficking
Targets: US Government, US-affiliated religious institutions

AKA: N/A

Description: Originating in Cochabamba and deriving its name from Alejo Calatayud, a Bolivian revolutionary figure, the group waged violent attacks against US targets in protest of antinarcotics activities. The group was urban based, but members recruited heavily from and found a support base among *campesinos* who depended on cocoa crops for livelihood. The group likely had an overlapping membership and leaders with the ELN and Zarate Willca Armed Forces of Liberation (FAL-ZW) and may have merged with the ELN.[695]

Anti-Imperialist Revolutionary Front/Frente Revolucionario Anti-Imperialista (FRA)

Founded: c. 1990
Disbanded: c. 1991
Ideology: Isolationist
Location: Chile
Tactics: Bombings
AKA: N/A

Description: The group was allegedly formed by members of the Movement of the Revolutionary Left (MIR) and the ELN, among other groups. The FRA quickly dissolved.[696]

Army of The People in Arms/Ejercito del Pueblo en Armas (EPA)

Founded: c. 2002
Disbanded: (Still active)
Ideology: Anti-globalization / anti-capitalist
Location: Venezuela
Tactics: Bombings (grenade)
Targets: Religious, US-affiliated institutions
AKA: N/A

Description: The group began when state efforts in Venezuela produced a large military reserve and two paramilitary organizations, one of which was the Army of the People in Arms. These groups were to leverage insurgency strategies and tactics to keep out foreign influences and reduce internal uprisings against Chavez and his followers.[697]

Eloy Alfaro Popular Armed Forces/Fuerzas Armadas Populares Eloy Alfaro

Founded: c. 1970
Disbanded: c. 1989
Ideology: Left Wing
Location: Ecuador, Colombia
Tactics: kidnapping/hostage-taking, armed assault, bombings
Targets: Religious, aid workers, NGOs, contractors, military, police
AKA: Alfaro Lives, Dammit!; ¡Alfaro Vive, Carajo!

Description: The group opposed perceived imperialism and foreign meddling. Group members became militaristic in the early 1980s and conducted at least 25 attacks in Ecuador and Colombia before disbanding and reforming into a legitimate political party. Members collaborated with other leftist organizations in South America and created a joint operations unit called America Battalion with the 19th of April Movement and the Tupac Amaru Revolutionary Movement (MRTA).[698]

Heroes of Palestine

Founded: c. 1991
Disbanded: c. 1991
Ideology: Left wing
Location: Colombia
Tactics: Bombings
Targets: Religious
AKA: N/A

Description: The small group operating in Medellin, Colombia bombed religious targets in protest of what they alleged to be American aggression against Palestinians and Arabs.[699]

Internationalist Brigade/Brigada Internacionalista (BI)

Founded: c. 1990
Disbanded: c. 1991
Ideology: Left wing
Location: Venezuela
Tactics: Arson (Molotov cocktail)
Targets: Religious
AKA: Internationalist Brigade Venezuela
Description: There is very little information on this organization, unknown to the US Department of State until a spokesperson for the group took credit for an attack against a Latter-day Saint meetinghouse. The group affiliated the Church with the United States, targeting meetinghouses in protest of US policies and perceptions of espionage operations within Venezuela.[700]

Islamic Revolutionary Command

Founded: c. 1990
Disbanded: c. 1991
Ideology: Jihadist
Location: Argentina
Tactics: Bombings
Targets: Religious
AKA: N/A
Description: The only attack attributed to this group is a hoax bomb emplaced at a Latter-day Saint meetinghouse. The group seemingly targeted the Church as a soft target in protest of US military involvement in the Middle East.[701]

Lautaro Youth Movement/Movimiento Juventil Lautaro (MJL)

Founded: c. 1988
Disbanded: c. 1994
Ideology: Left Wing (Marxist)
Location: Chile

Tactics: Robbery, assassinations, bombings, arson

AKA: Lautaro Faction of the United Popular Movement (MAPU/L), Lautaro Popular Rebel Forces (FRPL)

Description: Named for the famous chief of the Mapuche Indians who died resisting Spanish conquerors of Chile in 1557, the MJL sought to bring about political change through violent revolution. The group contained leaders from leftist factions and recruited heavily from poor communities, but also included criminals and alienated adolescents. The MJL formed as a militant member of the Popular Movement of United Action-Lautaro (MAPU/L), which broke away from the original United Popular Action Movement (MAPU), an extreme leftist splinter group that split off from the Chilean Christian Democratic Party in 1968. The MAPU/L formed additional groups to achieve objectives through violence. The MAPU/L formed the Lautaro Youth Movement (MJL) as a youth wing, as well as a military wing called the Lautaro Rebel Forces (FRPL). Chilean intelligence services referred to the three groups as the Complejo Partidario MAPU-Lautaro, or Multi-Partisan MAPU-Lautaro. The MJL mainly targeted political figures and sites, law enforcement figures, banks, stores, and Latter-day Saint chapels. The group's terror campaign began just prior to the presidential election and transfer of power on March 11, 1989 that ended the rule of General Augusto Pinochet. Members of the group assassinated Domingo Sarmiento, a member of the Party for Democracy (Chile).[702]

Manuel Rodriguez Patriotic Front/Frente Patriotico Manuel Rodriguez (FPMR)

Founded: c. 1983

Disbanded: c. 1991

Ideology: Left Wing (Maoist, Marxist, Communist, Socialist)

Location: Chile

Tactics: Assassinations, bombings, complex attacks

Targets: Political figures, religious, business

AKA: Manuel Rodriguez Patriotic Front–Dissidents (FPMR-D), a splinter-group from the original FPMR when the group divided in 1987. For the purposes of analysis, FPMR includes this splinter faction.

Description: The group was formed as the armed wing of the Chilean Communist Party. The group received external support in the form of training and weapons from Cuba. Analysts speculated the group may have trained with Peru's MRTA. At peak membership, the FPMR contained between 1,000 and 5,000 members.[703]

Maximiliano Gomez Revolutionary Brigade

Founded: c. 1987
Disbanded: c. 1988
Ideology: Left wing (anarchist, Marxist)
Location: Dominican Republic
Tactics: Bombings
Targets: Government, business, US-affiliated institutions
AKA: N/A

Description: Individuals created this group specifically to conduct attacks in July 1987, marking the 22nd anniversary of American intervention in the Dominican Republic.[704]

Movement of The Revolutionary Left/Movimiento de Izquierda Revolucionaria (MIR)

Founded: c. 1965
Disbanded: c. 1994
Ideology: Communist / Socialist / Marxist
Location: Chile
Tactics: Bombings, armed assault, hijacking
Targets: Business, religious, journalists, civilians, transportation
AKA: Movement of the Revolutionary Left – Chile (distinguishing the faction within Chile from other factions of the same name in other countries); Leftist Revolutionary Movement.

Description: The group supported reforms instituted by Salvador Allende's administration, and then strongly opposed the Augusto Pinochet dictatorship. Attacks targeting the Church amounted to a miniscule portion of attacks attributed to the MIR throughout the group's existence. Most attacks against the Church concerned protests against perceived imperialism and US military intervention in the Middle East.[705]

National Liberation Army/Ejercito de Liberacion Nacional (ELN)

Founded: c. 1965
Disbanded: (Still active)
Ideology: Communist / Socialist / Marxist / Leninist
Location: Colombia
Tactics: Kidnapping/hostage taking, bombings, assassinations
Targets: Infrastructure, transportation, military, aid workers, NGOs, contractors, religious
AKA: National Liberation Army of Colombia
Description: Urban-based group with origins in Cochabamba and other urban centers. The group likely contained around 100 members. Their objective was to bring about a general revolt through an armed faction.[706]

Nestor Paz Zamora Commission/Comision Nestor Paz Zamora (CNPZ)

Founded: c. 1990
Disbanded: c. 1991
Ideology: Left wing (Communist, Socialist)
Location: Bolivia
Tactics: Bombing, kidnapping
Targets: Business, infrastructure, monuments, government, religious
AKA: N/A
Description: Named after the brother of Jaime Paz Zamora, then president of Bolivia, this group conducted a handful of attacks, often claiming responsibility by leaving spray-painted initials of the group and the phrase, "Bolivia dignified and sovereign." The small group mainly targeted US Government facilities and plotted to take over mines with other extremist factions.[707]

Omar Torrijos Commando for Latin American Dignity

Founded: c. 1989
Disbanded: c. 1990
Ideology: Left Wing (Maoist, Marxist, Communist, Socialist)
Location: Panama, Colombia, Venezuela
Tactics: Bombings, arson
Targets: Religious, government
AKA: Omar Torrijos Anti-Intervention Command Group

Description: The organization emerged immediately after the US invasion of Panama. The group slogan was to take "a dead gringo for every assassinated Panamanian," but the group only conducted two registered attacks, one of which targeted a Latter-day Saint meetinghouse.[708]

Palestinian Support Group/Grupo de Apoyo a Palestina (GAP)

Founded: c. 1990
Disbanded: c. 1991
Ideology: Ethno-national
Location: Brazil
Tactics: Arson
AKA: N/A

Description: Little is known about this organization, as the Palestine Liberation Organization (PLO) in the locale where the GAP claimed responsibility for an attack denied association with the perpetrators. The Global Terrorism Database and other glossaries do not list a group by this particular name.[709]

People's Revolutionary Army—Argentina/ Ejercito Revolucionario del Pueblo (ERP)

Founded: c. 1969
Disbanded: c. 1991 (last registered attack)
Ideology: Communist / Socialist / Maoist
Location: Argentina, Chile

Tactics: Extortion, kidnapping, hostage taking, robbery, and armed assault

Targets: Military, police, government, business, religious

AKA: N/A

Description: This group began as the armed wing of the Workers' Revolutionary Party PRT, a communist party which later adopted a Maoist ideology. The group conducted at least 85 attacks over 22 years. Only one of these attacks took place in Chile, the target of which was a Latter-day Saint chapel.[710]

Revolutionary Armed Forces of Colombia—People's Army/Fuerzas Armadas Revolucionarias de Colombia—Ejercito del Pueblo (FARC-EP)

Founded: c. 1964

Disbanded: (Dissident groups remain active)

Ideology: Marxist-Leninist

Location: Colombia, Ecuador, Panama, Venezuela

Tactics: Kidnapping, ransom, extortion, drug trafficking activities, urban warfare, guerrilla warfare, ambush, mortar attack, armed assault, paramilitary operations, illegal mining

Targets: Civilians, government, schools, transportation, military, infrastructure, religious

AKA: Armed Revolutionary Forces of Colombia, Fuerzas Armadas Revolucionarias de Colombia

Description: The group was formed as the military wing of the Colombian Communist Party. Estimates of the group's size are as high as 8,000 core fighters and 30,000 militia forces. Of note, the group renamed itself "Common Alternative Revolutionary Force" on August 31, 2017, but all analysis and attributed acts of terrorism concern previous times under the name FARC or FARC-EP.[711]

Rodriguista Militias/Milicias Rodriguistas (MR)

Founded: c. 1990

Disbanded: c. 1991

Ideology: Left wing (anarchist), racist

Location: Chile

Tactics: Bombings

Targets: Religious

AKA: Rodriguistas Identity, Identidad Rodriguista

Description: The group opposed Pinochet's regime and policies in Chile. The MR targeted Latter-day Saint chapels, often with Molotov cocktails attempting to start an arson and cause physical damage to meetinghouses. Law enforcement stated adolescents establishing associations with the MR was the first step toward joining the widely known FPMR.[712]

Shining Path/Sendero Luminoso (SL)

Founded: Late 1960s

Disbanded: (Still active)

Ideology: Communist (Maoist), Socialist

Location: Peru

Tactics: Bombings, narcotics trafficking, armed assault, guerrilla/insurgency

Targets: Government, business, political figures, general civilian population, trade union organizers, religious, transportation

AKA: Communist Party of Peru (PCP)

Description: The group used brutal tactics to incite fear and intimidation among citizens and coerce them to support the organization. Recruiting and attacks began in the countryside, but later moved into Lima. The group used brutal tactics, which facilitated repressive government actions to counter the organization. Ultimately, Shining Path's objective was to overthrow the Peruvian government and install a communist revolutionary command. Activity sharply declined in 1992 with the arrest and imprisonment of the group's leader, Abimael Guzmán, but the group continued to attack law enforcement, military, and government targets into 2017.[713]

Simon Bolivar Guerrilla Coordinating Board/ Coordinadora Guerrillera Simon Bolivar (CGSB)

Founded: c. 1987
Disbanded: Early 1990s
Ideology: Left wing (Maoist, Marxist, Communist, Socialist)
Location: Colombia
Tactics: Bombings, kidnapping, armed assault, paramilitary operations
Targets: Oil facilities, government, religious, law enforcement, transportation, civilians
AKA: N/A
Description: This alliance consisted of the ELN, the Revolutionary Armed Forces of Colombia (FARC), and other groups at times began as a renegade cell of the Soviet Communist Party. The alliance conducted over 200 attacks, only three of which target the Church.[714]

Subversive Coordinator for a Popular Fatherland/ Coordinadora Subversiva por una Patria Popular (CSPP)

Founded: c. 1992
Disbanded: c. 1993
Ideology: Far-left (Communist, Maoist, Socialist)
Location: Chile
Tactics: Bombings, arson
AKA: Subversive Coordinating Board for a Free Fatherland, Subversive Coordinator for a Popular Fatherland
Description: The organization was seemingly an alliance or coalition, consisting of members of the Lautaro Youth Movement, the Movement of the Revolutionary Left (MIR), and the dissident faction of the Manuel Rodriguez Patriotic Front. Perpetrators left pamphlets with the organization name at attack sites, but members of the Lautaro Youth Movement later claimed responsibility for most of these attacks. The group referenced the struggle of the Mapuche Indians in their propaganda.[715]

The Extraditables/Los Extraditables

Founded: c. 1987

Disbanded: c. 1999

Ideology: Criminal (narcoterrorism)

Location: Colombia

Tactics: Bombings, hijackings, transnational crime, drug trafficking

Targets: Schools, religious, journalists, government, law enforcement, transportation, telecommunications

AKA: N/A

Description: Colombian drug lords created this group to persuade the Colombian government to do away with extradition. The group originally focused on media, publishing articles defending their position and seeking to influence political parties. Over time, these efforts turned violent and the group targeted law enforcement, politicians, and others through terrorism.[716]

Tupac Amaru Revolutionary Movement/Movimiento Revolucionario Tupac Amaru (MRTA)

Founded: c. 1983

Disbanded: Not publicly disbanded; no attacks since 1997

Ideology: Left Wing (Marxist)

Location: Peru

Tactics: Extortion, bombing, hostage taking, assassinations, urban terrorism

Targets: Government, journalists, business, schools, religious

AKA: N/A

Description: The group emerged when the Marxist-Leninist Revolutionary Socialist Party and the militant wing of the Revolutionary Left Movement fused in the early 1980s. Group propaganda indicates members were anti-imperialist and wanted to replace the government with socialist institutions. Evidence suggests the group "originated among public school teachers and college students, particularly sociology majors, at the University of San Andres."

The group sought to repel Americans and US institutions from their lands through violence. Around the time of the Gulf War, a portion of their fliers left at attack sites read, "there will be no peace for the Yankee imperialists. With the masses and arms fatherland or death, we shall win." The group consisted of hundreds of members when most active.[717]

Tupac Katari Guerrilla Army/Ejercito Guerrillero Tupac Katari (EGTK)

Founded: c. 1988
Disbanded: c. 1993
Ideology: Communist / Socialist / Left Wing
Location: Bolivia
Tactics: Bombings
Targets: Infrastructure (utilities, oil), religious (churches), government (facilities)
AKA: Tupac Katari
Description: This group, which broke away from a political party known as the Tupac Katari Revolutionary Movement-Liberation in favor of armed resistance, was largely rural-based. They established a base in the altiplano region north of Lake Titicaca and advocated for indigenous influence and power. The group contained as few as 30 members and struggled to recruit from among indigenous peoples.[718]

Zarate Willka Armed Forces of Liberation/Fuerzas Armadas de Liberacion Zarate Wilka (FAL-ZW)

Founded: c. 1988
Disbanded: c. 1991
Ideology: Left wing (Marxist)
Location: Bolivia
Tactics: Bombings, assassinations
Targets: religious, government
AKA: N/A

Description: Named after Pablo Zárate, a leader among indigenous peoples who led a famous rebellion in the early 1900s, this group used violence to promote indigenous rights. The group targeted entities affiliated with the United States, as their members believed US presence and policies encroached upon indigenous culture and rights.[719]

APPENDIX C

GLOSSARY OF ACRONYMS

ACH	Analysis of Competing Hypotheses
ANFO	Ammonium Nitrate/Fuel Oil
ATP	Army Techniques Publication
BBC	British Broadcasting Corporation
BI	Internationalist Brigade/Brigada Internacionalista
BYU	Brigham Young University
CAC	Alejo Calatayud Command/Comando Alejo Calatayud
CGSB	Simon Bolivar Guerrilla Coordinating Board/Coordinadora Guerrillera Simon Bolivar
CIA	Central Intelligence Agency
CNPZ	Nestor Paz Zamora Commission/Comision Nestor Paz Zamora
EGTK	Tupac Katari Guerrilla Army/Ejercito Guerrillero Tupac Katari
ELN	National Liberation Army/Ejercito de Liberacion Nacional
EPA	Army Of The People in Arms/Ejercito del Pueblo en Armas
ERP	People's Revolutionary Army—Argentina/Ejercito Revolucionario Del Pueblo
ETA	Basque Homeland/Fatherland and Liberty/Euskadi Ta Askatasuna
FAL-ZW	Zarate Willka Armed Forces Liberation/Fuerzas Armadas de Liberacion Zarate Wilka
FARC-EP	Revolutionary Armed Forces of Colombia—People's Army/Fuerzas Armadas Revolucionarias de Colombia—Ejercito del Pueblo

FBI	Federal Bureau of Investigation
FBIS	Foreign Broadcast Information Service
FPMR	Manuel Rodriguez Patriotic Front/Frente Patriotico Manuel Rodriguez
FPMR-D	Manuel Rodriguez Patriotic Front—Dissident/Frente Patriotico Manuel Rodriguez—Disidente
FRA	Anti-Imperialist Revolutionary Front/Frente Revolucionario Anti-Imperialista
GAP	Palestinian Support Group/Grupo de Apoyo a Palestina
GTD	Global Terrorism Database
IS	Islamic State
IRA	Provisional Irish Republican Army
LDS	Latter-day Saint(s)
MAPU	United Popular Action Movement/Movimiento de Accion Popular Unitaria
MIR	Movement of the Revolutionary Left/Movimiento de Izquierda Revolucionaria
MJL	Lautaro Youth Movement/Movimiento Juventil Lautaro
MR	Rodriguez Militias/Milicias Rodriguistas
MRTA	Tupac Amaru Revolutionary Movement/Movimiento Revolucionario Tupac Amaru
MSHARPP	Mission, Symbolism, History, Accessibility, Recognizability, Population, And Proximity
NATO	North Atlantic Treaty Organization
NCO	Non-Commissioned Officer
ORCLAD	Omar Torrijos Commando for Latin American Dignity
PCP	Communist Party of Peru/Partido Comunista Peruano
PLO	Palestine Liberation Organization
RDWTI	RAND Database of Worldwide Terrorism Incidents

RSO	Regional Security Officer
SL	Shining Path/Sendero Luminoso
START	National Consortium for the Study of Terrorism and Responses to Terrorism
TRAC	Terrorism Research & Analysis Consortium
TTP	Tactics, Techniques, and Procedures
TTP	Tehrik-E Taliban Pakistan
UPI	United Press International
US	United States
USAID	United States Agency For International Development

ENDNOTES

1 Jeffrey R. Holland, "Terror, Triumph, and a Wedding Feast," speech given at Brigham Young University, September 12, 2004.

2 "Data Collection Methodology," National Consortium for the Study of Terrorism and Responses to Terrorism (University of Maryland: College Park, MD, 2017), available at https://www.start.umd.edu/gtd/using-gtd/ (accessed November 21, 2017).

3 U.S. Department of State, "Country Reports on Terrorism 2013: Executive Summary," April 2014, available at https://www.state.gov/documents/organization/225050.pdf (accessed February 23, 2019).

4 David C. Rapoport, "The Four Waves of Modern Terrorism" in *Attacking Terrorism*, ed. Audrey Kurth Cronin and James M. Ludes, 46–73 (Washington, DC: Georgetown University Press, 2004), 47–48.

5 "Data Collection Methodology," National Consortium for the Study of Terrorism and Responses to Terrorism (University of Maryland: College Park, MD, 2017), available at https://www.start.umd.edu/gtd/using-gtd/ (accessed November 21, 2017).

6 "Database Scope," RAND Corporation, available at https://www.rand.org/nsrd/projects/terrorism-incidents/about/definitions.html (accessed March 31, 2019).

7 David Knowlton, "Missionaries and Terror: The Assassination of Two Elders in Bolivia," *Sunstone* (August 1989), 12.

8 Jorge Trujillo, interviewed by Matthew A. Hughes, Novemeber 14, 2019.

9 Moses 6:63.

10 Doctrine and Covenants 109:7.

11 "Preach My Gospel: A Guide to Missionary Service," (Salt Lake City, UT: The Church of Jesus Christ of Latter-day Saints, 2004), 113.

12 David Brent Marsh, "How Disciples of Christ Live in Times of War and Violence," *Ensign*, September 2012, 44.

13 Jack Anderson and Dale Van Atta, "Targets of Terrorism: Latin Mormon Churches," (Washington, DC: Washington Post, November 24, 1991), available at https://www.washingtonpost.com/archive/opinions/1991/11/24/targets-of-terrorism-latin-mormon-churches/ede6930c-5df8-4d82-82bc-190b5e474abe/?noredirect=on&utm_term=.4d9ff187d416 (accessed October 27, 2018).

14 Neal A. Maxwell, "All Hell Is Moved," Address presented at a Latter-day Saint Devotional, November 8, 1977.

15 *New Testament Institute Student Manual* (The Church of Jesus Christ of Latter-day Saints: Salt Lake City, UT, 2014), 543.

16 Dallin H. Oaks, "Scripture Reading and Revelation," *Ensign*, January 1995.

17 Boyd K. Packer, "Do Not Fear," *Ensign*, May 2004.

18 Duncan Green, "What if we allocated aid $ based on how much damage something does, and whether we know how to fix it?," March 7, 2013, http://www.oxfamblogs.org/fp2p/?p=13838 (accessed September 5, 2017).

19 Bruce C. Hafen, "For the Joy of Human Love," Brigham Young University-Idaho Devotional, November 13, 2001, available at http://www2.byui.edu/Presentations/Transcripts/Devotionals/2001_11_13_Hafen.htm (accessed September 17, 2017).

20 Rachel Zoll, "Was 9/11 religious resurgence just temporary?," *Deseret News*, January 12, 2002, available at https://www.deseretnews.com/article/889049/Was-911-religious-resurgence-just-temporary.html (accessed December 8, 2018).

21 Brigham Young, "Testimony to the Divinity of Joseph Smith's Mission—Elders Should Go to Their Missions Without Purse or Scrip—The Lord Deals with the Saints—Jesus Their President—Satan Angry," discourse delivered in Great Salt Lake City, August 31, 1856, in G.D. Watt et al., eds., *Journal of Discourses*, 4:41a, available at jod.mrm.org/4/33 (accessed December 2, 2017).

22 John Taylor, "The People of God in All Ages Led by One Spirit, and Subject to Persecution—Condition of the World," discourse delivered in Great Salt Lake City, January 10, 1858, in G.D. Watt et al., eds., *Journal of Discourses*, 7:125a, available at jod.mrm.org/7/118 (accessed December 2, 2017).

23 Bruce Hoffman, *Inside Terrorism*, (Columbia University Press: New York, 1998), 15–17.

24 Charles W. Penrose, "Elders Always Ready for Duty—No Salaried Preachers in the Church—No Compulsion in the Work of the Elders—The Liberty of Law—Sin Brings Its Penalties, Righteousness a Sure Reward," discourse delivered in Salt Lake City, UT, September 23, 1883, in G.D. Watt et al., eds., *Journal of Discourses*, 24:303b, available at jod.mrm.org/24/302 (accessed December 3, 2017).

25 John Taylor, "Man," discourse delivered in Great Salt Lake City, February 19, 1860 in G.D. Watt et al., eds., *Journal of Discourses*, 8:4b, available at jod.mrm.org/8/1 (accessed December 3, 2017).

26 Joseph B. Murdock, (no title) (1918).

27 Barbara B. Smith, "Women for the Latter Day," *General Conference* (October 1979).

28 M. Russell Ballard, "Duties, Rewards, and Risks," *General Conference* (October 1989).

29 Gordon B. Hinckley, "This Great Millennial Year," *General Conference* (October 2000).

30 Boyd K. Packer, "Do Not Fear," *General Conference* (April 2004).

31 Gordon B. Hinckley, "The Times in Which We Live," *General Conference* (October 2001).

32 *DoD Dictionary of Military and Associated Terms*, Joint Publication 1–02 (2017), 31.

33 John Adams, Letter to Hezekiah Niles, *National Humanities Center* (February 13, 1818), available at http://nationalhumanitiescenter.org/ows/seminars/revolution/Adams-Niles.pdf (accessed October 28, 2017).

34 Lyndon B. Johnson: "Remarks at a Dinner Meeting of the Texas Electric Cooperatives, Inc.," May 4, 1965, online by Gerhard Peters and John T. Woolley, *The American Presidency Project*, available at http://www.presidency.ucsb.edu/ws/?pid=26942 (accessed November 19, 2017).

35 Rick Atkinson, "Iraq Will Be Petraeus's Knot to Untie," *Washington Post* (January 7, 2007), available at http://www.washingtonpost.com/wp-dyn/content/article/2007/01/06/AR2007010601185_2.html (accessed November 19, 2017).

36 Doctrine and Covenants 77:2.

37 Abraham 3:28; Revelation 12:4.

38 Larry R. Lawrence, "The War Goes On," *Ensign*, April 2017.

39 Ibid.

40 2 Nephi 2:11.

41 Doctrine and Covenants 8:2.

42 Philippians 4:7.

43 Manuel Moises Sanchez, "Relatos de la historia de la Iglesia en el valle del Mantaro, 1990," microfilm of holograph, Church History Library.

44 "New Testament Study Guide for Home-Study Seminary Students," (The Church of Jesus Christ of Latter-day Saints: Salt Lake City, UT, 2016), 60.

45 Ibid.

46 "Book of Mormon Student Manual" (The Church of Jesus Christ of Latter-day Saints: Salt Lake City, UT: 2009), 344.

47 Ephesians 6:11, 14.

48 Malachi 4:6.

49 David A. Bednar, "Missionary, Family History, and Temple Work," *Ensign*, October 2014.

50 Genesis 4:5.

51 Moses 1:13.

52 Moses 6:15.

53 Hugh W. Nibley, "Nibley Commentary of the Book of Mormon Volume 1: Commentary of the Book of Mormon," 2014, Lecture 33.

54 Dallin H. Oaks, "Opposition in All Things," *LDS General Conference*, April 2016.

55 Doctrine and Covenants 45:33.

56 Ephesians 6:17.

57 George Q. Cannon, "Conflict of Truth Irrepressible—San Causes Fear, Then Apostasy," discourse delivered in Great Salt Lake City, May 6, 1866 in G.D. Watt et al., eds., *Journal of Discourses*, 11:229a, available at jod.mrm.org/8/1 (accessed December 8, 2017).

58 Fathali M. Moghaddam, "The Staircase to Terrorism: A Psychological Exploration," *American Psychologist* (February-March 2005) 60, no. 2: 161-169, DOI: 10.1037/0003-066X.60.2.161, 161.

59 Ibid.

60 Alma 47:18.

61 Rapoport, "The Four Waves of Modern Terrorism," 47–48.

62 Ibid, 50.

63 Ether 8:25.

64 Ether 8:15.

65 Ether 9:1, 6.

66 Ether 9:27.

67 "Cain," Bible Dictionary.

68 U.S. Department of State, "Foreign Terrorist Organizations," *U.S. Department of State Website*, https://www.state.gov/j/ct/rls/other/des/123085.htm (accessed January 27, 2018).

69 G. William Kirby and Joan S. Kirby, oral history, interviewed by Elder Steven Dinger and Sister Eileen Dinger, Long Jetty, New South Wales, Australia, February 22, 2016, Church History Library.

70 Headquarters, Department of the Army, *Antiterrorism*, FM 3-37.2 (February 2011), para. 2–24.

71 Compiled using multiple open sources (outlined in detail in Appendix A); categories based on information for each known perpetrator group listed by the Terrorism Research & Analysis Consortium (TRAC) at https://www.trackingterrorism.org.

72 Robert M. Gates. "International Terrorism: Challenge For The Future." *National Security and Risk Management Conference*. January 27, 1988. Declassified and approved for release June 4, 2012. CIA-RDP99-00777R000302580001-6.

73 David Clark Knowlton, "Mormonism and Guerrillas in Bolivia," *The Journal of Mormon History*, 187.

74 Charles E. Allen, Memorandum for Director and Deputy Director of National Intelligence, NIC 04409-85, (September 3, 1985), declassified and approved for release September 21, 2009, 2.

75 "Terrorism Review," *CIA Directorate of Intelligence* (January 24, 1991).

76 Sheila Sanchez, "2 missionaries shot by rebels, police say," *Deseret News*, August 24, 1990, B1-B2.

77 Michael Phillips, "Amid Bombs, LDS Church Reshaping Its Image in Chile," *Salt Lake Tribune*, April 20, 1992, A-1 and A-17.

78 Virginia Garrard Burnett, "Review: Protestantism in Latin America," (*Latin American Research Review* 27, no. 1 (1992), pp. 218–230), 220, JSTOR, www.jstor.org/stable/2503727 (accessed October 27, 2018).

79 Ibid., 224.

80 Ibid., 225–226.

81 David Clark Knowlton, "Mormonism and Chilean Exceptionalism," presented at the Society for the Scientific Study of Religion Meetings (Portland, OR, 2006), 16.

82 Burnett, "Review: Protestantism in Latin America," 225.

83 A. Delbert Palmer, "Establishing the LDS Church in Chile," MA Thesis, Brigham Young University (1979).

84 Samuel L. Huntington, "The Clash of Civilizations," (Simon & Schuster Paperbacks: New York), 99.

85 "Precautions taken against terrorism," *LDS Church News* (July 15, 1989), accessible at https://www.ldschurchnewsarchive.com/articles/18665/Precautions-taken-against-terrorism.html (accessed September 25, 2017).

86 Harrell Gwenden Fallis and Beverly Edith Fallis letter to friends and family, June 13, 1989, Correspondence, 1987-1989, Harrell G. Fallis correspondence, Church History Library.

87 "Mission History," *Peru Lima East*, available at http://www.mission.net/peru/lima/east/page.php?pg_id=908 (accessed July 13, 2017).

88 "Conversation with the South America North Area Presidency," *Ensign*, March 1994.

89 David Clark Knowlton, "Mormonism and Guerrillas in Bolivia," *The Journal of Mormon History*, 183.

90 Ibid., 207.

91 David Clark Knowlton, "Mormonism and Chilean Exceptionalism," presented at the Society for the Scientific Study of Religion Meetings (Portland, OR, 2006), 11.

92 "Terrorism Review," *Directorate of Intelligence*, July 13, 1989, 17, https://www.cia.gov/library/readingroom/docs/DOC_0000126946.pdf (accessed August 3, 2017).

93 Michael Phillips, "Amid Bombs, LDS Church Reshaping Its Image in Chile," *Salt Lake Tribune* (April 20, 1992), A-1, A-17.

94 Mark 12:17.

95 "The Articles of Faith of the Church of Jesus Christ of Latter-day Saints," 12.

96 David Clark Knowlton, interviewed by Matthew A. Hughes, May 31, 2018.

97 "Instituto Nacional de Estadísticas de Chile, Censo 2002," as quoted in David Clark Knowlton, "Mormonism and Chilean Exceptionalism," presented at the Society for the Scientific Study of Religion Meetings (Portland, OR, 2006), 23.

98 Alejandro Portes and Kelly Hoffman, "Latin American Class Structures: Their Composition and Change during the Neoliberal Era," *Latin American Research Review* 38:1:41–42, as quoted in David Clark Knowlton, "Mormonism and Chilean Exceptionalism," 23.

99 Lee Davidson and Jerry Spangler, "Were Slayings Really by Leftist Terrorists?," *Deseret News* (May 26, 1989).

100 "The Mormons' Ancestors and the FBI." November 25, 1953. *Izvestia* (Moscow). FBIS, Soviet European Service 53-231: CC1.

101 Ibid.

102 Ibid.

103 Kim B. Östman, "The Mormon Espionage Scare and Its Coverage in Finland, 1982–84," *Journal of Mormon History* 34: 1 (2008), 82–117, *JSTOR*, www.jstor.org/stable/23290718 (accessed July 28, 2017), 83.

104 "CIA Agents Said to be Flooding Latin America." October 25, 1975. *Izvestia* (Moscow). FBIS, Soviet European Service 75-214: B4.

105 "Reunion CP Leader Alleges CIA Activities." January 6, 1986. *TASS* (Moscow). FBIS, Soviet European Service 86-004: J2.

106 "'Wisely, cautiously,' missionary work proceeds in Bolivia," *LDS Church News* (June 24, 1989), accessible at https://www.ldschurchnewsarchive.com/articles/19002/Wisely-cautiously-missionary-work-proceeds-in-Bolivia.html (accessed September 25, 2017).

107 "Terrorism Review," *Directorate of Intelligence*, July 13, 1989, 17, https://www.cia.gov/library/readingroom/docs/DOC_0000126946.pdf (accessed August 3, 2017).

108 Ibid.

109 Dale Van Atta, interviewed by Fred Fiske, *The Fred Fiske Show* (WAMU-FM, NPR Network: Washington, DC, December 7, 1983), available at https://www.cia.gov/library/readingroom/docs/CIA-RDP88-01070R000201000002-5.pdf (accessed October 22, 2017).

110 Headquarters, Department of the Army, Department of the Army Pamphlet 550-66 ("Bolivia: a country study") (Washington, D.C.: Department of the Army, 1991), 92.

111 Néstor Curbelo, "Historia de los Santos de los Últimos Días en Chile" (Honeoye Falls, NY: Digital Legend Press, 2010), 118–119.

112 "Ghana Expels Missionaries, Bans Church," *Church News*, June 24, 1989, 12; Lawrence A. Young, "Confronting Turbulent Environments," in *Contemporary Mormonism: Social Science Perspectives*, ed. Marie Cornwall, Tim B. Heaton, and Lawrence Alfred Young (Champaign, IL: University of Illinois Press, 2001), 53.

113 Ben Ephson, "Spiritual Onslaught," *West Africa* (April 17–23, 1989), 584–85, as quoted in Lawrence A. Young, "Confronting Turbulent Environments," in *Contemporary Mormonism: Social Science Perspectives*, ed. Marie Cornwall, Tim B. Heaton, and Lawrence Alfred Young (Champaign, IL: University of Illinois Press, 2001), 53.

114 Néstor Curbelo, "Historia de los Santos de los Últimos Días en Chile" (Honeoye Falls, NY: Digital Legend Press, 2010), 118.

115 Michael Phillips, "Amid Bombs, LDS Church Reshaping Its Image in Chile," *Salt Lake Tribune* (April 20, 1992), A-1, A-17.

116 David Spencer and David Knowlton, *Panel Discussion*, Utah, 1991, sound recording available at https://www.sunstonemagazine.com/terrorism-and-the-church-in-south-america/ (accessed February 3, 2018).

117 Ibid.

118 Michael Phillips, "Amid Bombs, LDS Church Reshaping Its Image in Chile," *Salt Lake Tribune* (April 20, 1992), A-1, A-17.

119 Alma 32:2.

120 David Clark Knowlton, "Mormonism and Guerrillas in Bolivia," *The Journal of Mormon History*, 188.

121 David Clark Knowlton, "Mormonism and Guerrillas in Bolivia," *The Journal of Mormon History*, 192.

122 David Clark Knowlton, "Missionaries and Terror," *Sunstone*, no. 72 (August 1989): 10–15; "Zárate Willka amenaza matar a Alcalde y concejales de El Alto," *Hoy*, June 1, 1989, 7.

123 P. Scarlet, "LDS Church is a Top Target of Terrorists," *The Salt Lake Tribune* (January 18, 1992), retrieved from https://search-proquest-com.ezproxy2.apus.edu/docview/288497596?accountid=8289 (accessed September 19, 2017).

124 LTC Alvin D. Cantrell, "Drugs and Terror: A Threat to U.S. National Security," U.S. Army War College (Carlisle Barracks, PA), March 23, 1992: 10.

125 U.S. Department of State, untitled reporting cable (March 14, 1994), available at http://lum.cultura.pe/cdi/sites/default/files/documento/pdf/805.pdf (accessed December 28, 2017).

126 Jessica Stern, *Terror in the Name of God*, (New York: HarperCollins, 2003), 172.

127 Karl W. Haws and Julia Ann Waldrop Haws, oral history, interviewed by Marilyn Mills, Redlands, California, April 19, 2016, Church History Library.

128 Headquarters, Department of the Army, *Tactics*, Field Manual 3-90 (Department of the Army: Washington, DC, July 2001), 12.

129 "Bolivia: Potential for Terrorist and Insurgent Violence," Special Interagency Intelligence Memorandum, Officer of the Director of Central Intelligence, April 1989, declassified and approved for release March 24, 2014, CIA-RDP94T00885R000200140001-2, 3.

130 David Clark Knowlton, interviewed by Matthew A. Hughes, May 31, 2018.

131 David Clark Knowlton, interviewed by Matthew A. Hughes, May 31, 2018.

132 Jack Anderson and Dale Van Atta, "Targets of Terrorism: Latin Mormon Churches," *Washington Post*, November 24, 1991, https://www.washingtonpost.com/archive/opinions/1991/11/24/targets-of-terrorism-latin-mormon-churches/ede6930c-5df8-4d82-82bc-190b5e474abe/?utm_term=.aab18207befa (accessed July 30, 2017).

133 Lee Davidson, "Terrorists relatively easy on LDS targets," *Deseret News*, July 22, 1989, B1–B2.

134 Lee Davidson, "Were terrorist attacks related to the gulf war?," *Deseret News* (March 26, 1991), B1-B2.

135 Ibid.

136 Néstor Curbelo, "Historia de los Santos de los Últimos Días en Chile" (Honeoye Falls, NY: Digital Legend Press, 2010), 118.

137 Molina, "3 atentados," 2-A; "Explosions Damage Three Mormon Churches," *Bogota Radio Sutatenza Network* in Spanish, FBIS, LAT, 87-211: 35; "Significant Incidents: 1987," 38; RAND Database; National Consortium for the Study of Terrorism and Responses to Terrorism (START). (2017). Global Terrorism Database [Data file]. Retrieved from https://www.start.umd.edu/gtd.

138 Doctrine and Covenants 109:25.

139 Chip Parkinson, "Utahn Saddened by the Misuse of his Invention," *Deseret News* (May 17, 1995), available at https://www.deseretnews.com/article/421394/UTAHN-SADDENED-BY-THE-MISUSE-OF-HIS-INVENTION.html (accessed December 4, 2017).

140 "Global Terrorism Database Codebook," (University of Maryland: College Park, MD, June 2017), 23.

141 Benjamin George, "The Sicarii and Book of Mormon Secret Combinations," from *Selections from the BYU Religious Education Student Symposium 2003* (Religious Studies Center: Provo, UT, 2003), 72.

142 National Consortium for the Study of Terrorism and Responses to Terrorism (START). (2017). Global Terrorism Database [Data file]. Retrieved from https://www.start. umd.edu/gtd.

143 Martin and Idon Openshaw, interviewed by Matthew A. Hughes, May 30, 2018.

144 Lloyd Richmond and Julie Richmond, oral history, interviewed by Matthew K. Heiss, Solihull, England, May 17, 1999, James Moyle Oral History Program, Church History Library.

145 Martin and Idon Openshaw, interviewed by Matthew A. Hughes, May 30, 2018.

146 "Father, Thy Children to Thee Now Raise," *Hymns of the Church of Jesus Christ of Latter-day Saints* (Salt Lake City: The Church of Jesus Christ of Latter-day Saints, 1985), no. 91.

147 Martin and Idon Openshaw, interviewed by Matthew A. Hughes, May 30, 2018.

148 David Spencer and David Knowlton, *Panel Discussion*, Utah, 1991, sound recording available at https://www.sunstonemagazine.com/terrorism-and-the-church-in-south-america/ (accessed February 3, 2018).

149 "The Mormons' Ancestors and the FBI." November 25, 1953. *Izvestia* (Moscow). FBIS, Soviet European Service 53-231: CC1.

150 Headquarters, Department of the Army, *Antiterrorism*, FM 3-37.2 (February 2011), para. 2-102.

151 Jessica Stern, *Terror in the Name of God*, (New York: HarperCollins, 2003), 172.

152 W. Seth Carus, "Bioterrorism and Biocrimes: the Illicit Use of Biological Agents Since 1900," *Center for Counterproliferation Research* (National Defense University: Washington, D.C., February 2001), 129; "Anthrax Hoax Hits Church Offices," *Sunstone* (June 1999), 74.

153 Ben Winslow, "FBI: White powder mailed to Salt Lake Temple harmless," *Deseret News* (November 15, 2008), https://www.deseretnews.com/article/705382575/FBI-White-powder-mailed-to-Salt-Lake-Temple-harmless.html (accessed December 16, 2017).

154 U.S. Attorney's Office for the Northern District of Georgia, "Defendant sentenced to two years for mailing hoax anthrax threats," June 27, 2017, available at https://www.justice.gov/usao-ndga/pr/defendant-sentenced-two-years-mailing-hoax-anthrax-threats (accessed March 31, 2018).

155 Lloyd Richmond and Julie Richmond, oral history, interviewed by Matthew K. Heiss, Solihull, England, May 17, 1999, James Moyle Oral History Program, Church History Library.

156 Lloyd Richmond and Julie Richmond, oral history, interviewed by Matthew K. Heiss, Solihull, England, May 17, 1999, James Moyle Oral History Program, Church History Library.

157 Garry Russell Flake, oral history, interviewed by Jerald L. Taylor, Salt Lake City, Utah, July 7, 2011, James Moyle Oral History Program, Church History Library.

158 Lloyd Richmond and Julie Richmond, oral history, interviewed by Matthew K. Heiss, Solihull, England, May 17, 1999, James Moyle Oral History Program, Church History Library.

159 José Maria Gonzalez Sulca, oral history, interviewed by José Miguez Giraldez Rodriguez, Huamanga, Ayacucho, Peru, October 14, 2016, Church History Library.

160 Ibid.

161 Manuel Moises Sanchez, "Relatos de la historia de la Iglesia en el valle del Mantaro, 1990," microfilm of holograph, Church History Library.

162 David Spencer and David Knowlton, *Panel Discussion*, Utah, 1991, sound recording available at https://www.sunstonemagazine.com/terrorism-and-the-church-in-south-america/ (accessed February 3, 2018).

163 Ibid.

164 David Knowlton, "Missionaries and Terror: Assassination of Two Elders in Bolivia," *Sunstone* 72 (August 1989), 12.

165 "Death threats slow murder trial in Bolivia," *Deseret News*, June 2, 1991, A1, A4.

166 Headquarters, Department of the Army, *Antiterrorism*, FM 3-37.2 (February 2011), para. 1–33.

167 Martin and Idon Openshaw, interviewed by Matthew A. Hughes, May 30, 2018.

168 Sheridan R. Sheffield, "Fireside disrupted with threat of bomb," *Church News*, February 13, 1993, available at https://www.ldschurchnewsarchive.com/articles/22886/Fireside-disrupted-with-threat-of-bomb.html (accessed March 31, 2018).

169 United States of America v. Travis Ball, (N.D. Ga 2017).

170 Bureau of Diplomatic Security, "Significant Incidents of Political Violence Against Americans: 1987," United States Department of State, 14; RAND Database.

171 Christopher M. Schnaubelt, Eric V. Larson, and Matthew E. Boyer, "Vulnerability Assessment Method Pocket Guide," (The Rand Corporation: Washington, DC, 2014), 29.

172 Michael Phillips, "Amid Bombs, LDS Church Reshaping Its Image in Chile," *Salk Lake Tribune* (April 20, 1992), A-1, A-17.

173 Jack Anderson and Dale Van Atta, "Targets of Terrorism: Latin Mormon Churches," *Washington Post*, November 24, 1991, available at https://www.washingtonpost.com/archive/

opinions/1991/11/24/targets-of-terrorism-latin-mormon-churches/ede6930c-5df8-4d82-82bc-190b5e474abe/?utm_term=.aab18207befa (accessed July 30, 2017).

174 "Government Increases Guard on Mormon Churches," August 14, 1985, *Madrid EFE*, FBIS, LAM, 85-158: E3-E4.

175 Michael Phillips, "Amid Bombs, LDS Church Reshaping Its Image in Chile," *Salt Lake Tribune* (April 20, 1992), A-1, A-17.

176 Clayton M. Christensen, *The Power of Everyday Missionaries*, (Deseret Book: Salt Lake City, 2012), 5. Used by permission.

177 Jack Anderson and Dale Van Atta, "Targets of Terrorism: Latin Mormon Churches," *Washington Post*, November 24, 1991, https://www.washingtonpost.com/archive/opinions/1991/11/24/targets-of-terrorism-latin-mormon-churches/ede6930c-5df8-4d82-82bc-190xendib5e474abe/?utm_term=.aab18207befa (accessed July 30, 2017).

178 Robert M. Gates, "International Terrorism: Challenge For The Future," *National Security and Risk Management Conference*, January 27, 1988, declassified and approved for release June 4, 2012, CIA-RDP99-00777R000302580001-6.

179 James E. Faust, "The Great Imitator," General Conference, October 1987.

180 Ibid.

181 James Holmes, "Fabian Strategies, Then and Now," *War on the Rocks* (September 17, 2015), available at https://warontherocks.com/2015/09/fabian-strategies-then-and-now/ (accessed December 12, 2018).

182 Robert Bateman, "There are Three (And Only Three) Types of Military Strategy," *Esquire* (November 30, 2015), available at https://www.esquire.com/news-politics/politics/a40096/definitions-of-strategies/ (accessed December 11, 2018).

183 2 Nephi 2:11.

184 Harrell Gwenden Fallis and Beverly Edith Fallis letter to friends and family, February 27, 1989 and April 21, 1989, Correspondence, 1987-1989, Harrell G. Fallis correspondence, Church History Library.

185 Ibid.

186 Ibid.

187 Ibid.

188 Brian T. West, "LDS Church Reassigning Missionaries; Unrest in Bolivia and Peru," *Deseret News*, July 12, 1989, https://www.deseretnews.com/article/54960/LDS-CHURCH-REASSIGNING-MISSIONARIES.html (accessed November 23, 2018).

189 "Mission History," *Peru Lima East*, available at http://www.mission.net/peru/lima/east/page.php?pg_id=908 (accessed July 13, 2017).

190 Ibid.

191 Manuel Moises Sanchez, "Relatos de la historia de la Iglesia en el valle del Mantaro, 1990," microfilm of holograph, Church History Library.

192 Kevin M. Bulloch, "The War in Heaven and Satan's Continuing Battle for Power," *Religious Educator* 11, no. 1 (2010): 33-46.

193 George Q. Cannon, Untitled Discourse, delivered in Paris, Bear Lake County, Idaho (August 19, 1883), in "Journal of Discourses: Volumes 24-25," ed. George D. Watt (Liverpool: John Henry Smith, 1884), 255.

194 James E. Faust, "The Great Imitator," *LDS General Conference*, October 1987.

195 Moses 1:12; 1:4, 6, 7.

196 Moroni 9:20.

197 F. D. Richards, *Journal of Discourses* 26, April 4–5, 1885, http://www.Josephsmithfoundation.org/journalofdiscourses/speakers/franklin-d-richards/

present-conditions-the-hatred-of-the-world-toward-the-saints-why-the-leaders-of-the-church-are-attacked-the-purpose-of/ (accessed September 4, 2017).

198 Dale Christensen, ed., "The History of the Church in Peru," (editor, 1995), 159.

199 Ibid., 159–160.

200 Ibid., 160.

201 Ibid., 161.

202 David Clark Knowlton, "Mormonism and Guerrillas in Bolivia," *The Journal of Mormon History*, 207.

203 "Relacion de los hechos," *El Departamento de Derechos Humanos de la Organizacion para la solidaridad con Africa, Asia, y America Latina*, http://www.derechos.org/nizkor/bolivia/cdh/2.html (accessed September 23, 2017).

204 Alma 21:3; 43:6.

205 David Clark Knowlton, interviewed by Matthew A. Hughes, May 31, 2018.

206 Mosiah 10:12.

207 Milan Vego, "Clausewitz's Schwerpunkt: Mistranslated from German—Misunderstood in English," *Military Review* (Jan–Feb) 2007, 101.

208 C.S. Lewis, "The Screwtape Letters," (HarperCollins Publishers: New York, 2001), 114–115.

209 "Q and A with Dale Van Atta, an LDS Expert on Terrorism," *Meridian Magazine*, October 16, 2001, http://ldsmag.com/article-1-4534/ (accessed July 30, 2017).

210 *Messages of the First Presidency*, comp. James R. Clark, 6 vols., Salt Lake City: Bookcraft, 1965–75, 6:179.

211 George F. Gibbs, *Journal of Discourses* 23, December 18, 1881, http://www.Josephsmithfoundation.org/journalofdiscourses/reporters/george-f-gibbs/the-southern-states-mission-faithfulness-of-young-elders-opposition-to-the-truth-gradual-spread-of-the-gospel-changes-in-religious/ (accessed September 4, 2017).

212 "New Testament Institute Student Manual," (The Church of Jesus Christ of Latter-day Saints: Salt Lake City, UT, 2018), 551; Joseph Smith Translation, Revelation 12:7.

213 Ibid., 552.

214 Revelation 12:17.

215 *New Testament Student Manual*, 2nd ed. (Church Educational System manual). 2018. 553.

216 "Ayacucho," Peru Tourism Bureau, available at http://www.visitperu.com/visit-peruinfo/english/ciudades.php?cod_depa=3 (accessed October 30, 2018).

217 José Maria Gonzalez, oral history, interviewed by Brother José Miguel Giraldez Rodriguez, Ayacucho, Peru, October 14, 2016, Church History Library.

218 José Maria Gonzalez, oral history, interviewed by Brother José Miguel Giraldez Rodriguez, Ayacucho, Peru, October 14, 2016, Church History Library.

219 Ibid.

220 "Policies and Announcements," *Ensign*, March 1982.

221 "Government Increases Guard on Mormon Churches," August 14, 1985, *Madrid EFE* in Spanish, FBIS, LAM, 85–158: E3–E4.

222 "Conversation with the South America North Area Presidency," *Ensign*, March 1994.

223 *Los Angeles Times* (February 25, 1986) and *Atlanta Journal* (August 17, 1985), as quoted in Lawrence A. Young, "Confronting Turbulent Environments," in *Contemporary Mormonism: Social Science Perspectives*, ed. Marie Cornwall, Tim B. Heaton, and Lawrence Alfred Young (Champaign, IL: University of Illinois Press, 2001), 55.

224 Boyd K. Packer, "President Howard W. Hunter—He Endured to the End," *Ensign*, April 1995, 29.

225 Blair G. Van Dyke and LaMar C. Berrett, "In the Footsteps of Orson Hyde: Subsequent Dedications of the Holy Land, *BYU Studies* 47, no. 1 (2008), 64 and 91.

226 Gordon B. Hinckley, "This Great Millennial Year," *Ensign*, November 2000.

227 (Unknown title), (Church News: Salt Lake City, UT, November 2, 1991).

228 Robert O. Hickman, "Robert O. Hickman mission papers, 1991-2011," microfilm of holograph, Church History Library, The Church of Jesus Christ of Latter-day Saints, Salt Lake City, Utah.

229 William R. Bradford, "Righteousness," *General Conference* (October 1999).

230 Robert D. Hales, "Holy Scriptures: The Power of God unto Our Salvation," *General Conference* (October 2006).

231 Martin and Idon Openshaw, interviewed by Matthew A. Hughes, May 30, 2018.

232 "The History of the Church in Peru," 161.

233 Dale Christensen, ed., "The History of the Church in Peru," (editor, 1995), 161–163.

234 David Knowlton, "Missionaries and Terror: the Assassination of Two Elders in Bolivia," *Sunstone* (August 1989), 12; "Significant Incidents: 1988," 11; RAND Database.

235 Doctrine and Covenants 71:9.

236 David L. Cook, e-mail message to author, January 15, 2018.

237 Doctrine and Covenants 100:6.

238 W. Craig Zwick and Jan J. Zwick, "More to Your Story" (Salt Lake City, UT: Deseret Book, 2012), 18. Used by permission.

239 Ibid., 22. Used by permission.

240 Ibid., 17, 23. Used by permission; "They, the Builders of the Nation," *Hymns of The Church of Jesus Christ of Latter-day Saints* (Salt Lake City: The Church of Jesus Christ of Latter-day Saints, 1985), no. 36.

241 W. Craig Zwick and Jan J. Zwick, "More to Your Story," 23. Used by permission.

242 Doctrine and Covenants 103:12.

243 Scott Earl, interviewed by Matthew A. Hughes, January 2, 2020.

244 "Significant Incidents: 1990," 13.

245 "Mujer capitaneó nueva ola de atentados," *La Tercera* (December 3, 1990), 4.

246 Ibid.

247 Roberto Alejandro del Rio Troncoso, interviewed by Matthew A. Hughes by phone, September 10, 2017.

248 Ibid.

249 Ibid.

250 Lloyd Richmond and Julie Richmond, oral history, interviewed by Matthew K. Heiss, Solihull, England, May 17, 1999, James Moyle Oral History Program, Church History Library.

251 Martin and Idon Openshaw, interviewed by Matthew A. Hughes, May 30, 2018.

252 Isaiah 54:14, 17.

253 José Medina Cisternas, interviewed by Matthew A. Hughes by phone, July 20, 2017.

254 Ibid.

255 *The Teachings of Spencer W. Kimball*, 539.

256 José Medina Cisternas, interviewed by Matthew A. Hughes by phone, July 20, 2017.

257 Daniel 6:22–23.

258 Chris Wilson, "Oklahoma City Battalion Moves to New Building With Old Memories," *Recruiter Journal* 56, 4 (April), 2004: 18.

259 Julie A. Dockstader, "Faith, courage rise from the rubble," *Mormon Times* (April 29, 1995), https://www.ldschurchnewsarchive.com/articles/26065/Faith-courage-rise-from-the-rubble.html (accessed September 25, 2017).

260 Chris Wilson, "Oklahoma City Battalion Moves to New Building With Old Memories," *Recruiter Journal* 56, 4 (April), 2004: 19.

261 Ibid.

262 Jason Swensen, "LDS Spaniards mourn loss of bombing victims," *Mormon Times* (March 20, 2004), https://www.ldschurchnewsarchive.com/articles/45240/LDS-Spaniards-mourn-loss-of-bombing-victims.html (accessed September 29, 2017).

263 "In the News," *The Ensign*, June 2004.

264 William Blacoe, "Re: Madrid Bombs: members in the trains," message to Matt Heiss, Per Malm, Rick Ebert, and Yves Perrin, March 15, 2004, e-mail.

265 Ibid. This email included a letter from José Reina, President of the Madrid Spain East Stake, who stated members of the Guadalajara Branch, Azuqueca Ward, Alcalá de Henares First Ward, Alcalá de Henares Second Ward and Torrejón de Ardoz Ward used this train line to travel to work every day.

266 Alma 50:22.

267 Dallin H. Oaks, "Opposition in All Things," *General Conference*, April 2016.

268 "Peru missionaries 'eager to continue,'" *Church News*, September 15, 1990, 3–4.

269 Neal A. Maxwell, "Encircled in the Arms of His Love," *Ensign*, November 2002, 17.

270 Clayton M. Christensen, "The Power of Everyday Missionaries," (Deseret Book: Salt Lake City, 2012), 5. Used by permission.

271 M. Russell Ballard, "Duties, Rewards, and Risks," *Ensign*, November 1989.

272 M. Russell Ballard, "Duties, Rewards, and Risks," *Ensign*, November 1989.

273 Alma 60:13.

274 Mike McPheters, "Agent Bishop," (CFI: Springville, UT, 2009), 216.

275 Ibid., 217.

276 David Clark Knowlton, "Mormonism and Guerrillas in Bolivia," 197.

277 "More on Investigation," May 26, 1989, *La Paz La Red Panamericana* in Spanish, FBIS, LAT, 89–102: 53.

278 Lawrence A. Young, "Confronting Turbulent Environments," in *Contemporary Mormonism: Social Science Perspectives*, ed. Marie Cornwall, Tim B. Heaton, and Lawrence Alfred Young (Champaign, IL: University of Illinois Press, 2001), 50.

279 David Clark Knowlton, "Mormonism and Guerrillas in Bolivia," 198.

280 "Terrorists Kill Two U.S. Mormon Missionaries," May 25, 1989, *Hamburg DPA* in Spanish, FBIS, LAT, 89–101: 38–39.

281 Harrell Gwenden Fallis and Beverly Edith Fallis letter to friends and family, May 28, 1989, Correspondence, 1987–1989, Harrell G. Fallis correspondence, Church History Library.

282 Ibid.

283 *Eyewitness News*, KSL Television Channel 5, Salt Lake City, UT, 1989.

284 McPheters, "Agent Bishop," 221.

285 "Wisely, cautiously,' missionary work proceeds in Bolivia," *LDS Church News* (June 24, 1989), accessible at https://www.ldschurchnewsarchive.com/articles/19002/Wisely-cautiously-missionary-work-proceeds-in-Bolivia.html (accessed September 25, 2017).

286 Elayne Wells, "Work in South America continues to grow," *LDS Church News* (November 11, 1989), accessible at https://www.ldschurchnewsarchive.com/articles/18985/Work-in-South-America-continues-to-grow.html (accessed September 25, 2017).

287 David Clark Knowlton, "Mormonism and Guerrillas in Bolivia," 201.

288 Harrell Gwenden Fallis and Beverly Edith Fallis letter to friends and family, October 27, 1989, Correspondence, 1987-1989, Harrell G. Fallis correspondence, Church History Library.

289 David Clark Knowlton, "Mormonism and Guerrillas in Bolivia," 207.

290 McPheters, "Agent Bishop," 218.

291 John Hart, "Church leaders eulogize slain elders," *Mormon Times* (June 3, 1989), retrieved from http://www.ldschurchnewsarchive.com/articles/19505/Church-leaders-eulogize-slain-elders.html (accessed July 9, 2017).

292 M. Russell Ballard, "Duties, Rewards, and Risks," *Ensign,* November 1989.

293 Doctrine and Covenants 138:57.

294 "Bolivia tragedy plays role in conversions," *Church News* (September 9, 1989), http://www.ldschurchnewsarchive.com/articles/18682/Bolivia-tragedy-plays-role-in-conversions.html (accessed July 9, 2017).

295 "Families of Slain Peruvian Elders Share Testimonies, Encourage Work," *Ensign*, November 1990; Sheila Sanchez, "2 missionaries shot by rebels, police say," *Deseret News*, August 24, 1990, B1-B2.

296 Sanchez, "2 missionaries shot by rebels," B1-B2.

297 Dale Christensen, ed., "The History of the Church in Peru," (editor, 1995), 186.

298 Ibid., 186.

299 Ibid., 159.

300 Ibid., 159.

301 Ibid., 159.

302 Sanchez, "2 missionaries shot by rebels," B1-B2.

303 "Families of Slain Peruvian Elders Share Testimonies, Encourage Work," *Ensign*, November 1990.

304 Ibid.

305 Ibid.

306 Manuel Francisco Hidalgo Castro, oral history, interviewed by Alexander Nuñez, Arequipa, Peru, November 30, 2015, Church History Library.

307 "Families of Slain Peruvian Elders"; Manuel Francisco Hidalgo Castro, oral history, interviewed by Alexander Nuñez, Arequipa, Peru, November 30, 2015, Church History Library.

308 Manuel Francisco Hidalgo Castro, oral history.

309 Ibid.; "Families of Slain Peruvian Elders."

310 Cammy Lee Maughan, interviewed by Matthew A. Hughes by phone, October 8, 2017.

311 Ibid.

312 Kent Larsen, "LDS Bombing Victim's Family Remembers, Awaits Execution," *Mormons-News* (April 19, 2001), http://www.mormonstoday.com/010420/P2PBroxterman01.shtml (accessed September 30, 2017).

313 Cammy Lee Maughan, interviewed by Matthew A. Hughes by phone, October 8, 2017.

314 "Members Assist after Oklahoma Bomb Blast," *The Ensign,* July 1995.

315 Cammy Lee Maughan, interviewed by Matthew A. Hughes by phone, October 8, 2017.

316 Mosiah 18:9.

317 Cammy Lee Maughan, interviewed by Matthew A. Hughes by phone, October 8, 2017.

318 Julie A. Dockstader, "Faith, courage rise from the rubble," *Mormon Times* (April 29, 1995), https://www.ldschurchnewsarchive.com/articles/26065/Faith-courage-rise-from-the-rubble.html (accessed September 25, 2017).

319 "Paul Gregory Broxterman," *Find a Grave* (February 15, 2007), https://www.findagrave.com/cgi-bin/fg.cgi?page=gr&GRid=17940693 (accessed October 1, 2017).

320 *Teachings of Presidents of the Church: Spencer W. Kimball*, (2006), 82.

321 Alissa Parker, *An Unseen Angel*, (Ensign Peak: Salt Lake City, UT, 2017), 129–130.

322 Erin Walls, "Waves of Modern Terrorism: Examining the Past and Predicting the Future" master's thesis, Georgetown University, 2017, https://repository.library.georgetown.edu/bitstream/handle/10822/1043900/Walls_georgetown_0076M_13610.pdf?sequence=1.

323 Jeffrey Kaplan, "Terrorism's Fifth Wave: A Theory, a Conundrum and a Dilemma," in *Perspectives on Terrorism* 2, no. 2 (January 2008), 12.

324 Ibid., 48.

325 Ibid, 13.

326 Global Terrorism Database.

327 Walls, "Waves of Modern Terrorism," 57; Anthony N. Celso, "The Islamic State and Boko Haram: Fifth Wave Jihadist Terror Groups," Orbis 59, no. 2 (2015): 249-268, https://doi.org/10.1016/j.orbis.2015.02.010.

328 Malise Ruthven, "Historical Atlas of Islam," (Cambridge, MA: Harvard University Press, 2004), 14.

329 Ibid.

330 Headquarters, Department of the Army, Army Techniques Publication 2-33.4 (Intelligence Analysis), (Washington, D.C.: Department of the Army, 2014), paragraph A-2.

331 "Statistics: Nigeria," available at https://ldschurchtemples.org/statistics/units/nigeria/ (accessed March 21, 2018).

332 "Who, what, Why: Exactly what does the phrase Boko Haram mean?" *BBC News* (May 13, 2014), available at http://www.bbc.com/news/blogs-magazine-monitor-27390954 (accessed March 23, 2018).

333 Global Terrorism Database.

334 Ibid.

335 Ibid.

336 Jeffrey D. Simon, "Technological and Lone Operator Terrorism: Prospects for a Fifth Wave of Global Terrorism," in *Terrorism, Identity and Legitimacy*, ed. Jean E. Rosenfeld (New York: Routledge, 2011), 48.

337 Ibid.

338 Ibid., 59.

339 Walls, "Waves of Modern Terrorism," 76–77.

340 Ibid., 81.

341 Brynjar Lia, "Globalisation and the Future of Terrorism: Patterns and Predictions" (New York: Routledge, 2005), 19.

342 Walls, "Waves of Modern Terrorism," 74.

343 Ezra Taft Benson, "Prepare Yourself for the Great Day of the Lord," *New Era* (May 1982).

344 "Q and A with Dale Van Atta, an LDS Expert on Terrorism," *Meridian Magazine*, October 16, 2001, http://ldsmag.com/article-1-4534/ (accessed July 30, 2017).

345 M. Russell Ballard, "Duties, Rewards, and Risks," *Ensign,* November 1989.

346 Neal A. Maxwell, "All Hell is Moved," Devotional given at Brigham Young University, November 8, 1977.

347 Doctrine and Covenants 133:37, 90:11.

348 "The Philippines: Spiritual Strength upon the Isles of the Sea," *Ensign,* April 2014.

349 Ibid.

350 Ibid.

351 Michael Phillips, "Amid Bombs, LDS Church Reshaping its Image in Chile," *Salt Lake Tribune* (April 20, 1992), A-1, A-17.

352 "Facts and Statistics: Nigeria," *Newsroom*, The Church of Jesus Christ of Latter-day Saints, 2018, available at https://www.mormonnewsroom.org/facts-and-statistics/country/nigeria (accessed March 21, 2018).

353 Clayton M. Christensen, "The Power of Everyday Missionaries," (Deseret Book: Salt Lake City, 2012), 5. Used by permission.

354 Church Educational System, "Old Testament Student Manual: 1 Kings–Malachi," (Salt Lake City, UT: The Church of Jesus Christ of Latter-day Saints, 2003), 157.

355 Ibid.

356 Isaiah 19:18, footnote *a* in KJV used by The Church of Jesus Christ of Latter-day Saints.

357 Church Educational System, "Old Testament Student Manual: 1 Kings–Malachi," (Salt Lake City, UT: The Church of Jesus Christ of Latter-day Saints, 2003), 157.

358 Ibid.

359 Ibid.

360 Headquarters, Department of the Army, Army Techniques Publication 2–33.4 (Intelligence Analysis), (Washington, D.C.: Department of the Army, 2014), paragraph A-80.

361 Global Terrorism Database.

362 Thomas and Judith Parker, "Blessed Be Egypt My People," *Ensign,* September 1983.

363 Bureau of Democracy, Human Rights, and Labor, "International Religious Freedom Report 2005," available at https://www.state.gov/j/drl/rls/irf/2005/51598.htm (accessed March 11, 2018).

364 Global Terrorism Database.

365 Jeffrey M. Bale, "Islamism and Totalitarianism," *Totalitarian Movements and Political Religions* (2009) 10: 2, 73-96, DOI 10.1080/14690760903371313, 75.

366 Global Terrorism Database.

367 Bureau of Diplomatic Security, "Significant Incidents of Political Violence Against Americans: 1987," United States Department of State, 16; Bureau of Diplomatic Security, "Significant Incidents: 2001," 21; Bureau of Diplomatic Security, "Significant Incidents: 2011," 13, 15.

368 Bureau of Diplomatic Security, "Significant Incidents of Political Violence Against Americans: 1989," United States Department of State, 31.

369 Law 58 of 1937 (Criminal Code of 1937), art. 98(f), available in Arabic at http://www.mohamoon-montada.com/Default.aspx?action=ArabicLaw&ID=20 (accessed March 17, 2018).

370 Qu'ran, Sura 3, verse 110.

371 Arnold K. Garr, Donald Q. Cannon, and Richard O. Cowan, eds., Encyclopedia of Latter-day Saint History (Salt Lake City: Deseret Book, 2000), 549–51. Used with the permission of the Deseret Book Company. Used by permission.

372 "Statistics: Egypt," available at https://ldschurchtemples.org/statistics/units/egypt/ (accessed March 17, 2018).

373 Michael Phillips, "Amid Bombs, LDS Church Reshaping Its Image in Chile," *Salt Lake Tribune* (April 20, 1992), A-1, A-17.

374 Brigham Young, "Light of the Spirit—Coming Tribulations—Present Salvation," (July 15, 1860), in *Journal of Discourses* 8, ed. G.D. Watt, available online at http://www.Josephsmithfoundation.org/journalofdiscourses/volumes/volume-8/light-of-the-spirit-coming-tribulations-present-salvation/ (accessed March 24, 2018).

375 Reported by Amanda H. Wilcox, Prophetic Sayings of Heber C. Kimball to Sister Amanda H. Wilcox quoted by J. Golden Kimball in Conference, October 1930, Deseret News, Church Department, May 23, 1931, p. 3.

376 Blair G. Van Dyke and LaMar C. Berrett, "In the Footsteps of Orson Hyde: Subsequent Dedications of the Holy Land, *BYU Studies* 47, no. 1 (2008), 64 and 91.

377 "Police Injured Dispersing Protesters at U.S. Embassy," August 8, 1985, *Jerusalem Domestic Service* in Hebrew, FBIS, MEA, 85-154: I4.

378 Bruce R. McConkie, *Doctrinal New Testament Commentary*, (Salt Lake City: Deseret Book, 2012), 3:509. Used by permission.

379 Jairo Cala Otero, "Estallaron 3 bombas en Bucaramanga," *El Tiempo*, July 1, 1983, 1-A, 7-B; RAND National Security Research Division (2017); "ELN Attacks Organizations Linked to U.S.,"*Latin* (Buenos Aires), July 1, 1983, FBIS, LAM 83-129: F1; RAND Database of Worldwide Terrorism Incidents (data file), retrieved from https://www.rand.org/nsrd/projects/terrorism-incidents.html.

380 "ELN Commandos Attack Mormon Churches 28 NOV," November 28, 1983, *Caracol* Network in Spanish (Bogota Emisoras), FBIS, LAM 83-230: F1-2; Global Terrorism Database.

381 "ELN Commandos Attack Mormon Churches 28 NOV," November 28, 1983, *Caracol* Network in Spanish (Bogota Emisoras), FBIS, LAM 83-230: F1-2; Global Terrorism Database.

382 "ELN Commandos," F1-2; Global Terrorism Database.

383 "ELN Commandos," F1-2; Global Terrorism Database; "LDS church blasts blamed on leftists," *Deseret News*, November 29, 1983, 2A.

384 "ELN Commandos," F1-2; Global Terrorism Database; "LDS church blasts blamed on leftists," *Deseret News*, November 29, 1983, 2A.

385 Ibid.

386 "Eight LDS buildings damaged in bomb attacks," *Church News* (July 14, 1985), 6; "8 LDS chapels vandalized by Chilean Reds," *Deseret News* (July 7, 1985).

387 "Churches, Police Headquarters Targets of Bombs," July 5, 1985, *AFP* in Spanish (Paris), FBIS, LAM 85-130: E3; "Manuel Rodriguez Front Bombs Mormon Churches," July 7, 1985, *National News Feature* (Moscow), FBIS, SOV 85-132: K3; "Eight LDS buildings damaged in bomb attacks," *Church News* (July 14, 1985), 6; RAND Database; Global Terrorism Database; "8 LDS chapels vandalized by Chilean Reds," *Deseret News* (July 7, 1985).

388 "Churches, Police Headquarters Targets of Bombs," E3; "Manuel Rodriguez Front Bombs Mormon Churches," July 7, 1985, *National News Feature* (Moscow), FBIS, SOV 85-132: K3; "Eight LDS buildings damaged in bomb attacks," *Church News* (July 14, 1985), 6; RAND Database; Global Terrorism Database; "8 LDS chapels vandalized by Chilean Reds," *Deseret News* (July 7, 1985).

389 Ibid.

390 Ibid.

391 Ibid.

392 "Eight LDS buildings damaged in bomb attacks," *Church News* (July 14, 1985), 6; "8 LDS chapels vandalized by Chilean Reds," *Deseret News* (July 7, 1985).

393 "Churches, Police Headquarters Targets of Bombs," July 5, 1985, *AFP* in Spanish (Paris), FBIS, LAM 85-130: E3; "Manuel Rodriguez Front Bombs Mormon Churches," July 7, 1985, *National News Feature* (Moscow), FBIS, SOV 85-132: K3; "Government Issues Appeal Following Violent Attack," July 12, 1985, *Santiago Domestic Service* in Spanish, FBIS, LAM 85-136: E1; "Eight LDS buildings damaged in bomb attacks," *Church News* (July 14, 1985), 6; RAND Database; Global Terrorism Database; "8 LDS chapels vandalized by Chilean Reds," *Deseret News* (July 7, 1985).

394 "2 Banks, Mormon Church Bombed in Santiago," March 28, 1986, *Madrid EFE* in Spanish, FBIS, LAM, 86-062: E3; RAND Database.

395 "Bomb Explodes at Mormon Church in Southeast," April 19, 1986, *Hamburg DPA* in Spanish, FBIS, LAM, 86-076: L1; RAND Database; Global Terrorism Database.

396 RAND Database; Global Terrorism Database; "Explosions damage 5 meetinghouses," *Church News* (May 4, 1986), 14; "Bombs rip 5 Mormon chapels," *Deseret News* (April 24, 1986).

397 RAND Database; Global Terrorism Database; "Explosions damage 5 meetinghouses," 14; "Bombs rip 5 Mormon chapels."

398 Ibid.

399 Ibid.

400 Ibid.

401 "Further Details," June 27, 1986, *Bogota EL SIGLO* in Spanish, FBIS, LAM, 86-128: F3-F4.

402 Ibid.

403 RAND Database; Global Terrorism Database.

404 Bureau of Diplomatic Security, "Significant Incidents of Political Violence Against Americans: 1987," United States Department of State, 14; RAND Database.

405 "Significant Incidents: 1987," 14; RAND Database.

406 Ibid.

407 Ibid.

408 Ibid.

409 "Homemade Bomb Explodes at Peace Corps Office," April 30, 1987, *Paris AFP* in Spanish, FBIS, LAT, 87-123: N1; "Significant Incidents: 1987," 14.

410 "Homemade Bomb Explodes at Peace Corps Office," N1; "Significant Incidents: 1987," 14; RAND Database.

411 "Significant Incidents: 1987," 14; RAND Database.

412 "Significant Incidents: 1987," 24; RAND Database.

413 "Significant Incidents: 1987," 25; RAND Database.

414 Ibid.

415 Ibid.

416 Miguel Angel Molina, "3 atentados a mormones en Boyacá," *El Tiempo,* October 30, 1987, 2-A, https://news.google.com/newspapers?id=wM8cAAAAIBAJ&sjid=JF0EAAAAIBAJ&pg=4971%2C5168522 ; Significant Incidents: 1987," 38; "Explosions Damage Three Mormon Churches," *Bogota Radio Sutatenza Network* in Spanish, FBIS, LAT, 87-211: 35; RAND Database; Global Terrorism Database.

417 Molina, "3 atentados," 2-A; "Explosions Damage Three Mormon Churches," *Bogota Radio Sutatenza Network* in Spanish, FBIS, LAT, 87-211: 35; "Significant Incidents: 1987," 38; RAND Database; Global Terrorism Database.

418 Ibid.

419 "Significant Incidents: 1987," 39; RAND Database.

420 Ibid.

421 "Explosion Damages Mormon Church in Copiapo," December 9, 1987, *Santiago Domestic Service* in Spanish, FBIS, LAT, 87-239: 36; "Significant Incidents: 1987," 41; RAND Database.

422 "Mormon Church in Santiago Attacked," December 12, 1987, *Santiago EL MERCURIO* in Spanish, FBIS, LAT, 87-246: 39; "Significant Incidents: 1987," 41; RAND Database.

423 Bureau of Diplomatic Security, "Significant Incidents of Political Violence Against Americans: 1988," United States Department of State, 4; RAND Database.

424 U.S. Department of State, "U.S. Business Targets – 1988," December 30, 1988, on file at Church History Library, The Church of Jesus Christ of Latter-day Saints, Salt Lake City, Utah (accessed December 29, 2017), 2; "Significant Incidents: 1988," 11; RAND Database.

425 David Knowlton, "Missionaries and Terror: the Assassination of Two Elders in Bolivia," *Sunstone* (August 1989), 12; U.S. Department of State, "U.S. Business Targets," 2; "Significant Incidents: 1988," 11; RAND Database.

426 "Bomb Blast at Mormon Church Injures 3 Youths," July 20, 1988, *Santiago Domestic Service* in Spanish, FBIS, LAT, 88-140: 22; U.S. Department of State, "U.S. Business Targets – 1988," December 30, 1988, on file at Church History Library, The Church of Jesus Christ of Latter-day Saints, Salt Lake City, Utah (accessed December 29, 2017), 2; "Significant Incidents: 1988," 11–12; RAND Database; Global Terrorism Database.

427 "Bomb Explodes Near Mormon Church; No Injuries," August 23, 1988, *Santiago Domestic Service* in Spanish, FBIS, LAT, 88-164: 24; U.S. Department of State, "U.S. Business Targets–1988," December 30, 1988, on file at Church History Library, The Church of Jesus Christ of Latter-day Saints, Salt Lake City, Utah (accessed December 29, 2017), 2; "Significant Incidents: 1988," 12; RAND Database; Global Terrorism Database.

428 "Series of Terrorist Bombings Described," November 26, 1988, *Santiago Domestic Service* in Spanish, FBIS, LAT, 88-229: 32; U.S. Department of State, "U.S. Business Targets–1988," December 30, 1988, on file at Church History Library, The Church of Jesus Christ of Latter-day Saints, Salt Lake City, Utah (accessed December 29, 2017), 2; "Significant Incidents: 1988," 15; RAND Database; Global Terrorism Database.

429 "Device Explodes in Tarija Mormon Church," March 23, 1989, *La Paz La Red Panamericana* in Spanish, FBIS, LAT, 89-056: 24; "Significant Incidents: 1989," 4; RAND Database; Global Terrorism Database.

430 "Terrorists Kill Two U.S. Mormon Missionaries," May 25, 1989, *Hamburg DPA* in Spanish, FBIS, LAT, 89-101: 38-39; "More on Investigation," May 26, 1989, *La Paz La Red Panamericana* in Spanish, FBIS, LAT, 89-102: 53; "Emergency Meeting Called," May 26, 1989, *La Paz Radio Fides* in Spanish, FBIS, LAT, 89-102: 53; "Significant Incidents: 1989," 6; RAND Database; Global Terrorism Database.

431 Global Terrorism Database.

432 "Armed Group Attacks Mormon Church in Santiago," July 5, 1989, *Santiago Radio Chilena Network* in Spanish, FBIS, LAT, 89-128: 57; "Two Youths Indicted in Mormon Church Arson," October 17, 1989, *Santiago Domestic Service* in Spanish, FBIS, LAT, 89-200: 48-49; "Mormon chapel bombed in Bolivia," *UPI*, July 11, 1989, http://www.upi.com/Archives/1989/07/11/Mormon-chapel-bombed-in-Bolivia/2841616132800/ (accessed July 30, 2017); "Significant Incidents: 1989," 6; "Precautions taken against terrorism," *Deseret News* (July 15, 1989), https://www.ldschurchnewsarchive.com/articles/18665/Precautions-taken-against-terrorism.html (accessed September 25, 2017); David L. Cook, e-mail message to author, January 15, 2018; RAND Database; Global Terrorism Database; "Chilean leftists set fire to another LDS chapel," *Deseret News* (July 16, 1989), B1, B3; "3 held in attack on 1 LDS chapel," *Deseret News* (July 25, 1989), A5.

433 "Bomb Explodes in Santa Cruz Mormon Church," July 11, 1989, *La Paz La Red Panamericana* in Spanish, FBIS, LAT, 89-134: 54; "Mormon chapel bombed in Bolivia," *UPI*, July 11, 1989, http://www.upi.com/Archives/1989/07/11/Mormon-chapel-bombed-in-Bolivia/2841616132800/ (accessed July 30, 2017); "Significant Incidents: 1989," 7; "Precautions taken against terrorism," *Deseret News* (July 15, 1989), https://www.ldschurchnewsarchive.com/articles/18665/Precautions-taken-against-terrorism.html (accessed September 25, 2017); "Precautions taken against terrorism," *Church News* (July 15, 1989), 10; RAND Database; Global Terrorism Database; Brian T. West, "LDS Church reassigning missionaries," *Deseret News* (July 11, 1989), A1-A2.

434 "Terrorists Attack Mormon Church in Santiago," July 15, 1989, *Santiago Domestic Service* in Spanish, FBIS, LAT, 89-136: 57.

435 "Significant Incidents: 1989," 7; RAND Database; Global Terrorism Database; "Chilean leftists set fire to another LDS chapel," *Deseret News* (July 16, 1989), B1, B3.

436 "Osorno Mormon Church, Newspaper Offices Bombed," *Santiago Radio Chilena Network* in Spanish, July 20, 1989, FBIS, LAT, 89-140: 54; "Significant Incidents: 1989," 7; RAND Database; Global Terrorism Database.

437 "Significant Incidents: 1989," 7; RAND Database; Global Terrorism Database; "2 more LDS chapels are damaged in Chile," *Deseret News* (July 23, 1989), B4.

438 Ibid.

439 "Bomb Attack on Mormon Church in Osorno Reported," August 24, 1989, *Santiago Domestic Service* in Spanish, FBIS, LAT, 89-165: 56; "FPMR Pamphlets Found," August 24, 1989, *Santiago Radio Chilena Network* in Spanish, FBIS, LAT, 89-165: 56; "Significant Incidents: 1989," 7; RAND Database; Global Terrorism Database.

440 "Mormon Church Bombed 6 Sep; No Casualties," September 7, 1989, *Santiago Television Nacional de Chile Network* in Spanish, FBIS, LAT, 89-173: 24; "Significant Incidents: 1989," 8; RAND Database; Global Terrorism Database; "Bomb explodes at LDS chapel in Chile," *Deseret News* (September 8, 1989), B4.

441 "Significant Incidents: 1989," 10; RAND Database; Global Terrorism Database.

442 "Significant Incidents: 1989," 11; RAND Database; Global Terrorism Database; "Bogota chapel is bombed," *Deseret News* (November 17, 1989).

443 "Four Bombs Explode in Santiago; Two Casualties," November 23, 1989, *Santiago Domestic Service* in Spanish, FBIS, LAT, 89-225: 50–51; Global Terrorism Database.

444 "Significant Incidents: 1989," 12; RAND Database.

445 "Significant Incidents: 1989," 13; RAND Database; Brian T. West, "LDS Missionary Recuperating from Gunshot Injury to Knee," *Deseret News* (December 28, 1989), available at https://www.deseretnews.com/article/78804/LDS-MISSIONARY-RECUPERATING-FROM-GUNSHOT-INJURY-TO-KNEE.html (accessed November 11, 2017).

446 "Significant Incidents: 1989," 13.

447 "Significant Incidents: 1989," 15; RAND Database; Global Terrorism Database; "3 LDS chapels in Chile damaged by bomb blasts," *Deseret News* (December 25, 1989).

448 "Significant Incidents: 1989," 15; RAND Database; "3 LDS chapels in Chile damaged by bomb blasts," *Deseret News* (December 25, 1989).

449 Ibid.

450 "Significant Incidents: 1989," 15; RAND Database; U.S. Department of State, *Terrorist attacks against U.S. targets in Peru*, available at http://lum.cultura.pe/cdi/sites/default/files/documento/pdf/686.pdf (accessed December 29, 2017), 5.

451 "Significant Incidents: 1989," 15; RAND Database; U.S. Department of State, *Terrorist attacks against U.S. targets in Peru*, available at http://lum.cultura.pe/cdi/sites/default/files/documento/pdf/686.pdf (accessed December 29, 2017), 5; "Guerrillas bomb 2 LDS chapels, cultural center," *Deseret News* (December 27, 1989).

452 "Significant Incidents: 1989," 15; RAND Database; "Guerrillas bomb 2 LDS chapels, cultural center," *Deseret News* (December 27, 1989).

453 RAND Database; Global Terrorism Database.

454 "Significant Incidents: 1989," 15; Brian T. West, "LDS missionary recuperating from gunshot injury to knee," *Deseret News* (December 29, 1989), 20A; RAND Database.

455 Global Terrorism Database; "2 LDS buildings in S. America are targets of attacks," *Deseret News* (December 30, 1989).

456 "Mormon Church Attacked; No Injuries, Damage," December 29, 1989, *Santiago Domestic Service* in Spanish, FBIS, LAT, 89-249: 34; RAND Database; "2 LDS buildings in S. America are targets of attacks," *Deseret News* (December 30, 1989).

457 "Significant Incidents: 1989," 15; RAND Database; Global Terrorism Database.

458 "Terrorists Attack U.S.-Affiliated Properties," December 29, 1989, *Madrid EFE* in Spanish, FBIS, LAT, 90-001: 62; "Significant Incidents: 1989," 15; RAND Database; Global Terrorism Database.

459 "Significant Incidents: 1989," 16; RAND Database; Global Terrorism Database.

460 "More Bombings Reported," January 1, 1990, *Madrid EFE* in Spanish, FBIS, LAT, 90-001: 62; "Significant Incidents: 1989," 16; RAND Database; Global Terrorism Database.

461 RAND Database; Global Terrorism Database.

462 "Significant Incidents: 1990," 3; Global Terrorism Database.

463 Ibid.

464 "Molotov Cocktails Hurled at Mormon Church," January 2, 1990, *Havana PRENSA LATINA* in Spanish, FBIS, LAT, 90-004-A: 12–13; "Significant Incidents: 1990," 3; RAND Database; Global Terrorism Database; "Panama group says it bombed LDS chapel," *Deseret News* (January 3, 1990).

465 "Significant Incidents: 1990," 3; Global Terrorism Database.

466 "Bombs on 13 Feb in Bogota Protest Bush Visit," February 14, 1990, *Paris AFP* in Spanish, FBIS, LAT, 90-031: 31; "Significant Incidents: 1990," 4; Global Terrorism Database.

467 "Bombs on 13 Feb in Bogota Protest Bush Visit," February 14, 1990, *Paris AFP* in Spanish, FBIS, LAT, 90-031: 31; "Significant Incidents: 1990," 4.

468 "Significant Incidents: 1990," 4; RAND Database; Global Terrorism Database.

469 Ibid.

470 Global Terrorism Database.

471 Ibid.

472 Ibid.

473 "Several Bomb Attacks Reported, Three Injured," March 10, 1990, *Santiago Radio Chilena Network* in Spanish, FBIS, LAT, 90-048: 46; "Significant Incidents: 1990," 5; RAND Database; Global Terrorism Database.

474 "Significant Incidents: 1990," 5; Global Terrorism Database.

475 "Bombs Explode Near U.S. Consulate, Elsewhere," May 15, 1990, *Santiago Domestic Service* in Spanish, FBIS, LAT, 90-095: 38; "Significant Incidents: 1990," 5.

476 "Significant Incidents: 1990," 7; RAND Database; Global Terrorism Database.

477 Ibid.

478 "Seven Bomb Attacks Reported in Santiago," May 22, 1990, *Santiago Domestic Service* in Spanish, FBIS, LAT, 90-100: 26; "Significant Incidents: 1990," 7; RAND Database; Global Terrorism Database.

479 "Significant Incidents: 1990," 7; Global Terrorism Database.

480 Ibid.

481 Ibid.

482 Ibid.

483 Ibid.

484 Ibid,

485 Ibid.

486 Ibid.

487 Ibid.

488 "Significant Incidents: 1990," 7–8.

489 "Attack on Carabineros Patrol Car; Bombings," June 27, 1990, *Santiago Domestic Service* in Spanish, FBIS, LAT, 90-125: 29–30; "Significant Incidents: 1990," 8; Global Terrorism Database.

490 "Significant Incidents: 1990," 8; "Chile official deplores bombings that hurt 2, damaged LDS facilities," *Deseret News* (July 28, 1990).

491 Unknown periodical of Santiago (July 28, 1990), included in Henry Clay Gorton, "Santiago Chile MTC scrapbook, 1990-1992," microfilm of holograph, Church History Library, The Church of Jesus Christ of Latter-day Saints, Salt Lake City, Utah; "Significant Incidents: 1990," 8; Global Terrorism Database.

492 Unknown periodical of Santiago (July 28, 1990); "Significant Incidents: 1990," 8; Global Terrorism Database.

493 Ibid.

494 "Terroristas Incendiaron Templo Mormón en Stgo," Unknown periodical of Santiago (July 28, 1990), included in Henry Clay Gorton, "Santiago Chile MTC scrapbook, 1990-1992," microfilm of holograph, Church History Library, The Church of Jesus Christ of Latter-day Saints, Salt Lake City, Utah; "Significant Incidents: 1990," 8.

495 "Significant Incidents: 1990," 8; Global Terrorism Database.

496 "Political Party Office, Mormon Church Bombed," August 23, 1990, *Santiago Domestic Service* in Spanish, FBIS, LAT, 90-165: 29–30; "Significant Incidents: 1990," 9; RAND Database; Global Terrorism Database.

497 "Significant Incidents: 1990," 9; RAND Database; Global Terrorism Database; U.S. Department of State, *Terrorist attacks against U.S. targets in Peru*, available at http://lum.cultura.pe/cdi/sites/default/files/documento/pdf/686.pdf (accessed December 29, 2017), 5.

498 "Lautaro Group Claims Attack on Mormon Churches," August 27, 1990, *Santiago Domestic Service* in Spanish, FBIS, LAT, 90-168: 48; "Significant Incidents: 1990," 9; RAND Database; Global Terrorism Database.

499 Scott Earl, interviewed by Matthew A. Hughes, January 2, 2020. "Lautaro Group," 48; "Significant Incidents: 1990," 9; RAND Database; Global Terrorism Database.

500 Ibid.

501 Ibid.

502 Ibid.

503 "Four Bombs Explode; One Bomb Deactivated," September 12, 1990, *Santiago Radio Chilena Network* in Spanish, FBIS, LAT, 90-178: 29; "Significant Incidents: 1990," 9; RAND Database; Global Terrorism Database.

504 "Lautaro Group Bombs Mormon Church, Burns Bus," October 5, 1990, *Santiago Domestic Service* in Spanish, FBIS, LAT, 90-195: 48; "Significant Incidents: 1990," 10; RAND Database; Global Terrorism Database.

505 "Bomb Explodes at Mormon Church in Concepcion," November 1, 1990, *Santiago LA TERCERA DE LA HORA* in Spanish, FBIS, LAT, 90-217: 34-35; "Significant Incidents: 1990," 10; RAND Database; Global Terrorism Database.

506 "Significant Incidents: 1990," 10.

507 "Political Headquarters, Mormon Church Attacked," December 3, 1990, *Santiago Domestic Service* in Spanish, FBIS, LAT, 90-233: 54; "Mujer capitaneó nueva ola de atentados," *La Tercera* (December 3, 1990), 4; "Significant Incidents: 1990," 13; Global Terrorism Database.

508 "Significant Incidents: 1990," 13.

509 "Bomb Attacks Herald Bush's Arrival," 27; "Significant Incidents: 1990," 13; "Chilean Leftists Bomb LDS Chapels," *Sunstone* (April 1991), 63; RAND Database; Global Terrorism Database.

510 "Bomb Attacks Herald Bush's Arrival," 27; "Significant Incidents: 1990," 13; "Chilean Leftists Bomb LDS Chapels," 63; Global Terrorism Database.

511 Roberto Alejandro del Rio Troncoso, interviewed by Matthew A. Hughes by phone, September 10, 2017; "Bomb Attacks Herald Bush's Arrival," 27; "Mormon Churches Attacked; No Casualties," December 7, 1990, *Santiago Domestic Service* in Spanish, FBIS, LAT, 90-236: 34; "Chilean Leftists Bomb LDS Chapels," 63; "Significant Incidents: 1990," 13.

512 "Bomb Attacks Herald Bush's Arrival," 27; "Chilean Leftists Bomb LDS Chapels," 63; "Significant Incidents: 1990," 13.

513 "Significant Incidents: 1990," 13; "Coincidiendo con la visita del Presidente de EE.UU., sigue serie de bombazos contra mormones," *La Segunda*, December 7, 1990, 7.

514 "Significant Incidents: 1990," 13.

515 "Significant Incidents: 1990," 14; "Coincidiendo con la visita del Presidente de EE.UU.," 7.

516 Ibid.

517 Ibid.

518 Ibid.

519 "Mormon Church, Railway Bombed," December 15, 1990, *Santiago Domestic Service* in Spanish, FBIS, LAT, 90-242: 59; "Plot Against Officials Stopped; 2 Arrested," March 6, 1991, *Santiago Radio Chilena Network* in Spanish, FBIS, LAT, 91-045: 28; "Significant Incidents: 1990," 14; RAND Database; Global Terrorism Database.

520 "Terrorists Destroy Mormon Church," December 16, 1990, *Madrid EFE* in Spanish, FBIS, LAT, 90-242: 59.

521 "Leaders Saddened by Attack," *Mormon Times* (December 22, 1990), retrieved from https://www.ldschurchnewsarchive.com/articles/19760/Leaders-saddened-by-attack.html (accessed September 30, 2017); "Significant Incidents: 1990," 14; RAND Database; Global Terrorism Database.

522 "Significant Incidents: 1991," 4; RAND Database.

523 "Mormon Church Bombed To Protest U.S. in Gulf," January 16, 1991, *Santiago Radio Nacional de Chile Network* in Spanish, FBIS, LAT, 91-012: 20; "Significant Incidents: 1991," 4; Global Terrorism Database.

524 "Churches Bombed, Heavily Damaged," January 17, 1991, *Madrid EFE* in Spanish, FBIS, LAT, 91-013: 40; "Significant Incidents: 1991," 4; RAND Database; Global Terrorism Database; "Vigilan Embajadas: Atentados A Locales Vinculados Con EE.UU.," *El Mercurio* (January 18, 1991), C1, C6; "5 bombings in Chile," *Deseret News*, January 20, 1991.

525 "Churches Bombed, Heavily Damaged," January 17, 1991, *Madrid EFE* in Spanish, FBIS, LAT, 91-013: 40; "Significant Incidents: 1991," 4; RAND Database; Global Terrorism Database; "Vigilan Embajadas: Atentados A Locales Vinculados Con EE.UU.," *El Mercurio* (January 18, 1991), C1, C6.

526 "Significant Incidents: 1991," 4; "5 bombings in Chile," *Deseret News*, January 20, 1991.

527 "Molotov Cocktail Thrown at Mormon Church," January 18, 1991, *Madrid EFE* in Spanish, FBIS, LAT, 91-014: 34; "Significant Incidents: 1991," 4; RAND Database; Global Terrorism Database.

528 "Porto Alegre Synagogue Bombed; No Injuries," January 20, 1991, *Buenos Aires NOTICIAS ARGENTINAS* in Spanish, FBIS, LAT, 91-014: 34; "Police Chief Denies Bombings Linked to Terrorism," January 22, 1991, *Brasilia Domestic Service* in Portuguese, FBIS, LAT, 91-018: 32; "Significant Incidents: 1991," 4; "LDS Image Encourages South American Attacks," *Sunstone* 15, no. 2 (June 1991), 61; RAND Database; Global Terrorism Database.

529 "Two U.S. Companies, Mormon Churches Bombed," January 22, 1991, *Madrid EFE* in Spanish, FBIS, LAT, 91-015: 32; "Significant Incidents: 1991," 4–5; RAND Database; Global Terrorism Database; "Vigilan Embajadas: Atentados A Locales Vinculados Con EE.UU.," *El Mercurio* (January 18, 1991), C1, C6; "5 bombings in Chile," *Deseret News*, January 20, 1991.

530 "Two U.S. Companies, Mormon Churches Bombed," January 22, 1991, *Madrid EFE* in Spanish, FBIS, LAT, 91-015: 32; "Significant Incidents: 1991," 5; RAND Database; Global Terrorism Database.

531 "Two U.S. Companies, Mormon Churches Bombed," January 22, 1991, *Madrid EFE* in Spanish, FBIS, LAT, 91-015: 32; "Significant Incidents: 1991," 5; RAND Database; Global Terrorism Database.

532 "Significant Incidents: 1991," 5.

533 Ibid.

534 Ibid.

535 "Significant Incidents: 1991," 5; RAND Database; Global Terrorism Database.

536 "Bombs Explode at 2 Mormon Churches in Santiago," January 28, 1991, *Santiago Radio Nacional de Chile Network* in Spanish, FBIS, LAT, 91-019: 32; "Significant Incidents: 1991," 7; RAND Database.

537 Ibid.

538 "Significant Incidents: 1991," 7; Global Terrorism Database.

539 "Significant Incidents: 1991," 8; Global Terrorism Database.

540 RAND Database of Worldwide Terrorism Incidents (data file), retrieved from https://www.rand.org/nsrd/projects/terrorism-incidents.html.

541 "ELN Claims Responsibility for Terrorist Actions," February 4, 1991, *Bogota Inravision Television Cadena 1* in Spanish, FBIS, LAT, 91-024: 26-27; "Explosions Damage Mormon Temple, Leather Plant," February 4, 1991, *Hamburg DPA* in Spanish, FBIS, LAT, 91-043: 32; "Significant Incidents: 1991," 8; Global Terrorism Database.

542 "Significant Incidents: 1991," 9;

543 Ibid.

544 Ibid.

545 Ibid.

546 Ibid.

547 "Significant Incidents: 1991," 9; Global Terrorism Database.

548 "LDS chapel is bombed," *Deseret News* (February 14, 1991); "Significant Incidents: 1991," 9; Global Terrorism Database.

549 "Significant Incidents: 1991," 9; "LDS Image Encourages South American Attacks," *Sunstone* 15, no. 2 (June 1991), 61.

550 Ibid.

551 Ibid.

552 "Significant Incidents: 1991," 9; "LDS Image," 61.

553 "Significant Incidents: 1991," 10; Global Terrorism Database.

554 "Significant Incidents: 1991," 10; Global Terrorism Database.

555 "Significant Incidents: 1991," 11; Global Terrorism Database.

556 "Significant Incidents: 1991," 12; "Chilean Leftists Bomb LDS Chapels," *Sunstone* (April 1991), 63; Global Terrorism Database.

557 "Significant Incidents: 1991," 12; Global Terrorism Database.

558 Ibid.

559 Ibid.

560 Ibid.

561 Ibid.

562 Ibid.

563 Ibid., 14.

564 Ibid.

565 Ibid.

566 Ibid.

567 Ibid.; RAND Database; Global Terrorism Database.

568 "Significant Incidents: 1991," 14; RAND Database; Global Terrorism Database.

569 "Significant Incidents: 1991," 14; RAND Database; Global Terrorism Database.

570 "Significant Incidents: 1991," 15; Global Terrorism Database.

571 Ibid.

572 Ibid.

573 "Significant Incidents: 1991," 15; RAND Database.

574 Ibid.

575 Ibid.

576 Ibid.

577 "Significant Incidents: 1991," 16; RAND Database; Global Terrorism Database; "Bomb shatters windows in LDS chapel in Chile," *Deseret News*, July 8, 1991.

578 "Significant Incidents: 1991," 16; RAND Database; Global Terrorism Database.

579 "Bomb Explodes in Mormon Church in Santiago," July 8, 1991, *Santiago EL MERCURIO* in Spanish, FBIS, LAT, 91-137: 47-48; "Significant Incidents: 1991," 16-17; Global Terrorism Database.

580 "Bomb Thrown at San Cristobal Police Station," August 1, 1991, *Santo Domingo Radio-Television Dominicana Radio Network* in Spanish, FBIS, LAT, 91-149: 5; "Significant Incidents: 1991," 17; Global Terrorism Database.

581 "Significant Incidents: 1991," 18; Global Terrorism Database.

582 Ibid.

583 Ibid.

584 "Lautaro Group Responsible for Carabinero Shooting," September 19, 1991, *Madrid EFE* in Spanish, FBIS, LAT, 91-182: 27; "Significant Incidents: 1991," 19; "Mormon Church Bombed in Quinta Normal," September 20, 1991, *Santiago Radio Nacional de Chile Network* in Spanish, FBIS, LAT, 91-184: 37; Global Terrorism Database; RAND Database.

585 "Police Arrest FPMR Militants; Bombings Reported," October 7, 1991, *Santiago Radio Chilena Network* in Spanish, FBIS, LAT, 91-195: 31–32; "Significant Incidents: 1991," 19; RAND Database; Global Terrorism Database.

586 "Significant Incidents: 1991," 19.

587 "Terrorist Group Attacks 3 Mormon Temples," October 12, 1991, *Santiago Radio Cooperativa Network* in Spanish, FBIS, LAT, 91-202: 29; "Significant Incidents: 1991," 19.

588 "Significant Incidents: 1991," 19; Global Terrorism Database.

589 "Significant Incidents: 1991," 19; Global Terrorism Database.

590 "Significant Incidents: 1991," 20; Global Terrorism Database.

591 Ibid.

592 Ibid.

593 Ibid.

594 Ibid.

595 Ibid.

596 Ibid.

597 Ibid.

598 "Significant Incidents: 1992," 2; Global Terrorism Database.

599 Ibid.

600 "Significant Incidents: 1992," 6; RAND Database; Global Terrorism Database.

601 "Significant Incidents: 1992," 6; RAND Database; Global Terrorism Database.

602 "Attacks in Santiago, La Serena," March 27, 1992, *Santiago Radio Chilena Network* in Spanish, FBIS, LAT, 92-062: 20; "Significant Incidents: 1992," 6; RAND Database; Global Terrorism Database.

603 "Significant Incidents: 1992," 6; RAND Database; Global Terrorism Database.

604 "2 LDS chapels, courts bombed in Chile cities," *Deseret News* (March 29, 1992); "Significant Incidents: 1992," 6; RAND Database; Global Terrorism Database.

605 Ibid.

606 "Significant Incidents: 1992," 7; RAND Database; Global Terrorism Database.

607 "Significant Incidents: 1992," 7; RAND Database; Global Terrorism Database.

608 "Lautaro Members Bomb Mormon Temple in Santiago," May 16, 1992, *Santiago Radio Chilena Network* in Spanish, FBIS, LAT, 92-096: 18; "Significant Incidents: 1992," 8–9; RAND Database; Global Terrorism Database.

609 "Lautaro Members Bomb Mormon Temple in Santiago," May 16, 1992, *Santiago Radio Chilena Network* in Spanish, FBIS, LAT, 92-096: 18; "Significant Incidents: 1992," 9.

610 "Significant Incidents: 1992," 9; Global Terrorism Database.

611 José Medina Cisternas, interviewed by Matthew A. Hughes by phone, July 20, 2017; "Fourth Terrorist Attack Mounted on Mormon Church," May 19, 1992, *Santiago Radio Chilena Network* in Spanish, FBIS, LAT, 92-098: 41; "Significant Incidents: 1992," 9; RAND Database; Global Terrorism Database.

612 "Significant Incidents: 1992," 9; Global Terrorism Database.

613 "Significant Incidents: 1992," 9–10; RAND Database.

614 "Significant Incidents: 1992," 13; RAND Database; Global Terrorism Database.

615 "'Terrorist' Attack on Police Precinct, Church," June 26, 1992, *La Paz Television Boliviana Network* in Spanish, FBIS, LAT, 92-125: 21–22; RAND Database.

616 "Five Bombs Explode in Santiago; No Casualties," July 6, 1992, *Santiago Radio Chilena Network* in Spanish, FBIS, LAT, 92-153: 22.

617 Ibid.

618 "Five Bombs Explode in Santiago; No Casualties," July 6, 1992, *Santiago Radio Chilena Network* in Spanish, FBIS, LAT, 92-153: 22.

619 "Explosion in Paopote," July 17, 1992, *Santiago EL MERCURIO* in Spanish, FBIS, LAT, 92-146: 27; "Significant Incidents: 1992," 14; RAND Database; Global Terrorism Database.

620 "Lautaro Movement Claims Responsibility for Attack," July 21, 1992, *Santiago Radio Chilena Network* in Spanish, FBIS, LAT, 92-141: 29; RAND Database; Global Terrorism Database.

621 "Bomb blast damages LDS chapel in Chile," *Deseret News* (July 27, 1992); "Significant Incidents: 1992," 14; RAND Database; Global Terrorism Database.

622 "Several Bomb Attacks in Santiago 23 Jul," July 24, 1992, *Santiago Radio Chilena Network* in Spanish, FBIS, LAT, 92-144: 38; "Significant Incidents: 1992," 14; RAND Database; Global Terrorism Database.

623 "Several Bomb Attacks in Santiago 23 Jul," July 24, 1992, *Santiago Radio Chilena Network* in Spanish, FBIS, LAT, 92-144: 38; "Significant Incidents: 1992," 14; RAND Database; Global Terrorism Database.

624 RAND Database.

625 "Significant Incidents: 1992," 14–15; Global Terrorism Database.

626 "Significant Incidents: 1992," 15; RAND Database; Global Terrorism Database.

627 Global Terrorism Database.

628 "Significant Incidents: 1992," 15; Global Terrorism Database.

629 "Blast Causes Damage to Mormon Church," July 28, 1992, *Santiago Radio Chilena Network* in Spanish, FBIS, LAT, 92-146: 27; "Significant Incidents: 1992," 15; RAND Database.

630 "Significant Incidents: 1992," 15; Global Terrorism Database.

631 "Significant Incidents: 1992," 15; Global Terrorism Database.

632 Ibid.

633 Ibid.

634 Global Terrorism Database.

635 Ibid.

636 RAND Database; Global Terrorism Database.

637 RAND Database; Global Terrorism Database.

638 "Significant Incidents: 1992," 16; RAND Database; Global Terrorism Database.

639 "Significant Incidents: 1992," 16; RAND Database; Global Terrorism Database.

640 "Significant Incidents: 1992," 16; RAND Database; Global Terrorism Database.

641 "Significant Incidents: 1992," 17; RAND Database; Global Terrorism Database.

642 Ibid.

643 Ibid.

644 Ibid..

645 "Significant Incidents: 1992," 18; Global Terrorism Database.

646 "Significant Incidents: 1992," 18; Global Terrorism Database.

647 Global Terrorism Database.

648 RAND Database; Global Terrorism Database.

649 Global Terrorism Database.

650 Ibid.

651 "Significant Incidents: 1993," 3.

652 "EGTK Guerrilla Group Attacks Mormon Church," March 23, 1993, *Madrid EFE* in Spanish, FBIS, LAT, 93-056: 30; "Significant Incidents: 1993," 4; RAND Database.

653 "Significant Incidents: 1993," 6–7; RAND Database.

654 "Nine Bomb Attacks Reported," May 28, 1993, *Madrid EFE* in Spanish, FBIS, LAT, 93-103: 38–39; "Significant Incidents: 1993," 7; RAND Database.

655 "Significant Incidents: 1993," 7; RAND Database.

656 "Bomb Attacks Mark Anniversary of Military Coup," September 11, 1993, *Santiago EL MERCURIO* in Spanish, FBIS, LAT, 93-182: 31–32; "Significant Incidents: 1993," 11; RAND Database.

657 "Significant Incidents: 1993," 11; Global Terrorism Database.

658 Ibid.

659 RAND Database.

660 Jorge Trujillo, interviewed by Matthew A. Hughes, November 14, 2019; Pedro del Cardona, interviewed by Matthew A. Hughes, November 16, 2019; "Significant Incidents: 1994," 1; "Rebels Bomb Two LDS Chapels," *Sunstone* (February 1994), 81; "Rebels bomb 2 LDS chapels," *Deseret News* (January 25, 1994); RAND Database; Global Terrorism Database.

661 "Church, Bottling Plant Bombed To Protest U.S. Troops," January 25, 1994, *Santa Fe de Bogota Inravision Television Cadena 1* in Spanish, FBIS, LAT, 94-016: 36; "Significant Incidents: 1994," 1; "Rebels Bomb Two LDS Chapels," *Sunstone* (February 1994), 81; RAND Database; Global Terrorism Database.

662 "Anti-U.S. Groups Attack Baptist, Mormon Churches," February 18, 1994, *Santa Fe de Bogota Emisoras Caracol Network* in Spanish, FBIS, LAT, 94-035: 47; "Guerrillas Detonate Device at

American School in Cali," February 18, 1994, *Mexico City NOTIMEX* in Spanish, FBIS, LAT, 94-035: 46–47; "Significant Incidents: 1994," 2; RAND Database; Global Terrorism Database.

663 RAND Database; Global Terrorism Database.

664 RAND Database; Global Terrorism Database.

665 RAND Database; Global Terrorism Database.

666 Global Terrorism Database.

667 RAND Database.

668 Global Terrorism Database.

669 Ibid.

670 Ibid.

671 RAND Database; Global Terrorism Database.

672 RAND Database; Global Terrorism Database.

673 RAND Database; Global Terrorism Database.

674 RAND Database; Global Terrorism Database.

675 "Significant Incidents: 1994," 5; RAND Database.

676 "Mormon Churches Bombed," October 22, 1994, *Hamburg DPA* in Spanish, FBIS, LAT, 94-205: 55; "Significant Incidents: 1994," 5; RAND Database; Global Terrorism Database.

677 "Mormon Churches Bombed," October 22, 1994, *Hamburg DPA* in Spanish, FBIS, LAT, 94-205: 55; "Significant Incidents: 1994," 5; RAND Database; Global Terrorism Database.

678 "Significant Incidents: 1995," 4; Global Terrorism Database.

679 Jorge Trujillo, interviewed by Matthew A. Hughes, November 14, 2019; "Significant Incidents: 1996," 10; RAND Database; Global Terrorism Database.

680 "Significant Incidents: 1996," 11; RAND Database; Global Terrorism Database.

681 "Significant Incidents: 1996," 11; RAND Database; Global Terrorism Database.

682 W. Seth Carus, "Bioterrorism and Biocrimes: the Illicit Use of Biological Agents Since 1900," *Center for Counterproliferation Research* (National Defense University: Washington, D.C., February 2001), 129; "Anthrax Hoax Hits Church Offices," *Sunstone* (June 1999), 74.

683 "Significant Incidents: 1999," 9; Global Terrorism Database.

684 "Significant Incidents: 1999," 9; Global Terrorism Database.

685 Lucinda Dillon, "4 LDS chapels are bombed in Colombia," *Deseret News* (April 12, 2000), A1, A8; Carrie A. Moore, "Church praises efforts," *Deseret News* (April 13, 2000), B1-B2; "Significant Incidents: 2000," 8; Global Terrorism Database.

686 "4 LDS chapels are bombed," A1, A8; "Church praises efforts," B1-B2; "Significant Incidents: 2000," 8; Global Terrorism Database.

687 "4 LDS chapels are bombed," A1, A8; "Church praises efforts," B1-B2; "Significant Incidents: 2000," 8; Global Terrorism Database.

688 RAND Database; Daniel Shaw, e-mail message to author, October 31, 2017. Elder Shaw was a LDS missionary assigned to the Varazdin area at the time. He met with members in the local ward on behalf of the author and gathered relevant information.

689 RAND Database.

690 Ben Winslow, "FBI: White powder mailed to Salt Lake Temple harmless," *Deseret News* (November 15, 2008), https://www.deseretnews.com/article/705382575/FBI-White-powder-mailed-to-Salt-Lake-Temple-harmless.html (accessed December 16, 2017).

691 Ibid.

692 Global Terrorism Database.

693 "Man Attacks Latter-day Saints with Knives During Church Service," *LDS Living* (December 3, 2018), available at https://www.ldsliving.com/Man-Attacks-Latter-day-Saints-with-Knives-During-Church-Service/s/89850 (accessed December 4, 2018); Adry Torres, "'Everyone will die': Blood-soaked man is arrested for stabbing four during Sunday service at LDS church in Brazil," *Dailymail.com* (December 3, 2018), available at https://www.google.com/amp/s/www.dailymail.co.uk/news/article-6455203/amp/Four-men-stabbed-Mormon-church-Brazil-two-days-man-posted-threat-Facebook.html (accessed December 4, 2018).

694 Beacham Publishing's TRAC "Terrorism Research & Analysis Consortium); *14th of December Command*, available at http://www.trackingterrorism.org/group/14th-of-december-command (accessed November 26, 2018).

695 "Bolivia: Potential for Terrorist and Insurgent Violence," Special Interagency Intelligence Memorandum, Officer of the Director of Central Intelligence, April 1989, declassified and approved for release March 24, 2014, CIA-RDP94T00885R000200140001-2, 5; Beacham Publishing's TRAC (Terrorism Research & Analysis Consortium), *Alejo Calatayu*, available at http://www.trackingterrorism.org/group/alejo-calatayu (accessed November 28, 2018).

696 Robert Jackson Alexander, "International Trotskyism, 1929-1985: A Documented Analysis of the Movement," (Durham, NC: Duke University Press, 1991), 126.

697 Beacham Publishing's TRAC (Terrorism Research & Analysis Consortium), *Ejercito del Pueblo en Armas (EPA)*, available at http://www.trackingterrorism.org/group/ejercito-del-pueblo-en-armas-epa (accessed December 1, 2018); Max G. Manwaring, "Venezuela as an Exporter of 4th Generation Warfare Instability," (Carlisle Barracks, PA: U.S. Army War College Press, 2012), 7.

698 Beacham Publishing's TRAC (Terrorism Research & Analysis Consortium), Alfaro Vive, Carajo (AVC), available at http://www.trackingterrorism.org/group/alfaro-vive-carajo-avc (accessed August 22, 2020); Phil Gunson, Andrew Thompson and Greg Chamberlain, The Dictionary of Contemporary Politics of South America (London: Routledge, 1990), 3; Global Terrorism Database.

699 Michael Whine, "Terrorist Incidents against Jewish Communities and Israeli Citizens Abroad, 1968-2003," International Institute for Counter-Terrorism, December 20, 2003, available at https://www.ict.org.il/Article/893/Terrorist-Incidents-against-Jewish-Communities-and-Israeli-Citizens-Abroad-1968-2003#gsc.tab=0 (accessed December 1, 2018).

700 Daniel Masters, "The Origins of Terrorist Threats: Religious, Separatist, or Something Else?," *Terrorism and Political Violence* 20, no. 3 (July-September, 2008), pp. 396-414, "Appendix-Terrorist Groups and Ideological Categories," available at http://people.uncw.edu/mastersd/articles.html (accessed December 2, 2018); "Significant Incidents: 1991," 4.

701 Beacham Publishing's TRAC (Terrorism Research & Analysis Consortium), *Islamic Revolutionary Command*, http://www.trackingterrorism.org/group/islamic-revolutionary-command (accessed December 2, 2018).

702 Stephen Sloan and Sean K. Anderson, *Historical Dictionary of Terrorism* (Scarecrow Press: Lanham, MD, 2009), 378; Beacham Publishing's TRAC (Terrorism Research & Analysis Consortium), Lautaro Youth Movement, available at http://www.trackingterrorism.org/group/lautaro-youth-movement (accessed September 23, 2017); Lautaro Youth Movement." Encyclopedia of Terrorism, edited by Harvey W. Kushner, vol. 1, SAGE Reference, 2003, pp. 213–214. Gale Virtual Reference Library, go.galegroup.com/ps/i.do?p=GVRL&sw=w&u=char53948&v=2.1&id=GALE%7CCX3438800175&it=r&asid=30c197236b052ca57e2f69b169484005. Accessed July 15, 2017.

703 Beacham Publishing's TRAC (Terrorism Research & Analysis Consortium), *Manuel Rodriguez Patriotic Front*, available at http://www.trackingterrorism.org/group/manuel-rodriguez-patriotic-front (accessed December 1, 2018); Office of the Secretary of State and Office of the Coordinator for Counterterrorism, "Patterns of Global Terrorism: 1992," (Washington, DC: Office of the Secretary of State, April 30, 1993), Appendix B, available at https://fas.org/irp/threat/terror_92/index.html (accessed December 1, 2018).

704 Beacham Publishing's TRAC (Terrorism Research & Analysis Consortium), *Maximiliano Gomez Revolutionary Brigade*, http://www.trackingterrorism.org/group/maximiliano-gomez-revolutionary-brigade (accessed December 1, 2018).

705 Beacham Publishing's TRAC (Terrorism Research & Analysis Consortium), *Movement of the Revolutionary Left – Chile*, http://www.trackingterrorism.org/group/movement-revolutionary-left-chile (accessed December 2, 2018).

706 "Bolivia: Potential for Terrorist and Insurgent Violence," Special Interagency Intelligence Memorandum, Officer of the Director of Central Intelligence, April 1989, declassified and approved for release March 24, 2014, CIA-RDP94T00885R000200140001-2, 1; Beacham Publishing's TRAC (Terrorism Research & Analysis Consortium), *Ejercito de Liberacion Nacional (ELN)*, available at http://www.trackingterrorism.org/group/ejercito-de-liberacion-nacional-eln (accessed November 28, 2018).

707 Beacham Publishing's TRAC (Terrorism Research & Analysis Consortium), *Nestor Paz Zamora Commission*, available at http://www.trackingterrorism.org/group/nestor-paz-zamora-commission (accessed December 5, 2018); Stephen Sloan and Sean K. Anderson, *Historical Dictionary of Terrorism* (Scarecrow Press: Lanham, MD, 2009), 488–489.

708 Beacham Publishing's TRAC (Terrorism Research & Analysis Consortium), *Omar Torrijos Commando for Latin American Dignity*, http://www.trackingterrorism.org/group/omar-torrijos-commando-latin-american-dignity (accessed December 2, 2018); "Panama group threatens to attack Americans," *UPI* (December 27, 1989), available at https://www.upi.com/Archives/1989/12/27/Panama-group-threatens-to-attack-Americans/4267630738000/ (accessed December 2, 2018).

709 "Significant Incidents: 1991," 4; Global Terrorism Database.

710 Stephen Sloan and Sean K. Anderson, *Historical Dictionary of Terrorism* (Scarecrow Press: Lanham, MD, 2009), 378.

711 Beacham Publishing's TRAC (Terrorism Research & Analysis Consortium), *Revolutionary Armed Forces of Colombia (FARC)*, http://www.trackingterrorism.org/group/revolutionary-armed-forces-colombia-farc (accessed December 2, 2018).

712 Jaime Reyes Soriano, "La autodefensa de masas y las Milicias Rodriguistas: aprendizajes, experiencias y consolidación del trabajo militar de masas del Partido Comunista de Chile, 1982-1987," *Izquierdas* 26 (January 2016), available at https://scielo.conicyt.cl/scielo.php?script=sci_arttext&pid=S0718-50492016000100004 (accessed December 1, 2018).

713 Beacham Publishing's TRAC (Terrorism Research & Analysis Consortium), *Shining Path*, http://www.trackingterrorism.org/group/shining-path (accessed December 3, 2018).

714 Beacham Publishing's TRAC (Terrorism Research & Analysis Consortium), *Simon Bolivar Guerrilla Coordinating Board (CGSB)*, available at http://www.trackingterrorism.org/group/simon-bolivar-guerrilla-coordinating-board-cgsb (accessed November 28, 2018).

715 "Significant Incidents: 1992," 14; "Significant Incidents: 1993," 7.

716 Beacham Publishing's TRAC (Terrorism Research & Analysis Consortium), *Los Extraditables*, available at http://www.trackingterrorism.org/group/los-extraditables (accessed November 28, 2018).

717 Beacham Publishing's TRAC (Terrorism Research & Analysis Consortium), *Tupac Amaru Revolutionary Movement (MRTA)*, http://www.trackingterrorism.org/group/tupac-amaru-revolutionary-movement-mrta (accessed December 5, 2018); David Clark Knowlton, "Mormonism and Guerrillas in Bolivia," *The Journal of Mormon. History*, 201; Lee Davidson, "Were terrorist attacks related to the gulf war?," *Deseret News*, March 26, 1991, B1-B2.

718 "Bolivia: Potential for Terrorist and Insurgent Violence," Special Interagency Intelligence Memorandum, Officer of the Director of Central Intelligence, April 1989, declassified and approved for release March 24, 2014, CIA-RDP94T00885R000200140001-2, 1; Beacham Publishing's TRAC (Terrorism Research & Analysis Consortium), *Tupac Katari Guerrilla Army (EGTK)*, available at http://www.trackingterrorism.org/group/tupac-katari-guerrilla-army-egtk (accessed November 28, 2018).

719 Beacham Publishing's TRAC (Terrorism Research & Analysis Consortium), *Zarate Willka Armed Forces of Liberation (FAL-ZW)*, available at http://www.trackingterrorism.org/group/zarate-willka-armed-forces-liberation-fal-zw (accessed December 1, 2018).

ABOUT THE AUTHOR

Matthew Hughes is a Military Intelligence Officer and Foreign Area Officer in the United States Army. His undergraduate and graduate studies focused on foreign languages, terrorism, intelligence, and policy.

Matthew's military service ranges from leading linguists in intelligence collection and targeting efforts in Afghanistan to liaising with partner nations in Eastern Europe and Latin America. He has published and lectured on terrorist tactics and multiple intelligence disciplines.

Matthew has received professional and academic accolades for his numerous contributions to the intelligence field, especially for his original predictive analysis on terrorism and innovative approaches to analysis. Matthew has leveraged foreign language abilities to translate for refugees, preach the gospel on four continents, and strengthen international partnerships through his capacities in international diplomacy.

NOTES

NOTES

NOTES